Using Your *Texas Write Source* Book

Your *Texas Write Source* book is loaded with information to help you learn about writing. One section that will be especially helpful is the "Proofreader's Guide" at the back of the book. This section covers language and grammar rules.

Also helpful are the three units that cover the types of writing that you may encounter on state or district tests. At the end of each unit, there are samples and tips for writing in science, social studies, and math.

Your *Texas Write Source* book will help you with other learning skills, too—listening and speaking, giving presentations, and taking tests. This help makes the *Texas Write Source* book a valuable writing and learning guide in all your classes.

Your *Texas Write Source* guides . . .

With practice, you will be able to use the guides explained below to quickly find information in this book.

The **CONTENTS** lists the major sections of the book and the chapters found in these sections.

The **INDEX** (starting on page **649**) lists the topics covered in the book in alphabetical order. Use the index when you want to find where information about a specific topic can be found.

The **COLOR CODING** helps you keep track of the stages of the writing process and the Texas traits of writing. Color coding will make sections such as "Basic Grammar and Writing," "A Writer's Resource," and the "Proofreader's Guide" easy to find.

The **SPECIAL PAGE REFERENCES** in the book tell you where to turn for additional information about a specific topic.

TEXAS
WRITE
SOURCE

Authors
Dave Kemper, Patrick Sebranek, and Verne Meyer

Consulting Author
Gretchen Bernabei

Illustrator
Chris Krenzke

GREAT
SOURCE.

 HOUGHTON MIFFLIN HARCOURT

www.hmheducation.com/tx/writesource

Quick Guide

Contents

Texas Write Source

The Forms of Writing

DESCRIPTIVE WRITING

NARRATIVE WRITING

EXPOSITORY WRITING

RESPONDING TO TEXTS

CREATIVE WRITING

RESEARCH WRITING

The Tools of Language

Basic Grammar and Writing

WORKING WITH WORDS

A Writer's Resource

Proofreader's Guide

Why Write?

Writing won't help you become the star sprinter on the track team. And it won't give you a beautiful singing voice. However writing *will* help you in four very important ways.

Writing will help you . . .

- **become a better student.** Writing in a learning log about the subjects you are studying helps you understand and remember things better. Writing clear essays and paragraphs shows your teachers what you have learned.

- **understand your experiences.** Writing in a personal journal helps you sort out your thoughts about the everyday happenings in your life.

- **connect with others.** Writing e-mail messages and friendly letters keeps you in contact with the people that mean the most to you.

- **enjoy life.** Writing poems, stories, and plays allows you to be creative and have fun with the language.

Remember . . .

You can become a very good writer. All it takes is practice. That is why all of the writing that you do is important—whether you are writing for yourself or for an assignment.

⭐ **ELPS** 2C, 2G, 2H, 2I, 3D, 3E, 3G, 3H, 4C, 4G

The Writing Process

Writing Focus

- **Using the Writing Process**
- **Understanding the Texas Traits of Writing**
- **Evaluating Your Writing**

Learning Language

Work with a partner. Read the meanings aloud and share answers to the questions.

1. A process is a set of steps that have a certain outcome.
   Describe the process of making a tasty snack.

2. You show mastery of a skill if you use it well.
   How can you reach mastery when you are learning to do something new?

3. A holistic view looks at the whole thing together, instead of considering the separate parts.
   Why might a holistic approach be helpful when solving a problem?

4. People show off something they are proud of.
   Name something that you like to show off.

Using the

Writing Process

Baseball players have it tough, trying to hit an incoming fastball with a small, rounded bat. Even the best ballplayers usually get a hit only three out of ten times at bat.

Writers have it tough, too. They rarely come up with their best work in one try. In fact, writers may come to the plate many times before getting a "solid hit." That is why writing is often called a process. The best stories and essays have gone through a series of steps or stages before they are ready to share.

This chapter will explain the steps in the writing process and help you to build good writing habits along the way.

What's Ahead

- Becoming a Writer
- The Writing Process
- The Process in Action
- Working with the Texas Traits

Becoming a Writer

You can become a great writer, but you must work at it. The tips below will get you started.

Read! Read! Read!

Read books, magazines, and newspapers—and read them often! As you read, you will learn what the pros do, and how they do it.

> Read like a wolf eats.
> —Gary Paulsen

Write for yourself . . . and for other people.

Write in a personal journal. Also write stories, poems, . . . even plays! And make sure to share some of your writing with friends and family members.

> Write about what makes you want to write more. —Tamora Pierce

Celebrate the language!

Become aware of all the wonderful words in our language—and use them in your writing.

> Who could improve on splash, smash, ooze, shriek, slush, glide, squeak, coo?
> —Arville Schaleben

 Write about a quotation. Write nonstop for 3 to 5 minutes about one of the quotations on this page. Consider what it means to you. Discuss your thoughts with a partner.

TEKS 5.15A, 5.15C
ELPS 2G, 2H, 3E, 3G, 3H

The Writing Process

Good writers work on their writing in a step-by-step process. The steps in the writing process are described below.

The Steps in the Writing Process

Prewrite At the beginning of the writing process, you think about the purpose and audience to decide on the best writing form, or genre, to use. Then you select a topic, collect details about it, and plan how to use them.

Draft During this step, you write a first draft. This is the first chance to get all of the ideas down on paper while thinking about the purpose, audience, and form.

Revise After reviewing the first draft, you think about how well the questions of purpose, audience, and form were answered. Then you change the parts of the content that may be confusing or incomplete.

Edit Next, you check your revised writing for errors and write a final copy.

Publish In the last step, you share your final copy.

Think about writing. Suppose a student said, "Writing is easy. You just write everything down and then hand in your paper." What advice would you give to this student? Turn and discuss this with a partner.

TEKS 5.15A, 5.15C

The Process in Action

Prewriting

Selecting a Topic

- Think about your writing assignment: What do you want to do in your writing (share, inform, persuade, entertain, be creative)? Who is your audience? What form, or genre, of writing are you using? These are your questions of purpose, audience, and form.
- Select a specific topic that interests you.

Gathering Details

- Research or gather information about your topic.
- Think of a focus or main idea about the topic that you want to emphasize.
- Identify the details that support your focus and plan how to organize them.

Drafting

Developing the First Draft

- Use your prewriting as a guide.
- Get all of your ideas on paper.
- Include a beginning, a middle, and an ending.
- Think about your purpose, audience, and form, or genre, as you write.

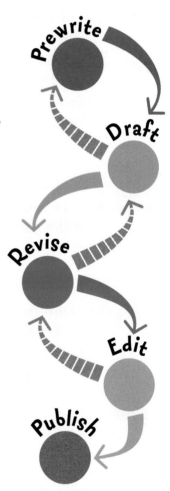

Revising **Improving Your Writing**

- Read your first draft once aloud and once silently.
- Think about how well you addressed the questions of purpose, audience, and form.
- Use these questions as a basic revising guide:
  - **Are my ideas clear and complete?**
  - **Does the beginning attract the reader?**
  - **Are the details in the middle organized and easy to follow?**
  - **Does the ending say something important about the topic?**
  - **Do I use specific words?**
  - **Do I sound interested in my topic?**
- Ask a classmate, family member, or teacher to read your work and give you feedback.
- Improve your writing by adding, cutting, moving, or rewriting parts based on feedback.

Editing **Checking for Conventions**

- Find and correct grammar, mechanics (punctuation and capitalization), and spelling errors.
- Also ask someone else to check your writing for errors.
- Write a neat final copy. Proofread this copy for errors.

Publishing **Sharing Your Writing**

- Share your finished writing with others.
- Decide if you will include the writing in your portfolio.

 Create a mini-poster. Design a writing-process poster on a piece of notebook or computer paper. Include a title, a short statement about the writing process, and an interesting graphic.

★ Working with the Texas Traits

Because writing is a process, you don't have to think about everything at once. Instead, you can deal with the five Texas traits of writing (shown below) when they become important. For example, *focus and coherence* is important right away, while *voice* becomes more important later on. Here are some of the key things you have to think about during your writing.

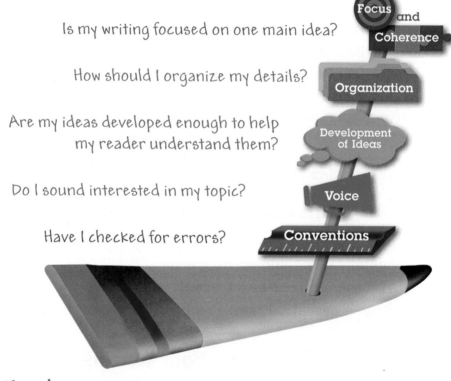

Is my writing focused on one main idea?   Focus and Coherence

How should I organize my details?   Organization

Are my ideas developed enough to help my reader understand them?   Development of Ideas

Do I sound interested in my topic?   Voice

Have I checked for errors?   Conventions

 Use the process. On your own paper, match each activity on the left to its proper place in the writing process on the right.

____ **1.** Rewrite some of your sentences.   **A.** Prewriting

____ **2.** Select an interesting topic.   **B.** Drafting

____ **3.** Post your story on your Web site.   **C.** Revising

____ **4.** Double-check your writing for errors.   **D.** Editing

____ **5.** Develop a creative beginning.   **E.** Publishing

One Writer's Process

Author James Howe says, "Writing is like digging in the sand for buried treasure: You have to be willing to do a lot of digging." Luckily, writing can be broken down into steps, which makes all of the "digging" more manageable. The steps in the writing process include *prewriting, drafting, revising, editing,* and *publishing.*

This chapter shows you how Max Koski used the writing process to write an expository essay explaining the importance of friends. As Max worked step-by-step on his essay, it became more detailed, more interesting, and more accurate.

What's Ahead

- **Previewing the Goals**
- **Prewriting**
- **Drafting**
- **Revising**
- **Editing**
- **Assessing the Final Copy**
- **Evaluating and Reflecting on Your Writing**

⭐ **ELPS** 2G, 2H, 2I, 3D, 3E, 3G, 3H, 4C, 4G, 4I, 4J, 4K

Previewing the Goals

Before Max began writing, he read the goals for the assignment. These goals helped him to get started. He also reviewed the *Write Source* Scoring Rubric on pages 34–35.

 **Focus and Coherence**
Focus on one idea and include only information about that idea.

Organization
Make sure that your essay is easy to follow from beginning to end.

Development of Ideas
Explain or describe your ideas with unique and thoughtful details.

Voice
Let readers know that you really care about the topic.

Conventions
Follow the rules for grammar, sentence structure, mechanics, and spelling.

 Answer these questions about Max's writing assignment. Discuss your answers with a partner. Be sure to explain your opinions, ideas, and feelings.

1 What type of topic should Max select?

2 How should he sound in his essay?

3 What should he remember about his sentences?

TEKS 5.15A

Prewriting Selecting a Topic

Max was given the following assignment: *Write an expository essay that explains something that is very important to you.* To think of topics, Max freely wrote about the assignment.

Freewriting

> Many things are important to me. I love sports, especially soccer and baseball. Of course, my family is important to me. My mom helps me in all kinds of ways. And how could I live without all my friends? Steve is . . .

Max decided to write about the importance of friends. He knew his classmates could identify with this topic.

Gathering Details

Ms. Lee, Max's teacher, helped the class think of different strategies that help explain a topic. They could . . .

✔ **1.** define the topic,
   2. share a quotation related to the topic,
✔ **3.** explain what the topic means to them,
✔ **4.** share what other people think about the topic,
   5. relate the topic to something they had read, or
✔ **6.** show the topic in action.

Max checked four strategies that he would like to use. Then he gathered details for his essay. He looked up the word *friend* in a dictionary and in a thesaurus. He also thought about the importance of friends in his own life. He asked others what they thought about friends. He took good notes along the way.

Drafting Completing Your First Draft

When Max wrote his first draft, he included the ideas he gathered during his prewriting on page 11. He tried to get all his thoughts down on paper. (Naturally, there are some errors in Max's first draft.)

The beginning paragraph introduces the main idea, or focus, of the writing. (underlined)

The writer shares his own thoughts.

The writer also shares the thoughts of other people.

The dictionary says what the word friend means. A few synonyms for friend include companion and classmate. You may also call your friends "amigos!" That's cool. <u>A friend is one of the most important things you can have.</u>

To me, maybe a friend is like a trusted baseball glove. That's how I think a friend shoud be: dependable, easy to be around, and helpful. I depend on my glove. It never lets me down. It helps me play good. I guess that having friends makes my life more fun, and it keep me going when I'm having a bad day.

Friends are different things to different people. My little sister thinks a friend shoud like to swim and ride bikes. My Mom's idea of a friend is Mrs.

ELPS 2C, 2G, 2H, 2I, 3D, 3E, 3H, 4C, 4G, 4I, 4K

Milanovich who walks and talks a lot with my mom. My Dad's friends are neighbors who do projects with him.

The writer adds details from his own experience.

Steve is definitely a best friend to me. We play soccer hang out and talk about sports. I broke my leg. He always came over to play video games. In school he carried my backpack and gets my lunch tray for me. I can always count on Steve. He knows that he can count on me.

A final thought supports the main idea.

Sum friends come and go in your life. Others will be there for a long time, maybe even forever I would hate to move, unless I coud take my friends with me. They are that important.

Practice

Review the goals for organization, ideas, and voice on page 10. Does Max meet these goals in his first draft? Explain to a partner. Listen to your partner's response.

TEKS 5.15C
ELPS 2G, 2H, 2I, 3D, 3E, 3H, 4C, 4I, 4J, 4K

Revising Improving Your Writing

After Max read through his first draft, he made the following changes to his essay.

> The dictionary says what the word friend means. A few synonyms for friend include companion and classmate. ~~Y~~ou may also call your ^(If you speak Spanish,) friends "amigos!" That's cool. A friend is one of the ^(In any langauge) most important things you can have.
>
> To me, ~~maybe~~ a friend is like a trusted baseball glove. That's how I think a friend shoud be: dependable, easy to be around, and helpful. I depend on my glove. ~~I~~t never lets me down. It helps ^(and) me play good. ~~I guess that~~ having friends makes my life more fun. I'm having a bad day. It keeps me going.

Phrases are added to clarify meaning.

Words are deleted to make the voice sound more confident.

Sentences are combined to include compound sentences.

Practice

Review Max's changes. Make one change to clarify meaning. Revise Max's draft to include another compound sentence. Explain your choices to a partner. Listen to your partner's response.

TEKS 5.15C, 5.15E
ELPS 2C, 2G, 2H, 2I, 3D,
3E, 3F, 3G, 3H, 4C, 4I, 4J, 4K

Revising Using a Peer Response

Max used a classmate's comments to make his essay clearer and to improve its style. He added, deleted, and rearranged sentences.

Could you add a definition and more synonyms?

The dictionary says ~~what~~ that the word friend
"a person someone knows and likes well"
means. A few synonyms for friend include
                                      pal and buddy.
companion ~~and~~ classmate. If you speak Spanish,

you may call friends "amigos!" ~~That's cool.~~ In any

langauge, a friend is one of the most important

things you can have.

Could you delete any unneeded sentences?

    To me, a friend is like a trusted baseball glove.

That's how I think a friend shoud be: dependable,

easy to be around, and helpful. I depend on my

Would rearranging some sentences make the order more logical?

glove and it never lets me down. It helps me play

good. Having friends makes my life more fun, and it

keep me going when I'm having a bad day. . . .

Practice

Suggest other ways that Max could add, delete, combine, or rearrange sentences to make his essay clearer. Explain your ideas to a partner.

TEKS 5.15D
ELPS 2C, 2G, 2H, 2I, 3D, 3E, 3G, 3H, 4C, 4G, 4I, 4J, 4K

Editing Checking for Conventions

Before writing a final copy, Max checked his essay for grammar, mechanics, sentence structure, and spelling. (See inside the back cover of this book for a list of editing and proofreading marks.)

Words being used in a special way are underlined.

Commas are placed between words in a series and in a compound sentence.

Spelling and usage errors are corrected.

The dictionary says that the word <u>friend</u> means "a person someone knows and likes well." A few synonyms for <u>friend</u> include <u>companion</u> <u>classmate</u> <u>pal</u> and <u>buddy</u>. If you speak Spanish, you may call friends "amigos!" In any ~~langauge~~ language, a friend is one of the most important things you can have.

To me, a friend is like a trusted baseball glove. I depend on my glove and it never lets me down. It helps me play ~~good~~ well. That's how I think a friend ~~shoud~~ should be: dependable, easy to be around, and helpful. Having friends makes my life more fun,...

Grammar Practice

Review Max's editing. Then discuss these questions as a class: Do you make some of the same errors? Do you use editing marks? Do you check for errors in the same way each time you edit your writing?

Max's Final Copy

Max felt great about his final essay. It captured how important friends are in his life.

Max Koski

The Power of Friends

The dictionary says that the word friend means "a person someone knows and likes well." A few synonyms for friend include companion, classmate, pal, and buddy. If you speak Spanish, you may call friends "amigos!" In any language, a friend is one of the most important things you can have.

To me, a friend is like a trusted baseball glove. I depend on my glove, and it never lets me down. It helps me play well. That's how I think a friend should be: dependable, easy to be around, and helpful. Having friends makes my life more fun, and it keeps me going when I'm having a bad day.

Koski 2

Friends are different things to different people. To my little sister, a friend is someone who likes to swim and ride bikes. My mom's idea of a friend is Mrs. Milanovich, someone who walks (and talks) with my mom every morning. My dad's friends are neighbors who help him with projects like building sheds and planting trees.

Steve is my best friend. We play soccer, hang out, and talk about sports. When I broke my leg, he always came over to play video games. In school, he carried my backpack and got my lunch tray for me. I know I can always count on Steve, and he knows that he can count on me.

Some friends may be in your life for just a little while. Others will be there for a long time, maybe even forever. I would hate to move, unless I could take my friends with me. They are too important to leave behind.

ELPS 2G, 2H, 2I, 3D, 3E, 3G, 3H, 4C, 4G, 4I, 4J, 4K

Assessing the Final Copy

Max's teacher used the *Write Source* Scoring Rubric on pages 34–35 to assess his final copy. A 4 is the very best score that a writer can receive. The teacher also included comments about his writing.

> Max, your writing is at a score point 3 because it expresses your ideas well, but it needs some improvements. Your use of focus and coherence is excellent. You maintained your focus on the importance of having friends, and all of your ideas are connected to the main idea and to each other. Your organization is mostly successful for your purpose and audience. Your writing generally flows well, but it would seem more logical if you switched the third and fourth paragraphs so that your personal ideas about friends flow together. Also, using more transitions would make it easier to understand how your ideas are related. You supported your ideas with specific details, but I wanted to know more about your sister's and dad's friends. Your writing is engaging and sounds original. You showed a strong command of the conventions of grammar, mechanics, sentence structure, and spelling. Overall, you did a great job!

Discuss the assessment with a partner. Do you agree with the score and the comments made by Max's teacher? Why or why not? What do you like in the essay? What would you do differently?

Evaluating and Reflecting on Your Writing

Once Max finished his essay, he filled out a reflection sheet.

> Thinking about your writing makes you aware of ways to improve as a writer.

Max Koski

My Expository Essay

1. The best score for my expository essay is . . .
   a 3.

2. It's the best score because . . .
   my essay stayed focused and coherent with a good development of my ideas, but my organization needs work.

3. The part that still needs work is . . .
   the organization. I should have switched the third and fourth paragraphs. Then I would be explaining my ideas about friends together, followed by others' ideas of friends.

4. The main thing I learned about writing an expository essay is . . .
   that it takes a lot of thinking and some research. It also must have a lot of good information.

5. The next time I write a expository essay, I would like to . . .
   compare my two favorite sports, soccer and baseball.

Understanding the
Texas Traits of Writing

To make a great pizza, you must work with the best ingredients: a homemade crust, tasty cheese, and fresh toppings. To write great stories or reports, you must also work with the best "ingredients." They include great ideas, specific details, colorful words, and smooth sentences.

This chapter reviews the traits found in all good writing. After learning how to use these traits, or ingredients, you'll be taking your writing from "bland" to "tasty" in no time.

What's Ahead

- **Introducing the Texas Traits**
- **Understanding the Texas Traits**

Introducing the Texas Traits

Keep the following traits in mind when you write. If you follow them, you will do your best work.

Focus and Coherence

The best writing is focused on one main idea, and all the sentences tell something about that idea. Readers can easily understand how the ideas in the composition are related. The writing feels complete.

Organization

Good writing is arranged in a logical order. Clear transitions make it easy for the reader to follow the ideas from beginning to end.

Development of Ideas

Excellent writing develops ideas with thoughtful details. The ideas are presented in a way that helps readers understand and appreciate them.

Voice

The best writing holds the reader's attention. It sounds original and lets the writer's personality shine through.

Conventions

Good writing follows the rules for grammar, sentence structure, mechanics (capitalization and punctuation), and spelling.

 tip One additional trait to consider is the **presentation** of your writing. Good writing looks neat and follows guidelines for margins, spacing, and indenting. (See pages **44–46**.)

Understanding Focus and Coherence

Good writing focuses on one important idea and includes only information that is related to that idea. All the sentences work together to achieve the writer's goal. The writing feels complete.

How can I create a strong focus?

You can create a strong focus by making sure your opening states your controlling or main idea. This sentence is called a focus statement. (See page 507.)

Beginning Paragraph

Interesting Opening

Focus Statement (underlined)

Believe it or not, I once dove into water that was full of sharks. But I wasn't afraid. That's because I was inside an underwater craft with my dad and a guide. I had a chance to do this when I was visiting my grandparents in Florida. I'll never forget the underwater sights.

How can I keep my writing focused?

Good writing stays on the topic. The writer leaves out any information that does not relate to the main idea.

Sample Middle Paragraph

Leave out details that don't belong.

It was dark as we dove down, and the lights on our craft lit up the sea. Brilliant-colored fish were darting in front of the thick glass window. A nurse shark bumped into the window with a thud. Nurse sharks move slowly, and they like to rest on the bottom of the ocean. Lobsters skittered away. With the help of our guide, we listed the names of the creatures we saw.

ELPS 2C, 3E, 3H, 4C, 5G

How can the ending sharpen the focus?

The ending part is very important because it supports the focus of your writing and makes it feel complete. It gives the reader a last look at your ideas. An effective ending does one or more of these things:

- Reminds the reader of the main idea.
- Summarizes the key points.
- Emphasizes one point.
- Answers any final questions the reader may have.
- Keeps the reader thinking about the topic.

Ending Paragraph

Summary of key points and reminder of main idea

From our underwater craft, we saw a whole world of ocean creatures. There were strange kinds of animals and plants that most people never see. Some of the creatures were very weird and looked nothing like the fish we see in Lake Erie. My deep sea adventure is an experience I'll remember for years to come.

Practice

Review one or two of your last pieces of writing. Rewrite the ending in one of the pieces, using the summary method or one of the other strategies listed above as a guide. Share your revision with a partner.

If you have trouble ending your writing, wait for a while. Then read what you've written so far. Taking a fresh look at your writing may give you ideas for your ending.

TEKS 5.15B
ELPS 2C, 3E, 3G, 3H, 4C

Understanding Organization

Organization is the way in which writers arrange their ideas. An organized essay moves smoothly from idea to idea. Writer Vicki Spandel states, "Effective organization keeps a piece of writing together and makes it easy to follow."

How should I arrange my ideas?

Before you begin to write, think about your audience and your purpose for writing.

- **Do you want to tell a story?** Arranging events in the order that they happen will help your readers follow the action.

- **Do you want to describe something unusual?** Comparing it with a familiar object might be an effective way to organize your description.

- **Do you want to persuade others to take action?** Stating the outcome you want and your reasons for it may work well.

- **Do you want to explain how to make something?** Giving the steps in the order they should be followed is a good plan.

Persuasive Paragraph

Are you looking for an exciting way to spend a Saturday afternoon? Jump on your bike and join the Fabulous Flyers for some outdoor fun. Every week we ride a different trail and explore a cool place, like the beach at Rocky Point. You won't find a better way to have adventures, keep in shape, and meet new friends!

Practice

How are the ideas arranged in the persuasive paragraph above? Do you think this organization is effective? Explain your ideas to a partner.

How are my ideas connected?

Your writing will be more effective if the reader can understand how your ideas are related. Are your thoughts presented in a logical order? Does one idea lead naturally to the next idea? Good writers use transition words or phrases to show how ideas are connected.

- **Time order** transitions are used in narrative and expository writing to show the order in which events take place.
  During the storm, **thunder rumbled and lightning flashed.**

- **Order of location** is often used in descriptive writing to help readers picture the details that are being described.
  Carlos noticed a tiny pink flower growing between **the rocks.**

- **Logical order** may be used in expository writing to organize details in a way that will make sense.
  Penguins are excellent swimmers. In fact, **some penguins spend up to 75 percent of their lives in the water.**

Learning Language

Some transition words and phrases help you understand the order in which events in a story take place. Work with a partner to orally summarize the events that happen in the paragraph below. Explain how transitions helped you follow the story.

> Every year Maria and her grandma grow all kinds of vegetables in a wonderful backyard garden. The work begins in early spring. As soon as the sun warms the earth, the gardeners prepare the soil. Then they plant the seeds in long rows—tomatoes, beans, carrots, and squash. Soon tiny sprouts appear, and before long, the vegetables start to form. Finally, it is time to harvest the crop.

ELPS 2C, 3H, 4C

Understanding Development of Ideas

Good writers develop their ideas with specific details based on their own unique thoughts and experiences.

What details should I include?

Include interesting facts and descriptive details that help readers understand and appreciate your ideas.

Explain: Share interesting facts about your topic.

Elaborate: Present ideas from your unique viewpoint.

Describe: Include sensory details about your topic.

Juan breathed in the earthy scent as he crumbled some lumps of moist soil between his fingers.

Which words should I choose?

As a writer, your goal is to use the best words to express your ideas. Specific nouns and vivid action verbs will give the reader a clearer, more detailed picture.

Strong Nouns and Verbs

General words: An animal walked up the hill.

Precise nouns and verbs: The llama trudged up the slope.

Colorful Modifiers

General modifiers: The dog barked when the doorbell rang.

Vivid adjectives and adverbs: The frantic dog barked wildly when the doorbell rang.

Practice

In one of your stories, circle your strongest nouns, verbs, and modifiers. Then change three words that could be more specific. Explain your changes to a partner.

ELPS 2C, 3G, 4C, 5G

Understanding Voice

Developing your own special way of saying things may take time, but as author Judy Blume says, "Eventually you'll come up with your own voice." Just read and write as much as you can.

Why is voice so important?

Writing that has voice interests readers. A strong voice helps bring the writer's thoughts and ideas to life and makes the reader say, "Hey, I like that."

Writing that lacks voice

I once got an autograph from a good tennis player. The player was Venus Williams. I was happy.

Writing that has voice

Suddenly, there was Venus Williams listening to headphones. I had butterflies in my stomach when I asked her for an autograph. I actually felt numb when she signed my paper. As I made my way to my seat, I pinched myself to make sure I wasn't dreaming.

How can I write with voice?

Follow these suggestions to develop an effective writing voice:

- **Read a lot.** Reading shows you how others express themselves.
- **Write a lot.** Your voice will develop as you continue writing.
- **Select good topics.** Write about topics that truly interest you.

Practice

Write freely for 3 to 5 minutes about the most exciting thing that has ever happened to you. When you finish, underline words and phrases that sound like you. Share your feelings with a partner.

ELPS 2C, 3E, 3G, 3H, 4C, 5F

Understanding Conventions

Conventions cover the rules of grammar, mechanics (punctuation and capitalization), sentence structure, and spelling. Good writing is enjoyable to read when it follows the rules and the sentences move smoothly from one to the next.

How can I make my sentences flow smoothly?

If you combine short, choppy sentences, your writing will be easier to read. (See pages **479–481**.)

Short, Choppy Sentences

We're having a family contest. Who can plan the best trip? My brother wants to go camping. I want to go camping. My sister wants to visit New York City.

Dad likes to fish. His plan is to rent a cabin near the lake.

Combined Sentences

We're having a family contest to see who can plan the best trip. My brother and I want to go camping, but my sister wants to visit New York City. Dad likes to fish, so his plan is to rent a cabin near the lake.

Learning Language

Often you can add a keyword or phrase to combine short, choppy sentences. Orally combine some sentences in the paragraph below so that the writing will flow more smoothly. Share your ideas with a partner.

I am on a soccer team. The team is called the Panthers. We listen to our coach. The coach is patient. The coach teaches us new skills. He makes up new plays. We could win. We could lose. We are always good sports.

Good writers edit their writing with the conventions in mind. When you follow the rules of grammar, mechanics (punctuation and capitalization), sentence structure, and spelling, your writing will be clear and easy to understand.

How can I make sure my writing follows the rules?

A conventions checklist like the one below can guide you as you edit and proofread your writing. When you are not sure about a rule, check the "Proofreader's Guide." (See pages **522–637**.)

Conventions

GRAMMAR

_____ **1.** Do I use the correct forms of verbs
    (*had seen,* not *had saw)*?

_____ **2.** Do I use the right words *(to, too, two)*?

MECHANICS

_____ **3.** Do I use end punctuation after every sentence?

_____ **4.** Do I use commas correctly in compound sentences?

_____ **5.** Do I start every sentence with a capital letter?

_____ **6.** Do I capitalize the names of people and places?

SENTENCE STRUCTURE

_____ **7.** Do I combine short, choppy sentences?

_____ **8.** Do I make sure that my sentences read smoothly?

SPELLING

_____ **9.** Have I checked my spelling?

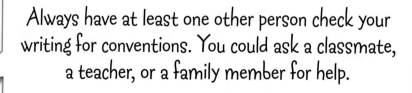

Always have at least one other person check your writing for conventions. You could ask a classmate, a teacher, or a family member for help.

Evaluating Your Writing

Car mechanics are lucky. They can use a diagnostic machine to evaluate the overall performance of an engine. If the machine finds a problem, the mechanic knows what to repair.

As a writer, you can use a scoring rubric, instead of a diagnostic machine, to evaluate your stories and essays. The *Write Source* Scoring Rubric lists four score points and describes the Texas Traits at each score point. This chapter explains how to use a holistic scoring rubric to rate and "repair" your writing.

What's Ahead

- **Understanding Holistic Scoring**
- **Reading a Rubric**
- **The *Write Source* Scoring Rubric**
- **Model Essay**
- **Evaluating an Essay**

ELPS 4C, 4K

Understanding Holistic Scoring

After you watch a movie, you can probably tell right away whether you liked it or not. You might notice good acting, realistic sets, or funny lines. However, the actors wouldn't have been so captivating without good lines to say, and stunning costumes wouldn't matter if the plot was boring. In a great movie, all of these things work together and enhance each other.

Holistic scoring works in the same way. Your writing is assessed as a whole. How well you focus, organize, and develop your ideas is influenced by your voice and command of grammar and mechanics. These individual writing traits work together to give an overall impression.

When the teacher evaluated Diego's essay about getting on the wrong school bus (pages **36–37**), she used holistic scoring and the Texas writing traits. Here's what she said.

Diego, I was immediately pulled into your story by the details you used to describe where you were and how you were feeling. Your writing is a score point 4 because I could hear your voice throughout as the story unfolded, and you organized your thoughts and experiences to build interest. I really felt your anxiety! You stayed focused on the topic of getting on the wrong bus, and each event flowed smoothly from one to another. You also chose interesting words that helped develop your ideas. Your description of the familiar sounds and movement of the bus was a nice contrast to the fear you felt about being in unfamiliar surroundings. You have an excellent command of grammar, mechanics, and spelling, and your sentences are interesting and varied. Finally, your ending was meaningful. More than just finding your way home, this experience helped you call this new place home. Great job!

ELPS 2C, 3G, 3H, 4C, 4G, 4K

Reading a Rubric

The scoring rubric on pages 34–35 is color coded for the four score points. Each score point includes five traits and a description of each trait. The descriptions will help you evaluate your writing.

The *Write Source* Scoring Rubric

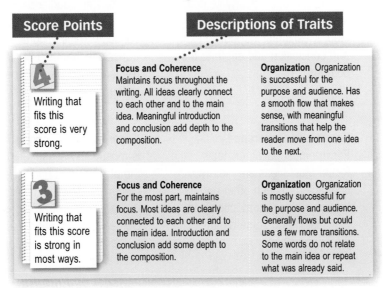

Score Points

Descriptions of Traits

4

Writing that fits this score is very strong.

Focus and Coherence
Maintains focus throughout the writing. All ideas clearly connect to each other and to the main idea. Meaningful introduction and conclusion add depth to the composition.

Organization Organization is successful for the purpose and audience. Has a smooth flow that makes sense, with meaningful transitions that help the reader move from one idea to the next.

3

Writing that fits this score is strong in most ways.

Focus and Coherence
For the most part, maintains focus. Most ideas are clearly connected to each other and to the main idea. Introduction and conclusion add some depth to the composition.

Organization Organization is mostly successful for the purpose and audience. Generally flows but could use a few more transitions. Some words do not relate to the main idea or repeat what was already said.

A Closer Look

When you use the holistic scoring rubric, follow these steps:

1. First, read the 3 description. (A 3 means that the writing is strong in most ways.)

2. Decide if your writing should get a 3.

3. If not, check the descriptions for 4, 2, and 1 until you find the rating that best fits your paper.

4. If you are still revising and your rating is a 2 or lower, make the changes needed to improve your score.

Review the complete scoring rubric. Review the rubric on pages 34–35. Which traits will be the hardest for you to achieve a 3 or 4 rating? Which will be the easiest? Express your ideas to a partner.

ELPS 4C, 4K

Texas Traits

The *Write Source* Scoring Rubric

Use the descriptions for each score to holistically evaluate your writing or that of your peers.

Writing that fits this score is very strong.

Focus and Coherence
Maintains focus throughout the writing. All ideas clearly connect to each other and to the main idea. Meaningful introduction and conclusion add depth to the composition.

Organization Organization is successful for the purpose and audience. Has a smooth flow that makes sense, with meaningful transitions that help the reader move from one idea to the next.

Writing that fits this score is strong in most ways.

Focus and Coherence
For the most part, maintains focus. Most ideas are clearly connected to each other and to the main idea. Introduction and conclusion add some depth to the composition.

Organization Organization is mostly successful for the purpose and audience. Generally flows but could use a few more transitions. Some words do not relate to the main idea or repeat what was already said.

Writing that fits this score is strong in a few ways.

Focus and Coherence Is somewhat focused. May suddenly shift from one idea to another, but the ideas are related. Some ideas do not add to the writing. Introduction and conclusion do not add depth.

Organization Organization may not match the purpose and audience. Thoughts do not always flow clearly or make sense. Unrelated or repeated words may interfere with ideas.

Writing that fits this score is weak.

Focus and Coherence Lacks focus. Includes a large amount of information not connected to the main idea. Is missing an introduction and/or conclusion.

Organization Has no organization or does not make sense. Has no transitions or uses ones that do not make sense. Unrelated or repeated words interfere with ideas.

ELPS 4C, 4K

Development of Ideas
Supports all ideas completely and with specific detail. Shows deep or creative thinking that adds to the overall quality of the writing.

Voice Engages the reader throughout the writing. Sounds original and expresses the writer's personality or unique viewpoint.

Conventions Shows a strong command of grammar, sentence structure, mechanics, and spelling.

Development of Ideas
Supports all ideas, but some need to be developed with more details. Development may be thoughtful but may not show creative thinking.

Voice Engages the reader for most of the writing. Sounds original and expresses the writer's unique viewpoint.

Conventions Includes only minor errors in grammar, sentence structure, mechanics, and spelling.

Development of Ideas
Support is general or lacks depth. Support may be only a list. Information may be missing. The message may be unclear.

Voice Engages the reader in some parts of the writing. Sounds original in only a few places and does not express a unique viewpoint.

Conventions Several errors in grammar, sentence structure, mechanics, and spelling. Errors may interfere with the reader's understanding.

Development of Ideas
Does not support ideas, or provides unclear support. Important information may be left out. The message is unclear.

Voice Does not engage the reader. Does not sound original and does not express a unique viewpoint.

Conventions Major errors in grammar, sentence structure, mechanics, and spelling. These problems interfere with the reader's understanding.

Model Essay

This essay is an example of writing that fits a score of 4 using the *Write Source* Scoring Rubric. Read the description for a score of 4 on pages 34–35. Next, read the essay. Remember to think about the quality of the writing as a whole. Decide how you would score this essay. Then read the teacher's evaluation of this writing on page 32.

Writing that fits a score of 4 is very strong.

New Kid Lost

Meaningful introduction and conclusion create focus and coherence.

After a day of unfamiliar hallways and new faces, I was relieved to sink into a creaky but familiar bus seat. This bus groaned and coughed as it started up just as my old school bus used to.

We rumbled down the street and I looked dreamily outside. It would be only a few minutes and then I'd be home. Finally.

My shoulder knocked against the window and brought me out of my daydream. But this time when I looked out the window, I saw stores and office buildings. My heart beat faster and I craned my neck to check the bus number in the front window.

Details and inner dialogue help add voice.

"Oh, no!" I mumbled. "I'm on the wrong bus." I was supposed to take bus three, not bus eight. My face flamed. What an end to my first day!

We had lived in Austin for only about a week, so I hadn't met many people. It was hard enough being the newest fourth grader. I didn't need my classmates finding out that I had done something so dumb. Getting on the wrong school bus was something a first grader might do!

Nothing on the streets looked familiar. We were probably heading miles and miles away. I felt like crying. Sweat beaded on my forehead and panic swelled in my stomach. I could feel the eyes of my classmates boring into me. How was I going to get out of this mess?

Organized ideas flow smoothly and logically.

Suddenly, I spied the library—my favorite place. The bus shuddered to a stop in the middle of town and I popped up like I had springs. There's nothing I like more than curling up with a book, so I knew I would be safe at the library.

The librarian at the front desk knew what was up as soon as she saw my scared, sweaty face. She offered to call my mom right away. I've never been so happy to hear my mom's voice.

Good control of conventions and varied sentences

When my mom arrived, she told me she was proud of me. "You were in a new place, but you knew just what to do," she told me. "Getting lost is no big deal!" I had to agree. After this experience, I knew I could find my way around Austin. It would soon become home.

ELPS 4G, 4I, 4K

Evaluating an Essay

As you read through the personal narrative below, pay special attention to the strengths and weaknesses in the writing. Then follow the directions at the bottom of the page.

Cousin Jake

"Do I have to go to the family reunion?" I asked my mom. Every summer, everything is the same.

"Yes, you have to go," Mom answered. So we packed up the car, and off we went to Montana.

When we arrived at Uncle Billy's house, I saw a new kid hanging around. He was about my age, but he didn't look like he belonged in our family. Most of us are tall and have red hair. This kid was short, and he had curly, black hair. His name was Jake, and he was my new cousin! Uncle Billy had gotten married, and Jake was his new wife's son.

Through the whole reunion, Jake and I had fun. He let me fly his Japanese kite. We built a skateboard ramp, rode our bikes, and played baseball. One night, Jake and some of his friends and I slept outside in a big tent. Jake was a nice kid, and I was happy that he was a part of my family.

When it was time to go home, I felt sad. I'm already looking forward to next year. With Jake around, family reunions will be a lot more fun.

Use the *Write Source* rubric. Assess the narrative you have just read, using the scoring rubric on pages 34–35. Record your ratings and comments on a separate sheet of paper.

Peer Responding

Sooner or later, writers need someone to read what they've written. At school, you might say, "LaKisha, please read my report." At home, you might ask for a parent's opinion. If you do, you are acting like a real author.

Getting someone else's response can help you improve a first draft. This chapter explains how to organize a peer-editing session.

What's Ahead

- **Peer-Responding Guidelines**
- **Making Helpful Responses**
- **Peer Response Sheet**

Peer Respon

Writer: ...Curtis Davis............ Re:

Title: ..."Flying Fish, Ocean Acroba

What I liked about your writing:

....*.Your opening is full of action.....

...*.The details really helped me learn

....*.The story about the fisherman is ir

....

Questions I have . . .

*.What do you know about their enemie

*.How could you begin some of your sen

...different ways?.....................

Peer-Responding Guidelines

When you first do a peer response, you may work with one classmate. Later, you may have a chance to work with a small group of classmates. Either way, you need to know how to share and respond to a piece of writing.

The Author's Role

As an author, share a piece of writing that you are working on. If possible, make a copy for each member of the group.

- **Introduce your writing,** but don't say too much about it.
- **Read your writing out loud,** or ask group members to read it silently.
- **Ask group members what they think.** Listen carefully.
- **Take notes** to help you remember what was said.
- **Ask for help** with any specific problems.

The Responder's Role

As a responder, make sure to show the writer the proper respect. Also follow these guidelines:

- **Listen (or read) carefully.** Take notes to help you remember what you want to say.
- **Tell what works** well in the writing.
- **Ask questions** if you are unsure about something or find a part that could be improved.

Be sure that you give the writer useful information. A response like "Nice paper!" may make the writer feel good, but it doesn't help the writer make the paper better. Be more specific.

TEKS 5.15E
ELPS 3E, 3G

Making Helpful Responses

Responses from your classmates are important when you are ready to revise your writing. Responders can help you find parts that work well or don't work well. Use responses to revise your writing.

Be Specific

The most useful responses help a writer improve his or her writing. Try to state your responses in the form of a question.

Instead of . . .	Try something like . . .
✗ Your writing is dull.	✔ How could you begin some of your sentences in different ways?
✗ Some of your facts are wrong.	✔ Do flying fish really "fly"?
✗ The third paragraph doesn't say anything new.	✔ What do you know about their enemies?

Ask Good Questions

The best questions cannot be answered with a simple yes or no. Instead, they ask the writer to think.

- What got you interested in your topic?
- What is your most important point?
- How do you want the reader to feel about your topic?

Learning Language

With a partner, discuss the types of comments that are most helpful to you during peer-responding sessions. Work with the class to make a chart of helpful comments or questions to post in the classroom.

Peer Response Sheet

Your teacher may want you to complete a response sheet like the one below. (Sample comments are included.)

Peer Response Sheet

Writer: Curtis Davis   Responder: Kim Lee

Title: "Flying Fish, Ocean Acrobats"

What I liked about your writing:

* Your opening is full of action.

* The details really helped me learn about flying fish.

* The story about the fisherman is interesting.

Questions I have . . .

* What do you know about their enemies?

* How could you begin some of your sentences in

   different ways?

Practice

Exchange an essay or a story with a classmate. Then fill out a response sheet like the one above for each other's writing.

Publishing and Portfolios

Publishing is the important final step in the writing process. It makes all of your prewriting, drafting, and revising worth the effort. Your writing is ready to publish once it says exactly what you want it to say.

This chapter will help you prepare your writing for publishing. It will show you how to design a great-looking final copy and how to assemble a classroom portfolio.

What's Ahead

- **Designing Your Writing**
- **Types of Portfolios**
- **Parts of a Portfolio**
- **Sample Portfolio Reflections**

ELPS 2H, 3E

Designing Your Writing

Once your writing is complete, think about how you want your paper to look. The guidelines below, and the example on pages **45–46**, will help you design and publish your writing using a computer.

Typography

- Use a clear and easy-to-read font for the body and any headings.
- Keep the title and any headings short. Follow the rules for capitalizing titles and headings. (See page **556.2**.)

Spacing and Margins

- Double-space your writing.
- Indent the first line of every paragraph.
- Use one space after every period.
- Avoid odd breaks between pages. For example, don't leave a heading or the first line of a paragraph alone at the bottom of a page.

Graphics

- Use numbered or bulleted lists to set off important points.
- Include a table, a chart, or an illustration if it helps make an idea clearer. Make sure that there is plenty of space for any graphics you use.

Practice

Find a page in one of your textbooks (including this one) that you feel is well designed. Share the page with your classmates and point out at least three features that you like.

Great-Looking Design in Action

Roy Wilson

Saving a Vanishing Falcon

The font is easy to read.

Imagine a bird dropping out of the sky at 200 miles an hour. That is what makes the peregrine falcon such a successful bird of prey. In fact, the Air Force Academy has made the falcon its official mascot. The peregrine falcon was placed on the Endangered Species list until 1999. A well-planned reintroduction effort has saved these amazing birds.

Why were falcons endangered?

Although a falcon pair may raise as many as four chicks, only two usually survive past their first year. The loss of these chicks from a variety of causes threatened the survival of the species. The main problems are listed here.

A bulleted list helps organize the essay.

- **Hunting and egg removal:** Before 1950, hunters shot falcons. Eggs were often taken from nests for falconry or food.
- **Pesticides:** Falcons ate birds that had eaten poisoned insects. The main poison, DDT, affected the thickness of eggshells. Eggs cracked, and the chicks died before hatching.

Wilson 2

What did falcons need?

The peregrine falcons needed a chance to raise enough chicks to replace their numbers. They also needed pesticide-free food.

How were falcons saved?

Several wildlife organizations and government programs worked to restore the peregrine population.

1. Falcons were placed on the Endangered Species list.
2. Pesticides such as DDT, which could last a long time in nature, were banned.
3. Safer pesticides were developed.
4. Eggs were taken from captive birds.
5. Newly hatched birds were fed and protected.

More than 6,000 falcons have been bred and released. They are successfully living in wild areas as well as in cities with tall buildings. This recovery of the fastest birds of the air shows what can be done if people become involved.

Margins are at least one inch all around.

A numbered list makes ideas easy to follow.

An illustration is added.

Types of Portfolios

A portfolio is a collection of your writing that you put together for a specific reason. There are four basic types of portfolios.

Showcase Portfolio

A showcase portfolio shows off your best writing for a grading period. This is the most common type of portfolio. (See page 48.)

Growth Portfolio

A growth portfolio shows your progress as a writer. It contains writing assignments that show how your writing skills are developing throughout the year.

Personal Portfolio

A personal portfolio contains writing that you want to save and share with others. You can include different types of writing—poetry, stories, reports, essays. You can have different themes—friends, animals, hobbies, sports.

Electronic Portfolio

An electronic portfolio is presented on a Web site or saved on a disk. In addition to your writing, you may include graphics and sound. Electronic portfolios make your writing available to many people.

Practice

Write a brief paragraph about your experience with portfolios. When did you put one together? How did you feel about it when you finished?

Parts of a Portfolio

You may be asked to keep a showcase portfolio. It should contain the parts listed below, but check with your teacher to be sure.

- **A table of contents** lists the writing samples you have included in your portfolio.
- **A short essay or letter** introduces your portfolio. It tells how you put it together and how you feel about it.
- **The writing samples** present your best work. Your teacher may ask you to include all of your work—from prewriting through editing—for one or two samples.
- **Reflection sheets or checklists** identify the writing skills that you have mastered and the ones that you still need to work on.
- **A creative cover for your portfolio** may include graphics and sketches that say something about you as a writer.

Gathering Tips

- **Date and save all your work,** including prewriting notes, first drafts, and revisions for each writing assignment.
- **Store your writing in a pocket folder.** Then you will have everything that you need in one place.
- **Take pride in your work.** Prepare a portfolio that shows you at your best.

Practice

Plan a showcase portfolio cover. Include your name and a title. Then add your own sketches and graphics.

Sample Portfolio Reflections

To reflect on your writing, think about the process that you used to develop it. The samples below will help you get started.

Student Reflections

My story called "Two Faces of Thanksgiving" taught me an important lesson about life. People change from year to year, and we can't do anything about it.

—Tina Sung

"Floating or Fishing?" was really hard to write because it was a comparison essay. I had to figure out how to organize the details about my two topics, Lake Superior and Great Salt Lake.

—Jon Worthy

Professional Reflections

"As I began writing what became my first book, *The Moves Make the Man,* I found that I loved writing in Jerome's voice about basketball."

—Bruce Brooks

"By the time I wrote *Catherine, Called Birdy,* I already knew a great deal about the Middle Ages, and when I wanted to learn more, I was able to find lots of books about everyday life during those times."

—Karen Cushman

ELPS 2C, 2G, 2H, 2I, 3D, 3E, 3G, 3H, 4C, 4G

Descriptive Writing

Writing Focus
- **Descriptive Paragraph**
- **Descriptive Essay**

Learning Language

Work with a partner. Read the meanings aloud and share answers to the questions.

1. A descriptive paragraph gives a detailed picture of a person, a place, a thing, or an event.
   What descriptive words would you use in a paragraph about your favorite place?

2. Sensory details use the five senses to describe something (see, hear, smell, taste, touch).
   How might you use sensory details to describe something in your classroom?

3. A quality is something special about a person, place, or thing.
   What quality do you have that is special?

4. Someone or something is one of a kind when there is nothing else like it.
   Name someone or something that is one of a kind and tell why.

Descriptive Writing

Descriptive Paragraph

No two people are exactly the same. Each person has a special personality, a special look, and a one-of-a-kind mind. One of the best ways to capture a person's individual qualities is by writing a description.

In this chapter, you will write a paragraph describing a person. Your goal is to help your reader "see" the person you have chosen and understand something special about him or her.

Writing Guidelines

Subject: A person you see often
Purpose: To describe a person
Form: Descriptive paragraph
Audience: Classmates

TEKS 5.15B
ELPS 2G, 2H, 2I, 3D, 3E, 3G, 3H, 4C, 4G, 4I, 4J, 4K

Descriptive Paragraph

A descriptive paragraph gives a detailed picture of a person, a place, a thing, or an event. It begins with a **topic sentence** that tells what the paragraph is about. The sentences in the **body** give all the details about the topic. In Juanita's paragraph below, many sensory details are used to describe a special school janitor. The **closing sentence** wraps up the paragraph.

Squeaky Clean

Topic Sentence (underlined)

Mr. Wolfe, our school janitor, is the cleanest one in school. At six feet three inches tall, he towers over everyone. His round, bald head shines under the hallway lights. His wide smile welcomes us each

Body

day. A crisp blue work shirt fits snugly across his broad shoulders. A gold, jingly key ring is attached to a belt loop of his khaki pants. His polished

Closing Sentence (underlined)

work shoes squeak as he cleans up our messy lunchroom. It is a wonder that someone who cleans up after all of us stays so clean himself.

Respond to the reading. On your own paper, answer each of the following questions. Discuss your answers with a partner.

- **Development of Ideas** (1) How does the writer introduce the topic?

- **Organization** (2) What method of organization does the writer use—order of importance, order of location, or time order? Explain.

- **Voice** (3) How does the writer make the paragraph sound authentic, or real? Name one example.

Prewriting **Selecting a Topic**

First, you need to choose a person to write about. You can use a "people chart" like the one Juanita used for the paragraph on page 52.

People Chart

Neighbors	School Staff	Relatives	Friends
Harold (Duke)	Mrs. Isley	Uncle Ray	Shannon
Mrs. Reyes	Mr. Wolfe	Cousin Marsha	Freddy
Soo and Jin		Grandpa John	

Select a topic. Create a chart listing some people you know. Then circle the name of the person you would like to describe in your paragraph.

Gathering Details

When you write your descriptive paragraph, your goal is to create a true-to-life picture for the reader. A cluster, like the one below, can help you gather details about the person you plan to describe.

Gathering Cluster

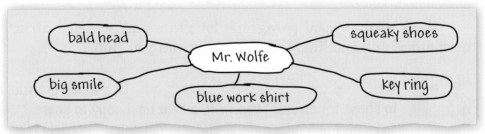

Make a cluster. Write the person's name in the center of your paper and circle it. Then write details about the person and connect them to the center circle.

★ **TEKS** 5.15B–D
ELPS 5G

Drafting Creating Your First Draft

The first draft of your paragraph is your chance to put all of your ideas on paper. Start with a topic sentence that catches the reader's interest. Then arrange the body sentences (details) by location, head to toe. End with a personal comment that wraps up your paragraph.

Write your first draft. Be sure to include the most important details about your person.

Revising Improving Your Paragraph

As you revise, you can add or rearrange details. You should cut details that don't help the reader see the person you are describing.

Revise your paragraph. You can use the following questions.

1. Does my topic sentence get the reader's attention?
2. Have I used order of location to organize my details?
3. Do I sound like I care about the person I am describing?
4. Do I use specific words to describe my subject?

Editing Checking for Conventions

Check your revised paragraph for grammar, sentence structure, mechanics, and spelling. Correct any errors you find.

Edit and proofread your paragraph. Use these questions to check for errors. Then write a neat final copy to share.

1. Do I use punctuation and capitalization correctly?
2. Are all my words spelled correctly?
3. Do I use the right words *(then, than)*?
4. Are my sentences complete? Do they flow smoothly?

Descriptive Writing

Descriptive Essay

Look around your classroom. Some of your classmates might have straight brown hair or curly black hair, some might wear glasses or earrings, some might be smiling or daydreaming. . . . No two classmates are exactly alike.

In this chapter, you will write an essay describing a person you admire. Besides physical characteristics, you'll describe something this person does that makes you admire him or her. All of these details will help the reader "see" the person and understand his or her personality.

Writing Guidelines

Subject: A person you admire

Purpose: To describe a person

Form: Descriptive essay

Audience: Classmates

TEKS 5.15B
ELPS 4I

Descriptive Essay

In the following essay, Natalia describes one of her favorite relatives. The notes on the side will help you to understand the different parts of this essay.

Beginning
The writer gets the reader's attention and names the subject of the essay.

Middle
Each middle paragraph describes something different about Aunt Frankie.

Aunt Frankie

Have you ever eaten pieces of warm pie crust sprinkled with cinnamon and sugar? Well, if you ever come to visit my favorite aunt, you will. Aunt Frankie is a fun, busy, and caring lady!

The thing I like best about Aunt Frankie is that she is always ready to have fun. After a long day at work, she usually comes in the door singing some tune. Sometimes she has a new dance step to share. Other times, she has a good story to tell as she hurries to change out of her work clothes.

Aunt Frankie is a woman who likes to be comfortable. At five foot three, she bounces out of her room with her shiny, dark brown hair pulled into a ponytail. She tucks the loose ends behind her tiny ears and smiles at me with sparkly blue eyes and a little mouth that looks just right on her small face. She almost always wears a big white T-shirt, old pink shorts, and no shoes. Purple nail polish glows from her bare toes.

TEKS 5.15B
ELPS 2G, 2H, 2I, 3D, 3E,
3G, 3H, 4C, 4G, 4I, 4J, 4K

Aunt Frankie's favorite pastime is baking. She's a genius with eggs, flour, milk, and salt. It's something she learned from her mom, and she promises to teach me someday. After gathering her baking supplies, she quickly mixes up some dough and rolls out the crust. Soon the smell of cinnamon and sugar fills the air.

Finally, she flops down next to me at the table. She puts her sticky hands on mine and asks me how my day was, how my classes are going, and what new friends I've made. Aunt Frankie always has time and treats to share at the end of the day.

Ending
The ending adds one final thought about Aunt Frankie.

Respond to the reading. After reading the essay, answer and discuss with a partner the following questions.

- **Development of Ideas** **(1) What details in the beginning get the reader's attention?**

- **Organization** **(2) In paragraph three, how does the writer organize the information—by order of importance or by order of location?**

- **Voice** **(3) List three words from the three middle paragraphs that show how the writer feels about Aunt Frankie.**

Prewriting **Selecting a Topic**

For your descriptive essay, you need to choose a person you know and admire. A chart like the one below can help.

Topic Chart

Person	Qualities I Admire
Ms. Grossman, grocery store owner	generous nice to customers keeps store clean and neat
Uncle Alex, Mom's brother who is a carpenter	smart plays catch with me builds houses
Raymond, our mail carrier*	positive attitude likes his job cares about people

Make a topic chart. List three people and the qualities you admire about them. Put a star (*) next to the person you choose. Discuss your choice with a partner.

Gathering Details

Think about the personality, the physical appearance, and the good qualities of the person you chose.

Gather details. Answer the following questions.

1 What one word best describes the person's personality? Why?

2 How would you describe the person from head to toe?

3 What does the person do that makes you admire him or her?

Using Sensory Details

A chart covering the five senses can help you gather specific details about your subject.

Sensory Chart

See	Hear	Smell	Taste	Touch
curly black hair eagle patch blue shirt	whistles cheerful stories	cologne	cool water cookies	heavy bag

 Prewrite

Create a sensory chart. Using the chart above as a guide, create your own sensory chart.

Organizing Your Details

Each paragraph in your essay has a different job to do. A list like the one below can help you organize the details for your paragraphs.

Directions   **Organized List**

Directions	Organized List
Name your subject.	Raymond, our mail carrier
List personality traits.	1. cheerful, friendly
Describe appearance.	2. curly black hair, blue shirt with patch, kneesocks
Name something you admire about the person.	3. cares about people, checks on Mrs. Jordan

 Prewrite

Create an organized list. Follow the directions above to create an organized list for your description.

TEKS 5.15B
ELPS 5G

Drafting Starting Your Essay

Your beginning paragraph should get the reader's attention and introduce the person you will describe.

Beginning
Middle
Ending

Beginning Paragraph

■ **Make a connection with the reader.**

> Everybody dreams of doing something important. Raymond dreamed of being a big-time drummer. He once played in the Narly Trees Band. When that band broke up, he had to find other work. Now Raymond is our mail carrier, and he's important to our whole neighborhood.

■ **Begin with a familiar saying.**

> Raymond lives by the saying "If you can't live the life you love, love the life you live." As a boy, Raymond dreamed of being a drummer in a band. Now he's living a different dream as the best mail carrier we've ever had.

Draft

Write your beginning paragraph. You can choose one of the approaches above to get you started. Keep the focus on your topic.

Texas Traits

⭐ Focus on the Texas Traits

Voice The special way you express your ideas is called *voice*. The voice in your essay should show that you know and care about the person you are describing.

Developing the Middle Part

The middle part of your essay should have three paragraphs that follow your organized list (from page 59). See the side notes below.

Middle Paragraphs

The person's personality is described.

Raymond is always cheerful. He greets everyone with a big smile and a friendly "Hi, how are you?" Best of all, he really wants to know! It's hard to be gloomy when we hear him whistling up and down the street.

The person's appearance is described.

Our mail carrier makes sure he always looks his best. Raymond wears a gray golfer's cap on his curly black hair, and silvery sunglasses hang on a chain around his neck. His blue postal shirt has a patch like a Boy Scout badge on the top of the left sleeve. It shows an eagle with a United States flag behind it. Blue suspenders hold up his gray shorts, and black kneesocks and shoes cover his legs and feet.

The writer shares a story about the person.

Raymond cares a lot about the people on his route. Every day, he knocks on Mrs. Jordan's door to ask for a drink of cool water. He's not really thirsty. Mrs. Jordan is old, and he just wants to make sure she's okay.

Draft

Write your middle paragraphs. Follow your organized list (from page 59) as you write your three middle paragraphs.

Drafting **Ending Your Essay**

The ending paragraph in your essay should share an interesting final thought with the reader.

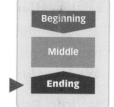
Beginning
Middle
Ending

Ending Paragraph

The writer gives a final thought about the person.

The U.S. Postal Service got a great employee when they hired Raymond. People depend on him for their mail, and they look forward to his friendly daily visits. In our neighborhood, Raymond is much more than just a mail carrier.

Draft

Write your ending paragraph. Try to leave the reader with an interesting final thought about the person.

Revising and Editing

Revise

Revise your description. Use the questions below as a guide when you revise your essay.

- **Focus and Coherence** Do I focus on the topic?
- **Organization** Do I have a clear beginning, middle, and ending?
- **Development of Ideas** Do I include sensory details?
- **Voice** Does my voice show that I care about my topic?
- **Conventions** Do my sentences flow smoothly?

Edit

Edit your description. Use the checklist on page 30 to guide your editing. Prepare a neat copy and have a classmate help you proofread it. Use the feedback to make necessary changes.

Descriptive Writing
Across the Curriculum

"Tell me all about it!" Friends want to know what you did over the weekend or what happened at the game. They want to know what things looked like, sounded like, and tasted like. So it's important to be able to describe things well.

You'll also be asked to describe things in your school subjects. You may need to write a description of a historical figure in social studies or a description of how a science topic relates to your everyday life. This chapter will help you sharpen your description skills.

What's Ahead

- **Social Studies**: Describing a Person from History
- **Science**: Describing a Chemical Change

TEKS 5.15B

Social Studies:
Describing a Person from History

Your teacher may ask you to write about a famous person from history. Notice how descriptive writing is used in the sample below.

Molly Pitcher

The **beginning** tells why the person is important.

During the Revolutionary War, Mary Hays McCauly earned the name "Molly Pitcher" at the Battle of Monmouth in 1778. She was a brave woman, and George Washington and his troops respected her.

Mary dressed like any other young woman of her time. She piled her long blond hair on top of her head and covered it with a dust cap. She often wore a white blouse and rust-colored skirt. That's what she wore on the day of the battle at Monmouth, New Jersey.

The **middle** describes the person and what she did.

June 18 was a hot, hot day. Soldiers were roasting in their heavy wool uniforms, and they were very thirsty. The metal gun barrels got so hot that the soldiers couldn't touch them. Mary helped the troops by carrying pitcher after pitcher of cool water to them. She raced back and forth across the battlefield with her skirt fluttering like a flag. Although she choked on the smoky air and bullets whizzed by her, Mary kept running.

The **ending** includes a final thought about the person.

Suddenly Mary dropped her pitcher. Her husband had fallen from heat stroke, so she took his place and helped his crew fire the cannon. She helped fire the cannon at the enemy again and again. Mary's strength and courage inspired the soldiers. From that day on, she was known as Molly Pitcher.

TEKS 5.15A, 5.15B
ELPS 5G

Writing Tips

Before you write . . .

- **Choose a person from history.**
  Select a person from a time you have studied.
- **Do your research.**
  Find information and pictures about the person and what he or she did to earn a place in history.
- **Take notes.**
  Focus on the person's appearance and actions.

During your drafting . . .

- **Organize your details.**
  Introduce your topic in the beginning. In the middle, give details about the person. End with a final thought about the person.
- **Show, don't tell.**
  Use descriptive details that help the reader see the person and understand why he or she is important.
- **Sound excited.**
  Use specific words that show you know a lot about this person.

After you've written a first draft . . .

- **Check for completeness.**
  Make sure to give the reader a clear picture of the person.
- **Check for correctness.**
  Proofread your essay for errors in grammar, sentence structure, mechanics, and spelling.

Plan and write an essay. Choose a person from history and write a detailed description of the person, following these writing tips.

Science: Describing a Chemical Change

Your science teacher may ask you to describe how science affects your everyday life. In the sample below, Ravi uses descriptive writing to tell what part science played at a family campfire.

S'more Changes

The **beginning** introduces a science topic.

Last Tuesday our science teacher told us about chemical changes. A chemical change makes a new substance that has different properties. Burning is an example of a chemical change. For example, when you burn wood, you change the properties of wood into the properties found in smoke, gases, and ashes.

This weekend my family built a campfire, and we made s'mores. To make a s'more, you have to heat a marshmallow on a pointed stick over a fire. If you take your time, the marshmallow will get soft and gooey. When you press it between two graham crackers along with some chocolate, the whole thing is sweet and crunchy. If you would let the s'more cool off, you could carefully separate the parts again.

The **middle** relates personal experience to the topic.

However, I was in too much of a hurry. I put my marshmallow too close to the heat. It caught on fire and turned black like charcoal. Instead of being soft and gooey, it was crackly and dry. It didn't smell sweet anymore. It tasted like ashes.

The **ending** summarizes the topic with a final thought.

So I learned that a chemical change doesn't happen when I slowly heat a marshmallow. Its properties are not permanently changed. A burned marshmallow, though, is the result of a chemical change because it will never be soft, sweet, and gooey again.

Writing Tips

Before you write . . .

- **Choose a topic that interests you.**
  Select something you have both studied in science class and experienced in your everyday life.
- **List the main ideas you want to include.**
  Consider what you know about your topic and how you experienced it.

During your drafting . . .

- **Write a clear beginning, middle, and ending.**
  Introduce the topic in the beginning, describe the experience in the middle, and end with a summary of your findings.
- **Organize your details.**
  Choose the best organization for your description— order of location, time order, or order of importance.
- **Use specific words.**
  Select specific nouns, action verbs, and adjectives.

After you've written a first draft . . .

- **Check for completeness.**
  Add details to make your topic clearer.
- **Check for correctness.**
  Proofread your description for errors in grammar, sentence structure, mechanics, and spelling.

Describe a science-related experience.
Use these tips to guide your writing.

ELPS 2C, 2G, 2H, 2I, 3D, 3E, 3G, 3H, 4C, 4G

Narrative Writing

Writing Focus

- **Narrative Paragraph**
- **Personal Narrative**

Grammar Focus

- **Subject-Verb Agreement in Simple Sentences**
- **Subject-Verb Agreement in Compound Sentences**

Learning Language

Work with a partner. Read the meanings aloud and discuss your answers to the questions.

1. A narrative essay tells a story.
   How is a narrative essay different from a descriptive essay?

2. Something that is challenging is difficult to do.
   Tell about a challenging experience you had last summer.

3. Success is achieving a goal.
   What success did you have recently?

4. When people get fired up, they become more enthusiastic.
   What happened that got you fired up?

Narrative Writing

Narrative Paragraph

Every time you finish a challenging job, you experience success. Think about some of your successes. Maybe you remembered all your lines in the school play, played your trombone solo well, or got a perfect score on a math test. It's successes like these that make you feel good about yourself.

You can share your success stories with others by writing about them. The following pages will help you write a narrative paragraph about a time when you succeeded at doing something you thought was challenging.

Writing Guidelines

Subject: Experiencing success
Purpose: To entertain
Form: Narrative paragraph
Audience: Classmates

 **TEKS** 5.15A, 5.15B
ELPS 2G, 2H, 2I, 3D, 3E,
3G, 3H, 4C, 4G, 4I, 4K

Narrative Paragraph

A narrative paragraph shares an event or experience. It begins with a **topic sentence** that introduces the main idea. The **body** of the paragraph contains details about what happened, and the **closing sentence** gives the reader something to think about. In the paragraph below, Tameeka shares an unexpected moment of success in gym class.

Topic Sentence (underlined)

Body

Closing Sentence (underlined)

A Successful Run

I never thought I was a good runner, until the day in gym class when I won the mile race. The course was marked with colorful flags, and the sight of the flags seemed to fire me up. When Ms. Holt, our gym teacher, blew her whistle, I charged ahead. To my surprise, I was one of the leaders right away. About halfway around the course, I noticed a few kids grabbing their sides. Some kids even started walking. I felt tired, too, but I kept running. Ms. Holt congratulated me when I was the first runner across the finish line. I thanked her and grinned. Now I think about running all the time. Maybe someday I'll even get the chance to run in the Olympics.

Respond to the reading. Answer the following questions on your own paper. Discuss your thoughts with a partner.

- **Organization (1) Does the writer organize the details by time or by location?**

- **Development of Ideas (2) What is the main idea of this paragraph?**

- **Voice (3) What words show the writer's personal feelings? Name two or three.**

TEKS 5.15A
ELPS 5G

Prewriting **Selecting a Topic**

The writer of "A Successful Run" used a topic chart to record her successes.

Topic Chart

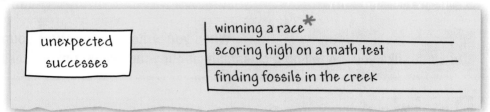

unexpected successes	winning a race*
	scoring high on a math test
	finding fossils in the creek

Prewrite

Make a chart like the one above. First, write "unexpected successes" in a box. Then, on the lines, write three examples. Put a star (✱) next to the one you want to write about.

Gathering Details

Next, Tameeka used a grid to gather details. She listed her moment of success, the events leading up to it, and how she felt afterward.

Gathering Grid

My moment of success	Events in the order they happened	How I felt afterward
• won a race	• mile run in gym class • course marked with flags • kept on running and passed other kids • finished first	• happy • wanted to run more races • dreamed about being in the Olympics someday

Prewrite

Make a gathering grid. Write down your moment of success, the events that led you to it, and how you felt afterward. Discuss your thoughts with a partner.

TEKS 5.15B, 5.15D
ELPS 5G

Drafting Developing the First Draft

Your narrative paragraph should include a topic sentence, a body, and a closing sentence. The topic sentence introduces the main idea, the body tells what happened, and the closing sentence gives the reader something to think about.

Write your first draft. When you write, try to make it sound like you are telling a classmate about your moment of success.

Draft

Revising Improving Your Paragraph

The tips that follow will help you revise your first draft.

- **Show, don't tell.** Instead of writing "I was happy," write "I threw my glove in the air."
- **Use time order.** Be sure the actions or details are arranged in the order in which they happened.

Revise your paragraph. Use the tips above to help you improve the first draft of your narrative paragraph.

Revise

Editing Checking for Conventions

It's important to check your writing for grammar, sentence structure, punctuation, capitalization, and spelling errors.

Edit and proofread. Use these questions as a guide when you edit. Then make a clean copy and proofread.

Edit

1 Have I used capital letters and end punctuation?
2 Have I checked for spelling errors?
3 Do all subjects and verbs agree?
4 Are all my sentences complete sentences?

Narrative Writing

Personal Narrative

How would you complete the following sentence? "I felt really proud when I . . . " Whenever you succeed at something, big or small, you should feel proud.

This chapter will help you recall times when you succeeded at something. Then it will guide you as you share your success story in a personal narrative.

Writing Guidelines

Subject: A time when you succeeded
Purpose: To share a true story
Form: Personal narrative
Audience: Classmates

 **Understanding Your Goal**

Your goal in this chapter is to write a narrative about a personal success. The traits listed below will help you meet that goal. The scoring rubric on pages **34–35** will also help to improve your writing.

Focus and Coherence
Write about a special personal achievement. Focus on the event by telling what happened and why this experience made you feel proud.

Organization
Start with an interesting beginning that grabs your readers' attention. Arrange the details of the event in time order. Use transition words to get from one idea to the next.

Development of Ideas
Include specific details so the reader understands why this success was important to you. Use specific nouns and vivid verbs.

Voice
Express your thoughts and feelings in a natural way so it sounds like you are telling your story to a friend.

Conventions
Be sure your grammar is correct. Use complete sentences. Check for correct capitalization, punctuation, and spelling.

 Literature Connection: For an example of a personal narrative, read about Travis's leg injury in the first part of Chapter 11 in *Old Yeller* by Fred Gipson.

TEKS 5.15B
ELPS 4I

Personal Narrative

In this narrative, Jamaal shares an important personal success—winning an award in an art contest.

What Is It?

Beginning
The beginning sets the scene.

When I paint, I love splashing bright colors and wild designs across the paper. That's my style. Last month, Ms. Robertson, my art teacher, told me about the school's art contest. She said, "Jamaal, entering this contest would be a good experience for you."

"Why?" I asked. "Most people think my art is weird."

"Well, I don't," Ms. Robertson replied.

The contest's theme was "The World: Its Continents and Countries." I immediately thought of Africa. Bright sunsets and patterns of wild animal hides rushed through my brain. Right then, I decided to enter the contest.

Middle
The middle includes colorful details (blue).

I sketched out my idea and worked hard on my painting. Streaks of red, orange, gold, and yellow spread across my paper. I zigzagged zebra stripes, made giant giraffe spots, and added gray ridges of elephant skin. Between the colors and patterns, I hid the letters A–F–R–I–C–A. After hours and hours of work, I stood back and took one last look. I saw Africa.

The very next day I took my painting to school. Ms. Robertson looked at it and said, "Well, Jamaal, I'm not at all surprised by your painting."

TEKS 5.15B
ELPS 2G, 2H, 2I, 3D, 3E, 3G, 3H, 4C, 4G, 4I, 4K

Middle
Each new paragraph builds suspense into the story.

"Is that good or bad?" I asked.

Instead of answering me, she just took my painting and hung it up next to all of the other ones.

During the day, I kept wondering what the judges thought of my painting. Then in the afternoon, I received an envelope. My heart pounded as I opened it. The first three judges wrote about how they liked my colors and my bold designs. As I unfolded the final sheet, my eyes shot to words in bright orange ink. "Africa! I can just see the sun setting on the Serengeti Plains." I was so surprised.

Ending
The ending tells how the writer felt.

I won a red ribbon for second place! But I almost felt like I had won first place because someone actually saw my Africa. After that, I felt more excited about painting. Now if people ask, "What is it?" I proudly tell them.

Respond to the reading. Answer the following questions about the narrative. Discuss your thoughts, opinions, and ideas with a partner.

- **Organization** (1) How is the middle part organized—by time order or by order of importance?

- **Development of Ideas** (2) What specific success does the author write about?

- **Voice** (3) What words and phrases reveal the writer's personal feelings? Name two or three.

Prewriting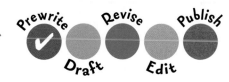

To get started, you need to choose a personal experience to write about. After that, you need to gather plenty of details.

Keys to Prewriting

1. **Think** of several personal successes you have had.

2. **Choose** one that will make a great story.

3. **Use** a time line to organize your story.

4. **Gather** sensory details about the experience.

5. **Think** about dialogue to include.

TEKS 5.15A
ELPS 5G

Prewriting **Selecting a Topic**

Anna, the writer of the essay on pages 85–88, used the sentence starter "I was proud when I . . . " to think of successes in her life.

Sentence Starter

> Personal Successes
>
> I was proud when I . . .
>
>   learned to play the guitar.
>
> * made tacos all by myself.
>
>   improved my grade in science.
>
>   finished a walkathon.

> You will do your best writing if you choose a topic you truly care about.

Brainstorm for topics. On your own paper, complete the sentence starter "I was proud when I . . . ." List four or five different personal successes. Put a star (*) next to the experience that would make the best story.

Reflecting on Your Topic

Thinking about your topic is an important part of prewriting. One way to think is to write freely about your success. Begin by explaining why the experience is special to you. Continue writing down whatever thoughts come to mind about it.

Reflect on your topic. Write freely for 5 minutes about your topic. Discuss your thoughts with a partner.

Finding the Basics

A 5 W's chart can help you gather basic details for your story. You may add H *(How?)* to your chart for even better coverage. Anna used the chart below to gather her details.

> Using graphic organizers will help you collect the best details for your story.

5 W's Chart

Topic: Making tacos by myself

Who?	My mom, my sister, and me
What?	I made supper when my mom sprained her ankle.
When?	Around supper time
Where?	At my house
Why?	I wanted to cook by myself and help my mom.

Make a chart. Create a 5 W's chart like the one above for your narrative.

Texas Traits

Focus on the Texas Traits

Development of Ideas A strong narrative includes (1) the *basic details* of what happened; (2) *sensory details* about what you saw, felt, and heard; and (3) *dialogue* to show what people said.

80

Prewriting Putting Things in Order

Just as a 5 W's chart works well for gathering basic details, a time line is handy for listing specific details in the order in which they happened.

Time Line

Topic: Making tacos by myself

- Mom hurt her ankle.
- She asked me to heat up leftovers for supper.
- I decided to make tacos instead.
- I searched the fridge for everything.
- I started peeling and chopping ingredients.
- I heated the meat and salsa in the microwave.
- The tacos were done, and we ate supper.

Create your time line. On your own paper, make a time line like the one above. List the main details in time order.

Focus on the Texas Traits

Organization For a narrative, you should arrange the details in time order, the order in which they happened. Ever since you heard your first story, you've been learning how to use this basic method of organization.

Collecting Sensory Details

There is more to writing a narrative than just telling what happens first, second, and third. A narrative needs **sensory details** that help the reader see, feel, smell, and hear an experience.

Sentences with effective sensory details:

> Using a dull table knife, I sawed into the tomato. Splat—red juice squirted onto my new white T-shirt!

The writer of the narrative on pages 85–88 used a sensory circle chart to collect sensory details for her narrative.

Sensory Circle Chart

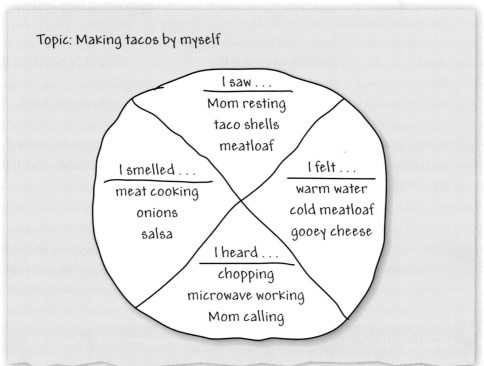

Topic: Making tacos by myself

I saw . . .
Mom resting
taco shells
meatloaf

I felt . . .
warm water
cold meatloaf
gooey cheese

I smelled . . .
meat cooking
onions
salsa

I heard . . .
chopping
microwave working
Mom calling

Prewrite

List sensory details. Draw a circle chart and label it with the same headings shown in the example above. Then list the sensory details connected with your own experience.

ELPS 5G

Prewriting Thinking About Dialogue

Dialogue makes an experience come alive for the reader. The chart below shows the three main things that dialogue can do.

		Without Dialogue	With Dialogue
1	Show something about a speaker's personality.	Mother sat in her chair while I worked in the kitchen. I told my mother to stay in her chair.	"How are things going in there?" she called from the other room. "Fine!" I said. "Just stay there and rest your foot."
2	Add details.	I quickly grabbed my sunglasses. My sister looked at me.	I quickly grabbed my sunglasses. "You look silly!" my sister said.
3	Keep the action moving.	It was time to eat supper.	"Supper is ready!" I called to Mom and my sister.

Prewrite **Plan some dialogue.** Think about what the people in your story should say to each other. Make your dialogue sound real.

 Texas Traits

Focus on the Texas Traits

Voice Your narrative voice will be strong if you write like you know the topic well and are truly interested in it. Also, using dialogue can make your voice sound more natural.

TEKS 5.15C
ELPS 5G

Drafting

Go Online!

Prewrite ○ ✓ Revise ○ Publish ○
Draft   Edit

Now that you have gathered details for your narrative, you are ready to write your first draft. Your goal is to get all of your thoughts about the topic down on paper.

Keys to Drafting

1. **Write** strong beginning and ending paragraphs. Keep the focus on your topic.

2. **Use** time order to organize events.

3. **Write** with your purpose, form, and audience in mind. Ask yourself:
   - Am I sharing a true story about a time in my life?
   - Does my story include my thoughts and feelings?
   - Do I keep my classmates interested?
   - Do I need to explain anything they won't know about?

TEKS 5.15B, 5.17
ELPS 5G

Drafting Getting the Big Picture

The chart below shows how the parts of a personal narrative fit together. (The examples are from the narrative on pages **85–88**.) You are ready to write your essay when you have . . .

- put the events of your story in time order and
- gathered enough details to express your thoughts and feelings.

Beginning	**Opening Sentence**
The **beginning** catches the reader's attention.	One day, my mom sprained her ankle and had to stay off her feet.
Middle	• We had everything I needed.
The **middle** part gives details about what happened during the experience.	• First, I washed my hands. • In our kitchen, kids can't . . . • Carefully, I started peeling . . . • Then I had to prepare . . . • Finally, it was time to eat.
Ending	**Closing Sentence**
The **ending** tells how you felt about the experience.	I felt great about doing something special for Mom, and she was proud of me for making supper all by myself.

TEKS 5.15B
ELPS 5G

Starting Your Personal Narrative

In the first paragraph, you should get the reader's attention and introduce your personal experience. Here are three ways to begin your paragraph.

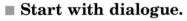

Beginning
Middle
Ending

- **Start with dialogue.**

  "I sprained my ankle," Mom said. "You will have to make supper tonight."

- **Begin with an interesting statement or fact.**

  One day, my mom sprained her ankle and couldn't walk.

- **Put yourself in the middle of the action.**

  When Mom asked me to heat up leftovers for supper, I had another idea. I decided to surprise her with tacos!

Beginning Paragraph

The writer begins with an interesting statement.

One day, my mom sprained her ankle and had to stay off her feet. She asked me to make supper. Mom said I could microwave the leftover meatloaf, but I wanted to surprise her with her favorite meal—tacos!

Remember to sound interested in your topic when you write.

Draft

Write your beginning paragraph. Use the ideas on this page to write two or three beginnings for your first paragraph. Choose the best one and finish the paragraph.

TEKS 5.15B, 5.17
ELPS 5G

Drafting Developing the Middle Part

The middle part of a narrative tells the story. It should be organized chronologically, or in time order. Here are some other things to keep in mind.

- **Arrange details** in a coherent way that makes sense to the reader.

- **Use dialogue**.

- **Share the thoughts and feelings** you experienced.

Middle Paragraphs

The writer immediately gets the story moving.

We had everything I needed. I'd seen a box of taco shells in the cabinet. In the fridge, there was leftover meatloaf. We had plenty of fresh tomatoes, onions, lettuce, and salsa, too. I also found a box of cheese, the kind that melts on cheeseburgers. I couldn't wait to get started!

Transition words (blue) help put the story in time order.

First I washed my hands. Then I crumbled the cold meatloaf into little pieces. I planned on zapping the meat and the salsa when it was time to eat. Next I shredded the lettuce into little pieces and piled it in a bowl.

In our kitchen, kids can't use sharp knives or the stove unless Mom is there to supervise. No problem. Using a dull table knife, I sawed into the tomato. Splat—red juice squirted onto my new white T-shirt! I hoped Mom didn't hear me groaning.

TEKS 5.15B, 5.17
ELPS 5G

Dialogue makes the characters real.

"How are things going in there?" she called from the other room.

"Fine!" I said. "Just stay there and rest your foot."

Carefully, I started peeling the onion. Ouch! The fumes burned my eyes. They really stung! Big tears streamed down my cheeks like a waterfall. I quickly grabbed my sunglasses. "You look silly!" my sister said. "But my eyes hurt," I cried. I realized the glasses didn't help.

Sensory details (green) help the reader "see" and "feel" the experience.

Then I had to prepare the cheese. I thought this would be the easy part. I tried to grate it, but it was too soft. Soon I had cheese goo all over my hands, and the grater was all clogged. I ended up using the knife on the cheese, too. It took forever to cut it into itty-bitty pieces.

Finally it was time to eat. I microwaved the meat and salsa, and then I put the tacos together. At the last minute, I remembered to grab the sour cream. Mom loves a big spoonful on her taco.

"Supper is ready!" I called to Mom and my sister.

Draft

Write your middle paragraphs. Before you start, review your details to make sure you shared all your thoughts and feelings.

 **TEKS** 5.15B, 5.17
ELPS 5G

Drafting Ending Your Personal Narrative

The final paragraph should bring your narrative to a close. Here are three strategies you can use to end your story.

Beginning

Middle

Ending

■ **Tell what you learned from the experience.**

My tacos tasted great, and Mom loved her surprise. In the beginning, I wasn't sure I could make tacos all by myself. But I learned that if I try, I can make supper for my family.

■ **Explain how the experience changed you.**

Mom said they were the best tacos she ever ate! That made me grin from ear to ear. I showed her that I'm a responsible kid. Now I want to help make meals more often.

■ **Tell how you felt about the experience.**

Ending Paragraph

The writer tells how she felt.

Mom smiled when she saw my tacos. They didn't look like Mom's tacos, but she said they were a wonderful surprise. I felt great about doing something special for Mom, and she was proud of me for making supper all by myself. I learned that I can make supper for my family and showed Mom that I'm a responsible kid.

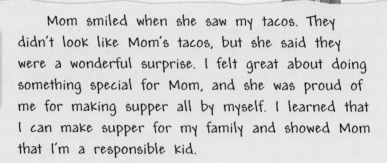

Write your ending. Use one of the three strategies listed above to end your narrative. Remember to include your thoughts and feelings about the experience.

⭐ **TEKS** 5.15C

Revising

Prewrite • Draft • Revise ✓ • Edit • Publish

Revising may be the most important step in the writing process. During this step, you can improve your narrative by adding details and by changing parts that sound confusing.

Keys to Revising

1. **Read** your narrative to yourself.

2. **Ask** yourself these questions:
   - Did I share a true story about a time in my life?
   - Does my story include my thoughts and feelings?
   - Will my classmates understand and want to read my narrative?

3. **Revise** for focus and coherence, organization, development of ideas, and voice.

Revising for Focus and Coherence

When you revise for *focus and coherence,* check to see that you have focused on one event. All details, descriptions, and dialogue in your narrative should be about that event. Be sure your beginning, middle, and ending paragraphs relate to each other and the main idea. A meaningful introduction and conclusion will also help make your narrative coherent.

Have I focused on one event?

You have focused on one event if all the ideas in your narrative are about that event. Be sure to only include details that relate to the one event.

Practice

Read this paragraph that tells about a personal experience. Identify the sentences that do not focus on that experience.

When the day of my oral report finally arrived, I thought about faking an illness. I have food allergies. The only problem with that plan was my mother knew about my speech. She had heard it so many times, she could probably recite it from memory! Though I was confident when I delivered my presentation to my parents, a classroom filled with students was a different story. My only choice was to get up and do my best. My best friend was supposed to give his speech today, too. I put on my favorite shirt, a new pair of jeans, and my lucky ring. If I was going to impress my classmates with my speech, I'd better look the part.

Check for focus. Read through your first draft or share with a partner. Are all your ideas about your personal experience? Are there any unrelated ideas that should not be included?

TEKS 5.15C

How do I know if my introduction and conclusion are meaningful and make my narrative coherent?

If your introduction gets the reader's attention and introduces the main idea, then you have a meaningful introduction. If your conclusion supports the focus of your writing and makes it feel complete, then you have a meaningful conclusion.

Your introduction is strong if it

- starts with some dialogue.
- begins with an interesting statement or fact.

A strong conclusion can

- remind the reader of the main idea.
- explain how you felt about the experience.

Revise

Check your introduction and conclusion. Do your beginning and conclusion work well? If not, rewrite them. Use one of the suggestions above.

Revising in Action

In the sample conclusion below, Anna added a simple sentence and a compound sentence. These changes improved the style of the narrative and gave more meaning to the conclusion.

Mom smiled when she saw my tacos. They didn't look

like Mom's tacos, but she said they were a wonderful
I felt great about doing something special for Mom, and
surprise. ∧She was proud of me for making supper all by

myself. I learned that I can make supper for my family and
∧ showed Mom that I'm a responsible kid.

Revising for Organization

When you revise for *organization,* make sure the ideas in your narrative are easy to follow. The order of your ideas should make sense to the reader. It is important that the ideas are connected. They should flow smoothly from sentence to sentence and paragraph to paragraph.

How do I know if my ideas are in the right order?

A personal narrative organizes ideas in time order. Details should be organized in the order in which they happened.

Practice

Read this narrative about a personal success. Identify the sentence that is out of order. Identify where it should go to make the story easy to follow.

I knocked down two hurdles, which slowed me down. I had been practicing every day after my cast was off. I wasn't sure I could run fast enough after breaking my ankle in the spring. I got set, the gun popped, and off I raced. When I crossed the finish line, I realized I was in second. Not bad for a kid who had a broken ankle four months earlier. I guess the practicing paid off.

Revise

Check your order. Is your narrative logically organized and easy to follow? If not, check the order of your sentences.

How do I know if my ideas flow smoothly?

Your ideas flow smoothly when one sentence or paragraph connects with the next. Transition words, phrases, and sentences help connect ideas. The following sets of transitions work well in narratives.

first then next	before after finally
now then soon	as soon as at last in the end

Revise **Review the sentences in your draft.** If you find that you have not used transitions, find a place where they could help the reader connect one idea to another.

Revising in Action

In the sample below, three transition words are added and an unrelated idea is deleted so that one paragraph connects to the next.

First
I washed my hands. Then I crumbled the cold meatloaf into little pieces. I planned on zapping the meat and the salsa when it was time to eat. Next I shredded the lettuce...

~~My neighbor likes tacos.~~ In our kitchen, kids can't use sharp knives or the stove in our kitchen unless Mom is there to supervise.

Revising for Development of Ideas

When you revise for *development of ideas,* make sure that the examples and details that you use help to tell the story and convey your thoughts and feelings to the reader.

Do my details move the story along?

Every detail should help you tell your story from beginning to end. Together, the details should answer any important questions a reader may have about your experience. Any detail that doesn't add to your story should be deleted.

Practice

Read the following paragraph. Then identify the two sentences (details) that should be deleted because they don't add to the story.

1   Dad said he would take me camping if I improved my math
2   grade. I really wanted to go, so I decided to work harder on my
3   math homework. After supper every night, I went to my room and
4   got right to work. Sometimes we have cheeseburgers for supper,
5   which I like a lot. Right away I started to understand things
6   better. At parent-teacher conferences, Mr. Cruz told my parents I
7   had raised my grade to a B. Mr. Cruz is a new teacher. The next
8   weekend my dad took me camping.

Check the details in your narrative. Does each detail add something important to your story? Delete any details that don't.

Revise

ELPS 5G

Do my details make the story seem real?

Your story will seem real if you include enough sensory details. Sensory details help a reader see, hear, feel, taste, or smell an experience. Add or delete sentences if necessary.

Practice

From the following paragraph, list one detail for each sense.

1   My mom finally let me take the subway by myself. The seat
2   feels cold on my legs. Everything looks and feels a little dirty.
3   The air smells of perfume and sweat. Across from me, a homeless
4   man is talking to himself. He looks like a bundle of rags. The train
5   suddenly screeches to a stop.

Revise

Review your details. Have you used sensory details in your narrative? If not, make sure to add some.

Revising in Action

In the sample below, sensory details are added and an unneeded detail is cut in order to make the story seem real.

Ouch! The fumes burned my eyes. They really stung!
Carefully, I started peeling the onion. Big tears streamed
down my cheeks like a waterfall. ~~I hated it~~ I quickly . . .

Revising for Voice

When you revise for *voice,* be sure your writing sounds natural—as if you were telling your story to a classmate.

Does my narrative have "voice"?

Your narrative will have voice if (1) you are excited about the experience and (2) you want to share it with your classmates.

Writing with Voice

Just then I felt a rush of wind, and I hit the ground facedown. But Bo pulled me right up by the T-shirt. He pointed his flashlight toward a big branch. Then I saw it. A huge great horned owl swiveled its head toward us. Wow! I was staring into a very spooky pair of yellow-gold eyes.

Practice

Freewrite for 4 minutes, starting with the following idea:

My friend and I...

After you finish your writing, underline parts that sound exciting or sound just like you.

Revise

Check for voice. Review your narrative to see if you sound excited and interested. Change any parts that sound dull.

Does my dialogue work well?

Your dialogue works well if it makes the people seem real and helps you tell your story. Add more if necessary.

Sample Dialogue

> We had climbed into a tree house about 20 feet off the ground.
> "Whoa! Is it safe up here?" I exclaimed.
>   "Safer than on the streets," Bo laughed.
>   Then I heard some bird squawking. "What's his problem?"
> I asked.
>   Bo whispered, "A raven has spotted an owl."

 Revise   **Check the dialogue.** Does the dialogue work well in your narrative? If not, rewrite it to make it sound more real.

Revising in Action

Dialogue adds personality and voice in the sample below.

> I quickly grabbed my sunglasses. "You look silly!" My sister said.
> "But my eyes hurt," I cried.
> ~~I looked silly.~~ I realized the glasses didn't help.

TEKS 5.15E
ELPS 5G

Revising Using a Checklist

Check your revising. Number a piece of paper from 1 to 10. If you can answer "yes" to a question, put a check mark after that number. If not, continue to work on that part of your essay.

Focus and Coherence

_____ **1.** Does my writing maintain focus throughout the story?

_____ **2.** Do all my ideas relate to my main idea?

_____ **3.** Is my narrative told in a clear, logical way?

Organization

_____ **4.** Do my beginning, middle, and ending work well?

_____ **5.** Do I use transitions to make ideas flow smoothly?

_____ **6.** Does my writing make sense to the reader?

Development of Ideas

_____ **7.** Are my ideas supported by enough details?

_____ **8.** Does my narrative include sensory details?

Voice

_____ **9.** Does my voice show my interest or excitement?

_____ **10.** Does my dialogue sound real?

Make a clean copy. Ask a classmate to read and respond to your narrative. Create a clean copy for editing.

Editing

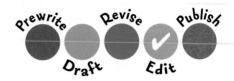

Editing is the next step in the writing process. When you edit, you make sure that you have followed the rules for grammar, sentence structure, mechanics, and spelling. These rules are called the "conventions" of writing.

Keys to Editing

1. **Use** a dictionary, a thesaurus, and the "Proofreader's Guide" in the back of this book for help.

2. **Edit** on a printed copy if you use a computer. Then make your changes on the computer.

3. **Use** the editing marks shown inside the back cover of this book.

4. **Ask** someone else to check your writing for errors, too.

Texas Traits · **Editing** for **Conventions**

Grammar

When editing for *grammar,* make sure that you use subjects and verbs correctly.

How do I make my subjects and verbs agree?

Decide if the subject in a sentence is singular or plural. Then make sure the verb in the sentence agrees in number. Most nouns ending in –s or –es are plural. Most verbs ending in –s are singular. (Also see pages **453**, **454**, and **472**.)

- If the subject is singular, the verb must be singular.
  Carlo eats **spaghetti for lunch.**
  (The subject *Carlo* and the verb *eats* are both singular.)

- If the subject is plural, the verb must be plural. Remember to look at the entire subject.
  Beans and peas sprout **in my garden.**
  (The subject *beans and peas* and the verb *sprout* are both plural.)

Grammar Practice

Decide if the subject in each sentence below is singular or plural. Then write each sentence, using the correct verb.

1. My brothers (go, goes) to the pool every Saturday.
2. Justin (practice, practices) complicated dives.
3. Carl (do, does) backflips in the air.
4. Martin and Ryan (watch, watches) with interest.

Edit

Check your subject-verb agreement. Make sure that the subjects and verbs in your sentences agree in number.

Do my subjects and verbs agree?

When editing for grammar, make sure the subject and the verb in each part of a compound sentence agree.

- Suri **wants a new puppy, but her** parents **do not.**
  (*Suri* and *wants* are singular; *parents* and *do* are plural.)

- **The** plants **in the window are healthy, and the** one **in the corner is, too.**
  (*plants* and *are* are plural; *one* and *is* are singular.)

Grammar Practice

Rewrite each sentence below so the verb in each part of the sentence agrees in number with the subject.

1. My sisters plan to go hiking, but I wants to stay at home.
2. Leah pack the lunches, and Jenny gather the gear.
3. Mother help them, and then they hurry toward the trail.

Edit

Edit for subject-verb agreement. Change your subjects or verbs if they do not agree in number.

Learning Language

Read the words below with a partner. Tell if each word is singular (one thing) or plural (more than one thing). Then match a subject with a verb to make a sentence. Say the sentence aloud.

Subjects	cats	car	teachers	doctor
Verbs	read	sleep	races	checks

 **TEKS** 5.21B(ii)

Mechanics: Punctuation

Is my dialogue spaced correctly?

Begin a new paragraph each time a different person speaks.

Dialogue That Runs Together

"Everyone line up," barked Mr. Brown. "It's time for physical fitness tests." "Do we have to do push-ups or chin-ups?" asked Sam. "You'll be doing chin-ups," Mr. Brown answered.

Dialogue Indented for Each New Speaker

"Everyone line up," barked Mr. Brown. "It's time for physical fitness tests."

"Do we have to do push-ups or chin-ups?" asked Sam.
"You'll be doing chin-ups," Mr. Brown answered.

Practice

Rewrite the dialogue below, beginning a new paragraph for each new speaker.

"How is the packing going?" called Mother from the other room. "Do you need anything else?" "I might need more boxes," I answered. "I'll bring some as soon as I get a chance," replied Mother.

Edit **Check your dialogue for proper spacing.** Make sure that you start a new paragraph each time a different person speaks.

TEKS 5.15C
ELPS 5F

Sentence Structure

When you edit for *sentence structure*, try to use different kinds of sentences.

How can I add variety to my sentences?

You can add variety to your writing and enhance style by using different kinds of sentences.

Kinds of Sentences

Declarative	I want to make the volleyball team.
Interrogative	Who will practice with me?
Imperative	Practice your serves.
Exclamatory	I scored the winning point!

Edit

Check for sentence variety. If you have used all declarative sentences, consider changing a few of them. Add or delete sentences as needed.

Editing in Action

In the sample below, changes are made to improve the sentences.

In the fridge,
^There was leftover meatloaf~~ in the fridge.~~ ~~There~~ ᵍWe had

~~were~~ᵍ plenty of fresh tomatoes, onions, lettuce,

and salsa, too. I also found a box of cheese,

I couldn't wait to get started!
the kind that melts on cheeseburgers. ^~~I was so~~ᵍ

~~hungry. It was time to get started.~~ᵍ

⭐ **TEKS** 5.15D
ELPS 5F

Editing **Using a Checklist**

 Check your editing. Number a piece of paper from 1 to 10. If you can answer "yes" to a question, put a check mark before that number. If not, continue to edit for that convention.

Conventions

GRAMMAR

_____ **1.** Do my subjects and verbs agree in number?
(He and I *were* running, not He and I *was* running.)

_____ **2.** Do I use the right words (*your* or *you're*)?

MECHANICS

_____ **3.** In dialogue, do I place the speaker's words within quotation marks?

_____ **4.** Do I begin a new paragraph each time a different person speaks?

_____ **5.** Do I start all my sentences with capital letters?

_____ **6.** Do I use end punctuation after all my sentences?

SENTENCE STRUCTURE

_____ **7.** Do I use different kinds of sentences?

_____ **8.** Have I deleted unnecessary sentences?

SPELLING

_____ **9.** Have I spelled all my words correctly?

_____ **10.** Have I double-checked the words my spell-checker might have missed?

Creating a Title

- Use strong, colorful words: **My Recipe for Success**
- Give the words rhythm: **Mom's Supper Surprise**
- Be imaginative: **Tasty Tacos, Anyone?**

TEKS 5.15E

Publishing

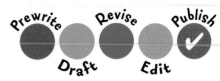

After you finish proofreading your story, make a neat final copy to share. You may also share your story online, in an interview, or with an oral reading. (See the suggestions below.)

Presentation

- Use blue or black ink and write neatly.
- Write your name in the upper left corner of page 1.
- Skip a line and center your title; skip another line and start writing.
- Indent every paragraph and leave a one-inch margin on all sides.
- Write your last name and the page number in the upper right corner of every page after the first one.

Share an Interview

Videotape a partner interviewing you about your successful experience. Show the tape to your class.

Go Online!

Upload your personal narrative for others to read.

Read Your Story to Others

Read your story to a younger class. Explain why your successful experience was important.

Publish

Make a final copy. Follow your teacher's instructions or use the guidelines above. (If you are using a computer, see pages 44–46.) Write a final copy of your narrative and proofread it.

Evaluating a Narrative

When you evaluate a narrative, use the scoring rubric on pages 34–35 and the narratives that follow. These narratives are examples of writing for each score on the holistic scoring rubric.

Notice that this first personal narrative received a score of 4. Read the description for a score of 4. Then read "Finding Sam." Use the same steps to study the other examples. Remember to think about the overall quality of the writing.

Writing that fits a score of 4 is very strong.

Finding Sam

I was lugging our trash out to the alley when I glimpsed the orange tail of Sam, our family cat. Fear closed my throat and I choked as he disappeared into the dark leafy bushes. Sam had disappeared into the night, and it was all my fault!

Bang! The screen door slammed shut behind me as I tore into the house and yelled for my mom to help me look for Sam. Quickly I dug through the cabinet under the kitchen sink, tossing dusters and spray bottles aside until I found our big flashlight. Mom ran past me with an open can of stinky tuna fish. If that didn't bring Sam back, nothing would!

Mom flipped on the back porch light, sending streams of yellow light across the yard. We both hollered so loudly for Sam that our nosy neighbor, Mrs. Garfinkle, flipped on her backyard light and stuck her

Specific details develop ideas and voice.

Every paragraph develops the story.

head out of her breakfast room window to watch us search.

The sharp leaves on our berry bushes scratched my arms as I stuck the flashlight through them, but I didn't care about the pain. All I could feel was my heart shaking at the thought of never seeing Sam again.

"Calm down!" I scolded myself. "Panicking won't help Sam at all."

I closed my eyes to settle my thoughts. When I opened them again, I noticed something important in the dirt in front of me. Paw prints! Sam had left a trail for us to follow in the soft earth of our backyard!

Good control of conventions

Feeling like a detective, I shone the flashlight on the ground and tracked Sam under our bushes, across Mrs. Garfinkle's lawn, and under her back fence. And there was Sam, digging old fish out of Mrs. Garfinkle's trash can!

I was so happy that I hugged Sam to my face, not even caring that his fur smelled like spoiled cod and tartar sauce. He meowed happily to see me, though I think he was even happier to see the tuna fish can Mom was still holding as I carried him back.

Focus maintained throughout.

Letting Sam escape was terrible, but I am proud of myself that I kept my cool and used my brains to find him again.

Writing that fits a score of 3 is strong in most ways.

It's Not So Scary After All

Right when my family just moved to a new place, I was sure I would never sleep again. Every night, I lay in bed all wide-eyed. Every time I closed my eyes, they flew back open because of another sound. Crash! Bang! Whistle! Woosh! Slam!

First there was the rattling train. It thundered and whooshed by on the tracks a couple of blocks away. It made a real commotion. I would sit up in bed every time it went by.

Transitions help organize ideas.

Then there were the slamming doors. The people living in the other apartments were walking in and out of their homes very late at night. They didn't care that other people might be sleeping! Slam! Sometimes they even knocked and knocked when they forgot their keys.

To make things worse, there was my dad's snoring. Just kidding! He does make lots of noise, like a swarm of angry bees is living in his nose, but I was used to that sound. Actually it reminded me of sleeping in my old room at our other place.

Focus established late in narrative.

But the most alarming sound by far was the strange clattering outside my window. I was so scared when I heard it! It sounded like a bunch of symbols had crashed-landed on the ground outside my window. I could hear scratching and clinking and a sound of breaking glass. What was going on?

A few errors in conventions

Oh no! Was someone breaking into our new home? I pulled my covers over my head. It was hot and scratchy under the blanket. My throat felt dry because also my mouth was hanging open in fear.

Then I realized that this was ridiculous. Even if some bad guy or robber was outside, someone needed to see that and call the police. So I crawled across the floor and peeped out the window.

Inner thoughts and personality create voice.

You will never guess what I saw! Not in a million years! It wasn't a bad guy or a robber, though it was wearing a mask. It was a raccoon!

The raccoon had knocked over our trash cans and was digging through our garbage. He had broken some old bottles we threw away. That was what I heard break. He stopped and looked back at me. He looked guilty.

"Shoo you old raccoon!" I yelled and pounded on my window.

He glared at me. I could see his shiny eyes in the night and I was so scared I couldn't breath for a minute. But then he leapt away and waddled down the driveway. I took a deep and free breath and I felt proud of myself.

Ending contains completed ideas.

That was the scariest thing outside, and I scared it away. I went back to bed and slept well that night.

Writing that fits a score of 2 is strong in a few ways.

Focus is clearly established.

Some unrelated ideas

Several errors in conventions

Details add to development.

The Star of the Show

It was my proudest moment. I was the star of our class play. Or I was about to be the star. All I had to do was step onto the stage. But I couldn't make my feet move. They felt like big bricks, they were so heavy.

We tried out for parts and I knew I would do good as the head cowboy. I wish we did the play about animals. It would be fun to be the king of the jungle too. But we only had cowboy costumes, so we did the rodeo play. I said my lines really good and even threw in a whoop.

I wish I hadnt done so good now. I had so many lines and my family was in the audience. I didn't remember wether my first line was about cows or sheep.

Maria poked me in the back. Her finger was telling me it was time to go on. The music was telling me to go on too. I swallowed so hard I almost choked. Then I stepped out into the bright lights. I said my first line. It wasnt so bad. People laughed! I knew then it would all be OK. I felt better so I bellowed my next line.

I did great and Maria was jealous she had to be a sheep. Once I started talking I said all my words almost right. I didnt fall off the stage even. I would be the star of the play again next year I was so proud.

Writing that fits a score of 1 is weak.

Surprize!

It is hard to plan a surprize party, but my party was a good surprize party. Dad got a new job and we were proud and I wish I had a job too. I want to wash pets for money. I like to be around dogs and cats especially when they don't bite or scratch on me. Mom says maybe when I am older but I want to be old now and I mean right now.

Anyway back to the party. I helped Mom plan the party. I got some things for the party like blue and silver streamers cause those are the colors of his favorit football team. I got some cool black plates and a poster. And of course lots and lots of balloons. I almost forget noise makers. Of course you have to have those! I tested them out to make sure they were loud. Noise makers at a surprize party have to be loud.

We hid the party food and we hid us too. Dad come home and we jump out and yell SURPRIZE and we were loud and Dad surprize and we show him food. Surprize! There were lots of people there and they ate food they liked the noise makers and really liked balloons.

I like to hide and jump out and surprize Mom and my friends and my dog. Surprize! That is my favorit thing to do.

Focus is not clear.

Details and personality create voice.

Many errors in conventions

Ending loses focus.

ELPS 4I, 4K

Evaluating and Reflecting on Your Writing

Take time to think about your writing. On your own paper, finish each sentence starter below. To score your writing, refer to the rubric on pages **34–35** and the examples you just read.

My Personal Narrative

1. The best score for my personal narrative is . . .

2. It's the best score because . . .

3. The best part of my essay is . . .

4. The part that still needs work is . . .

5. The main thing I learned about writing a personal narrative is . . .

Narrative Writing
Across the Curriculum

The world is full of stories, and narrative writing can help you tell them. For example, you can write a narrative that shares an important event in history. You can also write about your personal experiences with a challenging subject like math. You can even write a letter to tell an absent classmate what happened in class.

On the following pages, you'll learn how you can use narrative writing in social studies class and math class. You will also learn how to take class minutes and answer a narrative prompt on a writing test.

What's Ahead

- **Social Studies:** Sharing a Moment in History
- **Math:** Sharing a Personal Experience
- **Practical Writing:** Drafting a Friendly Letter

Social Studies:
Sharing a Moment in History

In the following narrative, Dominic shares the moment when two explorers, Lewis and Clark, finally reached the Pacific Ocean. Dominic writes his narrative from the point of view of William Clark.

Lewis and Clark Reach the Pacific

Beginning
The main characters are introduced.

I wipe the pouring rain off my face. Most explorers hope to find land, but Meriwether Lewis and I, William Clark, came all the way from St. Louis to reach the Pacific Ocean. I turn around and face the rest of our crew, the Corps of Discovery.

"We did it!" I shout. Everyone cheers as loudly as the sound of the huge waves crashing on the rocky shore. "We've paddled upstream, hiked over snowy mountains, and faced hunger and many other dangers."

Middle
Action and dialogue move the story along.

Out of the corner of my eye, I see Sacagawea. She is calm, as usual. "Of course, without the help of our Indian friend, Sacagawea, we wouldn't have made it. Thank you, Sacagawea." The men cheer again, and Sacagawea smiles shyly.

Ending
A surprising twist in the story adds interest.

I look back at the Pacific and notice that Meriwether looks unhappy. I truly can understand why. We had hoped to spot Asian trading ships at sea, but there are no ships anywhere. We planned to sail home by sea. Maybe the ships will come soon. If not, we'll have to go back the same way we came.

Prewriting Selecting a Topic

To find a topic, you can skim your social studies book for interesting historical events. Dominic wrote the following list.

Topics List

> –Thomas Jefferson writes <u>Declaration of Independence</u>
> –George Washington elected first president
> –Meriwether Lewis and William Clark reach Pacific *

Prewrite List topic ideas. Skim your social studies book and list three or four important events and the people involved. Put a star (*) next to the event you would like to write about.

Gathering Details

To gather details about your topic, check your social studies book and the Internet for help. Dominic used the 5 W's to guide him.

5 W's Chart

Who?	Meriwether Lewis, William Clark, Corps of Discovery
What?	Reached Pacific
Where?	At the mouth of the Columbia River
When?	November 1805
Why?	President Jefferson wanted them to find route to Pacific

Prewrite Gather details. Answer the 5 W's for your topic. Review the names you have listed after "who." Choose one who you would like to be for your story. Explain your choice to a partner.

⭐ ELPS 5G

Prewriting **Bringing Your Story to Life**

Next, you need to think of details that can help bring to life the people in your story. To do this, Dominic made the following cluster.

Details Cluster

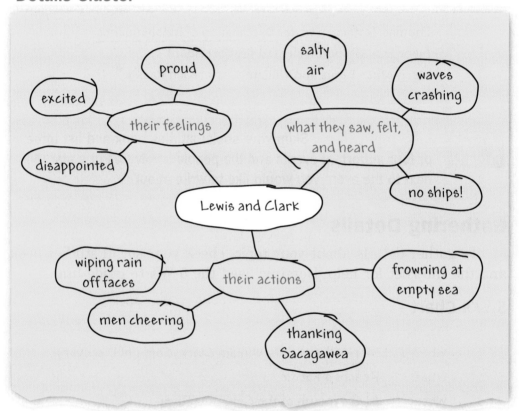

Create a cluster. Follow these instructions:

1 Write the main person or people at the center of your paper and circle it.

2 Create circles for "their feelings," "what they saw, felt, and heard," and "their actions." Connect the circles.

3 List three or four details for each new circle.

TEKS 5.15B
ELPS 5G

Drafting Creating Your First Draft

Imagine being one of the people in your story and begin writing. In the first paragraph, introduce the people and the event. In the middle paragraphs, include feelings, sensory details, and actions to make the story interesting. In the last paragraph, include a final thought.

Draft

Write your first draft. Use your prewriting as a guide to help you bring the event to life.

Revising Improving Your Writing

Keep the following traits in mind as you revise your narrative.

- **Focus and Coherence** Do all my ideas connect to each other and to the main idea?
- **Organization** Does my story use transitions to help the reader know the order of events?
- **Development of Ideas** Did I choose specific details to support and develop my ideas?
- **Voice** Does my voice express my viewpoint? Does it sound like the person who's telling the story?

Revise

Improve your writing. Ask yourself the questions above as you review your story. Make any revisions needed.

Editing Checking for Conventions

When you are done revising, edit for conventions.

- **Conventions** Have I checked for errors in grammar, sentence structure, mechanics, and spelling?

Edit

Edit your work. Also have someone else check your work. Then make a neat final copy and proofread it.

Math: Sharing a Personal Experience

A math narrative shares an adventure—or a misadventure—you've had with math. In the following narrative, Winona writes about a time she used math in her everyday life.

The **beginning** sets the scene.

The **middle** gives details about the experience.

The **ending** shows what the student has learned.

Math Memory

I use addition and subtraction a lot in my everyday life, but now I'm learning harder things like multiplying fractions. When would I ever use that? Well, last week our school had a bake sale, and I wanted to help my mom bake my favorite cookies. That's when I found out how important it is to know how to multiply fractions.

Mom said we needed to make a double batch of cookies. First, we multiplied the measurements for each ingredient by two. Next, we reduced the measurements to the lowest denominator. For example, 1/4 multiplied by two equals 2/4. Then 2/4 can be reduced to 1/2. Mom showed me how the 1/4 cup of brown sugar fit into the 1/2 cup twice. We knew we did it right. The cookies were delicious.

When I use math in my everyday life, it makes my homework easier to understand. I can remember what I learned and get the right answer. Math can be tough at first, but once I understand it, I don't forget it.

Writing Tips

Before you write . . .

- **Think of how you use math in everyday life.**
  List times outside of school when you've used math.
- **Pick a specific event for your narrative.**
  Choose a time that sticks out in your memory. It may be a time when you first understood a math concept. Think about how the experience made you feel.

During your drafting . . .

- **Set the scene.**
  In the first paragraph, give the important background information to introduce the experience.
- **Focus on the details.**
  In the middle part, provide details about how you used math.
- **Share your feelings.**
  In the closing, reflect on how the experience changed your thinking.

After you've written a first draft . . .

- **Revise your writing.**
  Add any important details that are missing.
- **Check your organization.**
  Make sure that you have arranged the details in the best order.
- **Edit for conventions.**
  Have a partner read your paper. Correct any grammar, sentence structure, mechanics, and spelling errors based on his or her feedback.

> Write your math narrative. Focus on a specific time that you used math in your everyday life.

Practical Writing:
Drafting a Friendly Letter

Alicia sent a friendly letter to a friend about a class he missed. Notice how she follows the principles of narrative writing.

The heading provides the sender's address and date.

The salutation begins with a capital letter and ends with a comma.

The body conveys ideas and information. Paragraphs are indented.

The closing concludes the letter. It includes the signature.

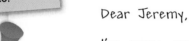

2400 Waller St.
El Paso, TX   79925
November 8, 2010

Dear Jeremy,

I'm sorry you got sick before science class today. I thought you should know what happened so you don't get behind. Today, we talked about the planet Mars.

First, Mrs. Alderson handed out fact sheets. They said that Mars is half the size of Earth and is rocky and covered with dust. Since the atmosphere is so thin, the average temperature is −81 degrees F!

Then Mrs. Alderson showed us a video about missions to Mars. The first one landed in 1971 and the last one in 2008. They found signs of water once being there.

Finally, Mrs. Alderson gave us an assignment. Each student must write a story about being the first astronaut to land on Mars. The stories are due Friday.

I hope you feel better soon. See you in class tomorrow!

Your friend,
Alicia

Writing Tips

Before you write . . .

- **Know your goal.**
  Think about your reason for writing and what your reader needs to know.

During your writing . . .

- **Write a heading.**
  Include your address and the date.
- **Choose a salutation.**
  Greet the person you are writing and use a comma.
- **Organize your details.**
  Make sure your reader can understand the information.
- **Close politely.**
  Let the reader know what to do, write a closing, and politely include your name.

After you've written a first draft . . .

- **Read your message carefully.**
  Make sure your letter uses correct capitalization and punctuation before sending.

> **Write a friendly letter.** Write to a friend, telling about the best thing that happened today during school.

ELPS 4I, 4J, 4K

Narrative Writing

Writing for the Texas Assessment

When you take state tests in Texas, you often have to write. The prompt tells you what to write about and gives some things to remember. Read the following prompt.

Prompt

> Write a composition about a time when you were responsible.

Use the information below to help you write your composition.

REMEMBER THAT YOU SHOULD---

☐ write about a time when you were responsible and tell what you learned from the experience.

☐ make sure each sentence helps readers understand your composition.

☐ write about your ideas in detail so that the reader fully understands what you are saying.

☐ try to use correct grammar, sentence structure, punctuation, capitalization, and spelling.

TEKS 5.15A
ELPS 4I, 4J, 4K, 5G

Prewriting Select a Form

The prompt doesn't tell you what form, or genre, of writing to use. How can you decide which one? Think about which form best fits what you want to say.

Do you want to—
■ describe a person or place?
■ offer a solution to a problem?
■ explain an object?
■ share a personal experience?
■ give information?
■ persuade someone to do something?

Answering these questions will help you decide on a form, or genre. (Also see page **503**.)

Hector saw that the prompt asked him to tell about something that happened to him. Since he wanted to share an experience, he decided the best form was a narrative.

Putting Events in Order

Hector decided to write about taking care of a neighbor's dog. He thought he was very responsible because it was hard work and he had to remember to take care of Sammy every day. To plan his draft, Hector used a time line. It helped him choose events and organize them in time order.

Time Line

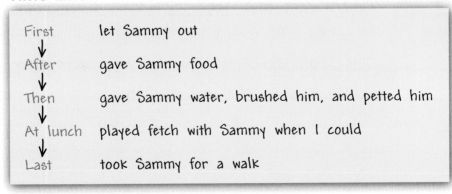

First	let Sammy out
After	gave Sammy food
Then	gave Sammy water, brushed him, and petted him
At lunch	played fetch with Sammy when I could
Last	took Sammy for a walk

ELPS 4I, 4K

Drafting **Writing the Narrative**

Next, Hector used his time line to write his personal narrative.
Read Hector's narrative.

> ### You Can Count on Me!
>
> Last summer I had a golden opportunity when our neighbors, the Ortegas, asked me to be their dog sitter while they were on vacation. I always wanted a dog, so I thought it would be fun. Mrs. Ortega gave me the house key and instructions for taking care of Sammy, a golden retriever. <u>Taking care of Sammy would be a big responsibility, but I knew I could handle it.</u>
>
> Every morning I let Sammy out into the Ortega's backyard. After I let him back in, I gave him two cups of dry food just like the instructions said. Then I filled his water bowl, brushed him, patted him on the head, and locked the door. Whenever I could, I went over after lunch to play fetch with Sammy.

The **beginning** introduces the focus (underlined).

The **middle** paragraphs tell about the experience.

ELPS 2G, 2H, 2I, 3D, 3E, 3G, 3H, 4C, 4G, 4I, 4K

The **middle** part is organized by time.

The last thing I did each day was walk Sammy around the neighborhood. He liked to stop and sniff the ground like crazy. Maybe he smelled a rabbit trail. After we got back to his house, I gave him one cup of food and filled his water bowl before I left. I double-checked that the door was locked.

The **ending** tells what the writer learned.

My two weeks with Sammy went quickly, even though it was hard work. It helped that Mrs. Ortega paid me for my work. I hope I get to take care of Sammy the next time they go on vacation. I learned that being responsible means that people and pets can count on me!

Respond to the reading. Answer the following questions about the response. Discuss your answers with a partner.

- **Focus and Coherence** (1) What is the topic of the response? (2) What key words from the prompt are used?
- **Organization** (3) How does the writer organize the details of the narrative?
- **Voice** (4) What words and phrases help make the writer sound responsible?

Literature Connection: See the May 16, 1850 entry in *Rachel's Journal* by Marissa Moss for an example of a personal narrative.

TEKS 5.15A, 5.15C
ELPS 4I, 4J, 4K, 5G

Writing Tips

Before you write . . .

- **Understand the prompt.**
  Make sure you understand what you are supposed to write. Think about your purpose and audience. Select the form that will help you best convey your meaning.
- **Use your time wisely.**
  Plan your narrative before you begin to write.

During your drafting . . .

- **Find key words.**
  Use words from the prompt to introduce the experience.
- **Choose carefully.**
  Select details that will keep your story focused and coherent on one event.
- **Stay focused and organized.**
  Make sure your ideas are focused, in the right order, and flow smoothly.
- **Write a strong ending.**
  Explain the importance of this experience to you.
- **Rethink the form.**
  Make sure you chose the right form for your purpose and audience.

After you've written a first draft . . .

- **Check your essay against the prompt.**
  Make sure you have done what the prompt asks.
- **Check for conventions.**
  Correct any errors you find.

Plan and write a response. Respond to the prompt on page 122. Remember to select a form and use the tips above as you write.

Narrative Writing in Review

In narrative writing, you tell a story about something that has happened. You may write about your own personal experiences.

Prewrite

Select a topic from your life that you truly care about. (See page 78.)

Gather important details about the people and events in your narrative. Use a graphic organizer. (See pages 79–81.)

Draft

In the beginning part, give background information and introduce your topic. (See page 85.)

In the middle part, tell your story using dialogue and sensory details. (See pages 86–87.)

In the ending part, tell what you learned from the experience, how it changed you, or how you felt about the experience (See page 88.)

Revise

First, review your focus and coherence, organization, and **development of ideas.** Then, check for **voice.** (See pages 90–98.)

Edit

Also check your writing for conventions. Correct any errors in grammar, mechanics, sentence structure, and spelling. (See pages 100–104.)

Publish

Make a final copy and proofread it for errors before sharing it. (See page 105.)

Use the scoring rubric to assess your finished writing. (See pages 34–35.)

ELPS 2C, 2G, 2H, 2I, 3D, 3E, 3G, 3H, 4C, 4G

Expository Writing

Writing Focus

- Expository Paragraph
- Expository Essay

Grammar Focus

- Using the Right Word
- Indefinite Pronouns

Learning Language

Work with a partner. Read the meanings aloud and discuss your answers to the questions.

1. An expository essay is written to explain something. **What information would you include in an expository essay about a favorite hobby?**

2. A strategy is a plan for accomplishing a goal. **Describe a strategy that works well in a game or sport that you play.**

3. You get the big picture when you understand how all the parts of something fit together to make sense. **How can a diagram help you get the big picture when you're making a model airplane?**

Expository Writing

Expository Paragraph

Think of a favorite game: freeze tag, soccer, thumb wrestling, dodgeball, four-square. . . . Now imagine that a friend from another country wants to learn the rules. Could you explain your game in a single paragraph?

An expository paragraph provides plenty of information in a small space. In the following chapter, you'll write an expository paragraph explaining a favorite game.

Writing Guidelines

Subject: A favorite game
Purpose: To explain the rules
Form: Expository paragraph
Audience: Classmates

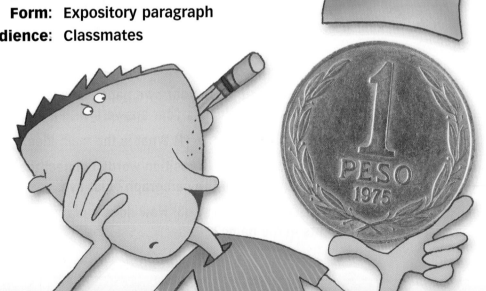

TEKS 5.15A
ELPS 2G, 2H, 2I, 3D, 3E, 3H, 4C, 4G, 4I

Expository Paragraph

An expository paragraph starts with a **topic sentence**, which contains the main idea and explains the general meaning of the paragraph. The sentences in the **body** develop the main idea with important details. The **closing sentence** completes the explanation. In the following paragraph, Marco tells about his favorite game back in Chile.

Topic Sentence (underlined)

Body

Closing Sentence (underlined)

Hit the Penny

In Chile, kids play a game called "hit the penny." The game requires just a few pennies and a stick or broom handle with one flat end. First, set up the stick by pushing one end into the ground. Then lay a penny on the flat top end of the stick. Around the stick, draw a circle about six feet wide. Next, have each player stand outside the circle and take turns throwing another penny to knock the penny off the stick. If the knocked-off penny falls in the circle, the player gets one point, and if it falls outside, the player gets two points. Hit the penny takes only a couple minutes to learn but a long time to master!

Respond to the reading. On your own paper, answer each of the following questions. Discuss your answers with a partner.

- **Focus and Coherence** (1) What is the main idea?

- **Organization** (2) What transition words connect the sentences in the body of the paragraph? List two.

- **Development of Ideas** (3) How does a player score points in the game?

 **TEKS** 5.15A, 5.23A
ELPS 2I, 3E, 5G

Prewriting Selecting a Topic

Brainstorm with others to come up with topics. Marco worked with a partner to create the following cluster about his favorite games.

Topic Cluster

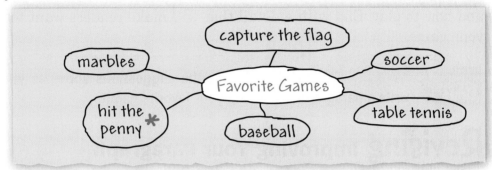

 Create a cluster. Work with a partner to make a cluster like the one above. In it, list your favorite games. Put a star (✳) next to the game you want to write about. Be sure to choose a topic you can explain completely in a paragraph.

Writing a Topic Sentence

To be an effective introduction for your paragraph, a topic sentence should name the game and tell something interesting about it.

name of the game		something interesting		a good topic sentence
hit the penny	**+**	my friends and I played it in Chile	**=**	In Chile, kids play a game called "hit the penny."

 Write your topic sentence. Follow the pattern above to write the topic sentence for your paragraph. Try two or three different versions until the sentence sounds just right.

 **TEKS** 5.15B
ELPS 5G

Drafting **Creating Your First Draft**

Your first draft should sound as if you were explaining your favorite game to a friend. Start with a topic sentence and build on ideas to create a well-organized paragraph focused on one topic. Include the equipment needed, how to set up the game, the rules to follow, and how to play. End with a detail that will make readers want to try your game.

 Write your first draft. Use the suggestions above as you write a paragraph explaining your favorite game.

Revising **Improving Your Paragraph**

When you revise, consider the *focus and coherence, organization, development of ideas,* and *voice* of your paragraph.

 Revise your paragraph. Let the questions below guide you.
1. Does my topic sentence clearly state my main idea?
2. Have I used transitions to connect the details in the body?
3. Have I used specific nouns and verbs?
4. Does my voice show my interest in the topic?

Editing **Checking for Conventions**

Review your paragraph one last time. Focus on *conventions.*

 Edit and proofread your work. Answer these questions.
1. Does each sentence begin with a capital letter and include end punctuation?
2. Have I checked my spelling?
3. Have I used words correctly *(to, too, two)*?
4. Are my sentences clear and complete?

Expository Writing

Expository Essay

Do you know how a seed grows? Do you know how leaves make food for trees? Do you know how flowers turn into fruit? When you tell how something works, you are explaining a process.

In this chapter, you will write an expository essay that explains how something works. Your goal is to share interesting information with the reader. Along the way, you may just learn something yourself!

Writing Guidelines

Subject: A process (how something works)

Purpose: To inform

Form: Expository essay

Audience: Classmates

Understanding Your Goal

Your goal in this chapter is to write an essay that clearly explains a process (how something works). The traits listed below will help you meet that goal. The scoring rubric on pages **34–35** will also help you. Refer to it often to improve your writing.

Focus and Coherence
In the beginning, introduce your topic with a clear focus statement. Then, in the middle, explain the process. In your ending, make sure you support the main idea.

Organization
Arrange the information in a logical way that is easy to follow. Use transitions to show how ideas are connected.

Development of Ideas
Include interesting facts, details, and examples that clearly explain the process.

Voice
Use a voice that holds the attention of your audience and shows that you know your topic well.

Conventions
Be sure your grammar is correct. Use a variety of sentences. Check for correct capitalization, punctuation, and spelling.

Literature Connection: You can find expository text that explains a process in "Living honey jars," a section in *Exploding Ants* by Dr. Joanne Settel.

TEKS 5.18A(i), 5.18A(iii)
ELPS 4I

Expository Essay

In the following expository essay, Terrell explains how the process of photosynthesis works.

Food for Everybody

Beginning
An effective introduction captures the reader's attention and gives the focus statement (underlined).

Kids are always saying "I'm starving!" They probably hope to get some potato chips or oatmeal cookies. Moms may give them apples or oranges. All of these foods come from plants, but where do plants get their food? <u>Plants actually make their own food through a process called photosynthesis.</u>

Photosynthesis begins when a plant takes in water and carbon dioxide. The plant gets water from the ground through its roots. It gets carbon dioxide from the air through its leaves. Carbon dioxide is a gas that animals breathe out but that plants breathe in.

Middle
Each middle paragraph includes specific details organized to tell about a different part of the process.

In the next part of the process, the water and carbon dioxide are changed into sugar in the leaves. Each leaf has cells full of a green substance called chlorophyll. Chlorophyll uses sunlight first to break down the water and carbon dioxide. It then combines these two elements into sugar.

TEKS 5.18A(i), 5.18A(iii–iv), 5.20A(viii),
ELPS 2G, 2H, 2I, 3D, 3E, 3G, 3H, 4C, 4G, 4I

Middle
Transitions (in blue) help organize an essay by linking specific details and paragraphs.

In the end, photosynthesis supports all life on earth. It creates the sugar that lets all green plants live. It also feeds the plant-eating animals, and eventually the animals that eat the plant eaters.

When photosynthesis breaks down carbon dioxide, it releases oxygen. Without photosynthesis, humans and animals couldn't even breathe!

Ending
The concluding paragraph wraps up your explanation and gives the reader something to think about.

Bite into an apple and taste the sweetness. That taste comes from photosynthesis. Take a deep breath of fresh air. That freshness comes from photosynthesis, too. Next time you say, "I'm starving," remember that photosynthesis is the process that makes food for everybody.

 Respond to the reading. Answer and discuss the following questions with your partner.

- **Focus and Coherence** (1) How does the writer introduce the topic?

- **Organization** (2) What transitions help connect the middle paragraphs?

- **Voice** (3) What words or phrases show that the writer understands and cares about the topic? Find two and explain why.

Prewriting

Go Online!

Prewrite · Draft · Revise · Edit · Publish

The writing process begins with planning, or prewriting. Prewriting starts when you think of possible writing topics and ends when you are ready to write your first draft.

Keys to Prewriting

1. **Select** a topic to write about.

2. **Gather** key evidence, such as facts and details, about the topic.

3. **Find** a few special details to include.

4. **Write** a focus statement and topic sentences.

5. **Create** an organized list of your key ideas.

 **TEKS** 5.15A, 5.23A
ELPS 2I, 3E, 5G

Prewriting Using a "Basics-of-Life" List

Latonya was going to write an essay about a process (how something works). She began by brainstorming a "Basics-of-Life" list. She discussed the list with a partner and then chose two categories that interested her: food and environment.

"Basics-of-Life" List

agriculture	education	food *	love
animals	energy	freedom	machines
art/music	environment *	friends	money
books	exercise	health	plants
clothing	faith	housing	science/technology

Prewrite

Choose two categories. Consult with a partner about the "Basics-of-Life" list. Choose two categories that interest you.

Selecting a Topic

Next, Latonya needed a specific topic to explain. She wrote down her two chosen categories and listed possible topics under each of them.

Topic List

Food	Environment
popcorn popper	global warming
the stomach	water cycle *
an ice-cream maker	hurricanes
the food chain	rock cycle

Prewrite

Select a topic. Write down the two categories you have chosen. Under each, list specific topics (things you can explain by telling how they work). Put a star (*) next to the topic you like the best. Discuss your choice with a partner.

TEKS 5.18A(ii–iii),
5.23A, 5.23B, 5.24A, 5.26A
ELPS 5G

Gathering Details

Latonya made a plan for gathering key evidence about her topic. She created a KWL chart to organize her ideas, listing details she **K**nows and open-ended questions she **W**onders about. Latonya used her science book and the Internet to fill in what she **L**earned.

KWL Chart

How the Water Cycle Works

K – What do I know?	W – What do I wonder about?	L – What did I learn?
1. Water can be solid ice or a cloud.	1. Does Earth lose any water?	1. Earth just recycles water.
2. Temperature makes the form of water change.	2. What words describe how water changes?	2. "evaporation," "condensation," and "precip-itation"
3. Water is in lakes, rivers, and oceans, under the ground, and in the air.	3. How much of the earth's water is in the oceans?	3. Oceans contain 97% of earth's water.

Prewrite

Create a KWL chart. Make a KWL chart to find and organize key evidence that will guide the reader's understanding of your topic. Check books, magazines, or the Internet.

1 In the first column, list details you already know.

2 In the second column, list what you wonder about.

3 In the third column, write new information you learn.

⭐ **TEKS** 5.18A(ii), 5.26B
ELPS 5G

Prewriting **Including Amazing Details**

An expository essay uses key evidence, such as facts and details, to support conclusions about a topic. One way to keep readers interested and guide their understanding of the key evidence is to include amazing details.

Practice

Which details below provide the best key evidence to support conclusions about the water cycle? Explain your ideas to a partner.

1. Clouds hold water.
2. Water freezes at 32 degrees Fahrenheit.
3. The water that humans drink was once drunk by *Tyrannosaurus rex*.
4. Underwater volcanoes help make the sea salty.
5. The average American uses 100 gallons of water per day.

Check your details. Review the key evidence you have gathered on your KWL chart (from page 139). Did you find some amazing details to support your conclusions and inform your readers? If not, keep looking.

Focus on the Texas Traits

Development of Ideas Amazing details keep readers interested and guide their understanding of the evidence.

TEKS 5.18A(ii), 5.26B
ELPS 5G

Writing Your Focus Statement

Your focus statement appears at the end of your first paragraph. The focus statement names your topic and focuses on one part of it.

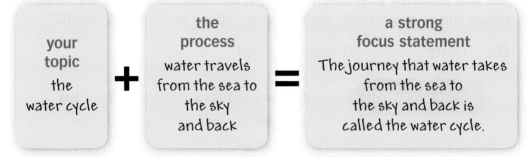

| your topic the water cycle | **+** | the process water travels from the sea to the sky and back | **=** | a strong focus statement The journey that water takes from the sea to the sky and back is called the water cycle. |

Prewrite

Write your focus statement. Use the pattern above and try different versions until you are satisfied.

Writing Topic Sentences

Each topic sentence introduces key evidence that supports conclusions about a specific part of the process. Clear topic sentences guide the reader's understanding of the key ideas and evidence. Here are some sentence starters to help you write your topic sentences.

| To start, Next, Finally, | In the first stage, During the next stage, In the last stage, | The process begins when . . . The next step in the process . . . The end of the process comes when . . . |

You may also use Latonya's topic sentences as models.

The water cycle begins with evaporation.
The next step in the water cycle is condensation.
When droplets in a cloud get big enough, precipitation begins.

Prewrite

Write topic sentences. Complete three of the sentence starters above. Remember that your topic sentences should support conclusions and help readers understand the evidence.

Prewriting Organizing Your Key Ideas

Now that you have written a focus statement and topic sentences, you can organize your essay. Latonya followed the directions below to create an organized list, including key ideas and specific details.

Directions	Organized List

Focus statement
> The journey that water takes from the sea to the sky and back is called the water cycle.

First topic sentence
> 1. The water cycle begins with evaporation.

List of details
> – One trillion tons each day
> – Gets rid of salt
> – No water lost

Second topic sentence
> 2. The next step in the water cycle is condensation.

List of details
> – Cools off/sticks to dust
> – Cloud, fog, dew, frost
> – Lemonade glass, mirror

Third topic sentence
> 3. When droplets in a cloud get big enough, precipitation begins.

List of details
> – Rain, sleet, snow
> – Falls in ocean or flows to ocean
> – Oceans contain 97 percent

Prewrite

Make an organized list. Follow the model above to create your own organized list of topic sentences and details.

TEKS 5.15B, 5.15C, 5.18A(i), 5.18A(iii)
ELPS 5G

Drafting

Prewrite Revise Publish
Draft Edit

Once you have gathered and organized your details, you are ready to write your first draft. You will put all your thoughts on paper or on the computer as you build on ideas to create a focused essay.

Keys to Drafting

1. **Write** strong beginning and ending paragraphs.

2. **Organize** facts, details, and examples in each middle paragraph.

3. **Write** with your purpose, form, and audience in mind. Ask yourself:
   - Am I informing my readers about how something works?
   - Does my essay include details that clearly explain a process?
   - Do I keep my classmates interested?

TEKS 5.15B, 5.18A(i–iii)
ELPS 5G

Drafting Getting the Big Picture

The chart below will help you to draft a focused expository essay by building on key ideas. (The examples are from the sample essay on pages 145–148.) You are ready to begin writing when you have . . .

- gathered enough specific facts and details,
- written your focus statement and topic sentences, and
- created an organized list or outline.

Beginning

The **beginning** introduces the topic and gives the focus statement.

Focus Statement

The journey that water takes from the sea to the sky and back is called the water cycle.

Middle

Each **middle** paragraph explains one key idea in the process.

Topic Sentences

- The water cycle begins with evaporation.
- The next step in the water cycle is condensation.
- When droplets in a cloud get big enough, precipitation begins.

Ending

The **ending** summarizes your thoughts and supports the main idea.

Closing Sentence

Better yet, just take a sip from a drinking fountain and think of the journey that this water has taken!

TEKS 5.15B, 5.18A(i–iii)
ELPS 5G

Starting Your Essay

A good introduction builds on ideas to create focus and catch the reader's attention. Try these strategies.

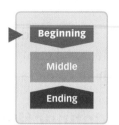

Beginning

Middle

Ending

- **Ask a question.**
  How many gallons of water do you use each day?

- **Give a surprising fact or example.**
  People drink the same water dinosaurs once drank.

- **Present a descriptive detail.**
  The world is like a giant terrarium.

- **Tell a one- or two-sentence anecdote.**
  Once I went sledding on a mountain and swimming in the ocean—during the same week.

Beginning Paragraph

The first sentence catches the reader's attention.

The focus statement (underlined) helps readers grasp a key idea.

> Once I went sledding on a mountain and swimming in the ocean—during the same week. That was an amazing journey, but water makes that journey all the time. After all, the snow that fell on the mountain once was in the sea! <u>The journey that water takes from Earth's surface to the sky and back is called the water cycle.</u>

Draft

Write your beginning paragraph.
Use one of the four strategies above to write a sentence that grabs the reader's attention. Then write sentences that lead up to your focus statement.

TEKS 5.15B, 5.18A(ii), 5.18A(iii), 5.20A(viii)
ELPS 5G

Drafting **Developing the Middle Part**

The middle paragraphs build on ideas to create a focused essay. Each one includes facts and details that help readers understand key ideas about the topic.

> Beginning
>
> Middle
>
> Ending

Connecting Your Sentences

One way to connect ideas is to use transition words or phrases. Another way is to fit sentences together like the pieces of a puzzle. Notice how the words in italics connect the sentences.

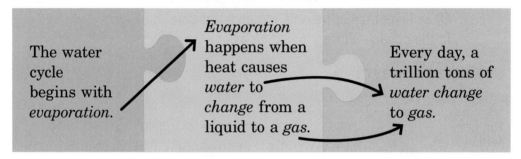

The water cycle begins with *evaporation.*

Evaporation happens when heat causes *water* to *change* from a liquid to a *gas.*

Every day, a trillion tons of *water change* to *gas.*

Middle Paragraphs

Topic Sentence 1

Sentences are connected with repeated words.

The water cycle begins with evaporation. Evaporation happens when heat causes water to change from a liquid to a gas. Every day, a trillion tons of water change to gas. When ocean water evaporates, it leaves its salt behind. The water that evaporates has no salt in it. If water only evaporated, the oceans would eventually dry up, as they did on Mars. But Earth's water cycle doesn't end with evaporation.

TEKS 5.15B, 5.18A(ii–iv), 5.20A(viii)
ELPS 5G

Topic Sentence 2

Details, facts, and examples from the organized list of key ideas are included.

The next step in the water cycle is condensation. Condensation is water vapor (evaporated water) turning back into drops of liquid. This happens if water vapor cools or water molecules stick to dust particles in the air. When water condenses in the air, it forms clouds or fog. When it condenses on the ground, it forms dew or frost. Water can also condense onto a cold lemonade glass or a cool bathroom mirror.

Topic Sentence 3

Each paragraph informs readers about a different part of the cycle.

When droplets in a cloud get big enough, precipitation begins. Precipitation is just falling water. Different temperatures create different kinds of precipitation. Rain, sleet, and snow are forms of precipitation. Most precipitation ends up back in the ocean. That's where 97 percent of Earth's water is. Then the water cycle is ready to begin again!

Draft

Write your middle paragraphs. Build on key ideas from the organized list you created on page 142 to write focused middle paragraphs. Organize facts, details, and examples, using an appropriate strategy. Try connecting your ideas and linking paragraphs with transitions and repeated words.

TEKS 5.15B, 5.18A(i–iii)
ELPS 5G

Drafting Ending Your Essay

As you wrap up your explanation, continue to guide your reader's understanding of the key ideas. Use these strategies to create a strong ending that builds on ideas to complete an organized essay.

Beginning

Middle

Ending

- **Connect with the reader.**
  Better yet, just take a sip from a drinking fountain and think of the journey that this water has taken!

- **Add a final surprising fact, detail, or example.**
  Water makes up 60 percent of the human body, so everyone is part of the water cycle.

- **Tell why the topic is important.**
  Without the water cycle, nothing could live on land—and that means all of us.

- **Use the strategy you used in your beginning.**
  So, get out and enjoy the water cycle. Try sledding on a mountain or swimming in the sea.

Ending Paragraph

> The writer used two of the strategies above.

> Get out and enjoy the water cycle. Try sledding on a mountain or swimming in the sea. Better yet, just take a sip from a drinking fountain and think of the journey that this water has taken!

Draft

Write your ending. Organize specific facts, details, or examples to reinforce the reader's understanding of key ideas. Use one or more of the strategies above, or invent your own.

Form a complete first draft. Write your first draft on every other line so you have room to revise.

TEKS 5.15C
ELPS 5G

Revising

Prewrite ● ● ✓ ● ● Publish
Draft   Revise   Edit

Go Online!

Revising may be the most important step in the writing process. When you revise, you think again about your purpose, form, and audience. You check your essay for *focus and coherence, organization, development of ideas,* and *voice.*

Keys to Revising

1. **Read** your essay to yourself.

2. **Ask** yourself these questions:
   - Did I inform my readers about how something works?
   - Does my essay include details that clearly explain a process?
   - Will my classmates understand and want to read my essay?

3. **Revise** for focus and coherence, organization, development of ideas, and voice.

TEKS 5.15C, 5.18A(i), 5.18A(ii)
ELPS 5G

Revising for Focus and Coherence

When you revise for *focus and coherence,* you review your essay to make sure the topic is clear throughout. You check that each paragraph presents information that helps readers understand your key ideas and evidence and that the beginning and ending work well.

How do I know if my beginning works well?

You know your beginning works well if it introduces the process that you are going to explain in a way that captures your reader's attention. Remember the strategies below. (Also see page 145.)

- Ask a question.
- Give a surprising fact or example.
- Present a descriptive detail.
- Tell a short story or anecdote.

Practice

Replace each beginning sentence below with a new sentence that grabs the reader's attention. Use a different strategy for each sentence beginning.

1. A hurricane is a storm that goes in a circle.
2. One process that people care about is how a volcano works.
3. If cream is churned, it will turn into butter.
4. Sometimes snow on a mountainside comes loose.

Revise

Review your beginning with a partner. Does the first sentence capture the attention of your audience? If not, rewrite it using one of the strategies above.

How do I know if my ending works well?

You know your ending works well if it's interesting to read and supports the key ideas in your essay. A good concluding paragraph gives the reader something to think about.

> On Earth 95 percent of all animal species are insects, and all of them go through metamorphosis. You might not want to be born as a worm, but wouldn't it be great to grow wings and fly.

> Can you add a sentence or two that sum up the main idea or tell why the topic is important?

 Revise

Check your ending. Do you leave your reader with something to think about? If not, revise your ending by adding one or more sentences, using the strategies on page 148 as a guide.

Revising in Action

In the sample below, a weak ending is revised.

Get out and enjoy the water cycle. ~~There's not much~~ Try sledding on a mountain or swimming in the sea. Better yet, ~~else to say.~~ Just take a sip from a drinking fountain and think of the ~~water.~~ journey that this water has taken.

TEKS 5.15C
ELPS 5G

 **Revising** for  Organization

When you revise for *organization,* you check to be sure your essay is easy to follow from beginning to end. You make certain that your ideas are arranged in a logical order and that they are stated only once. To connect your ideas in a clear and logical way, delete extra sentences, improve wordy sentences, and add transition words, phrases, or sentences.

How can I remove wordiness from my essay?

Words that don't mean much and just take up space can make your essay confusing. Remove wordy words and phrases like these to improve your organization.

kind of	really	There is . . .
sort of	very	There are . . .
a little bit	totally	It is . . .

Practice

On your own paper, remove the wordiness from each sentence.

1. It is true that the human heart is really really important.
2. When blood needs a little bit of oxygen, it turns sort of a little dark red.
3. Blood that is totally full of oxygen is really very bright red.
4. It is interesting that the heart and lungs sort of work as a kind of team.

 Revise

Remove wordiness. Read your writing and watch for the wordy words and phrases above. Remove any you find. Also delete any sentences that contain repeated ideas.

TEKS 5.15C, 5.18A(iv)
ELPS 5G

How can transitions improve my writing?

You can use transition words or phrases to move smoothly from one thought to the next and to show how ideas are connected.

> The first transition links this paragraph to other paragraphs in the essay.

> To begin the process, the team unrolls the hot-air balloon on the ground. The burner and the basket are attached, and then a big fan starts blowing air into the balloon. Once it is partly full, the pilot uses the burner to heat up the air. After the balloon is upright, the crew climbs aboard.

Check your transitions. Is it easy to follow from one idea to the next? If not, try adding transitions to show how paragraphs are linked and how ideas are connected within a paragraph.

Revising in Action

You can also use sentences to connect from one paragraph to another. In the sample below, a transition sentence is added to show how this paragraph is connected to the next paragraph.

> The next step in the water cycle is condensation.
> ∧When salt water evaporates, it leaves its salt behind,
>
> so evaoporation of salt water gives the world freshwater. If
>
> water only evaporated, the oceans would eventually dry up,
>
> as they did on Mars.

Revising for Development of Ideas

When you revise for *development of ideas,* you check to be sure that you have included plenty of interesting details, organized in a way that will help readers understand and appreciate your ideas.

How do I know if I included enough details?

You know you have included enough details if your essay answers all the main questions. Here is a list of those questions.

1. What process am I explaining?
2. How does the process begin?
3. How does the process continue?
4. How does the process end?
5. Why do I think the process is interesting?

Practice

Read the paragraph below and then answer the five questions above.

Snails have a one-of-a-kind way to get around. First, a gland on the snail's stomach releases slime. It makes the ground slick and also protects the snail's soft body. Then the motion begins. Rows of muscles on the snail's stomach start to flex. These ripples push the snail over the slimy ground. The snail belongs to a group of animals known as gastropods. *Gastropod* means "stomach foot," so the snail's stomach really is a foot. After the snail moves on, the slime trail dries. Often snails leave trails in gardens. A snail can move only two or three inches in a minute—but during a year, it could go 17 miles!

Revise

Check your details. Read your essay and then answer the five questions above. If you can't find an answer to a question, add supporting details to your essay to provide an answer.

TEKS 5.15C, 5.18A(iii)
ELPS 2I, 3E, 3G, 5G

How do I know if my details are interesting?

Your essay will hold your reader's attention if you develop your ideas with lots of interesting details. One way to find out whether your details are interesting to your audience is to ask a classmate or another reader.

Partner Conference Sheet

My favorite detail is _gastropod means "stomach foot."_

An amazing detail is _snails can travel 17 miles a year!_

What I wonder is _how do snails crawl up walls?_

Revise

Hold a partner conference. **Trade essays with a partner and read each other's work. Then write your favorite detail, an amazing detail, and what you wonder. Discuss your answers. Make changes based on your partner's feedback.**

Revising in Action

Notice in the sample below that an unneeded detail is taken out and an important detail is added.

Most precipitation ends up back in the ocean.
That's where 97 percent of the earth's water is.
~~Only 1 percent of all water on earth is drinkable . . .~~
∧

Revising for Voice

When you revise for *voice,* you make sure your writing voice fits your audience, purpose, and form, or genre. You let readers know that you are well-informed and interested in your topic.

Does my writing voice fit my audience?

Your essay will hold the attention of your audience if your writing voice sounds lively and interesting. However, be sure your voice is also suitable for the classroom.

Too Casual for an Essay

C'mon. Don't you know what double dribbling is? You can't just dribble and stop and dribble again. It's our ball. Give it here.

More Formal for an Essay

The rules of basketball don't allow "double dribbling." Double dribbling happens when a player dribbles the ball, holds it, and then begins dribbling again. A player who double dribbles gets called for a foul, and the ball is given to the other team.

> When you talk to friends, you sound very casual. An expository essay should have a more formal voice.

TEKS 5.15C

How can I make my voice suitable for an essay?

The purpose of an expository essay is to inform your audience about a specific topic. Because you are writing to inform, you can make your voice suitable by changing words or phrases that sound too casual. The choices you make about what words to use and how to arrange those words in sentences contribute to your writing style.

Practice

The paragraph below is too casual for an expository essay. Find three words, phrases, or clauses that make the voice too casual.

The baler goes rolling over a bunch of hay and gobbles up the stuff and squeezes it into a block. Some balers make wimpy little bales, but others make these huge ones that could crush a guy! The baler wraps the hay up, and you have got yourself a bale.

 Revise

Review your voice. Read your essay. To enhance the style, replace overly casual words, phrases, or clauses with more suitable language that fits your purpose, audience, and genre.

Revising in Action

Casual words, phrases, and clauses are replaced in the sample below. The changes enhance the style and make the writing more informative.

When droplets in a cloud get big enough, ~~they go~~ precipitation begins.

Precipitation is just falling water.

~~"Hasta la vista!"~~ Different temperatures create . . .

TEKS 5.15C, 5.15E
ELPS 5G

Revising Using a Checklist

Revise

Check your revising. Number your paper from 1 to 9. If you can answer "yes" to a question, put a check mark before the number. If not, continue to work with that part of your essay.

Focus and Coherence

_____ **1.** Does my beginning capture the reader's attention?
_____ **2.** Does all the information relate to the key ideas?
_____ **3.** Does my ending leave readers with something to think about?

Organization

_____ **4.** Have I removed wordiness from my essay?
_____ **5.** Have I used transitional words and sentences to show how ideas are connected?

Development of Ideas

_____ **6.** Do I include enough facts and examples?
_____ **7.** Are my details interesting?

Voice

_____ **8.** Does my writing voice fit my audience?
_____ **9.** Is my language suitable for an essay?

Revise

Make a clean copy. Ask a classmate or your teacher to read and respond to your expository essay. Make any needed revisions. Create a clean copy for editing.

Editing

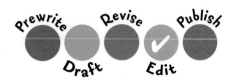
Prewrite • Draft • Revise • Edit • Publish

Editing becomes important after you've revised your first draft. When you edit, you make sure you have followed the rules for grammar, sentence structure, mechanics, and spelling. These rules are called the "conventions" of writing.

Keys to Editing

1. **Use** a dictionary, a thesaurus, and the "Proofreader's Guide" in the back of this book for help.

2. **Edit** on a printed copy if you use a computer. Then make your changes on the computer.

3. **Use** the editing marks shown inside the back cover of this book.

4. **Ask** someone else to check your writing for errors, too.

★ **TEKS** 5.15D
ELPS 5E

 **Editing** for **Conventions**

Grammar

When you edit for *conventions,* you check for errors in grammar, sentence structure, capitalization, punctuation, and spelling.

Am I using the right words?

To use the *right* words listed below, you must pay attention to the apostrophe. If the word has an apostrophe, it is a contraction. Otherwise, it shows possession. (See pages **534–537**.)

Misused Words	What They Mean
it's/its	*It's* means "it is." *Its* means "belonging to it."
you're/your	*You're* means "you are." *Your* means "belonging to you."
they're/their	*They're* means "they are." *Their* means "belonging to them."

Grammar Practice

For each of the sentences below, two words are shown in parentheses. Choose the correct one for each sentence.

1. A submarine floats when (*it's, its*) lighter than water.
2. To dive, the submarine takes water into (*it's, its*) tanks.
3. (*They're, Their*) pumped out when it's time to surface.
4. Submarines carry compressed air in (*they're, their*) tanks.
5. Maybe (*you're, your*) wondering if fish do the same.
6. (*You're, Your*) guess is right: Fish use swim bladders to dive.

Use the right word. Read your essay. Look for commonly misused words. Make sure you have used the right word.

TEKS 5.15D, 5.20A(vi)
ELPS 2C, 3C, 3D

Do I use indefinite pronouns correctly?

Indefinite pronouns can be singular, plural, or either singular or plural. (See page **446**.)

Singular: anything, no one, one, somebody

Plural: both, few, many, others

Singular or Plural: all, any, more, most, none

When you use an indefinite pronoun as the subject in a sentence, the verb must agree with it in number.

Grammar Practice

Name the indefinite pronoun in each sentence. Rewrite each sentence so the verb agrees in number with the pronoun.

1. Both boys likes to play soccer.

2. Everyone are ready for the test.

3. Several of us was late for school.

4. A few of my friends is not on the team.

Edit

Check for agreement. Make sure the indefinite pronouns and verbs in your essay agree in number.

Learning Language

The indefinite pronouns in the sentence pairs below may be singular or plural. Read each sentence to a partner and tell what the pronouns refer to. Explain which form, singular or plural, each pronoun takes.

None of the clothes were the right size.
After the movie, none of the popcorn was left.

All of the children want to stay up late.
All of this newspaper article is about the storm.

 **TEKS** 5.15C, 5.18A(iv)
ELPS 5F

Sentence Structure

When editing for *sentence structure,* check for a variety of sentence structures and different sentence lengths to make your writing flow smoothly.

How can I use a variety of sentence structures?

Using a variety of sentence structures, or patterns, makes your writing more interesting to the reader. All essays should have simple, compound, and complex sentences. (See pages **476–478**.)

Types of Sentences

Simple	**We ate dinner early.**
Compound	**We ate dinner early, and then our friends came over.**
Complex	**Because we knew our friends were coming over, we ate dinner early.**

Practice

Rewrite each pair of sentences to create a compound or complex sentence. Use the connecting words *because, when, but,* and *although.*

1. I opened the mailbox and saw a butterfly. I was surprised.
2. I forgot to get the mail out. I was watching the butterfly.
3. I wanted to watch the butterfly longer. It flew away.
4. It happened yesterday. I wrote about it in my journal.

Edit

Check sentence variety. Check your essay to make sure you have used a variety of sentence structures. Combine sentences or add connecting words to create simple, compound, and complex sentences.

TEKS 5.18A(iv)
ELPS 5F

How can I check the lengths of my sentences?

You can check sentence lengths by counting words in each sentence. You may need to combine short sentences to create a variety of lengths.

Practice

Count the words in each sentence below. How many sentences are short (up to 8 words), medium (8 to 12 words), and long (more than 12)?

(1) The team unrolls the hot-air balloon on the ground. **(2)** The burner and the basket are attached. **(3)** A big fan starts blowing air into the balloon. **(4)** Once it is partly full, the pilot uses the burner to heat up the air. **(5)** After the balloon is upright, the crew climbs aboard.

Check your sentence lengths. Count the number of words in each sentence of one paragraph in your essay. Combine sentences as needed to create a variety of sentence lengths.

Editing in Action

In the sample below, three short sentences are combined.

> Once I went sledding on a mountain. ~~Then I went~~ and
> swimming in the ocean. ~~This happened~~ during the same
> week. That was an amazing journey, but water . . .

TEKS 5.15D
ELPS 5E, 5F

Editing **Using a Checklist**

Edit

Check your editing. Number a piece of paper from 1 to 10. If you can answer "yes" to a question, put a check mark before that number. If not, continue to edit for that convention.

Conventions

GRAMMAR

_____ **1.** Have I watched for commonly misused words such as *its* and *you're*?

_____ **2.** Do indefinite pronouns and verbs agree in number?

MECHANICS

_____ **3.** Do I start all my sentences with capital letters?

_____ **4.** Do I use commas after introductory word groups?

_____ **5.** Do I use commas in all my compound sentences?

_____ **6.** Do I use end punctuation after all my sentences?

SENTENCE STRUCTURE

_____ **7.** Have I used a variety of sentence structures?

_____ **8.** Have I used a variety of sentence lengths?

SPELLING

_____ **9.** Have I spelled all my words correctly?

_____ **10.** Have I looked for words my spell-checker might miss?

Creating a Title

Here are some ideas for writing a title.

- Repeat a sound: **Wet, Wild, and Wonderful**
- Use a common expression: **Water, Water, Everywhere**
- Find a phrase from your essay: **From the Sea to the Sky**

TEKS 5.15E

Publishing

Prewrite • Draft • Revise • Edit • Publish ✓

It's time to proofread your essay and make a neat copy to share. You could also turn your writing into a diagram, a speech, or a Web page. (See the suggestions below.)

Presentation

- Use blue or black ink and write neatly.
- Write your name in the upper left corner of page 1.
- Skip a line and center your title; skip another line and start writing.
- Indent every paragraph and leave a one-inch margin on all sides.
- Write your last name and the page number in the upper right corner of every page after the first one.

Create a Diagram

Make an illustration to show how your process works. You might model your diagram on one you find in a book, in a magazine, or on a Web site.

Give a Speech

Present your essay to the class as a speech. (See pages 367–372 for more about giving a speech.)

Go Online!
Upload your expository essay for others to read.

 Publish

Make a final copy. Follow your teacher's instructions or use the presentation guidelines above. (If you are using a computer, see pages 44–46.) Create a clean final copy of your essay.

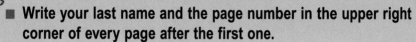

⭐ ELPS 4I, 4K

Evaluating an Expository Essay

To learn how to evaluate an expository essay, you'll use the scoring rubric on pages **34–35** and the essays that follow. These essays are examples of writing for each score on the rubric.

As you read each essay, think about the traits of good expository writing. Does the beginning capture the reader's attention and include a clear focus statement? Are the middle paragraphs well-organized? Do they include interesting facts, details, and examples? Does the essay have a meaningful ending? Always remember to think about the overall quality of the writing.

Writing that fits a score of 4 is very strong.

Blowing Its Top!

In 1980, Mount Saint Helens exploded with the force of a nuclear bomb. The eruption blew off a 1,300-foot chunk of the mountain and spat out an enormous cloud of ash. Lava and hot gas burnt the trees, plants, and lakes. Rocks the size of small buildings tumbled down the mountain. An explosion like that doesn't just happen. The eruption of a volcano like Mount Saint Helens is the result of a long process.

The process begins out at sea. That's where the Pacific plate gets shoved under the North American plate. Over thousands of years, one plate is pulled underneath the other, forming a deep trench in the ocean. This movement is called subduction. The plate that slides downward melts in the hot mantle beneath the surface of the Earth. It turns into hot liquid rock called magma.

Interesting introduction includes a clear focus statement.

Facts, details, and examples explain the process.

Soda bottle comparison shows creative thinking.

Magma doesn't stay in place like solid rock. It pushes up through cracks, trying to escape. The magma under Mount Saint Helens has a great deal of air trapped in it. As magma hardens, air is released. But that air has no place to go. The pressure builds up more and more. It's like soda in a bottle. Mount Saint Helens was acting like a cap on a soda bottle, keeping everything inside. But what happens when you take the cap off of a shaken-up soda bottle?

Mount Saint Helens began to rumble ominously in March. A series of earthquakes shook the mountain, and scientists urged people to stay away. Then, steam and ash began to escape from the ground. These earthquakes and eruptions caused landslides. One side of the mountain began to crack and bulge under the pressure.

Transitions are used to show causes and order.

Magma finally broke through solid rock on May 18. An earthquake caused a huge landslide on one side of the mountain. With all that weight gone, lava shot out like soda out of a shaken bottle. Ash, steam, and rock destroyed lakes and forests, and killed people and animals. The eruption was even visible from space!

Conclusion gives a final detail and tells why the topic is important.

The Mount Saint Helens eruption destroyed things, but it also created new life. Gophers, mice, beetles, and elk returned and now the mountain is alive with flowers and plants. Life returns every time a volcano erupts. Our world would not look the same without volcanoes.

ELPS 4I, 4K

Writing that fits a score of 3 is strong in most ways.

3

Around the Rock Cycle

Nothing on Earth is as solid and unchanging as a rock, right? Wrong! Over the years, rocks break down into tiny pieces, melt, and turn into new kinds of rocks. The process rocks follow where they change from one kind of rock to another is called the rock cycle, and it is going on all the time around us. Rocks are always being formed, breaking down, and then reforming as new rocks.

Imagine you are touching a hard rock on a hill. It will never go anywhere, right? Wrong again! Over time, it will be eroded. That means that things like the blowing wind, falling water, and ice will slowly wear bits of the rock off and move them away. Bits of animal bones, salt, or plants also mix with the rock and are carried away.

Where are these tiny bits going? On a ride around the rock cycle! If the stream slows, the glacier moves, or the wind dies down, the particles stop moving. They settle somewhere. This is the first step in making a rock. It starts with bits of sediment piled loosely together.

Next, other bits of sediment build up and up. Sometimes there are layers and layers of stuff. These layers press down on each other really, really hard. Give them some time and they all stick together and turn into a type of rock called a sedimentary rock. All sedimentary rocks are formed from squishing layers of tiny sediments together. Eventually those sediments harden into hard rock.

Information is organized by types of rock.

What if, deep under the surface of the Earth, a sedimentary rock is put under a lot of heat and pressure? It might be near a volcano, or it might be buried deep where it is hot. If this happens, it turns into a second kind of rock, a metamorphic rock. Things inside the rock react and make something new. All metamorphic rocks are formed from changing a sedimentary rock or an igneus rock with heat and pressure.

Few errors in conventions

Oh, wait, what's an igneus rock? That's the third kind of rock in the rock cycle. Igneus rocks are formed when melted rock called magma cools. If a sedimentary or a metamorphic rock is melted into magma, it can become an igneus rock, too.

Any rock can turn into another kind of rock in the right circumstances. It's pretty common for one rock to turn into another kind of rock. An igneous rock or a metamorphic rock can erode into the tiny sediments that form a sedimentary rock. A sedimentary rock or a metamorphic rock can melt into magma to form an igneous rock. And an igneous rock or a sedimentary rock can feel heat and pressure and become a metamorphic rock.

Ending supports topic but repeats information.

The rock cycle is amazing because rocks seem like they would never change. But with just a little wind, water, heat, and pressure, rocks really can change. They really can change colors and textures and everything. You might not recognize a rock after a few hundred or a few thousand years!

Writing that fits a score of 2 is strong in some ways.

Where Does Your Food Go?

Beginning introduces the topic.

The food you eat doesn't stay in your stomach forever. That would be horrible. It would just build up and you would never get rid of it. Instead, it goes through your body in the digestive system.

First you chew your food to make your food mushy and small. Then you swallow it. It doesn't get lost. It goes through a tube in your throat. The tube takes your food to your stomach.

Several errors in conventions

Your stomach mixes the food around and around. Like a washing machine. Your food is nice and soft and mushy.

Ideas are repeated, not developed.

Time for another tube. In this tube, your body takes out nutrients from the food that it needs. Your body needs vitamins and energy. So you can do stuff like running. That is what happens in this tube. That is what happens to your food.

And now your food leaves your body. It goes through a big tube. You get rid of the part of food you don't need. It is waste.

Ending wavers from the focus.

If we didn't have food we wouldn't have energy to do things. Plants make food for us to eat. We are lucky plants grow on Earth.

Writing that fits a score of 1 is weak.

Voice is narrative, not expository.

Knowledge of topic is not clear.

Many errors in conventions

Unrelated details

The Moon is Glowing

The other day I saw a lunar eclipse. I thought it was really cool. Part of the moon turned reddish orange and it glowed! I thought it looked like my dog had taken a bite out of the moon. How weird is that? My teacher said it was okay to look at the moon during a lunar eclipse, but not during a solar eclipse.

The Earth takes the sun's light in a lunar eclipse. We block the Sun. The moon can't see the sun. A little light gets past, maybe, and the moon turns orange. Sometimes the whole moon glows orange like a car headlight!

I like when the moon its like half up there only. Sometimes the moon looks really big and then I think that sometimes the moon must go on a diet because it gets so skinney!

But the moon looks super bright during the lunar eclipse. Next time I see a lunar eclipse I will take a picture. Maybe I can paint a picture. Even maybe a flashlight? My friend Juliana broke my flashlight. That made me mad.

I am so excited I got to see a lunar eclipse. Do they happen a lot? I am usually in bed at night. But maybe if I stay up late some other night I will see a lunar eclipse. You could look for one too!

Evaluating and Reflecting on Your Writing

You're done! If you can, set your essay aside for a few days. Then, on your own paper, complete each sentence starter below. To score your writing, refer to the scoring rubric on pages **34–35** and the examples you just read.

My Expository Essay

1. The best score for my expository essay is . . .

2. It's the best score because . . .

3. The best part of my essay is . . .

4. The part that still needs work is . . .

5. The main thing I learned about writing an expository essay is . . .

Expository Writing
Across the Curriculum

Expository writing is useful in all your classes. For example, the expository writing in your math book explains how a pie chart or circle graph is divided up, and the expository writing in your history book helps you understand actual events. Expository writing could even help you on a writing test!

On the following pages, you'll get the chance to try four different types of expository writing.

What's Ahead

- **Social Studies:** Writing a Comparison-Contrast Essay
- **Math:** Creating a Circle Graph
- **Practical Writing:** Taking Two-Column Notes
- **Assessment:** Writing for the Texas Assessment

TEKS 5.15B, 5.18A(i)

Social Studies:
Writing a Comparison-Contrast Essay

Rosa chose to build on ideas about George Washington and King George III to create a focused comparison-contrast essay.

Beginning
The beginning introduces the two leaders. The focus statement (underlined) presents a key idea about them.

Middle
In this comparison-contrast essay, one paragraph explains how the two men were alike. The other explains how they were different.

Ending
The ending gives the reader something to think about.

Worlds Apart

During the American Revolutionary War, King George III led Great Britain, while George Washington led the 13 colonies. Could these enemies have anything in common besides their first names? Though the two Georges private lives were very similar, they disagreed about governing the colonies.

At home, the Georges could have been friends. Both were the oldest sons in their families and were young when their fathers died. They each were tutored and worked hard on their schoolwork. As they got older, they enjoyed math, science, and farming. King George III was nicknamed "Farmer George," and Washington loved to work at his farm called Mount Vernon.

When it came to politics, these leaders were very different. Washington wanted freedom for the colonies, but King George III wanted them to be taxed and ruled by Great Britain. George III turned out to be unpopular after losing the war. Washington's victory led to his becoming one of the most popular presidents ever.

George Washington and King George III grew up in different worlds, but if they could have talked, they might have become good friends. Maybe if they had been neighbors, they could have given each other farming tips.

TEKS 5.15A, 5.23B, 5.24A
ELPS 5G

Prewriting **Selecting a Topic**

First, you need to find two people from history to compare and contrast. Rosa began by listing historical leaders she knew about.

Topic List

Leaders

Clara Barton	Thomas Jefferson	John Adams
George Washington	Abraham Lincoln	King George III

Prewrite

Select a topic. Choose a type of historical person (explorers, inventors, artists) and list names. Then choose two people who have some similarities and some differences.

Gathering Details

Next, make a plan for gathering information about your topic. You can use your history book or the Internet, visit the library, or interview experts. Rosa used a T-chart to list details she collected.

T-Chart

George Washington	King George III
Was young when father died *	Oldest son *
Liked math, science *	Called "Farmer George" *
Liked farming *	Liked math, agriculture, science *
Wanted independence for colonies	Was young when father died *
Popular president	Wanted British rule of colonies
Defeated Great Britain	Lost against colonies
Oldest son *	Unpopular king after the war

Prewrite

Make a T-chart. Plan your research. Use books, magazines, and the Internet to gather data. Talk to experts. Write things you find out in a T-chart. Put a star (*) next to the similarities.

Prewriting **Writing a Focus Statement**

In a comparison-contrast essay, your focus statement should tell how the subjects are alike and different. Rosa used this formula.

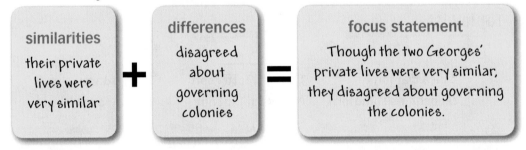

similarities		differences		focus statement
their private lives were very similar	**+**	disagreed about governing colonies	**=**	Though the two Georges' private lives were very similar, they disagreed about governing the colonies.

Prewrite | **Write your focus statement.** Sum up the similarities and differences. Then write a focus statement like the one above.

Organizing Your Ideas

Rosa created the organized list below to put her details in order. Then she used this strategy to build on ideas to organize her essay.

Directions　　**Organized List**

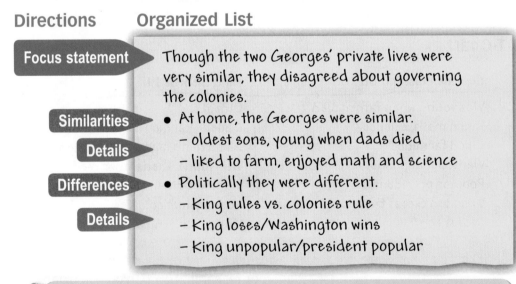

Focus statement　Though the two Georges' private lives were very similar, they disagreed about governing the colonies.

Similarities　● At home, the Georges were similar.

Details　　　– oldest sons, young when dads died
　　　　　　　– liked to farm, enjoyed math and science

Differences　● Politically they were different.

Details　　　– King rules vs. colonies rule
　　　　　　　– King loses/Washington wins
　　　　　　　– King unpopular/president popular

Prewrite | **Create an organized list.** Write an organized list of ideas that you can build on as you draft your comparison-contrast essay.

TEKS 5.18A(i)
ELPS 5G

Drafting Creating Your First Draft

Now you are ready to write your first draft. First, introduce your topic and give your focus statement. Then focus on similarities in one paragraph and differences in another. Start each paragraph with a topic sentence. In the end, sum up the similarities and differences.

Write your first draft. Use your organized list from page 176 as a guide. Remember to create effective beginning and concluding paragraphs. See pages 145 and 148 for strategies.

Revising Improving Your Writing

Next, you need to revise your work using the following traits.

- **Focus and Coherence** Is all the information in my essay clearly related to the main idea?
- **Organization** Do I explain similarities in one paragraph and differences in another?
- **Development of Ideas** Do I include interesting details?
- **Voice** Does my voice show my interest in the topic?

Improve your work. Use the checklist above to revise your first draft. Then make a clean copy for editing.

Editing Checking for Conventions

When you have finished revising, edit your paper for conventions. Check for errors in grammar, sentence structure, capitalization, punctuation, and spelling.

Check your work. Edit your essay using the questions above. Have someone else check your work, too. Then make a final copy and proofread it before you hand it in.

Math: Creating a Circle Graph

A circle graph can make writing about percentages much easier. Tamika created the circle graph below to show the different sources used to make electricity.

A paragraph introduces and explains the topic.

A circle graph "shows" the percentages for each source of electricity.

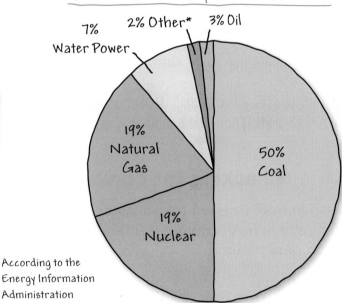

Making Electricity

Turning on a light or a TV is easy because of electricity. But where does all that electricity come from? Most power plants produce electricity by using energy sources like coal, oil, natural gas, and nuclear energy. Other plants make electricity by using sources such as sunlight, wind, water, or even heat from underground! That means there are eight different sources of electricity in use today.

Sources of Electricity in the U.S. in 2005

7% Water Power

2% Other*

3% Oil

19% Natural Gas

50% Coal

19% Nuclear

According to the Energy Information Administration

*Sunlight, wind, and heat from the earth

Writing Tips

Before you write . . .

- **Select a topic.**
  Choose a topic that focuses on different percentages of a whole, such as surveys or statistics.
- **Research your topic carefully.**
  Add up your percentages to make sure they equal 100%.
- **Do the math.**
  Figure out the right size for each piece of the pie. Multiply 360 (the number of degrees in a circle) by the percentage. For example, to draw a piece of pie to show 20 percent, your equation would be $360° \times .20 = 72°$.

During your writing . . .

- **Introduce your topic.**
  Write a paragraph to explain your topic.
- **Draw your circle using a compass.**
  Create each segment using a protractor to measure the number of degrees.
- **Color-code your graph.**
  Use colors to make your graph clear.
- **List your source.**
  Tell where you got your information.

Create a circle graph. Follow the directions above and look at the sample graph on page 178 as you make your own circle graph.

After you've written a first draft . . .

- **Check your layout.**
  Make sure that your numbers are correct.
- **Make a final version of your graph.**
  Remember to proofread your work.

TEKS 5.24C

Practical Writing:
Taking Two-Column Notes

These two-column notes show how ideas about water molecules are related. You may want to use a computer to record your data.

Main ideas appear on the left and details on the right.

Len Hankavara   February 19
                     Water Molecules

Made of three atoms	– 2 hydrogen atoms – 1 oxygen atom
Always moving	– atoms move faster when heated
Solid	– vibrate but can't move around • Ice 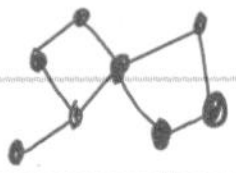
Liquid	– vibrate and can move around • Water 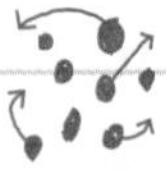
Gas	– vibrate and move very fast – particles escape – free to move anywhere • Steam 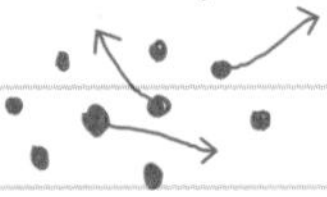

Drawings help to explain the details.

A question is added.

Why do the particles escape?

Writing Tips

Before you write . . .

● **Create a heading.**
Write your name, the date, and a topic heading at the top of your paper, or use a computer to create your note-taking chart.

● **Create two columns.**
Make the left column narrow and the right column wide.

During your writing . . .

● **Place the main ideas in the left column.**
Leave space between each main idea so that you have plenty of room to fit the details on the right side.

● **Place the details in the right column.**
Use words and phrases instead of complete sentences.

● **Use drawings and visual data.**
Illustrate your notes to make information clear. You may want to include visual data, such as graphs or diagrams.

After you've written . . .

● **Review for completeness and correctness.**
Be sure important facts are correctly written down.

● **Write any questions you still have.**
Jot down questions in your notes. Then check your book or ask your teacher for help to find answers.

● **Use your notes to help you study.**
Read over your notes before a test. Have a friend or family member ask you questions from your notes.

Take notes. Use the tips above as you take notes in one of your classes. Afterward, review your notes.

Expository Writing

Writing for the Texas Assessment

When you take state tests in Texas, you often have to write. The prompt tells you what to write about and gives some things to remember. Read the following prompt.

Prompt

> Write an essay that explains interesting facts about an animal.

Use the information below to help you write your composition.

REMEMBER THAT YOU SHOULD---

☐ explain interesting facts about an animal.

☐ capture your reader's attention at the beginning and wrap up your ideas at the end.

☐ include specific facts, details, and examples to make sure readers fully understand what you are saying.

☐ try to use correct sentences, grammar, punctuation, capitalization, and spelling.

Prewriting **Selecting a Form**

The prompt doesn't tell you what form, or genre, of writing to use. Which form best fits what you want to say? (Also see page **497**.)

Do you want to:

- describe a person or place?
- offer a solution to a problem?
- explain an object or process?
- share a personal experience?
- give information?
- persuade someone to do something?

Niki chose to explain the life cycle of a frog. She decided the best form was an expository essay.

Organizing Key Ideas

Niki wanted to organize her thoughts before she began to write. First, she wrote a focus statement. Then, she wrote topic sentences and jotted down details, facts, and examples she planned to include.

Organized List

Because a frog goes through metamorphosis, the baby looks completely different than an adult.

1. A tiny, finned tadpole is a long way from an adult frog.
   - Eats plants and algae
   - Has a strong tail and gills
2. The tadpole changes inside and out as it becomes a frog.
   - Develops hard skull and strong tongue
   - Lungs and legs form
3. Once metamorphosis is over, the frog can live and hop on land.
   - Eats different things
   - Can start the cycle again

TEKS 5.18A(i), 5.18A(iii), 5.18A(iv)

ELPS 4I, 4K

Drafting **Writing an Expository Essay**

Next, Niki used her organized list to write an expository essay. Read Niki's essay.

From Egg to Frog

The beginning introduces the topic and has a focus statement (underlined).

Usually when you look at a baby, you can tell what it will look like when it grows up. But you would never know that from looking at a baby frog. Because a frog goes through metamorphosis, the baby looks completely different than an adult.

Middle paragraphs include facts, details, and examples.

The tiny, finned tadpole is a long way from an adult frog. A tadpole begins as a jelly-like egg. Once it wriggles out of the egg, special teeth help the tadpole chew pond plants and algae. Its strong, long tail propels it around the pond, and gills help it suck oxygen from the water.

Sentences are different lengths and begin in different ways.

The tadpole changes inside and out as it becomes a frog. A skull hardens inside its head. Instead of remaining a pond plant vegetarian, the tadpole develops a strong tongue to help it capture tasty flies. It forms air-breathing lungs as its gills go away. As its

TEKS 5.18A(i–iv)
ELPS 2G, 2I, 2H, 3D, 3E, 3G, 3H, 4C, 4G, 4I, 4K

> **Transitions and explanations make key ideas and evidence easy to understand.**

> **The ending completes the life cycle and adds depth to the focus statement.**

tail shrinks and eventually disappears, the new frog grows strong legs that will help it travel on land.

Once metamorphosis is over, the frog can live, eat, and hop on land. Some frogs add mice, snakes, and other small animals to their insect diet. When the frog is completely mature, it can lay or fertilize eggs and start the whole cycle again. It's hard to believe that slick, nimble frog started as a fishy-looking tadpole!

Respond to the reading. With a partner, discuss and answer the following questions.

- **Focus and Coherence** (1) How does Niki introduce her topic? (2) Why is her concluding paragraph effective?

- **Organization** (3) How does Niki organize the key ideas, details, and evidence in her essay? (4) What transitions does she use to link and organize ideas?

- **Voice** (5) What words or phrases make this essay lively and interesting?

Literature Connection: You can find expository text that gives information in "A Way of Life," a section in *Vaqueros: America's First Cowboys!* by George Ancona.

TEKS 5.15A, 5.15C, 5.18A(i–iv)

ELPS 4J, 4K, 5G

Writing Tips

Before you write . . .

- **Understand the prompt.**
  Make sure you understand what you are to write. Think about your purpose and audience. Select the best form that will help you convey your meaning.
- **Gather your key ideas and evidence.**
  Make a list or simple graphic organizer.
- **Form a focus statement.**
  Write your main point in a single sentence.
- **Use your time wisely.**
  Plan time at the end to check your work.

During your drafting . . .

- **Begin with a strong opening paragraph.**
  Clearly state your main idea.
- **Organize your details, examples, and key evidence.**
  Put information into well-organized paragraphs. Use transitions and a variety of sentences.
- **End effectively.**
  Leave the reader with something to think about.
- **Rethink the form.**
  Make sure the form you chose is correct.

After you've written a draft . . .

- **Check for clarity and conventions.**
  Rewrite any confusing ideas and correct any errors.

Respond to an expository prompt. Respond to the prompt on page 182 within the amount of time your teacher gives you. Remember to select a form and use the tips above as you write.

Expository Writing in Review

In expository writing, you explain something to readers.

Prewrite

Select a topic that truly interests you and will also interest your reader. (See page 138.)

Gather and organize details and key evidence about your topic using a graphic organizer. (See pages 139–140.)

Write a focus (thesis) statement, identifying an important part of the topic that you plan to cover. (See page 141.)

Draft

In the beginning part, introduce your topic and state your focus. (See page 145.)

In the middle part, give details, examples, and key evidence that help the reader understand. Use transitions and a variety of sentences. (See pages 146–147.)

In the ending part, summarize your main points and make a final comment about the topic. (See page 148.)

Revise

First, review your focus and coherence, organization, and **development of ideas.** Then check for **voice.** (See pages 150–158.)

Edit

Check your writing for conventions. Correct any errors in grammar, mechanics, sentence structure, and spelling. (See pages 160–164.)

Publish

Make a final copy and proofread it for errors before sharing it. (See page 165.)

Use the scoring rubric to assess your finished writing. (See pages 34–35.)

ELPS 2C, 2G, 2H, 2I, 3D, 3E, 3G, 3H, 4C, 4G

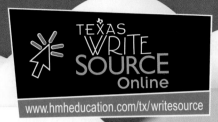

TEXAS **WRITE SOURCE** Online

www.hmheducation.com/tx/writesource

Persuasive Writing

Writing Focus

- Persuasive Paragraph
- Persuasive Essay

Grammar Focus

- Comparative and Superlative Adjectives
- Collective Nouns

Learning Language

Work with a partner. Read the meanings aloud and discuss your answers to the questions.

1. Being persuasive is convincing someone to agree with you.
   Tell about a persuasive person you know.

2. Reasons are explanations that support an opinion, or position.
   What reasons would you give to convince someone to try your favorite food?

3. If you kick a habit, then you stop doing it.
   Did you kick a habit lately? Tell your partner about it.

Persuasive Writing

Persuasive Paragraph

Commercials on TV advertise all kinds of health-related products. The problem is that some of those products may do nothing at all—and some may even do harm.

What truly healthy habit would you suggest to your friends? In this chapter, you will write a persuasive paragraph that gives your opinion about a healthy habit. Think of it as a short commercial for a habit that is good for you.

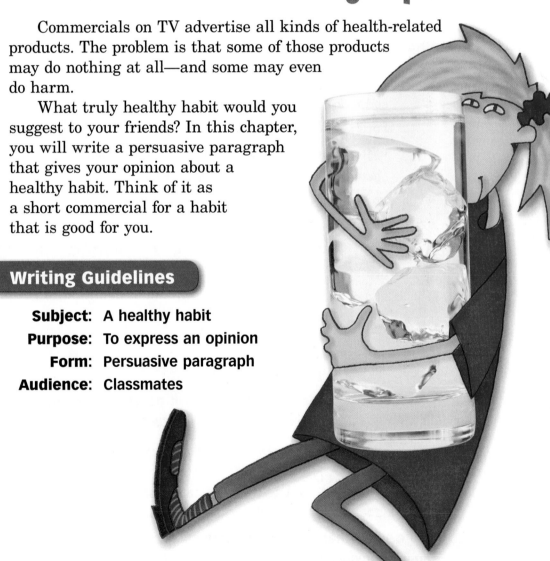

Writing Guidelines

Subject: A healthy habit
Purpose: To express an opinion
Form: Persuasive paragraph
Audience: Classmates

TEKS 5.19
ELPS 2G, 2H, 2I, 3D, 3E, 3H, 4C, 4G, 4I

Persuasive Paragraph

A persuasive paragraph starts with a **topic sentence** that gives the writer's opinion, or position. The sentences in the **body** support the topic sentence, and the **closing sentence** restates the writer's opinion. The following paragraph expresses an opinion about a healthy habit.

Topic Sentence (underlined)

Body

Closing Sentence (underlined)

The Best Health Drink of All

<u>Young people should drink more water and less soda.</u> Soda is full of ingredients people don't need. For example, a regular soda has caffeine and about 10 teaspoons of sugar! A diet soda is full of weird chemicals. On the other hand, everyone needs to drink up to half a gallon of water every day. Water helps blood flow, helps brains work, and helps bodies cool off. Without water, a person can get dehydrated or have heatstroke. <u>Young people should do their bodies a favor and drink plenty of water!</u>

Respond to the reading. On your own paper, answer the following questions. Discuss your answers with a partner.

- **Focus and Coherence** (1) What is the topic of this paragraph? What is the writer's position?

- **Development of Ideas** (2) What reasons and details does the writer give for drinking water?

- **Voice** (3) What words or phrases make the voice sound convincing?

Prewriting **Selecting a Topic**

First, you need to find a health-related topic to write about. The writer of the sample paragraph on page 190 used freewriting to think about what she did to be healthy.

Freewriting

What I do for my health. Hmm. Well, I try to eat good things, and I walk to school. That's good, except when I get caught in the rain. I also drink lots of water. That's a good thing. Most people don't even think about . . .

Freewrite. **Write freely about things you do to be healthy. Keep going until you find a topic you can write a paragraph about.**

Gathering Reasons

Now that you have chosen a topic, you need to write an opinion about it and give reasons that support your opinion. The writer of the sample paragraph used a table diagram.

Table Diagram

Opinion	Young people should drink more water and less soda.		
Supporting Reasons	soda has sugar, caffeine, chemicals	need half a gallon of water a day	avoid dehydration, heatstroke

Gather supporting reasons. **Make a table diagram like the one above. In the tabletop, write your opinion using the word *should*. Then write reasons that support your opinion in the table legs.**

Drafting Creating Your First Draft

The following guidelines can help you persuade your reader. Start with a sentence that states your opinion, or position. Remember to use the word *should*. Write body sentences that include detailed and relevant evidence to show sound reasoning. End with a sentence that restates your opinion as a command or *call to action*.

Write your first draft. Use the guidelines above to write your paragraph. Connect your ideas with transition words and phrases.

Revising Improving Your Paragraph

When you revise, check your paragraph for *focus and coherence, organization, development of ideas,* and *voice.*

Revise your paragraph. Ask yourself the following questions.

1. Is my paragraph focused on my main idea?
2. Is my evidence relevant and detailed?
3. Is my reasoning sound enough to persuade readers?
4. Is my voice appropriate for my audience?

Editing Checking for Conventions

When you edit your paragraph, you should focus on *conventions.*

Edit and proofread your work. Answer these questions.

1. Does each sentence begin with a capital letter and include end punctuation?
2. Have I checked my spelling?
3. Is each sentence complete with a subject and a verb?
4. Are my sentences written clearly and correctly?

Persuasive Writing

Persuasive Essay

George Washington knew how to fight for independence, but he didn't know how to fight cavities. Nobody back then did. Washington was one of many people in those days who lost all of his teeth.

People nowadays know more about being healthy. In this chapter, you will write about a health-related issue. Of course, no matter how persuasive you are, you'll be too late to save President Washington's teeth!

Writing Guidelines

Subject: A health-related issue
Purpose: To express an opinion
Form: Persuasive essay
Audience: Classmates

 Understanding Your Goal

Your goal in this chapter is to write a persuasive essay about a health-related issue. The traits below will help you meet that goal. Refer to the scoring rubric on pages 34–35 to improve your writing.

Focus and Coherence
Choose one health-related issue that is important to children. Create an attention-grabbing introduction to establish your opinion, or position, and conclude in a way that inspires action.

Organization
Organize your ideas in a way that persuades readers to agree with your opinion. Use transition words to help readers move from one idea to the next.

Development of Ideas
Choose reasons and use specific details that will appeal to readers' logic and to their emotions.

Voice
Keep your readers' attention throughout the essay. Use a voice that sounds original and expresses your personality.

Conventions
Errors in your writing can weaken your efforts to persuade readers. Use complete sentences. Check for correct grammar, capitalization, punctuation, and spelling.

 Literature Connection: You can find persuasive writing in campaign advertisements in *Vote for Me!* by Pamela Zorn.

TEKS 5.19
ELPS 4I

Persuasive Essay

The following persuasive essay establishes Ladonna's opinion, or position, about dental hygiene. The side notes point out what each part of the essay does.

Beginning
The beginning gets the reader's attention and states the opinion, or position (underlined).

Middle
Each middle paragraph supports the opinion statement with sound reasons.

Polish Your Pearly Whites

George Washington had many great successes in his life, but he didn't succeed in keeping his own teeth! Back then, many people lost their teeth. They didn't understand dental hygiene the way people do now. <u>For the sake of their teeth, people should brush, floss, and eat right every day.</u>

The most important thing people should do for their teeth is brush. Brushing removes pieces of food that can feed bacteria. Brushing also helps get rid of plaque, which is where bacteria live. Some toothpastes can even help stop tartar, or minerals that build up on teeth. A person should brush after every meal to keep cavities from starting.

In addition, people should floss to clean their teeth. Flossing helps get rid of food and plaque. It prevents tartar from developing between teeth. It also helps keep the gums clean so that they don't bleed or become diseased. People should floss at least once a day.

TEKS 5.19
ELPS 2G, 2H, 2I, 3D, 3E, 3G, 3H, 4C, 4G, 4I

Middle
The body paragraphs list sound reasons in order, from most important to least important.

One other important thing people should do to keep teeth strong is to eat a healthy diet. For example, milk and cheese give teeth calcium, which they need to be strong. Fruits and vegetables also help by providing vitamins A and D. On the other hand, sugary foods rot teeth. People who want strong teeth should eat right.

Ending
The ending gives a command or call to action.

If people follow this advice, they'll be able to have excellent teeth for their whole life. That's one success that even George Washington didn't have!

Respond to the reading. On your own paper, answer these questions about the model essay. Discuss with a partner.

- **Organization** (1) What transition words or phrases in the topic sentences help to show the importance of each reason?

- **Development of Ideas** (2) What details does the writer use to give sound reasoning? Name two.

- **Voice** (3) Find at least four places where the word *should* is used. How does it help the writer sound persuasive?

Prewriting

Go Online!

Prewrite Revise Publish
Draft Edit

The writing process begins with the prewriting steps that are listed below. Prewriting starts when you consider what to write about. It ends when you are ready to create your first draft.

Keys to Prewriting

1. **Select** a topic that you have an opinion about.

2. **Gather** sound reasons to support your opinion.

3. **Think** about the order in which you will present your reasons.

4. **Write** an opinion, or position, statement and topic sentences.

5. **Create** an organized list of reasons and details.

 **TEKS** 5.15A, 5.19
ELPS 5G

Prewriting **Selecting a Topic**

First, you'll need to select a health-related topic. For her essay, Joelle used a line diagram to discover a health-related topic that she wanted to write about.

Line Diagram

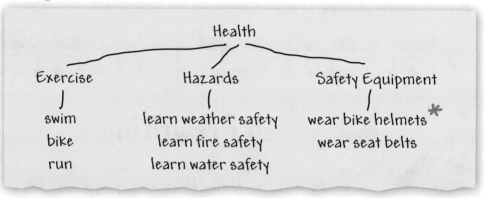

Health

Exercise   Hazards   Safety Equipment

swim   learn weather safety   wear bike helmets *
bike   learn fire safety   wear seat belts
run   learn water safety

Prewrite

Create a line diagram. Use the sample above as a model to create your own line diagram. Follow the steps below.

1 Write "Health" at the top of the diagram.

2 Next, write three categories of health issues. You can use the categories above or ones such as these: "Diets," "Hygiene," "Safety Rules," "Diseases," or "Emotions."

3 Then write specific things people should do to be healthier. Put a star (✳) next to the topic you'd like to write about.

Texas Traits

Focus on the Texas Traits

Development of Ideas Your topic is something people should do to be healthy. The word *should* makes this statement an opinion. Choose a topic you can support with at least three sound reasons. Discuss your choice with a partner.

Gathering Detailed and Relevant Evidence

Gather evidence to support your position. Evidence should be detailed and relevant. Detailed evidence includes facts, examples, and anecdotes. Evidence is relevant when it focuses on the main idea. Joelle used a T-chart to write down her position and evidence.

T-Chart

Opinion	Evidence
I think . . .people who ride bikes should always wear bike helmets.	Because . . . —bike injuries cost our country a lot. —helmets prevent brain injuries. —helmets prevent neck injuries. —helmets save lives.

Prewrite

Create a T-chart. Use the sample above as a model. In the left column, give your opinion. In the right column, list supporting evidence.

Selecting Sound Reasons

A well-organized persuasive essay provides at least three sound reasons to support the opinion. Joelle reviewed her evidence and noticed that a couple of them belonged together.

List

Sound Reasons
- bike injuries cost a lot
- helmets save lives
- helmets prevent injuries (brain, neck)

Prewrite

Group your reasons. Review your T-chart and try to group your evidence into three or four main sound reasons.

Prewriting
Understanding Order of Importance

Think of the last time you tried to persuade someone:

> Our family should go to Fun Land this June for three reasons.
> First of all, we can get cheap tickets through the school.
> Secondly, we all enjoy Fun Land.
> Most importantly, my birthday is in June!

These three sentences try to persuade by building up to the most important reason. The transition words help show the organization: "First of all, . . . Secondly, . . . Most importantly, . . . "

Practice

Read the opinion below. Then match each transition on the left with a reason on the right. Afterward, write one sentence that tells why you chose a particular reason as the most important.

Opinion: Families should hold fire drills at home.

Transitions:	Reasons:
1. First of all,	**a.** Smoke from a fire makes a house very dark.
2. Also,	**b.** Practice can prevent terrible injuries.
3. Most importantly,	**c.** The whole family needs to follow the same plan.

> Organizing your reasons by order of importance can make your writing more persuasive.

Prewrite Find your most important reason. Review your sound reasons from the bottom of page 199. Put a star next to the reason that you think is most important. Then arrange your other reasons in the best possible order.

TEKS 5.19, 5.20A(viii)
ELPS 5G

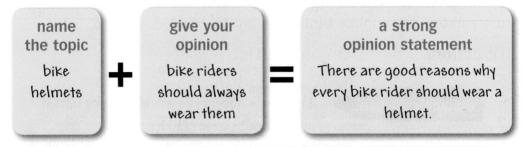

Writing an Opinion (Position) Statement

Next, you need to write an opinion, or position, statement. This statement will appear at the end of your beginning paragraph.

name the topic		give your opinion		a strong opinion statement
bike helmets	**+**	bike riders should always wear them	**=**	There are good reasons why every bike rider should wear a helmet.

Prewrite

Write your opinion statement. **Use the pattern above to write your opinion statement. Be clear, but also be creative.**

Writing Topic Sentences

Now is a good time to write topic sentences. Each one should focus on one sound reason that supports your opinion. Transition words can help you arrange your topic sentences by order of importance.

Transitions: Least to Most Important

To begin with,	One reason	For one thing,
Another reason	A second reason	In addition,
Most importantly,	The main reason	The biggest reason

Topic Sentences

To begin with, wearing bike helmets can save money.

Another reason for wearing bike helmets is they can prevent injuries.

Most importantly, wearing bike helmets can save lives.

Prewrite

Write your topic sentences. **Review your main reasons from page 199. Then write a topic sentence for each one. Remember to use transition words and phrases to show order of importance.**

TEKS 5.19
ELPS 5G

Prewriting Organizing Your Ideas

Now you can organize your whole essay. Following the directions below, Joelle created an organized list. Notice that the topic sentences are written as complete sentences, but the evidence is not.

Directions   **Organized List**

Opinion statement
There are good reasons why every bike rider should wear a helmet.

First topic sentence
1. To begin with, bike helmets can save money.

Evidence (Details)
   – bike accidents can cause serious injuries
   – doctor/hospital visits
   – $81 million in medical costs

Second topic sentence
2. Another reason for wearing bike helmets is they can prevent injuries.

Evidence (Details)
   –67,00 head injuries a year
   – 27,000 hospital stays
   – brain and neck injuries

Third topic sentence
3. Most importantly, wearing bike helmets can save lives .

Evidence (Details)
   – 800 people/year die in bike crashes
   – most die from head injuries
   – helmets protect head

Prewrite

Organize your essay. Make your own organized list. Include detailed and relevant evidence for each reason.

Drafting

In the next part of the process, you will follow the steps below to write your first draft. When you write your first draft, you put all your ideas on paper (or enter them in the computer).

Keys to Drafting

1. **Write** strong beginning and ending paragraphs.

2. **Start** each middle paragraph with a topic sentence and include supporting details.

3. **Write** with your purpose, form, and audience in mind. Ask yourself:
   • Am I taking a strong position?
   • Am I providing sound reasons?
   • Am I including details and solid evidence?

TEKS 5.15B, 5.19
ELPS 5G

Drafting Getting the Big Picture

The chart below shows how the parts of a persuasive essay build an idea to create an organized and coherent piece of writing. You are ready to draft your essay when you have . . .

- gathered enough detailed and relevant evidence,
- written a position statement and topic sentences, and
- created a list to help with the organization.

Beginning

The **beginning** introduces the topic and gives the position statement.

Position Statement

There are good reasons why every bike rider should wear a helmet.

Middle

Each **middle** paragraph gives one main reason with evidence. One should also consider alternatives.

Topic Sentences

To begin with, wearing bike helmets can save money.

Another reason for wearing bike helmets is they can prevent injuries .

Most importantly, wearing bike helmets can save lives.

Ending

The **ending** summarizes your opinion and calls the reader to action.

Call to Action

If you don't wear a helmet, it's time to start. You can get a new helmet, but you can't get a new head!

Starting Your Essay

The first paragraph in your essay should grab the reader's attention and establish your opinion, or position. Here are four ways to get your reader's attention and build a coherent and organized essay.

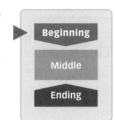

- **Give surprising information.**
  In the US, about 700 bike riders die every year in accidents.

- **Refer to an expert.**
  Safety experts report that most bike deaths could be avoided if all riders wore helmets.

- **Ask a question.**
  Who looks more foolish than a kid riding a bike and wearing a bike helmet?

- **Be creative.**
  It's easy to get a new helmet but tough to get a new head.

Beginning Paragraph

The topic is introduced.	Who looks more foolish than a kid riding a bike and wearing a bike helmet? How about a kid riding a bike and NOT wearing a helmet? Right! In fact, wearing a helmet isn't foolish. It's smart. <u>There are good reasons why every bike rider should wear a helmet.</u>
The last sentence shares the opinion statement (underlined).	

Draft

Write your beginning paragraph. Try one of the strategies listed above to get the reader's attention. Then introduce your topic and write your opinion, or position, statement.

TEKS 5.20A(viii)
ELPS 5G

Drafting **Developing the Middle Part**

Each middle paragraph begins with a topic sentence. The sentences after it support the topic sentence with details. Your organized list can guide you.

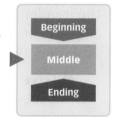

Connecting Your Sentences

Arrange sentences in a coherent way that makes sense to the reader. Use transition words and phrases to connect the body sentences in your paragraphs. Here are the transitions Joelle used within her middle paragraphs.

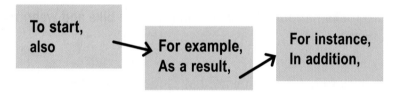

Middle Paragraphs

Topic Sentence 1 **Supporting details are added.**	To begin with, wearing bike helmets can save money. <u>To start</u>, bike accidents happen often. Some result in serious injuries or even lifetime care for injured bikers. Injured bikers not using helmets generate medical costs estimated at $81 million each year! Lawsuits, insurance, and special
Transitions (underlined) connect the sentences. **Topic Sentence 2**	help for permanently injured riders <u>also</u> push yearly costs up to more than two billion dollars. Another reason for wearing bike helmets is that they can prevent injuries. <u>For example</u>, bike accidents often cause serious brain and neck damage. 67,000 bike riders have head or neck

Additional details support the second reason.

injuries of some kind every year. <u>As a result</u>, more than 27,000 riders wind up in the hospital for some time. Thousands of those people have brain or neck injuries that seriously limit them for the rest of their lives. If they had worn a helmet, between 45 and 88 percent of brain injuries could have been prevented.

Topic Sentence 3

The most important reason is given last.

　　Most importantly, wearing bike helmets can save lives. <u>For instance</u>, every year 800 or so riders who jump on a bike and race off someplace don't make it back home. They lose their lives in bike accidents, primarily from head injuries. Most would have survived if they had worn a helmet. Why? The hard outside shell of a helmet and the soft cushion inside are designed to protect your head. <u>In addition</u>, it protects your brain! The only

Show readers that you have considered alternatives.

alternative is not to ride your bike. But wouldn't it be more fun to ride AND be protected?

Organize your paragraphs by order of importance and include strong supporting details.

Draft

Write middle paragraphs. Follow your organized list from page 202. Use transition words and phrases to connect sentences. Remember to include alternative ideas if possible.

TEKS 5.15B
ELPS 5G

Drafting **Ending Your Essay: A Call to Action**

The ending of your essay should restate your opinion, or position. Your ending should also ask the reader to do something. This is known as a *call to action*. A call to action uses a command verb such as "listen," "throw out," or "say no." Here are three sample calls to action.

- Help make wearing bicycle helmets a law in every state!
- Come back safely from your ride. Wear a helmet!
- Say "yes" to safety and wear a helmet!

For her ending paragraph, Joelle continues to build on her ideas to complete an organized and coherent essay. She includes a strong call to action. She also connects with the reader with a twist on another bit of evidence.

Ending Paragraph

> **A call to action is given.**
>
> **The reader is given something to think about.**
>
> If you don't wear a helmet, it's time. If you do and have a bike crash in which you hit your head, replace the helmet immediately. Even a slight hit can seriously damage it. If you're not wearing a helmet, a slight hit will seriously damage your head. You can get a new helmet, but you can't get a new head!

Draft

Write your ending. Continue to build on your ideas, create a call to action, and give your reader a final interesting thought.

Form a complete first draft. If necessary, write a complete copy of your essay. Write on every other line to make room for your revising changes.

TEKS 5.15C
ELPS 5G

Revising

Prewrite   Revise   Publish

Draft   Edit

In this part of the process, you will revise your work following the steps listed below. When you revise, check your essay for *focus and coherence, organization, development of ideas,* and *voice.*

Keys to Revising

1. **Read** your essay to yourself.

2. **Ask** yourself these questions:
   - Does my introduction support my purpose?
   - Is my persuasive essay organized?
   - Have I persuaded my audience to take action?

3. **Revise** for focus and coherence, organization, development of ideas, and voice.

TEKS 5.15C
ELPS 5G

Texas Traits

Revising for Focus and Coherence

To revise your essay for *focus and coherence,* check to see if your meaning is clear and how well your ideas are connected to each other. Remember that a persuasive essay tries to persuade your audience to believe your opinion, or position. To keep focus in your essay, add sentences that are meaningful and delete those that do not support your opinion.

Do my ideas clearly connect to each other and to the main idea?

The answer is yes IF, as you reread your essay, there are no details or sentences that distract from your main idea.

Practice

Read the following paragraph and find the sentence that might distract readers from the essay's main idea.

A person's attitude can shape his or her overall health. Optimists expect good things to happen, and their expectations often come true. Why is this? People usually find what they are looking for. Most people have heard that laughter is the best medicine, but doctors have proven it. Doctors have found that patients who think the best will happen heal more quickly. Therefore, everyone should try to be more optimistic.

Revise

Check for focus. Read your essay to look for sentences that might distract readers from your main idea. Add or delete sentences to strengthen the focus of your opinion and clarify your meaning.

TEKS 5.15C
ELPS 5G

Have I made my introduction and conclusion meaningful and supportive of my main idea?

Does your introduction state your opinion, or position? Good! You have a meaningful introduction. Does your conclusion restate your opinion in a way that is coherent with the rest of the essay? Then you have a supportive conclusion.

Your introduction can be more meaningful if it

- grabs the readers' attention.
- gives surprising information.

Your conclusion can be more supportive if it

- sums up your ideas.
- inspires readers to take action.

Revise

Remove unnecessary text. Read your essay and delete text that is not meaningful or does not support your position.

Revising in Action

When Joelle reread her introduction, she deleted a large unit of text that was not meaningful and might confuse readers.

Who looks more foolish than a kid riding a bike and wearing a bike helmet? How about a kid riding a bike and NOT wearing a helmet? Right! In fact, wearing a helmet isn't foolish. It's smart. ~~I wear a pink helmet with stickers all over it. I think it's pretty. It keeps my hair from blowing around.~~ There are good reasons why every bike rider should wear a helmet.

TEKS 5.15C
ELPS 5G

Revising for Organization

When you revise for *organization,* you check the order of your paragraphs and sentences.

How can I check the organization of my paragraphs?

Beginning Paragraph

1. Does my first sentence grab the reader's attention?
2. Does my beginning paragraph include my opinion statement?

Middle Paragraphs

3. Does each middle paragraph start with a clear topic sentence?
4. Are sentences in the right order to make sense?

Ending Paragraph

5. Does the ending paragraph contain a call to action?

Revise

Check the organization. **Ask yourself the five questions above. Revise until you can answer "yes" to all.**

Revising in Action

The example is moved closer to the topic sentence.

> Another reason for wearing bike helmets is that they can prevent injuries. 67,000 bike riders have head or neck injuries of some kind every year. For example, bike accidents often cause serious brain and neck damage.

How can transitions help organize my paragraphs?

Carefully chosen transitions help clarify meaning and improve the style and overall organization of a paragraph. (See also pages 515–516.)

Practice

Find places where transitions could improve the following paragraph. Here are some transitions: *also, for example, finally, most importantly.*

Seat belts provide protection in different situations. Child seats keep toddlers in place instead of climbing all over the driver. Riders wearing seat belts are protected on bumpy roads and during quick stops. Seat belts often keep people in accidents from hitting their heads. If a car rolls over, seat belts keep riders from being thrown out.

Revise

Check your transitions. Read your essay and then add any transitions needed to connect your ideas.

Revising in Action

Notice how a transition connects the ideas in the sentences.

The hard outside shell of a helmet and the soft cushion

                              In addition,

inside are designed to protect your head. ∧ It protects your

brain!

TEKS 5.15C
ELPS 5G

Revising for Development of Ideas

When you revise for *development of ideas,* you want to make sure that your examples and details support your topic sentences. Since your purpose is to persuade readers to agree with your opinion, or position, your details should be convincing!

Do my details support my topic sentences and persuade my readers?

Details are supportive if they answer the question "How?" or "Why?" See how these details are persuasive and support the topic sentence (underlined).

First of all, swimming is great for overall health. [How?] It gives the swimmer's heart and lungs a workout. That's called cardiovascular exercise. Swimming is also good for the joints. [Why?] Other sports may damage feet, knees, and hips, but swimming doesn't hurt them. [How?] Finally, swimming strengthens all the major muscles of the body—legs, back, stomach, and arms.

Practice

Which details answer "How?" or "Why?" Which two details do not?

Topic sentence: **Learning to swim can help prevent bad accidents.**
  Detail 1: **Experienced swimmers know not to swim alone.**
  Detail 2: **Swimming pools require much maintenance.**
  Detail 3: **Strong swimmers understand their limits and don't go too deep.**
  Detail 4: **Chlorine kills bacteria in the water.**

Revise

Reread your essay's topic sentences. Revise your paragraphs so that details support your purpose for writing.

TEKS 5.19
ELPS 5G

Do I include detailed and relevant evidence?

Just as a table needs at least three legs to stand up, your purpose and topic sentences need at least three supporting pieces of evidence to be convincing. Your evidence should be detailed and relevant. Detailed evidence includes facts, examples, and anecdotes. Evidence is relevant when it focuses on the main idea.

Practice

Read the following paragraph. Decide whether the topic sentence is well supported. If not, think of other details that could give it more support.

The most important reason people should swim is to have fun together. Young kids enjoy playing Marco Polo. Older kids join swim teams and compete in meets.

Check your evidence. Review each of your body paragraphs. Do you have at least three strong pieces of detailed and relevant evidence to support each topic sentence? If not, add more.

Revising in Action

Notice how Joelle added more detailed and relevant evidence to support her purpose.

Injured bikers not using helmets generate ~~huge~~ estimated at $81 million.
medical costs. Lawsuits, insurance, and special help for
to more than two billion dollars.
permanently injured riders push yearly costs up

Revising for Voice

When you revise for *voice,* you focus on how your writing sounds. Because you are writing to persuade, you can make your voice suitable by using words or phrases that have a serious and convincing tone. The choices you make about what words to use and how to arrange those words in sentences contribute to your writing style.

Do I use the right voice in my writing?

The voice of your writing shows how you feel about your topic. A persuasive essay should have a serious voice.

Words such as silly, serious, angry, confused, worried, **and** excited **describe voice.**

Practice

Match each sentence below with the word that best describes the voice of the writing. Then, for each sentence, identify the words that help create the voice.

1. I can't stand it when people don't wash their hands.
2. Hand washing prevents serious diseases.
3. Run your hands under the water and then wipe them off.
4. Fine! Don't wash your hands. You might as well eat your lunch off the floor.
5. Even Rufus Raccoon washes his hands before he eats.

a. cutesy
b. careless
c. disgusted
d. serious
e. sarcastic

How can I create a serious and convincing voice?

You can create a more serious and convincing voice by showing that you believe in your opinion and want your reader to agree with you. Carefully chosen words can help you create such a voice.

Practice

Find words or phrases that help create a serious, convincing voice.

Hand washing can prevent sickness. However, one person out of every three doesn't wash his or her hands after using the bathroom! When that person shakes hands with someone else, germs are likely to get passed. Just 30 seconds at the sink can help people stay healthy.

 Check your voice. Revise your draft to create a serious and persuasive voice. To enhance the style, add or delete words or sentences to make the purpose of your essay more serious.

Revising in Action

A careless voice is made more serious and persuasive by adding and deleting words and sentences. These changes enhance the writing style.

To start, bike accidents happen ~~often~~. ~~There's nothing you can do about it~~ Some result in ~~crazy~~ serious injuries or ~~can make you permanently messed up~~ even lifetime care for injured bikers.

TEKS 5.15E
ELPS 5G

Revising Using a Checklist

> **Check your revising.** Number a piece of paper from 1 to 8. If you can answer "yes" to a question, put a check mark before that number. If not, continue to work on that part of your essay.

Focus and Coherence

_____ **1.** Does my essay have an introduction that states my position and a conclusion that is meaningful?

_____ **2.** Do all my ideas connect to each other?

Organization

_____ **3.** Do my paragraphs follow a logical order?

_____ **4.** Have I used transitions to help the reader move from one idea to the next?

Development of Ideas

_____ **5.** Do I use examples and details to support my ideas?

_____ **6.** Does my essay persuade readers to agree with my position?

Voice

_____ **7.** Have I used a serious voice?

_____ **8.** Does my essay express my personality and viewpoint?

> **Make a clean copy.** Ask a classmate or your teacher to read and respond to your essay. Make any needed revisions. Create a clean copy for editing.

TEKS 5.15D

Editing

Prewrite Draft Revise Edit Publish

Editing becomes important after you've revised your first draft. When you edit, you make sure you have followed the rules for grammar, sentence structure, mechanics, and spelling. These rules are called the "conventions" of writing.

Keys to Editing

1. **Use** a dictionary, a thesaurus, and the "Proofreader's Guide" in the back of this book for help.

2. **Edit** on a printed copy if you use a computer. Then make your changes on the computer.

3. **Use** the editing marks shown inside the back cover of this book.

4. **Ask** someone else to check your writing for errors, too.

TEKS 5.15D, 5.20A(iii)
ELPS 5E

Editing for Conventions

Grammar

When you edit for *conventions*, you need to check your essay for errors in grammar. These two pages will show you how to correctly use comparative and superlative adjectives and collective nouns.

Do I use comparative and superlative adjectives correctly?

Adjectives are words that describe nouns or pronouns. (See pages 457–459.) Comparative and superlative adjectives can be formed by adding -er and -est. You can put *more* and *most* in front of most multisyllable adjectives to also make these forms.

Positive	**Misha is a** generous **person.**
Comparative	**José is** more generous **than Misha.**
Superlative	**Ramon is the** most generous.

Some forms of comparative and superlative adjectives are irregular.

Positive	Comparative	Superlative
good	better	best
bad	worse	worst

Grammar Practice

Rewrite each sentence using a comparative or superlative adjective.

1. Maria is a kind person in my class.
2. My new fleece jacket is colorful.
3. Jean did a good job on her report.
4. Ken's painting is impressive.

Edit

Check your use of adjectives. Make sure you have used comparative and superlative adjectives properly in your essay. For more help, see pages 458 and 626.

TEKS 5.15D, 5.20A(ii)
ELPS 3C, 3D

Do I use collective nouns correctly?

A *collective noun* is a word that refers to people, animals, or things as a group. (See page 604.)

Collective Nouns

People: audience, class, department, team
Animals: colony, pack, swarm, herd
Things: bundle, bunch, clump, range

Grammar Practice

For each description below, write the correct collective noun using the list above.

1. a group of busy ants
2. people who work in the same section of a company
3. students together in a classroom
4. several sticks tied together
5. a number of animals living together

Edit

Check collective nouns. Make sure you have used collective nouns properly in your essay.

Learning Language

Collective nouns can be used to simplify and clarify a sentence. Read the sentences below. Tell a partner how to change each sentence so it uses a collective noun.

The people watching the play clapped loudly.
The soccer players practiced hard before the game.
New people who are related to each other just moved next door.

Sentence Structure

When editing for *sentence structure,* you need to expand choppy sentences and correct sentence errors such as run-ons.

How can I expand a choppy sentence?

A choppy sentence is a short sentence that doesn't say much. One way to expand a choppy sentence is to ask the 5 W questions *(who, what, when, where, why)* and add details to answer them.

> Bike riders should learn the rules.

When? **Before heading out,** bike riders should learn the rules.

Where? Before heading out, bike riders should learn the rules **at bike camp.**

Why? Before heading out, bike riders should learn the rules at bike camp, **so they can be safe.**

Practice

Expand each of the following choppy sentences by adding details.

1. Bikes need maintenance.
2. Rules are important.
3. Riders should use signals.
4. Reflectors help visibility.
5. Bikers should wear safety gear.

Edit **Expand choppy sentences.** Answer some of the 5 W's to expand any choppy sentences in your essay.

How can I fix run-on sentences?

A run-on sentence is two sentences written together without the correct punctuation or a connecting word. (Also see page **471**.)

Reflectors make bike riders visible wearing bright clothes helps, too.

You can fix a run-on by turning it into two sentences.

Reflectors make bike riders visible. **W**earing bright clothes helps, too.

You can also turn a run-on into a compound sentence.

Reflectors make bike riders visible, **and** wearing bright clothes helps, too.

Practice

Make each run-on below into two sentences. Then make it a compound sentence. (See page **634** for a list of coordinating conjunctions.)

1. Hand signals are easy to learn they alert drivers.
2. Bikes have the right of way riders should watch traffic.

Edit

Correct run-ons. Read your essay and watch for run-on sentences. Fix any you find by using one of the methods above.

Editing in Action

The run-on sentence below has been corrected.

> If you don't wear a helmet, it's time if you do and have a
>
> bike crash in which you hit your head, replace the helmet
>
> immediately.

TEKS 5.15D
ELPS 5E, 5F

Editing **Using a Checklist**

Check your editing. On a piece of paper, write the numbers 1 to 10. If you can answer "yes" to a question, put a check mark before that number. If not, continue to edit for that convention.

Conventions

GRAMMAR

_____ **1.** Do I use correct forms of comparative and superlative adjectives?

_____ **2.** Do I use collective nouns when appropriate?

MECHANICS

_____ **3.** Do I use end punctuation after all my sentences?

_____ **4.** Do I use commas after introductory word groups?

_____ **5.** Do I start all my sentences with capital letters?

_____ **6.** Do I capitalize all names (proper nouns)?

SENTENCE STRUCTURE

_____ **7.** Have I expanded choppy sentences?

_____ **8.** Have I fixed run-on sentences?

SPELLING

_____ **9.** Have I spelled all my words correctly?

_____ **10.** Have I checked for words my spell-checker might miss?

Creating a Title

Write a title using one of these suggestions.

- Be creative: **Hard Hats Unite!**
- Use a common saying: **Use Your Head!**
- Repeat a sound: **Brainy Biking**

TEKS 5.15E

Publishing

Prewrite · Draft · Revise · Edit · Publish ✓

Now that you have finished editing your essay, it's time to make a final copy to share. You may also want to include a copy in your portfolio, create a poster, or send your essay to your school newsletter.

Presentation

- Use blue or black ink and write neatly.
- Write your name in the upper left corner of page 1.
- Skip a line and center your title; skip another line and start writing.
- Indent every paragraph and leave a one-inch margin on all sides.
- Write your last name and the page number in the upper right corner of every page after the first one.

Create a Poster

Turn your call to action into a slogan and design a poster around it.

Go Online!

Upload your persuasive essay for others to read.

Add to Your Portfolio

Make a clean final copy of your essay for your writing portfolio. Include a reflection page. (See page 232.)

Make a final copy. Follow your teacher's instructions or use the guidelines above to format your essay. (If you are using a computer, see pages 44–46.) Create a clean final copy.

Evaluating a Persuasive Essay

To evaluate a persuasive essay, use the scoring rubric on pages 34–35 and the essays that follow. These essays are examples of writing for each score on the rubric.

As you read each essay, think about the traits of good persuasive writing. Is the writer's opinion, or position, clearly stated? Does each paragraph give a sound reason and evidence to support that opinion? Does the writer consider the other side of the issue? Does the ending summarize the essay and include a call to action? Always remember to think about the overall quality of the writing.

Writing that fits a score of 4 is very strong.

Creative beginning includes a focused opinion statement.

Thoughts and reasons flow smoothly.

Take Five to Stretch

When I started jogging with my mom, she made me stretch when we ran. "How come I have to waste time stretching?" I asked. Mom told me that stretching makes me a better runner. To improve their performance and maintain muscle health, athletes should stretch.

If you are having trouble even finding time to exercise, it can be hard to find time to stretch, too. Busy runners might want to just hit the pavement and start running. After all, is stretching really worth the time?

Actually, yes. Stretching is different than running, and it has many benefits. When running or during any exercise, people should stretch to get their bodies ready to move. Stretching warms up tendons and gets blood going. It makes joints more flexible.

Another important reason to stretch is to keep from getting hurt and to help you if you are hurt. Muscles that are cold can cramp up. That's no fun. For another thing, joints that aren't ready to move can get strains or sprains. If you do get hurt while exercising, the extra blood flow from stretching can help your muscles recover faster.

Ideas are supported with evidence and sound reasoning.

The most convincing reason to stretch is that it can help a person do better! This is because stretching improves your range of motion and balance, and it lengthens your muscles. If your legs are flexible and your muscles are loose, you will be able to take longer strides as you run. Your arm muscles will be toned and ready to lift heavier loads. Your body will work more efficiently. Stretching might help you finish a longer workout, run a faster mile, or heave a bigger weight!

Good command of conventions

Stretching can help you even if you're not exercising. Think about how your muscles feel if you are worried or stressed out. They might feel tight or cramped. Next time, try stretching those muscles slowly. It can improve your mood and help you relax. Then you can face the things you need to do with a better attitude.

Ending includes a personal comment and a call to action.

When I first started running with Mom I thought pro runners were great because of their special shoes. Really they're great because of their training, which always includes stretching. So, remember to stretch. It'll help you feel good, avoid getting hurt, perform better, and relax.

Writing that fits a score of 3 is strong in most ways.

Attention-grabbing beginning with focused opinion statement

Few errors in conventions

Most paragraphs are developed with thoughtful examples.

Check Out That Label

Do you usually study the nutrition labels on your food? Admit it. It's more fun to read about the contest or play the games on the back of the box, look at the pictures, or read about how great the food tastes. But that boring nutrition label is the most important part of your snack. Everyone should read the nutrition labels to make sure they're eating right.

That number at the top of a nutrition label is more important than it looks because it is the serving size. It's an important thing to know. Otherwise, you might think you were being really healthy eating a bag of crackers, when really you just ate four whole servings! Look at all the serving size on the label and multiply that number by four. That's what you just ate!

Now look at the list of ingrediants. If an ingrediant is listed first, second, or third, that means there is a lot of it inside. Watch out for sugar because it sometimes goes by other names like corn syrup, sucrose, or glucose. If one of those things are high on the list of ingrediants, it's a really sugary food and you probably shouldn't eat too too much of it. Watch out because some breakfast cereals can be really sugary.

To be a really smart eater, you should look through the percentages. Keep your eyes pealed for the stuff listed at the top—calories, fat, cholesterol, and sodium. All of those can be bad if you have too much. One bag of chips can have 17 percent of the fat you should eat in a day. That's just too much! Percentages are pretty easy to read because they all add up to 100. It just takes a little bit of mind excercise to find out whether something is good for you.

Reading nutrition labels might even help you find food that is good for you. You might find a hidden bonus in your favorite foods. The best foods have a lot of vitamins—look for vitamin A and C especially. Also look for foods with lots of fiber, calcium, and iron. For example, I know milk is rich in calcium. Drinking it regular can help your bones and muscles. So pour yourself a tall glass and use some tasty milk to wash down your breakfast

Nutrition labels are super helpful if you want to compare different foods. They can help you compare some foods like yogurt or potato chips. How can you tell which potato chips are better? You can compare them. Look at the numbers and look at the ingredients and try to see which one is better. That's how you compare stuff.

Next time you go to the grocery store or sit down to eat, flip the box and look at those numbers, percentages, and ingrediants. Do a little math and find what secrets your food is hiding. Those numbers can tell you a whole bunch of information about the food that's going to be inside of you soon.

Some extraneous or repeated information

Ending summarizes key ideas and has a call to action.

ELPS 4I, 4K

Writing that fits a score of 2 is strong in some ways.

2

Be a Good Recycler

Direct, passionate voice

Don't be messy and lazy when you recycle. That is rude to people at the recycling plant. It is also wasteful. If one kind of recycled item messes up another, the other one can't be recycled anymore.

Repetition is not effective.

Recycling goes to a plant where different things are recycled. Plastic can make new bottles or containers. Paper can make new paper. Cardboard can make new cardboard. We don't want to run out of resources. That is why we recycle.

Evidence needs further development.

Some people threw all their recycling together. I saw my sister throw a soda can in the box for newspaper and many plants don't take wet paper because they don't have people to sort through recycling. Now that paper is wasted and it can't be used again. Probably.

Ideas are not organized clearly.

There's a reason we have different bins for kinds of recycling and the recycling people don't want to deal with paper that is covered with yucky, sticky soda. They don't want to open newspaper bins and have glass fall out. That would be dangerous!

Several errors in conventions

This is why it is important to recycle and this is why it is important to keep our stuff seperate. People should look where their putting recycle things. They should pay attention. Don't be like my sister.

Writing that fits a score of 1 is weak.

Watch Out For the Sun!

Guess waht? Its time to go to the beach! It is important to stay safe from the sun. The sand is really fun too, and sometimes we swim in the water. But the sun is always there, and you have to watch out for it!

Lacks focus and strong reasoning

The sun can burn. One time my sunscreen wash off in the water. I was so red I was the color of my swimsuit. I couldn't even sit in a chair my back was burned so much. Everytime I moved it hurt lots. Then my skin pealed too it got all itchy and started bleeding some when I scratched it more. I was really sorry that I didn't put on sunscreen that day. I wish I had went to the movies instead of the beach!

Many errors in conventions

I think my sunglasses are important to. Mine are super cool. They protect me to. I like to wear those at the beach to.

Ideas are not supported with evidence.

I get why people don't like to wear sunscreen. I think it feels yucky and greasy. And sometimes I miss a spot to! Also I dont' like to wear a hat it mess up my hair. Sometimes mom has us wear a white shirt over our swim suit!

Unrelated ideas

The beach is fun but you have to be careful. Sometimes I see people in the water when they can't swim very well and I think that is really kinda scary to!

Evaluating and Reflecting on Your Writing

Now that you've finished your persuasive essay, take a moment to reflect on the job you have done. On your own paper, complete each sentence starter below. To score your writing, refer to the scoring rubric on pages **34–35** and the examples you just read.

My Persuasive Essay

1. The best score for my persuasive essay is . . .

2. It's the best score because . . .

3. The best part of my essay is . . .

4. The part that still needs work is . . .

5. The main thing I learned about persuasive writing is . . .

Persuasive Writing

Across the Curriculum

Most newspapers feature an editorial page, a page where opinions about current events or issues are expressed.

In this section, you will write an opinion or editorial of your own. Maybe you have noticed that recycling programs need more community support. Perhaps the city is planning to close your favorite park. An editorial lets you give your opinion about things going on around you.

You'll also get to try your hand at other forms of persuasive writing and even prepare for writing persuasively on a test.

What's Ahead

- **Science:** Writing an Editorial
- **Social Studies:** Creating a Brochure
- **Practical Writing:** Drafting a Persuasive Letter
- **Assessment:** Writing for the Texas Assessment

Science: Writing an Editorial

An editorial establishes an opinion, or position, about a current issue. The following editorial was written by Akeem and published in his local newspaper.

Beginning
The issue is introduced, and the opinion statement (**underlined**) is given.

Middle
The middle paragraphs support the writer's opinion and also offer an alternative.

Ending
The last paragraph sums up the opinion.

Beyond the Bins

Most people in Elmwood recycle. They sort out paper, plastic, metal, and glass and put them in the right bins. <u>However, recycling must not stop with throwing things into recycling containers.</u>

People should help the environment by buying reusable items. For example, if a family of four uses paper napkins twice a day, that equals 2,920 napkins a year! Instead of paper napkins, families should switch to washable cloth napkins.

People also should buy recycled products. Then there would be no reason to recycle. Clothing and shoes can be made from recycled materials.

Finally, people should reduce waste. One fast-food meal can include a bag, a box, a cup, a straw, napkins, and other packaging. One alternative is to bring lunch from home in reusable containers. Home cooked meals are easier on the environment.

Recycling isn't just about filling the bins. People also have to buy reusable items and products made from recycled materials. They also need to reduce waste. If everyone develops some new recycling habits, it will help save our planet.

TEKS 5.15A, 5.19
ELPS 5G

Prewriting **Selecting a Topic**

One way to find an editorial topic is to read a newspaper. After finding interesting headlines, Akeem wrote an opinion about each.

Our school needs a program like this one.

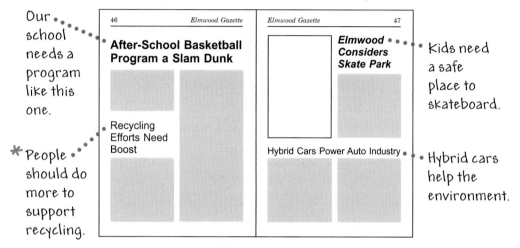

46   *Elmwood Gazette*

After-School Basketball Program a Slam Dunk

Recycling Efforts Need Boost

Elmwood Gazette   47

Elmwood Considers Skate Park

Hybrid Cars Power Auto Industry

Kids need a safe place to skateboard.

* People should do more to support recycling.

Hybrid cars help the environment.

Prewrite

Read headlines. Find four headlines in a local newspaper and write an opinion about each. Choose one to write about.

Gathering Sound Reasons

Freewriting helped Akeem gather sound reasons for his opinion.

Freewriting

It's really important to recycle. It protects the earth. People put stuff in bins, but that's not enough. So much stuff gets thrown away, like napkins. How many per day? Per year? And what about buying recycled products and . . .

Prewrite

Freewrite. Write freely for five to ten minutes about your topic. Write whatever comes to mind, getting your ideas and sound reasons down on paper.

Prewriting **Researching the Topic**

Akeem wrote down questions about his topic. He checked books, magazines, and Web sites to collect detailed and relevant evidence.

> What kinds of items are reusable?
> People could use cloth napkins, washable towels, cloth diapers.
>
> What things are made from recycled material?
> Cans and bottles, but also watches, shoes, clothing, and even school supplies can be made of recycled materials.
>
> What's one way to reduce waste?
> Don't buy things with too much packaging—like fast food.

Do your research. Write questions. Check books, magazines, and Web sites to collect detailed and relevant evidence.

Organizing Your Editorial

To organize his thoughts, Akeem made a table diagram. The "tabletop" gives his opinion, and the "legs" list supporting evidence.

Table Diagram

Opinion: Recycling shouldn't stop at the recycling bins.

Supporting Evidence: reuse products | buy recycled products | avoid waste

Create a table diagram. Write your opinion in a box and your supporting evidence underneath. Find at least three reasons.

Drafting Creating Your First Draft

The following tips can help you write your first draft. Write an opinion statement in your first paragraph. Give detailed evidence in the middle paragraphs. The ending should summarize your opinion, offer alternatives, and leave readers with an interesting final thought.

Draft

Write your first draft. Using the guidelines above, write a first draft of your editorial.

Revising Improving Your Writing

Keep the following traits in mind as you revise your first draft.

- **Focus and Coherence** Do my ideas connect to the main idea? Do I maintain focus throughout my writing?
- **Organization** Do my transitions create a smooth flow?
- **Development of Ideas** Do I offer alternative ideas?
- **Voice** Does my voice show my interest in the topic?
- **Conventions** Do I use complete sentences?

Revise

Improve your writing. Ask yourself the questions above as you revise your writing.

Editing Checking for Conventions

When your revising is done, edit your paper for conventions.

- **Conventions** Have I checked for errors in grammar, sentence structure, capitalization, punctuation, and spelling?

Edit

Check your work. Edit your essay using the question above. Have someone else check it over, too. Then make a final copy and proofread it before you hand it in.

Social Studies: Creating a Brochure

Travel brochures use words and pictures to invite others to visit a certain place. One student created the following brochure to convince readers to come to his hometown, Madison, Wisconsin.

> **The cover uses words and pictures to encourage people to visit the city.**

Madison, Wisconsin

A City for Explorers!

> **The headings help create interest.**

> **Inside, details persuade visitors to come.**

CATCH SOME WAVES

Madison is practically surrounded by lakes. In the summer, you can swim, sail, or water-ski. When the lakes are frozen, enormous kites sail and snap overhead.

HEY, SPORTS FANS

If you love sports, don't miss the Wisconsin Badgers! At Camp Randall, you can yell and scream for the football team. Make sure to bring extra money for some crispy nachos and ice-cold soda!

MUSEUM MANIA

For fun on a rainy day, visit the Madison Children's Museum. Exhibits are regularly changed, so there is always something new to discover. Make a rain stick or a miniature suspension bridge. This museum lets you learn with your brain, hands, and feet!

Come and explore for yourself!

Writing Tips

Before you write . . .

- **Review tourist information.**
  Find brochures or Web sites that advertise your area or state. Notice how they use pictures and words to convince people to visit.

- **Brainstorm a list of favorite places.**
  Think about all the special places to visit and things to do where you live. List as many as you can. Then pick three or four to focus on.

During your drafting . . .

- **Select snappy language.**
  Choose words that will excite the reader. Use a thesaurus. For example, instead of using the word *hot,* try the word *sizzling,* or instead of *delicious,* try *scrumptious.*

- **Use exciting pictures.**
  Draw pictures or include photographs.

After you've written a first draft . . .

- **Experiment with your layout.**
  Think about whether you have put each picture, paragraph, and heading in the best place to create a balanced look.

- **Check for conventions.**
  Correct any errors in grammar, sentence structure, capitalization, punctuation, and spelling.

Create a brochure.
Make a brochure about a favorite place. Draw pictures or use photos to add interest.

★ TEKS 5.18B

Practical Writing:
Drafting a Persuasive Letter

Sometimes letters are written to make requests. The letter that follows was written by Trisha to the editor of a local newspaper.

32114 West Lake Street
Elkhorn, WI 53100
June 4, 2010

Xenia Campos
Walworth County Week
Box 360
Delavan, WI 53110

Dear Ms. Campos:

I'm a fifth grader in Elkhorn who volunteers with my dad at Lakeland Animal Shelter. The shelter is having its annual Adoptathon on June 23 and 24, and we need your help. Could you please send a reporter to write a story about the Adoptathon and to take pictures of some of the animals?

All of the animals in the shelter need good homes, but right now, the shelter has more kittens than it can handle. There are dozens of adorable kittens to choose from. Even if some people can't adopt pets, they can donate money or pet supplies to help the shelter.

Your help with the Adoptathon will be greatly appreciated. An article in your paper will let your readers know about this important event and maybe help find good homes for many wonderful animals.

Sincerely,

Trisha Edwards
Trisha Edwards

The **opening** introduces the topic and states the opinion.

The **body** provides ideas, information, and supporting details.

The **ending** demonstrates closure by including a call to action.

Writing Tips

Before you write . . .

- **Know what you want from the reader.** Write down what you want your reader to do (or think).
- **Do your research.** Make sure you have all the ideas and important information your reader needs.

During your writing . . .

- **Use the proper format.** See pages 242–243.
- **Make your request (or state your opinion).** Ask the reader to do something, or let the reader know your feelings.
- **Provide support.** Give the reader details he or she needs to be convinced.
- **Demonstrate closure.** Give the reader a sense of closure by restating your opinion and including a call to action. This is a signal that your letter is ending.

After you've written a first draft . . .

- **Ask someone to review the letter.** Does your reader understand the letter? What feedback does the person have? Incorporate any changes that are needed.
- **Check for organization.** Make sure each sentence leads naturally to the next.
- **Check for conventions.** Make sure the heading, salutation, and closing are capitalized and punctuated correctly.

Write a letter. Use the model letter and the tips above to write a formal letter that makes a request. One idea would be to ask store owners in your town to help with the littering problem.

TEKS 5.18B
ELPS 4C, 4F

Parts of a Business Letter

1 The **heading** includes your address and the date. Write the heading at the left margin, at least one inch from the top.

2 The **inside address** includes the name, title, and address of the person or organization you are writing to.

- Put short titles on the same line as the name. Put longer titles on the next line.

- If you are writing to an organization, use the organization name.

3 The **salutation** is the greeting. Put a colon after it.

- If you know the person's name, use it:

   Dear Mr. Medina:

- Otherwise, use a salutation like one of these:

   Dear Store Owner:

   Dear Palo Alto Soccer Club:

4 The **body** is the main part of the letter. Do not indent your paragraphs; instead, skip a line between them.

5 The **closing** is placed after the body. Use **Yours truly** or **Sincerely**. Capitalize only the first word and put a comma after the closing.

6 The **signature** ends the letter. If you are using a computer, leave four spaces after the closing; then type your name. Write your signature between the closing and the typed name.

Try It Use the guidelines above and the letter format on the next page to write a business letter to someone with information and your ideas for a new club. Remember to give your reader a sense of closure. Make sure the heading, salutation, and closing are capitalized and punctuated correctly.

Formal Business-Letter Format

1

⎯⎯⎯⎯⎯⎯
⎯⎯⎯⎯⎯⎯⎯⎯⎯⎯
⎯⎯⎯⎯⎯⎯⎯⎯⎯⎯   ⎬— **Four to Seven Spaces**

2

⎯⎯⎯⎯⎯⎯
⎯⎯⎯⎯⎯⎯⎯⎯⎯⎯
⎯⎯⎯⎯⎯⎯⎯⎯⎯⎯
⎯⎯⎯⎯⎯⎯⎯⎯⎯⎯

3

⎯⎯⎯⎯⎯⎯ :   ⎬— **One Space**
                  ⎬— **One Space**

⎯⎯⎯⎯⎯⎯⎯⎯⎯⎯⎯⎯⎯⎯⎯⎯⎯⎯⎯⎯⎯⎯⎯⎯
⎯⎯⎯⎯⎯⎯⎯⎯⎯⎯⎯⎯⎯⎯⎯⎯⎯⎯⎯⎯⎯⎯⎯⎯
⎯⎯⎯⎯⎯⎯⎯⎯⎯⎯⎯⎯⎯⎯⎯⎯⎯⎯⎯⎯⎯⎯⎯⎯   ⎬— **One Space**

4

⎯⎯⎯⎯⎯⎯⎯⎯⎯⎯⎯⎯⎯⎯⎯⎯⎯⎯⎯⎯⎯⎯⎯⎯
⎯⎯⎯⎯⎯⎯⎯⎯⎯⎯⎯⎯⎯⎯⎯⎯⎯⎯⎯⎯⎯⎯⎯⎯
⎯⎯⎯⎯⎯⎯⎯⎯⎯⎯⎯⎯⎯⎯⎯⎯⎯⎯⎯⎯⎯⎯⎯⎯   ⎬— **One Space**

⎯⎯⎯⎯⎯⎯⎯⎯⎯⎯⎯⎯⎯⎯⎯⎯⎯⎯⎯⎯⎯⎯⎯⎯
⎯⎯⎯⎯⎯⎯⎯⎯⎯⎯⎯⎯⎯⎯⎯⎯⎯⎯⎯⎯⎯⎯⎯⎯

5

⎯⎯⎯⎯⎯⎯⎯⎯⎯⎯ ,   ⎬— **One Space**

6   ⎬— **Four Spaces**

⎯⎯⎯⎯⎯⎯⎯⎯⎯⎯

(Leave a 1-inch margin on all sides.)

Persuasive Writing

Writing for the Texas Assessment

When you take state tests in Texas, you often have to write. The prompt tells you what to write about and gives some things to remember. Read the following prompt.

Prompt

> Write a composition about a rule in your community that you support or oppose.

Use the information below to help you write your composition.

REMEMBER THAT YOU SHOULD---

☐ write a strong beginning that includes a statement of your opinion.

☐ consider the other side of the issue.

☐ include sound reasons and evidence to support your opinion.

☐ end by summarizing and restating your opinion.

☐ try to use correct grammar, sentence structure, punctuation, capitalization, and spelling.

Prewriting **Selecting a Form**

The prompt doesn't tell you what form, or genre, of writing to use. How can you decide? Thinking about which form will help you say what you want to say.

Do you want to:
- describe a person or place?
- offer a solution to a problem?
- explain an object or process?
- share a personal experience?
- give information?
- persuade someone to do something?

Answering these questions will help you decide on a form. (Also see page **497**.)

Diego decided to write about a new law in his community that required that people wear safety equipment in skate parks. He supported the law, and he wanted to explain why.

Plan the Writing

Diego knew that the opinions in his persuasive essay needed to be supported by sound reasons and evidence. He used a three-legged table diagram to gather his reasons.

Table Diagram

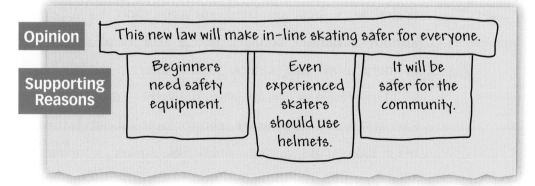

Opinion	This new law will make in-line skating safer for everyone.		
Supporting Reasons	Beginners need safety equipment.	Even experienced skaters should use helmets.	It will be safer for the community.

TEKS 5.19
ELPS 4I, 4K

Drafting **Writing the Persuasive Essay**

Next, Diego used his table diagram to write his essay. He made sure to consider why people might disagree with his point of view.

Safe Skating in the City

> The **beginning** includes the opinion, or position, statement (underlined).

The city of Hamilton wants to require in-line skaters to wear protective gear. Kids without protective gear won't be allowed to skate in city parks. This new law will make in-line skating safer for everyone.

> Each **middle** paragraph gives a sound reason and evidence that supports the opinion.

Protective gear is a must for beginners. Young skaters are still learning how to balance, turn, and stop. They fall often, and their wrists, elbows, and knees can get hurt. The right equipment can keep them safe while they learn the sport.

Even skillful skaters need helmets. In-line skates work best on hard surfaces, and a fall without a helmet could cause a bad head injury. Helmets allow all skaters to be safer.

The new law would also help the community. Parents would feel more comfortable about letting their kids skate on city sidewalks. Fewer injuries may set an example for other communities to make the same rule.

TEKS 5.19
ELPS 2G, 2H, 2I, 3D, 3E,
3G, 3H, 4C, 4G, 4I, 4K

The writer considers the other side of the issue.

Some people say they don't need knee pads or a helmet because they never fall. But an injury can happen to anyone, and it can happen very fast.

The **ending** summarizes and gives a call to action.

In-line skating is fun, but it should also be safe. The leaders in Hamilton have the right idea. People should be required to grab their safety gear before they get rolling!

Respond to the reading. Discuss and answer the questions below with a partner.

■ **Focus and Coherence** (1) What is Diego's opinion, or position, about the new rule?

■ **Development of Ideas** (2) What three sound reasons does he use to support his position? (3) In your opinion, which evidence is the strongest? (4) What other idea does Diego consider? How does he argue against it?

■ **Voice** (5) How would you describe Diego's voice— humorous, sarcastic, serious, or angry?

Literature Connection: For an example of persuasive writing, read de Zavala's powerful speech in *De Zavala: A Voice for Texas.*

TEKS 5.15A, 5.15C, 5.15D, 5.19
ELPS 4J, 4K, 5G

Writing Tips

Before you write . . .

- **Understand the prompt.**
  Make sure you understand what you are being asked to write. Think about your purpose and audience. Select the form that will help you best convey your meaning.
- **Use your time wisely.**
  Use a graphic organizer such as a line diagram to plan your essay before you write.
- **Form an opinion statement.**
  Choose an opinion, or a position, that you can support.

During your drafting . . .

- **Build your argument.**
  Use sound reasons and detailed and relevant evidence to support your opinion. Think about why people might disagree with you.
- **End effectively.**
  Summarize your argument and restate your opinion.
- **Rethink the form.**
  Make sure the form, or genre, you chose is correct.

After you've written a first draft . . .

- **Check for clear ideas.**
  Rewrite any ideas that sound confusing.
- **Check for conventions.**
  Correct any errors you find in grammar, sentence structure, punctuation, capitalization, and spelling.

 Plan and write a response. Respond to the prompt on page 244. Remember to select a form and use the tips above as you write.

Persuasive Writing in Review

In persuasive writing, you try to *convince* people to agree with you.

Prewrite

Select a topic that you feel strongly about and one that will interest your reader. (See page 198.)

Gather and organize sound reasons to support your opinion, or position, statement. You may use a graphic organizer. (See pages 199–200 and 202.)

Write a position statement that identifies your cause and your feeling about it. (See page 201.)

Draft

In the beginning part, get your reader's attention and state your opinion, or position. (See page 205.)

In the middle part, each paragraph should list a sound reason and support it with detailed and relevant evidence. Think about the other side of the issue and include alternatives. (See pages 206–207.)

In the ending part, repeat your opinion and give a call to action. (See page 208.)

Revise

Review focus and coherence, organization, and **development of ideas.** Then check **voice.** (See pages 210–218.)

Edit

Check for conventions. Correct grammar, mechanics, sentence structure, and spelling. (See pages 220–224.)

Publish

Make a final copy and proofread it before sharing it. (See page 225.)

Use the scoring rubric to assess your finished writing. (See pages 34–35.)

ELPS 2C, 2G, 2H, 2I, 3D, 3E, 3G, 3H, 4C, 4G

Responding to Texts

Writing Focus

- **Response Paragraph**
- **Book Review**

Learning Language

Learning these words and expressions will help you understand this unit. Work with a partner. Read the meanings and share answers to the questions.

1. A response is a reaction to something.
   Tell your response to a favorite meal.

2. Literary text usually tells a story.
   Name a type of literary text.

3. A review is a report that gives an opinion.
   Why might you read a review of a movie?

4. If you describe something in a nutshell, you describe it in very few words.
   Describe last weekend in a nutshell.

Responding to Texts

Response Paragraph

When your friends ask you about a story you've read, they don't want to know everything—especially the ending! In fact, they just want the story "in a nutshell."

In a response paragraph, you want to encourage others to read the story. You can do this by highlighting important parts without giving away the whole story.

Writing Guidelines

Subject: Key parts of a novel
Purpose: To preview a novel
Form: A paragraph
Audience: Classmates

TEKS 5.18C
ELPS 2G, 2H, 2I, 3D, 3E,
3G, 4G, 4I, 4K

Response Paragraph

Your response paragraph should begin with a **topic sentence** that names the novel and the author. The **body sentences** share evidence from the text to show understanding, and the **closing sentence** includes the author's message, or theme.

Topic Sentence (underlined)

Body

Closing Sentence (underlined)

Keeper of the Doves

Keeper of the Doves is a novel by Betsy Byars. The story is told by eight-year-old Amen McBee, who loves writing. Amen lives with her parents and her four sisters in Kentucky in the late 1800s. Mr. Tominski lives on their property in an old chapel in the woods, and he takes care of some doves. He scares the McBee sisters, and they tease him and call him names. Amen notices little things about people, and she decides that Mr. Tominski is a gentle, caring person. When something unexpected happens, Amen must decide if Mr. Tominski is to blame. This story is about accepting people who are different.

Respond to the reading. On your own paper, answer each of the following questions. Discuss answers with a partner.

- **Organization** (1) How does the writer organize the paragraph (time order, logical order, or order of importance)?

- **Development of Ideas** (2) What details does the writer share to spark the reader's interest in the novel?

- **Voice** (3) What words or phrases show that the writer really understands the characters' personalities and actions? Name two.

Prewriting **Selecting a Topic**

Your first step in writing a response is to choose a novel to write about. Brainstorm to come up with ideas.

Ideas List

Novels I Have Read and Liked

Bud, Not Buddy | Keeper of the Doves

Island of the Blue Dolphins | The Castle in the Attic

Choose a novel. Brainstorm a list of novels you know and like. Think of novels you have read recently. Place a star (✳) next to the one that interests you the most.

Summarizing the Plot

In any novel, there are characters in a certain place and time (the setting) who are dealing with a problem. To summarize the plot, you must tell *who* the main characters are, *where* and *when* the story takes place, and *what* the problem is.

Collection Sheet

Characters	Setting (where and when)	Problem
McBee family Mr. Tominski	Kentucky in the late 1800s	The McBee girls are scared of Mr. Tominski.

Make a collection sheet. Fill it in with the information for the novel you have chosen.

TEKS 5.15D, 5.18C, 5.21C
ELPS 5G

Drafting Creating Your First Draft

A response paragraph contains the following ideas. The topic sentence gives the book title and the author's name. The body tells about the novel's characters, setting, and problem. These sentences should include evidence from the text. Finally, the closing sentence explains the author's main message.

Draft

Write the first draft of your response paragraph. Use the tips above to guide you as you write your paragraph.

Revising Improving Your Paragraph

The next step is to make changes in the first draft to improve your *focus and coherence, organization, development of ideas,* and *voice.*

Revise

Revise your paragraph. Use the questions below as you revise your first draft.

1. Do I include enough information about the main action?
2. Do I organize the details clearly?
3. Do I sound interested in the book?
4. Do I support my ideas with relevant details?

Editing Checking for Conventions

Now it's time to check your paragraph for *conventions.*

Edit

Edit and proofread your work. Use the questions below as you edit. Then make a neat copy and give it a final proofreading.

1. Have I checked my punctuation, grammar, and spelling?
2. Have I underlined the title?

Responding to Texts

Writing a Book Review

When you read a new novel, you're like an explorer in uncharted oceans. When you review a novel, you're like a mapmaker, sharing your journey.

In this chapter, you will write a review of a novel. A book review explores important parts of a novel, without giving away the ending, and tells what you like about it.

Writing Guidelines

Subject: Review of a novel
Purpose: To show your understanding
Form: An essay
Audience: Classmates

TEKS 5.18C
ELPS 4I

Writing a Book Review

The beginning paragraph in a review names the novel's title and author and includes a sentence or two to introduce the novel. The two middle paragraphs tell what the novel is about and explain the novel's theme or message. The ending paragraph includes evidence and explains why the writer likes the novel.

Beginning
The writer introduces the novel.

Middle
The first middle paragraph tells what the novel is about.

<u>Treasure Island</u>

<u>Treasure Island</u> was written by Robert Louis Stevenson way back in 1883. The novel is very old, but that doesn't mean that it isn't good. It is one of the best pirate adventures ever written.

A 12-year-old boy named Jim Hawkins tells the story. At his parents' inn, Jim meets a mysterious old pirate. When introducing himself, the pirate says, "You mought call me Captain." Jim discovers that Captain has a map of an island that shows exactly where a valuable treasure is buried. A bunch of bad guys are after Captain because they want the map and the treasure, too. Jim and some men from his town sail to the island to search for the treasure. They are surprised to learn that some of the men traveling with them are really evil pirates. The pirates will do anything to get the treasure.

TEKS 5.18C
ELPS 2G, 2H, 2I, 3D, 3E, 3G, 3H, 4C, 4G, 4I

Middle
The second middle paragraph explains the book's theme, or message.

Treasure Island may be an adventure story, but it also teaches something. Good people can win out. Many times it looks like Jim and his friends will be killed by the pirates. Then something surprising happens, and the pirates are stopped.

Ending
The final paragraph includes evidence and tells what the writer likes about the book.

I like Treasure Island because it is filled with action and adventure. Almost every chapter ends with a surprise that makes you want to keep reading. Robert Louis Stevenson describes the characters so well that it seems like the reader is right there with Jim. Here is how Stevenson has Jim describe some sailors: "I saw besides, many old sailors, with rings in their ears, and whiskers curled in ringlets and tarry pig-tails, and their swaggering, clumsy sea-walk." Your parents, your grandparents, and even your great-grandparents probably read Treasure Island. Now it's your turn.

Respond to the reading. Answer the following questions about the model response. Discuss your answers with a partner. Add evidence to support your answers.

- **Focus and Coherence** (1) How does the conclusion support the main idea?

- **Organization** (2) Are the ideas arranged in a way that makes the writing easy to follow? Explain.

- **Voice** (3) What words and phrases will make others want to read this book?

 **TEKS** 5.15A, 5.23A
ELPS 5G

Prewriting **Selecting a Topic**

Brainstorm a list of novels. Select one you like and know well for your review. You should be able to summarize the story and explain why you liked it. Completing sentence starters is a way to record ideas.

 Complete sentence starters. Read the sample below. Then complete sentence starters for two books you have enjoyed.

Sentence Starters

BOOK 1: The Birchbark House

The story is about . . . a Native American girl in Minnesota during the pioneer days.
I like this book because . . . I like reading about pioneer times and Native American customs.

✓ BOOK 2: In the Year of the Boar and Jackie Robinson

The story is about . . . a Chinese girl who moves from China to New York.
I like this book because . . . my family has moved a lot, so I understand how the character feels.

 Choose your topic. Review your sentence completions for both books. Put a check mark by the book you want to write about.

Gathering and Organizing Details

The events you include in your review should be in time order. A time line, like the one below for *In the Year of the Boar and Jackie Robinson,* will help you.

Time Line

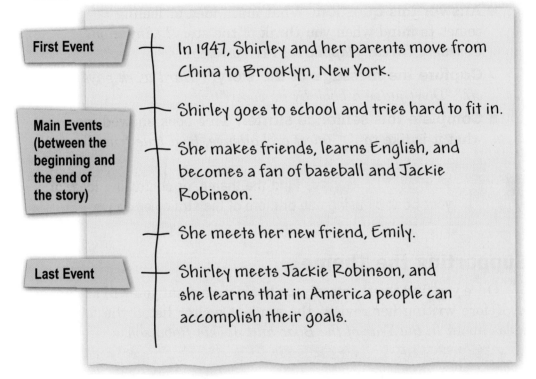

First Event — In 1947, Shirley and her parents move from China to Brooklyn, New York.

Main Events (between the beginning and the end of the story)

— Shirley goes to school and tries hard to fit in.

— She makes friends, learns English, and becomes a fan of baseball and Jackie Robinson.

— She meets her new friend, Emily.

Last Event — Shirley meets Jackie Robinson, and she learns that in America people can accomplish their goals.

tip Use present-tense verbs in your book review to bring life to your writing. Notice the verbs in the time line above (*move, goes, tries, makes, learns, becomes, meets*).

Prewrite **Create your time line.** Make a time line like the one above. Look back through the story and write the main events in their order from beginning to end. Be sure to use the present tense. Try to include at least five events.

 TEKS 5.15A
ELPS 5G

Prewriting Thinking About the Theme

All novels have a theme—a message or controlling idea. To identify the theme, try one of these strategies.

Strategies for Identifying the Theme

- **Answer this question:** What main idea or feeling comes to mind when you think of the story? *(Ambition? Courage? Greed? Happiness? Peer pressure?)*
- **Capture the message of the story:** *("Hard work pays off." "Don't judge a book by its cover.")*
- **Complete this sentence starter:** This book showed me what it is like to . . . *(meet a challenge, be a true friend).*

 Identify the theme. Find the theme, or controlling idea, of your book by using one or more of the strategies above.

Supporting the Theme

Once you find the theme of your book, plan what you will say about it. Before writing her review, the student writer listed the following ideas about *In the Year of the Boar and Jackie Robinson*.

Theme: People can accomplish their goals.

Supporting Ideas:
- Shirley learned English and made a friend.
- Jackie Robinson became the first black major-league baseball player.

 Support the theme. List details from your book that support the theme, or controlling idea, that you have chosen.

TEKS 5.18C, 5.24A
ELPS 5G

Drafting Starting Your Book Review

The beginning paragraph of your book review should name the book's title and the author. It should also include details that catch the reader's interest.

Beginning

Middle

Ending

Knowing Your Book

Follow a plan to research interesting or unusual facts about your book and its author.

1. The Newbery and Coretta Scott King awards are given each year. An expert such as your librarian can tell you if your book has won any awards.

2. Many authors have Web pages. If your author has one, try to find out what inspired him or her to write the book.

Beginning Paragraph

Try using the kinds of evidence shown above to grab the reader's interest in your beginning paragraph. (Review the following opening paragraph as well as the one on page 256.)

> **The beginning paragraph introduces the story and its author.**
>
> Bette Bao Lord wrote the book <u>In the Year of the Boar and Jackie Robinson</u>. It is the story of one year in the life of a Chinese girl who moves to America with her family. The author was born in Shanghai, China. She moved to the United States with her family in 1947. This story is really about her own life!

Draft

Write your beginning. Write the first paragraph of your book review. Be sure to include some interesting evidence that will make the reader want to learn more about the story.

Drafting **Developing the Middle Part**

The middle paragraphs should tell what the book is about and explain the story's theme. Your planning will help you write these paragraphs. Adding sentences from the book as evidence will help you show your understanding.

First Middle Paragraph

Summarize the story in the first middle paragraph. It should highlight key events without telling everything.

The first middle paragraph summarizes the story. Using exact words from the text shows how Shirley feels.

The story begins with Shirley Temple Wong in China in the Year of the Boar, 1947. That January, she and her parents move from Chungking to Brooklyn, New York. At first, the 10-year-old girl feels sad, lonely, and bored. The author describes Shirley in this way: "She hardly spoke, not even in Chinese, to her mother." But little by little, Shirley makes friends and learns to speak English and play baseball. That summer, she becomes a fan of the Brooklyn Dodgers and Jackie Robinson. He is the first black man to play baseball in the major leagues. By the end of the year, Shirley learns that America is a land of opportunity.

TEKS 5.18C
ELPS 5G

Second Middle Paragraph

The next middle paragraph should tell about the book's theme. Compare the paragraph below with the second middle paragraph in the review on pages **256–257**. As you will see, they both name the theme in the topic sentence. The other sentences in the paragraph support or explain the book's theme.

The second middle paragraph explains the book's message.

> The message of this book is that anything is possible, if you take advantage of an opportunity. Learning about Jackie Robinson gives Shirley confidence. As the author says, "Shirley felt as if she had the power of ten tigers, as if she had grown as tall as the Statue of Liberty." Shirley realizes she can learn English and make friends in America.

Draft

Write the middle part of your review. Use your prewriting notes to guide your writing. Also remember to provide evidence from the text.

Adding direct quotations as evidence can make your book review come alive. This evidence can show your understanding.

Drafting Ending Your Book Review

In the closing paragraph, you should tell why you like the novel and why you would recommend it to your friends. Your answers to the following questions will help you write this paragraph.

> Beginning
>
> Middle
>
> ▶ Ending

- What did I learn from the story?
- What personal connection do I have with a character?
- Why should my classmates read this book?

Ending Paragraph

Read the ending paragraph below. The writer shares an experience that helped her identify with the main character of the book.

The writer's reasons for liking the book show understanding of the text.

> I like <u>In the Year of the Boar and Jackie Robinson</u> because my family has moved a lot, and I know what it's like to be the new kid in school. Shirley has some funny experiences learning English. If you enjoy baseball and learning about Chinese traditions and customs, I think you will like this book.

Draft

Write your ending. Use the questions at the top of this page as a guide for writing your closing paragraph. Provide evidence from the text to show you understand it.

Form a complete first draft. If necessary, write a complete copy of your first draft. Write on every other line to make room for changes.

TEKS 5.15C
ELPS 5G

Revising Using a Checklist

Revise

Revise your first draft. Number your own paper from 1 to 8. If you can answer "yes" to a question, put a check mark before that number. If not, work with that part of your essay.

Focus and Coherence

_____ **1.** Do I name the book's title and author in paragraph one?

_____ **2.** Do I include the main events in the next paragraph and explain the theme in the paragraph after that?

_____ **3.** Does my conclusion tell why I like the book and why I would recommend it?

Organization

_____ **4.** Is my summary of events in time order?

_____ **5.** Do any sentences need rearranging in order to clarify meaning?

Development of Ideas

_____ **6.** Do I support my ideas with direct quotations and specific facts, details, and examples from the book?

Voice

_____ **7.** Do I sound knowlegable about the book?

_____ **8.** Do I sound as though I like the book?

Revise

Make a clean copy. After revising your review, make a clean copy for editing.

TEKS 5.15D
ELPS 5D, 5F

Editing **Using a Checklist**

Edit

Edit your revised copy. Number your own paper from 1 to 9. If you can answer "yes" to a question, put a check mark before that number. If not, edit for that convention.

Conventions

GRAMMAR

_____ **1.** Do I use correct verb forms *(had gone*, not *had went)*?

_____ **2.** Do I use the right words *(to, too, two)*?

MECHANICS

_____ **3.** Do I start all my sentences with capital letters?

_____ **4.** Do I capitalize proper nouns and words in titles?

_____ **5.** Do I use end punctuation after all my sentences?

_____ **6.** Do I use commas after introductory word groups?

SENTENCE STRUCTURE

_____ **7.** Do I use a variety of sentence lengths and patterns?

SPELLING

_____ **8.** Have I spelled all my words correctly?

_____ **9.** Have I double-checked the words my spell-checker may have missed?

Creating a Title

- Use the title of the book: *In the Year of the Boar and Jackie Robinson*
- Share the theme of the story: **Opportunity at Bat**
- Be creative: **Not a Boring Year**

Publish

Make a clean final copy. Check your paper one last time.

Reflecting on Your Writing

Now that you've finished your book review, take a moment to reflect on it. Complete each sentence starter below on your own paper.

Your thoughts will help you prepare for your next writing assignment.

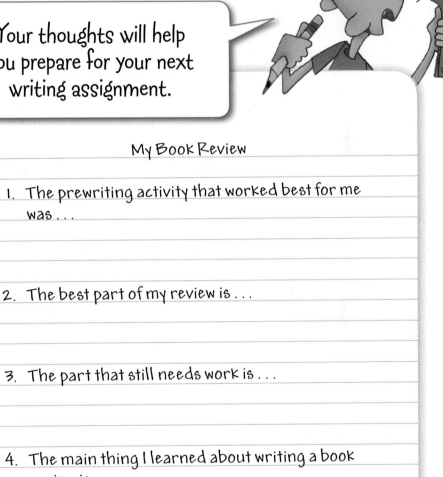

My Book Review

1. The prewriting activity that worked best for me was . . .

2. The best part of my review is . . .

3. The part that still needs work is . . .

4. The main thing I learned about writing a book review is . . .

5. In my next book review, I would like to . . .

TEKS 5.18C
ELPS 2E, 4C, 4F

Additional Ideas for Book Reviews

Listed below are additional ideas for book reviews. You can focus on one or two of these ideas in your writing. Remember to provide evidence from the text to show you understood the plot, characters, setting, and theme.

Plot (the action of the story)

- The story includes several surprising events.
- The climax (the most important event) of the story is interesting, believable, or unbelievable.
- Several important events lead to the outcome or ending of the story.
- The ending is surprising, predictable, or unbelievable.

Characters (the people—and sometimes animals—in the story)

- A main character changes from _____ to _____ by the end of the story.
- Certain people, settings, events, or ideas affect how the main character or characters act.
- _____ is the main character's outstanding personality trait. (You may point out more than one outstanding trait.)

Setting (the time and place of the story)

- The setting has an important effect on the main character.
- The setting (in a historical novel) increased my knowledge of a certain time in history.
- The setting (in a science-fiction novel) creates a different world.

Theme (the author's statement or lesson about life)

- *Ambition . . . courage . . . greed . . . happiness . . . jealousy . . .* is clearly a theme in (title of book).
- The moral, "Look before you leap" . . . "Haste makes waste" . . . "Pride comes before a fall," is developed in (title of book).
- This book showed me what it is like to be . . .

Writing in a Response Journal

There are many ways to respond to the books you read. One of the best ways is to keep a **response journal**. In your journal, you may write about the main character, try to guess what will happen next in the story, or relate some part of the story to your own life. Don't forget to include evidence from the book to show you understood.

How to Respond

Try to write in your journal at least three times for every book you read—four or five times for long books. Your journal ideas will come in handy when you write book reviews. Use the following questions to help you respond as you read. (Also refer to the additional questions on page 270.)

First Feelings
What did you like best about the first few chapters? How do you feel about the characters?

On Your Way
Are the events in the story clear? Do you still feel the same way about the characters? What do you think will happen next?

The Second Half
What seems to be important now? Is the book still interesting? How do you think it will end?

Summing Up
How do you feel about the ending? How has the main character changed? What do you like most about the book? What do you like least? Why?

Reflections
How does the book connect with today's world? How does the book relate to your own life?

Additional Questions for Responding

Whenever you need a starting point for writing in your response journal, check this page for ideas.

Before and After

- What happens in the first part of the book? What were your feelings after reading this part?
- What important things happen in the middle of the book? (Name two or three.) Why were they important?
- How does this book end? What were your overall feelings about this book?

Favorites

- What was the best part of this book? Explain.
- Which illustration in the book was your favorite? Describe it in detail.

Making Changes

- Are there any parts of the book that you would like to change? Explain.
- Could you write a new ending for this book? What would it be?
- Do you think the title of the book is a good one? Why? Can you think of a better title? What is it?

Author! Author!

- What do you think the author wants you to learn from this story?
- What would you say in a short, friendly letter to the author?

Cast of Characters

- What is the main character in the story like? Write about him, her, or it.
- Are you like any of the characters in the book? Explain your answer by telling a story about how you and the character are alike.
- Do any of the characters remind you of friends or family members? Explain by writing a comparison.
- Which character in the book would you like to write a letter to? Write it!
- Would you like having one of the characters in the story as a friend? Explain why.
- What would you say in a poem about one character, scene, or event in the story?

Responding to Texts

Other Forms of Responding

Think about the literature you come across every day. There are novels, short stories, articles, poems, plays, and reports. That's just the beginning of the list! It is safe to say that literature takes many different forms.

In this section, you will learn how to respond to four forms of literature: a quotation, a poem, an article, and an anecdote. These forms are often included on writing assessments.

What's Ahead

- Responding to a Quotation
- Responding to a Poem
- Responding to a Nonfiction Article
- Responding in a Letter to an Anecdote

TEKS 5.18C
ELPS 4I

Responding to a Quotation

A **quotation** is a passage from a piece of literature that can make you think. One way to respond to a quotation is to relate it to an experience in your own life. In the sample below, the student writer related a personal experience to this quotation: *"It is far easier to start something than it is to finish it."*

The **beginning** introduces a quotation that has meaning to the writer.	A few years ago, when my family moved to Lansing, I got into soap-box racing. That's when I discovered that "it is far easier to start something than it is to finish it."
The **middle** relates the quotation to an experience the writer had.	Dad bought a kit to make a sleek race car. I was very impatient to get it done. One day, while Dad was at work, I decided to get going on my car. I looked at the plans, and I said to myself, "You can do this." I got out Dad's toolbox, and I started building. Part A easily fit into Part B. Part C was a little harder to connect to Part D. By the time I got to Part G, I'd made a real mess of things. It took Dad and me two hours to undo what I had done.
The **ending** explains what the quotation means to the writer.	What did I learn from this experience? I was lucky I didn't ruin my race car. Now I know that before I start something, I better be sure I know how to finish it.

Prewriting **Planning Your Response**

To plan a response to a quotation, follow these three steps.

1 **Select a quotation.** Your teacher may have examples for you to choose from. If not, look for one in a book of quotations.

2 **Think about the quotation.** Once you select a quotation, restate it in your own words. This rewriting will show if you really understand the quotation.

"It is far easier to start something than it is to finish it."

> When you start something, you should have a good idea of what it will take to finish it.

3 **List personal experiences related to the quotation.** Then choose the one that you think will work best.

> * Last year I ran in an eight-mile race with my dad. I didn't train very hard because I thought the run would be easy. I didn't make it to the finish line.
>
> * I thought it would take a few hours to clean my room. Once I got started, it took the whole weekend.

Prewrite **Plan your response to a quotation.** Use the information above as your planning guide. If you have trouble finding a quotation, use one of these:
- *"Full effort is full victory."*
- *"Honesty is the best policy."*

ELPS 5G

Drafting Developing Your Response

In the **beginning** part, capture the reader's interest and restate the quotation.

> I admit it. My room barely had a path from the door to my bed. One day, I decided to straighten it up. That's when I found out that "it is far easier to start something than it is to finish it."

In the **middle** part, show the details of your experience.

> After piling, sorting, and putting away things all day, my room was still full of books, magazines, and clothing. Some of this stuff had to go. It took a whole weekend for me to decide what to keep, what to give away, and what to throw out. I finally got rid of two boxes of stuff.

In the **ending**, explain what the quotation means to you. Do this by relating the quotation to the experience you described in the middle part.

> When I started cleaning my room, I had no idea it would take a whole weekend to finish the job. I learned that I should have thought more about the neatness and order of my room all along. For me, there'll be no more living like a pack rat in a cluttered room.

Draft

Write a first draft. Write the beginning, the middle, and the ending of your response based on the guidelines above.

ELPS 5G

Revising and Editing Checklist

Once you finish your first draft, use the following checklist to revise and edit your response.

Focus and Coherence

_____ **1.** Do all of my sentences clearly relate to the idea expressed by the quotation?

Organization

_____ **2.** Does my first paragraph introduce the quotation?

_____ **3.** Does the ending explain the meaning of the quotation?

_____ **4.** Are the sentences in the right order to make sense?

_____ **5.** Are the paragraphs in the right order to make sense?

Development of Ideas

_____ **6.** Do I relate the quotation to one experience?

_____ **7.** Do I use interesting details to share that experience?

Voice

_____ **8.** Do I sound interested in my quotation?

Conventions

_____ **9.** Do I use a variety of sentence lengths and beginnings?

_____ **10.** Have I checked capitalization, spelling, and punctuation?

Revise

Revise and edit your response. Make the necessary changes in your response. Proofread your final copy before sharing it.

TEKS 5.18C
ELPS 4C, 4I

Responding to a Poem

A **poem** is a special type of literature that uses only a few words to express an idea or an emotion. To respond to a poem, you should think about its form, the special words that the poet uses, and the main idea or message of the poem. In the essay below, the writer responds to the poem "Fireball."

> **Fireball**
> Superior star
> Warms the earth
> Melting icicles, creating deserts
> Sun

The **beginning** introduces the subject and names the form of the poem.

"Fireball" is a word cinquain poem. The poem has five lines that follow this pattern: one word, two words, three words, four words, and one word. The last line is a synonym of the first line.

The **middle** explains how the words are used.

Each line shares different ideas about the topic. The words "Superior star" in line two say that this ball of fire is better than the other stars. In line three, "Warms the earth" describes the value of this star. Line four, "Melting icicles, creating deserts," describes its power.

The **ending** explains the message of the poem.

The main message of this poem is that the sun is both helpful and harmful. This poem describes the sun as the most powerful star in our sky.

Prewriting Planning Your Response

1 **Choose a poem.** Make sure to select a poem that you truly enjoy and understand.

2 **Read the poem several times.**

> **Silence**
> Faithful trees stand guard
> as the forest sleeps under
> a blanket of snow.

3 **Decide what form the poem takes** (*free verse, limerick, haiku, cinquain*). If you're not sure of the form, note the number of lines in the poem, if rhyme is used, and if the poem follows a pattern of some type.

4 **List ideas for your response.** Use an organizer like the one below to gather ideas and evidence to show understanding.

Gathering Chart

form	haiku–nature poem line 1–five syllables; line 2–seven syllables; line 3–five syllables
special words	trees "stand guard" like people "forest sleeps"–everything quiet
main message	In winter the trees look like they protect the forest.

Prewrite

Plan your response. Use the information above as your planning guide. Provide evidence from the text. If you have trouble finding a poem, consider this one:

> **Full Moon**
> Wakes when darkness comes
> climbs a tall starry ladder
> lights the earth below.

 **TEKS** 5.15B, 5.18C
ELPS 5G

Drafting **Developing Your Response**

Organize the paragraphs of your response by building on ideas. In the **beginning**, discuss the form of the poem and explain how it is put together.

> "Silence" is a haiku. Haiku poems are about nature. They are three lines long. The first line has five syllables, the second line has seven, and the third line has five.

In the **middle**, to show understanding, explain how the poet uses special words. Refer to a few specific parts of the poem as evidence.

> This poem is about a forest in winter. In the first line, the trees seem like real people "standing guard" over the forest. In the second and third lines, "forest sleeps" tells us that everything is quiet "under a blanket of snow."

In the **ending** paragraph, explain the poem's main message.

> I think that the poet's message in "Silence" is that even though the trees are bare, they still protect the forest. Even in the winter, they shelter everything on the forest floor.

Draft

Write a first draft. Write the beginning, the middle, and the ending of your response based on the guidelines and examples. Remember to include evidence to show your understanding.

TEKS 5.15D
ELPS 5G

Revising and Editing Checklist

Once you finish your first draft, use the following checklist to revise and edit your response.

Focus and Coherence

_____ **1.** Do all of my sentences focus on explaining the meaning of the poem?

Organization

_____ **2.** Are my sentences in the right order to make sense?

_____ **3.** Do my ideas flow smoothly from beginning to end?

Development of Ideas

_____ **4.** Do my ideas show a clear understanding of the poem?

_____ **5.** Do I quote specific words or phrases from the poem as evidence and explain their meaning?

Voice

_____ **6.** Do I sound like I understand and enjoy the poem?

Conventions

_____ **7.** Do I use correct capitalization, punctuation, and grammar?

_____ **8.** Do I spell all my words correctly?

Revise and edit your response. Make the necessary changes in your response. Proofread your final copy before sharing it.

 **TEKS** 5.18C
ELPS 4C, 4I

Responding to a Nonfiction Article

A **nonfiction article** often shares important information about a real person, place, or event. One way to respond to a nonfiction article is to point out interesting facts, or evidence, that helped you understand the subject as well as questions you still have about it.

Turkey Talk

By Margarita Hernandez

What bird best symbolizes the spirit of the United States of America? Chances are, people wouldn't say "turkey." Yet in the 1770s, Ben Franklin proposed to Congress that the wild turkey be named the national bird. The turkey lost to the bald eagle by only one vote.

Flocks of wild turkeys once roamed free in woodlands, grasslands, swamplands, and forests from southern Canada to Guatemala. Native peoples valued this clever and curious bird for its meat, eggs, and feathers.

Wild turkeys were first domesticated, or tamed, in Mexico. Spanish explorers introduced the bird to Europe where it became a popular choice for holiday meals. Colonists continued this tradition when they came to America, so it is no surprise that the turkey is an honored "guest" in many homes at Thanksgiving time.

The **beginning** names important facts from the article.

The **middle** names more evidence.

The **ending** tells what the writer still wants to know.

"Turkey Talk" is about the history of the wild turkey in America. I was surprised to learn that Benjamin Franklin wanted the wild turkey to be named the national bird of the United States. It lost by just one vote in Congress. I wouldn't have thought turkeys were that popular!

One reason for their popularity could be that wild turkeys were everywhere, from Canada to Guatemala. They were a source of food for many people.

Once Europeans learned about the bird they began serving turkey for holiday meals, just like we do today. I like turkey, but I don't eat it that often. I'd be interested in learning about different ways to cook a turkey. I wonder how native peoples across the Americas prepared it.

Prewriting **Planning Your Response**

Follow these steps when you plan a response to an article.

1 Select an interesting article to read, like the one below.

A True Survivor

By Curtis Reynolds

The Western diamondback rattlesnake lives in the desert-like regions of the southwestern United States. How has it adapted to survive in this hot, rocky environment?

When the temperature is very hot or very cold, heat-sensing organs located near the rattlesnake's eyes help it find shelter. These "pits" also help the rattlesnake track warm-blooded prey and avoid predators, even in the dark.

Another adaptation is the rattlesnake's deadly venom. When a snake bites, the venom works quickly to thin the victim's blood and destroy its nervous sytem. As a result, the rattlesnake uses less energy when chasing prey or defending itself.

Most notably, this reptile grows a hard "rattle" at the end of its tail for protection. A rapid shake warns others to stay away.

Adaptations like these make this snake a true survivor.

2 List the most important facts, or evidence from the article.

Facts List

–The diamondback rattlesnake lives in a desert-like environment.
–"Pits" help the snake find shelter, locate prey, and avoid predators.

3 Think of any questions that you have about the article.

<u>My questions</u>

What do the pits look like and how do they work?
How long does it take venom to work?

Prewrite

Plan your response. Use the information above as a guide. If you have trouble finding an article, ask your teacher for help.

Drafting Developing Your Response

In the **beginning**, name the important facts, or evidence, that helped you understand the first part of the article.

> The Western diamondback rattlesnake is an amazing creature. It has developed many clever and useful adaptations that help it survive in the desert-like region of the southwestern United States.

In the **middle** part, identify evidence that helped you understand the rest of the article.

> What makes this reptile so special? Heat-sensing organs help it find shelter from the heat and cold, track prey, and avoid predators. The rattlesnake conserves energy by using venom to kill its prey and its enemies. In addition, it has a funny way of avoiding trouble. It shakes a rattle that grows on its tail as a warning to other creatures to beware.

In the **ending** paragraph, state any key question that you have after reading the article.

> The rattlesnake's heat sensors, or pits, interest me the most. I would like to find out how they work. I wonder if scientists got the idea for night goggles from studying rattlesnakes. Perhaps other rattlesnake adaptations will help people, too.

Draft

Write a first draft. Write the beginning, middle, and ending of your response using the information above as a guide.

TEKS 5.15D
ELPS 5G

Revising and Editing Checklist

Once you finish your first draft, use the following checklist to revise and edit your response.

Focus and Coherence

____ **1.** Do I state the main idea in the first paragraph?

____ **2.** Do the rest of the sentences relate to the main idea?

Organization

____ **3.** Does my beginning name important information, or evidence, from the first part of the article?

____ **4.** Do I give more evidence in the middle part?

____ **5.** Do I ask a question related to the article at the end?

____ **6.** Are my sentences and paragraphs in an order that makes sense?

Development of Ideas

____ **7.** Does my response show that I understand the article?

Voice

____ **8.** Do I sound interested in my response?

____ **9.** Do I use specific words to keep the reader's interest?

Conventions

____ **10.** Do I use correct capitalization and punctuation?

____ **11.** Have I corrected spelling or grammar errors?

Revise and edit your response. Make the necessary changes in your response. Proofread your final copy before sharing it.

 **TEKS** 5.18B

ELPS 4C, 4I

Responding in a Letter to an Anecdote

An **anecdote** is a brief, interesting story. Anecdotes are written about real people. The following anecdote is about Oprah Winfrey.

> **Oprah's Letter**
>
> On Oprah's first day of kindergarten, her teacher got a letter saying that Oprah belonged in the first grade. After reading the letter, the teacher agreed. Do you know who wrote the letter? Oprah did! At five years old, she knew how to read and write.

In the letter below, a student responds to this prompt: *Read the anecdote "Oprah's Letter." What word do you think best describes the person being written about? Write a letter to a friend using information from the anecdote to support your choice. Include all parts of an informal letter: the greeting, closing, and signature.*

What key word in paragraph one describes the person's character?	Dear Judy, Oprah Winfrey is a <u>clever</u> person. She knew how to read when she started school, so she thought she should skip kindergarten.
What evidence supports the writer's opinion of the person?	On the first day of school, she wrote her teacher a letter to prove that she should be moved up to first grade. Her letter showed how, even as a child, she wanted a good education.

How does the ending show the value of the character trait?	Today she is one of the most famous women in the world, Her story shows me the importance of finding creative ways to reach my goals.
	
	                    Sincerely,
	
	                    Ella Ellison

TEKS 5.18B
ELPS 5G

Prewriting Gathering Details

Your teacher may ask you to write a letter in response to an anecdote. The following ideas will help you get started.

1 Read the anecdote and the prompt carefully.

> ### Jim's Dream
>
> Jim Abbott wanted to play Little League baseball. However, he was born with his right arm missing just below the elbow. Yet Jim spent hours throwing tennis balls against a wall. He learned to throw left-handed while holding his glove under his right arm. Then he quickly switched the glove to his left hand so he could catch. Before long, Jim's dream came true. He made a Little League team as a pitcher.

2 Based on this story, what word or phrase would best describe the person's character or personality?

3 Write a statement that identifies the topic of your response. (Include the word or phrase that would best describe the person in your statement.) Then think of three reasons from the anecdote to explain your statement.

> I think Jim Abbott was very determined.
> REASONS:
> 1. He wanted to play baseball, even though he had a birth defect.
> 2. He spent hours throwing a tennis ball.
> 3. He learned to throw and catch with his left hand.

Respond to an anecdote. Plan a letter in response to an anecdote provided by your teacher. Discuss your plan with a partner.

 **TEKS** 5.18B, 5.18C
ELPS 5G

Drafting Developing Your Response

To write a letter in response to an anecdote about a person, focus on a key word that describes his or her character. Write sentences from the anecdote (evidence) that show your understanding.

In the **beginning**, write a statement that describes the person.

> I just read about a very determined man named Jim Abbott. He was born missing his right arm below the elbow, but he found a way to overcome his disability.

Write a **middle** paragraph that supports the opening statement.

> Jim dreamed of playing Little League baseball. He spent hours throwing tennis balls against a wall. He threw and caught left-handed. Jim held his glove under his right arm when he threw. Then he quickly switched the glove to his left hand so he could catch. Because of hard work, Jim became a pitcher.

Write an **ending** that reemphasizes the character trait and demonstrates a sense of closure.

> Do you agree that Jim Abbott showed what a determined person can do? His goal was to play baseball, and through hard work, he reached that goal.

Draft

Write a first draft. Write the beginning, the middle, and the ending of your response letter based on the guidelines above.

Texas Traits

Revising and Editing Checklist

Use the following checklist to revise and edit your letter.

Focus and Coherence

_____ **1.** Does my letter focus on one key character trait that describes the person?

Organization

_____ **2.** Does my beginning describe the person's character?

_____ **3.** Does my middle support the opening statement?

_____ **4.** Does my ending give the reader one final thought?

_____ **5.** Are my sentences in an order that makes sense?

Development of Ideas

_____ **6.** Do I use one key word or phrase to describe the person?

_____ **7.** Do I refer to details in the anecdote as evidence?

Voice

_____ **8.** Does my writing sound like me?

_____ **9.** Do I sound interested in the topic?

Conventions

_____ **10.** Do I use correct capitalization and punctuation?

_____ **11.** Have I checked for errors in spelling and grammar?

 Revise

Revise and edit your response. Make the necessary changes in your response. Proofread your final copy before sharing it.

ELPS 2C, 2G, 2H, 2I, 3D, 3E, 3G, 3H, 4C, 4G

TEXAS WRITE SOURCE Online
www.hmheducation.com/tx/writesource

Creative Writing

Writing Focus
- **Writing Stories**
- **Writing Poems**

Learning Language

Work with a partner. Read the meanings and share answers to the questions.

1. **Fiction** is a story about an imaginary person or event.
   Which is fiction, an encyclopedia or a novel?

2. Something **historical** has to do with events or people in the past.
   What historical event interests you?

3. The standpoint from which a story is told is the **point of view**.
   Tell about your day in first-person point of view. Then tell about a partner's day in third-person point of view.

4. A **tall tale** is a story that has characters with special powers and events that are hard to believe.
   What tall tales have you heard or read?

Creative Writing

Writing Stories

Try to imagine living long ago at some other time in history. What would it have been like to sail on the *Mayflower* or to travel with Harriet Tubman on the Underground Railroad to freedom? What would it have been like to help Ben Franklin discover electricity or invent bifocals?

Fictional stories set in another time and place allow the writer and the reader to have adventures in history. This chapter will help you write a believable historical fiction story. Afterward you can create a tall tale or even a play!

Writing Guidelines

Subject: Historical fiction story

Purpose: To entertain

Form: Short story, tall tale, play

Audience: Classmates

Historical Fiction Story

In the following story, Clayton imagines being the best friend of a young Benjamin Franklin. He uses action, dialogue, and sensory details to set the scene and bring his story to life.

Beginning
The beginning introduces the setting and the main characters and shows the point of view from which the story is told.

Rising Action
A conflict between the characters creates tension.

Dialogue
Dialogue refers to the words characters speak to each other. How does the dialogue help you understand this story?

My Best Friend, Ben

The summer of 1716 was a hot one in Boston. Almost every afternoon, I went swimming in Fresh Pond with my best friend, Ben Franklin. We loved those long, hot days.

On one particular afternoon, Ben was late. I went to his house and climbed the stairs to his cluttered bedroom. He was sitting there messing with a kite.

"What's with the kite?" I said. "I thought we were going swimming."

Ben smiled at me as he tied one more knot in the kite string. "We need the kite for swimming."

"Who goes swimming with a kite?" I asked.

"I do," Ben said. His blue eyes twinkled.

When you're the friend of a genius, you get used to hearing crazy ideas. I just shook my head. "I'd like to see you do it."

Half an hour later, we were standing on the shore of Fresh Pond. Ben held his crazy kite in one hand and an

TEKS 5.16A(iii)
ELPS 2G, 2H, 2I, 3D, 3E, 3G, 3H, 4C, 4G, 4I, 4J

old log in the other. He sat on the muddy shore, slipped off his shoes, and tied the end of the kite string to one big toe. Then he flipped the kite into the air and let a breeze catch it. The kite rose over Fresh Pond.

"This is ridiculous," I said.

My friend Ben grinned at me and hopped into the pond. He threw one arm over his log, leaned back, and let the kite pull him across the pond.

"Oh, I get it!" I cried as Ben drifted away. "It's a flying sail!"

"Meet you on the other side!" he called back.

Sure enough, I did! That was my friend Ben's first famous kite trick, and I was there to see it. I only wish I'd been with him years later when he used another kite to discover electricity!

High Point
The conflict is resolved when the main character understands the mystery.

Ending
The ending reflects on the events of the story.

Respond to the reading. **Answer the following questions about the story. Then discuss them with a partner.**

- **Organization** **(1) How is this story organized? (2) Does the organization fit the purpose? Why or why not?**

- **Development of Ideas** **(3) What do you think happened next? Write more dialogue to develop the story.**

- **Voice** **(4) Find three specific action verbs or phrases. Tell how they strengthen the voice of the story.**

TEKS 5.16A(i)
ELPS 5G

Prewriting **Selecting a Topic**

One way to find a topic is to list historical people and events. Clayton paged through his social studies book to create the list below.

Topic List

> ### Historical People and Events
>
> Paul Revere riding to warn of the British attack
> Pocahontas saving John Smith from execution
> Ben Franklin using a kite to cross a lake *

List topic ideas. Use a history book or the Internet to find topic ideas. Star (*) the one that will be the focus of your story.

Choosing a Point of View

Clayton decided to use first-person point of view because he wanted a friendly, informal voice. He decided to tell the story as if he were Ben Franklin's best friend. Clayton began to freewrite.

Freewriting

> If I were Ben Franklin's best friend, I'd be used to his crazy ideas. But I bet I'd still doubt him if he tried to tie a kite to his foot and cross a lake. If we were just about to going swimming, I'd feel hot and impatient. Maybe I'd just roll my eyes and shake my head at Ben's latest weird idea.

Freewrite about point of view. Choose first-person or third-person point of view. Then freewrite about what your narrator will think, feel, and want during your story.

 **TEKS** 5.16A(i)
ELPS 5G

Creating a Plot

The actions that take place during a story make up the plot line. Each part of the plot plays an important role in the story.

- The **beginning** introduces the characters and the setting.

- The **rising action** develops the conflict—a problem or challenge for the characters.

- The **high point** is the most exciting part.

- The **ending** tells how the conflict worked out.

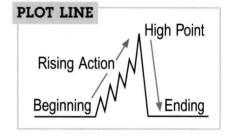

PLOT LINE

High Point

Rising Action

Beginning / Ending

Clayton used a plot chart to help him think about what would happen during each part of his story.

Plot Chart

Beginning	Rising Action	High Point	Ending
I show up at Ben's house to go swimming. He's building a kite instead.	Ben says the kite is for swimming. I dare him to show me.	Ben ties the kite to his big toe and floats across Fresh Pond.	I laugh at my friend and think of other things he would do with kites.

 Prewrite

Create a plot chart. In each column, write what will happen in the beginning, in the rising action, at the high point, and in the ending of your story.

 **TEKS** 5.16A(i–iii)
ELPS 5G

Drafting Creating Your First Draft

Use the tips below to begin writing your story.

1 **Set the scene by using sensory details to answer *when* and *where*.**

Instead of . . . **Ben and I were going to go swimming.**
Write . . . The summer of 1716 was a hot one in Boston.

2 **Use dialogue to let characters speak for themselves.**

Instead of . . . **I didn't know why he had a kite.**
Write . . . "What's with the kite?"

3 **Tell your story from a unique point of view.**

Instead of . . . **It was kind of a crazy idea.**
Write . . . When you're the friend of a genius, you get used to hearing crazy ideas. I just shook my head.

4 **Use sensory details to create the setting and make the story come alive.**

Instead of . . . **He got ready for his experiment.**
Write . . . He sat on the muddy shore, slipped off his shoes, and tied the end of the kite string to one big toe.

5 **Show actions and build to a high point.**

Instead of . . . **Ben Franklin tried his idea.**
Write . . . "This is ridiculous," I said.
My friend Ben grinned at me and hopped into the pond.

 Write your first draft. Use your prewriting charts and the tips above as you create a draft of your historical fiction story.

TEKS 5.15D, 5.16A(i), 5.16A(ii)
ELPS 5G

Revising Improving Your Writing

Once you finish your first draft, set it aside for a while. When you are ready to revise, the following questions can help.

- **Focus and Coherence** Did I focus on a specific historical event or person?
- **Organization** Does my story have a plot with a beginning, rising action, a high point, and an ending?
- **Development of Ideas** Did I use sensory details to create a believable setting?
- **Voice** Is my story told from a clear point of view?

Revise your writing. Use the questions above as a guide when you revise your first draft.

Editing Checking for Conventions

The following questions can help you edit your story.

- **Conventions** Have I corrected spelling and capitalization errors? Have I included end punctuation for each sentence? Have I checked for easily confused words (*to, too, two*)?

Edit your story. Edit using the questions above. Use the tips below to write a title. Create a clean final copy to proofread.

Creating a Title

- Use a repeated sound: **My Best Friend, Ben**
- Be playful: **Towed by a Flying Sail**
- Use a line from the story: **Swimming with a Kite**

TEKS 5.16A(i)
ELPS 5G

Creating a Tall Tale

Have you ever bragged about something you did? Tall tales can begin with facts, but the writer includes so many exaggerations that the story becomes wild and wacky. Here are the steps for creating a tall tale about a historical figure.

❶ Make your hero larger than life.

Focus on one idea or trait about your main character and then exaggerate it until it is unbelievable. Decide on a point of view from which your story will be told.

Betsy Ross, famous flag maker, designed a flag big enough to be seen by all the original 13 states at once.

❷ Give your hero a powerful challenge.

For the plot, come up with a villain, a monster, or a natural event that the hero must fight against.

While traveling the Missouri River, Lewis and Clark had to fight a 50-foot killer sturgeon that had just swallowed three canoes.

❸ Exaggerate.

Make your story as wild as it can be.

Because her plane's engine was damaged, Amelia Earhart overinflated her tires and bounced across the country.

Write a tall tale. Exaggerate one of your main character's traits. Then give him or her a great challenge. Use exaggeration to tell the story of how your character succeeds.

Creating a Play

Another creative way to share a story is to write it as a play. A play depends on dialogue to tell a story. Actions are stated in parentheses. Here is the beginning of a play that Clayton wrote based on his Ben Franklin story.

Franklin, the Flying Fish

Characters: Clayton Jones, 10 years old
Ben Franklin, 10 years old

Setting: The shore of a large pond; a breezy afternoon

ACT I

(Ben sits under a tall oak tree and ties the last bit of string onto a kite he has just made. Clayton, in a swimsuit, rushes up.)

Clayton: Sorry I'm late.

Ben: No problem. I had time to finish my kite.

Clayton: (scratching his head) What's with the kite? I thought we were going swimming.

Ben: (tying the kite string onto his big toe) We are . . . with a kite.

Clayton: Who swims with a kite?

Ben: (standing up and grinning) I do. . . .

 Write your story as a play. Use the sample play above as a guide. Choose a topic, list your characters, create the setting, and then write dialogue to tell your story.

Story Patterns

Story plots often follow patterns. Here are five popular story patterns that you could try.

The Rescue

In a *rescue* story, a character is either the rescuer or someone who needs to be rescued.

> A boy and his dog are trapped on the roof of a house in a flood.

The Quest

In a *quest* story, a character travels into unknown places to achieve a goal.

> Daniel Boone searches for a pass through the mountains.

The Mystery

In a *mystery* story, a character must answer a puzzling question.

> A girl who finds a ring with strange markings tries to find out where the ring came from and what the markings mean.

The Underdog

In an *underdog* story, a character overcomes real difficulty to succeed.

> A boy faces his fear of water and learns to swim.

The Rivalry

In a *rivalry* story, two characters compete for a single object or goal.

> Luis and Jamal try to outdo each other to win the position of starting quarterback.

Check the story pattern. Think of a favorite story. Does the plot follow one of the story patterns above? If not, how would you describe the story pattern? Discuss with a partner.

TEKS 5.16A(i)
ELPS 4C, 4F

Elements of Fiction

Writers use specific terms to talk about the parts of a story. In the following list, you'll find words that will help you as you write stories and read the stories of others.

Action The **action** is everything that happens in a story.

Antagonist An **antagonist** (sometimes called a villain) is a person or thing that fights against the hero.
> The wolf is the antagonist of the three little pigs.

Character A **character** is a person or humanlike animal in a story.

Conflict **Conflict** is a problem or challenge for the characters. There are five basic types of conflict:

- **Person vs. Person:**
  Two characters have opposite goals.
  > A supervillain wants to sink a ship, but a superhero wants to save it.

- **Person vs. Society:**
  A character has a problem with a group of people.
  > A student has trouble fitting in at a new school.

- **Person vs. Himself or Herself:**
  A character has an inner struggle.
  > A young detective wonders what to do when the clues in his current case point toward his best friend.

- **Person vs. Nature:**
  A character has to battle an element of nature.
  > A mountain climber gets caught in a blizzard.

- **Person vs. Fate:**
  A character faces something he or she can't control.
  > After falling from a horse, an injured man fights to walk again.

TEKS 5.16A(i), 5.16A(iii)
ELPS 4C, 4F

Dialogue   **Dialogue** refers to the words characters speak to each other in a story.

Mood   **Mood** is the feeling a reader gets from a story— happy, sad, frightened, peaceful.

Moral   A **moral** is a lesson the writer wants readers to learn from a story. The moral of "The Boy Who Cried Wolf" is that if you tell lies, no one will believe you even when you tell the truth.

Narrator   The **narrator** is the one who tells the story. Harold the dog tells the story in the book *Bunnicula,* so Harold is the narrator (even though he is a dog!).

Plot   The **plot** is the action or series of events that make up the story. Most plots follow a plot line with four parts: beginning, rising action, high point, and ending. (See page **293**.)

Point of View   **Point of view** is the angle from which a story is told.

- A story about the writer uses *first-person point of view.*
   I went swimming in Fresh Pond with my best friend, Ben Franklin.

- A story about other people uses *third-person point of view.*
   Clayton and Ben went swimming in Fresh Pond.

Protagonist   The **protagonist** is the hero of the story.

Setting   The **setting** is the time and place of a story.

Theme   The **theme** is the main idea or message of a story. The theme of *Charlotte's Web* is the importance of friendship.

Tone   The **tone** is the feeling the author creates in a story. For example, the tone of a story may be serious, funny, or angry.

Creative Writing

Writing Poems

Think of a special place, somewhere you love to be. Then think of how exciting it is to tell someone about it.

A poem is a great way to tell someone about a favorite place. Poems focus on sights, sounds, and feelings. In this unit, you will write a poem about your own favorite place, inviting readers to join you in this special spot.

Writing Guidelines

Subject: A favorite place
Purpose: To entertain
Forms: Free-verse poem, diamanté, limerick, list poem
Audience: Classmates and family

TEKS 5.16B(i), 5.16B(ii)
ELPS 2G, 2H, 2I, 3D, 3E, 3G, 3H, 4C, 4G, 4I, 4J

Free-Verse Poem

Not all poems have to rhyme. All poems *do* use language in a special way. Dina Lazeric wrote the following free-verse (nonrhyming) poem about her favorite part of a zoo.

Aviary

Glass dome above,
like an eggshell
filled with green branches

where rainbow-colored birds
flutter, squawk, and fly!

Stone path leading
through the trees,
crossing a blue pool

where rainbow-colored fish
chase bird reflections.

Respond to the reading. Answer and discuss with a partner the following questions about the poem "Aviary."

- **Organization** (1) Which two similar lines tie the poem together?

- **Development of Ideas** (2) What details in this poem best help you imagine the aviary? List at least three.

- **Voice** (3) Find an example of onomatopoeia in this poem. (4) Find a simile. What two things are being compared?

Prewriting **Selecting a Topic**

To write a poem, first you need a topic. Dina brainstormed ideas by writing a list of her favorite places.

Brainstorming List

my room on rainy days	the playground on Elm Street
✓ the aviary at the zoo	the swimming pool in Ash Park

Make a list. List some of your own favorite places. Check
(✓) the one that you are most interested in writing about.

Gathering Details

Poems use sensory details to create pictures for the reader. Dina gathered details about the aviary in a sensory chart.

Sensory Chart

See	Hear	Smell	Taste	Touch
Stone path	Birds chattering, singing, squawking	Dirt	none	Damp air
Green leaves and branches		Plants		Cold cement bench
Blue pool	Wings fluttering			Soft flowers and ferns
Bright-colored birds and fish	Water splashing			
Clear glass dome				

Gather sensory details. Make a chart like the one above and
list details about your topic.

 **TEKS** 5.16B(i), 5.16B(ii)
ELPS 5G

Prewriting Using Poetry Techniques

Poets use special techniques and figurative language in their writing. Dina used a *simile* and *onomatopoeia* in her poem.

- A **simile** *(sĭm´ə-lē)* uses the word *like* or *as* to compare two things.

  Glass dome above,

  like an eggshell

- **Onomatopoeia** *(ŏn´ə-măt´ə-pē´ə)* uses words that sound like the noises they name.

  where rainbow-colored birds

  flutter, squawk, and fly!

Prewrite Use poetry techniques and figurative language. Try to think of one simile to use in your poem. List two words that use onomatopoeia.

Drafting Developing Your First Draft

Now it's time to write your poem! Follow these tips.

- **Imagine being in your favorite place.** Review your sensory chart for details.
- **Write whatever comes to mind.** If you're not sure how to start, begin with the most important detail.
- **Play with words.** Capture sights, sounds, and feelings.

Draft Write the first draft of your poem. Use poetry techniques to describe your favorite place so the reader can experience being there, too.

TEKS 5.15E, 5.16B(i), 5.16(ii)
ELPS 5G

Revising Improving Your Poem

Revise your draft by answering these questions about the traits.

- **Focus and Coherence** Is my poem focused on describing a place?
- **Organization** Do I arrange my ideas in an interesting and logical way?
- **Development of Ideas** Do I use figurative language, such as similes and metaphors, to develop my ideas?
- **Voice** Do I use alliteration or onomatopoeia?

> **Revise your writing.** Keep working with your poem until you're happy with every word. Use the traits above. Ask a classmate or your teacher for feedback. Make revisions based on this feedback.

Editing Fine-Tuning Your Poem

You want your poem to flow smoothly and be easy to read.

- **Conventions** Are my words spelled correctly? Have I used the right words (*there, they're, their*)?

> **Edit your work.** Correct any errors in your poem.

Publishing Sharing Your Poem

Here are a few ways to share your poetry.

- **Perform it.** Read it aloud to friends and family.
- **Post it.** Display it on a bulletin board or on your refrigerator.
- **Send it out.** Submit it to a newspaper, magazine, or Web site.

> **Present your work.** Make sure to share your poem. Use one of the ideas above or come up with an idea of your own.

TEKS 5.16B(iii)
ELPS 4I, 5G

Writing a Diamanté

A diamanté *(dē'ə-män-tā')* is a five-line poem written in a diamond shape. The lines follow a specific formula, as shown below.

Outside
bright, breezy
running, shouting, jumping
loud, excited, calm, quiet
sitting, whispering, giggling,
warm, cozy
inside

Title: One noun
Two adjectives about the first noun
Three *-ing* words about the first noun
Two words about the first noun and two
about the final noun
Three *-ing* words about the final noun
Two adjectives about the final noun
Ending: One noun (the title's opposite)

Writing Tips

- **Select a topic.** Think of an interesting place or idea and its opposite (attic and basement, summer and winter).
- **Gather details.** List contrasting details about these two places or ideas. Make a chart like the one below.
- **Follow the pattern.** Fill in your diamanté. Make sure your poem flows smoothly from the title to the ending.

Planning Chart

1 noun	2 adjectives	3 -ing words	2 more adjectives
Outside inside	bright, breezy warm, cozy	running, shouting, jumping sitting, whispering, giggling	loud, excited quiet, calm

Create your diamanté. Choose two opposite ideas and write your diamanté using the writing tips above.

TEKS 5.16B(ii), 5.16B(iii)
ELPS 4I, 5G

Writing Other Forms of Poetry

Here are two more types of poems for you to try.

Limerick

Limericks tell funny stories. The first, second, and fifth lines rhyme. Try to include one or two similes.

My Race Car Cat

When my cat has a mouse in her thrall
Like a race car she'll whiz down the hall
But when I see her trail
I let out a wail
It looks like huge beasts had a brawl!

List Poem

If you like making lists, try writing a list poem. Each item begins with a capital letter and helps build a word picture.

Waiting

Buttery popcorn
Giant drink
Cushiony seats
Dim lights
High ceiling
Hushed talking
Let's start the show!

Write a poem. Choose a funny event or favorite activity and write your own limerick or list poem. Remember to check capital letters.

TEKS 5.16B(i), 5.16B(ii)
ELPS 4C, 4F

Using Special Poetry Techniques

The next two pages explain the special techniques that poets use. Try using some of these in your poems.

Figurative Language

- A **simile** *(sĭm´ə-lē)* compares two different things using the word *like* or *as*.

  A dresser like a sunken treasure chest

- A **metaphor** *(mĕt´ə-fôr)* compares two different things without using *like* or *as*.

  My closet is a time machine.

- **Personification** *(pər-sŏn´ə-fĭ-kā´shən)* makes something seem human that isn't.

  The breeze whispers through the porch screens.

- **Hyperbole** *(hī-pûr´bə-lē)* is an exaggeration.

  Their lunchroom stretches to another county.

Poetry Techniques

Poets use the following techniques to add interesting sounds to their work. (Also see page 304.)

- **Alliteration** *(ə-lĭt´ə-rā´shən)* means repeating beginning consonant sounds.

  flutter, squawk, and fly

- **Assonance** *(ăs´ə-nəns)* is the repetition of vowel sounds in words.

  On Saturdays, I wake to kitchen sounds.

- **Consonance** *(kŏn´sə-nəns)* is the repetition of consonant sounds anywhere within words.

  On Saturdays, I wake to kitchen sounds.

TEKS 5.16B(i–iii)
ELPS 4C, 4F, 5G

- **Graphic elements** such as line length, color, spacing, letter size, and other visual elements can emphasize how the poem sounds and what it means.

  The old teapot let out a SCREECH!

- **Line breaks** help slow down the reader, focusing attention on individual words and phrases.

  Stone path leading
  through the trees

- **Onomatopoeia** *(ŏn´ə-măt´ə-pē´ə)* means the use of words that sound like the noise they name.

  flutter, squawk, **and fly**

- **Repetition** means using the same word, idea, or phrase for rhythm or emphasis.

  Dad making biscuits. Mom making coffee.

- **Rhyme** means using words whose endings sound alike.

  End rhyme happens at the ends of lines.

  Janice sings
  while she swings.

  Internal rhyme happens within lines.

  Teachers left the bleachers.

- **Rhythm** *(rĭth´əm)* is the way a poem flows from one idea to the next. In free-verse poetry, the rhythm follows the poet's natural voice.

  Ă dréssĕr likĕ ă súnkĕn tréasurĕ chést

 Write a poem. Write about a favorite time or place. Use figurative language, a poetry technique, and a graphic element.

ELPS 2C, 2G–2I, 3D, 3E, 3G, 3H, 4C, 4G

TEXAS
WRITE
SOURCE
Online

www.hmheducation.com/tx/writesource

Research Writing

Writing Focus

- **Research Report**
- **Speech**
- **Multimedia Presentation**

Grammar Focus

- **Prepositions**

Learning Language

Work with a partner. Share answers. Remember to summarize information and listen carefully.

1. When you surf the Web, you search for information on the Internet.
   What do you learn when you surf the Web?

2. A bibliography tells the books, magazines, Web sites and interviews you used to write your report.
   What information do you need for your bibliography?

3. Something multimedia uses pictures and sound.
   Which is multimedia, a movie or a textbook? Explain.

Research Writing

Building Research Skills

Good research is like detective work. As you research, you'll search high and low to find what you want. There's a lot of information out there, and you'll need solid research skills to find what you need.

The key to effective research is having a plan for gathering information and knowing where and how to find the best sources for that information. This chapter guides you through the process of finding sources on the Internet, in the library, and even from experts. You'll search for answers to your research questions. Soon, you'll be able to turn the information you find into an effective research report.

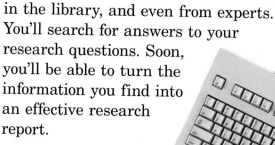

TEKS 5.23A, 5.23B, 5.24A–E
ELPS 3E, 3G

The Research Process

Create a Research Plan

- First, choose a topic. Brainstorm by yourself or consult with other students. More brains mean more ideas!

- Decide what you want to research and form open-ended research questions about your topic. If your question can be answered with just one word, it's not open ended.

- Make a plan for how you will research your questions.

Try IT Here are some questions about the topic, "dogs that work." Work with a partner to decide which questions are open ended. Together, create three more open-ended questions about dogs that work.

> **What tasks can dogs do?**
> **What is the most popular breed of dog in America?**
> **What remarkable dogs are in your town?**
> **Can dogs help people in wheelchairs?**

Gather Sources

- Collect information from reference books, magazines, and newspapers. Do an online search. Look for charts, diagrams, and maps. Take notes on what you learn.

- Make a special effort to find a primary source. You might even find an expert who can help you!

- Always use sources that you can trust, and make sure you are collecting information that you can use.

- Take notes carefully and paraphrase information. Don't plagiarize! Write down works-cited information as you go.

Try IT Find an expert who can tell you about dogs that work. Do dogs help the police or fire fighters in your community? Can you find an organization that trains dogs to help people?

TEKS 5.24C, 5.25A, 5.25B, 5.26A–D
ELPS 3G

Synthesize Information

■ Think about what you found and decide on a focus. You might need to revise your research questions. Use a computer, a grid, and note cards to organize your ideas.

■ Go through each source to make sure it is trustworthy, accurate, and relevant to your topic.

 Which of the following sources is relevant, valid, *and* reliable?

A newspaper article about therapy dogs in your town

A Web site about tricks that terriers can do

An encyclopedia article about wheelchairs

Organize and Present Your Ideas

Written Presentations

■ Develop a thesis statement. Then write topic sentences that summarize your findings.

■ Include quotations and evidence from multiple sources.

■ Create a works-cited page to acknowledge your sources.

Oral Presentations

■ Plan a speech using presentation software. Create slides with topic sentences that summarize your findings. Use facts and quotes as evidence. Choose pictures and sounds.

■ Include a slide that lists the sources you used. Make sure to use multiple trustworthy sources.

■ Practice your oral presentation until you're ready to go. Remember to speak slowly and clearly.

 Find a quote in a book or online that supports this idea: *Dogs do some of the most important work in our communities.* Acknowledge your source when you cite the quote.

TEKS 5.24A, 5.24E, 5.25B
ELPS 2G, 2H, 3H, 4G, 4K

Gathering Sources

When you are researching a topic, don't rely on one source. Instead, gather information from many different sources.

Reading . . . Learn facts and details by reading about your topic in books, encyclopedias, and magazines.

Surfing . . . Explore the Internet for information.

Viewing and Listening . . . Watch TV programs and videos about your topic.

Interviewing . . . Ask an expert questions about your topic.

Guidelines for Interviewing

Use the following tips as a guide when you conduct an interview.

■ Write a list of questions to ask during the interview. Make sure the questions ask for more than a "yes" or "no" answer.
What do police dogs do?
How are police dogs trained?
Which breeds make the best police dogs? Why?

■ When taking notes, don't try to write down every single word of the interview. If you hear something interesting, say, "I want to write that down." Ask how to spell any unfamiliar words.

Evaluating Sources

Before you use information in your writing, ask yourself these questions. Then explain why it is important to use valid, reliable, and relevant sources.

- Is the source someone who knows a lot about the subject?
- Is the information current or posted recently?
- Is the information complete and dependable?
- Is the source unbiased? Does it tell both sides of the story?

Primary and Secondary Sources

Primary sources, or original sources, give you firsthand information. Here are a few examples of primary sources.

Diaries, Journals, and Letters

Reading the diaries, journals, and letters of other people (especially historical figures) is the best way to learn about their experiences.

Historic Sites and Artifacts

Visiting historic places will let you see where history happened. Museum artifacts such as photographs, tools, artwork, clothes, and furniture can tell you about how people used to live.

Interviews

In an interview, you can talk to someone who is an expert on your topic. You can do this in person, by phone, or through e-mail.

Surveys and Questionnaires

You can use a survey or questionnaire to gather firsthand information. Make a list of questions and give out copies. Then collect the surveys and study the results.

Observation and Participation

Observing people, places, or things can tell you a lot about their lives. Or you can try an activity for yourself.

Try IT Which of these primary sources could you use in a report about dogs that work? Work in small groups to come up with ideas.

Secondary sources contain information that has been gathered by someone else. Most nonfiction books, magazines, and Web sites are secondary sources of information.

Try IT Which of these is a primary source? Which is a secondary source? Explain how you know.

A newspaper story about dogs helping visually impaired people

A discussion with a visually impaired person about her dog

TEKS 5.24A
ELPS 2C, 3E, 3H

Researching on the Internet

The easiest way to find out about a topic on the Internet is to use a **search engine**. Common search engines are easy to use. Just type in your topic, and links to many sites will appear.

> Always ask yourself: Is this Web site trustworthy?

Helpful Hints

- **Use the Web carefully.** Find Web sites that will give you reliable information. Look for sites that have *.edu, .org,* or *.gov* in the address. These are educational, nonprofit, or government Web sites. If you are not sure about a site, check with your teacher or librarian.

- **Look for links.** Web pages often include links to other pages about your topic. Use these links to find even more information.

- **Be patient.** Searches can get complicated. Sometimes a search engine will list sites that have little, if anything, to do with your topic. If this happens, try the search again using different keywords about your topic.

- **Know your school's Internet policy.** Be sure to follow your school's Internet policy. Also follow the guidelines that your parents may have set up for you.

Practice

Surf the Web to find information about an occupation that you find interesting. Find at least two Web sites that tell you about the training required. Describe to a partner what you found.

TEKS 5.24A
ELPS 2I, 3E, 4C

Using the Library

Find out where everything is located in your school or public library. Your library will have labels or signs, such as "Fiction" or "Reference," telling where the different sections are located.

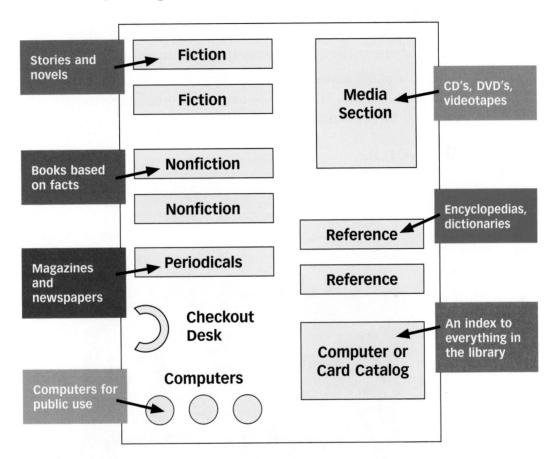

Stories and novels → Fiction

Fiction

Media Section ← CD's, DVD's, videotapes

Books based on facts → Nonfiction

Nonfiction

Reference ← Encyclopedias, dictionaries

Magazines and newspapers → Periodicals

Reference

Checkout Desk

Computer or Card Catalog ← An index to everything in the library

Computers

Computers for public use

Practice

Make a map of your school library, labeling where each section is located. Give a partner oral directions on how to find the library sections. Then go on a scavenger hunt. Pick a subject that interests you and write down the title of a useful book, magazine, or video.

Searching a Computer Catalog

In a **computer catalog**, you can find information about the same book in three ways:

1 If you know the book's title, enter the title.

2 If you know the book's author, enter the author's name. (When the library has more than one book by the same author, there will be more than one title listed.)

3 Finally, if you know only the subject you want to learn about, enter either the subject or a keyword. (A *keyword* is a word or phrase that is related to the subject.)

Using Keywords

If your subject is . . .	your keywords might be . . .
dogs that work	dogs, therapy, healing

Computer Catalog Screen

Author:	Crawford, Jacqueline
Title:	Therapy Pets: The Animal-Human Healing Partnership
Published:	Prometheus Books, 2003
Subjects:	Dogs, therapy
STATUS: Available	CALL NUMBER: 716.8 CRA
LOCATION: Recreation, Nonfiction	

Practice

Create a catalog screen like the one above for a book in the classroom. Then practice using the catalog in your library to find books.

TEKS 5.24A
ELPS 4C

Finding Books

Nonfiction Books ● Nonfiction books are arranged on library shelves according to **call numbers**.

- **Some call numbers contain decimals.**
  The call number 973.19 is a smaller number than 973.2 (973.2 is really 973.20). The number 973.19 would appear on the shelf before the number 973.20.

- **Some call numbers include letters.**
  The number 973.19D would appear on the shelf before 973.19E.

- **Most call numbers are based on the Dewey Decimal System.**

The Ten Classes of the Dewey Decimal System			
000	General Topics	500	Pure Science
100	Philosophy	600	Technology (Applied Science)
200	Religion	700	The Arts, Recreation
300	The Social Sciences	800	Literature
400	Language	900	Geography and History

Biographies ● Biographies are arranged according to the last name of the person they are written about. They are shelved in alphabetical order under the call number 921. A biography of astronaut John Glenn would have **921GLENN** on its spine.

Fiction Books ● Fiction books are arranged alphabetically according to the first three letters of the author's last name. A book by Katherine Paterson would have the letters **PAT** on the spine.

Practice

Find your favorite book in the computer or card catalog of the library. Write down the call number and see if you can find the book on the shelves. Use the labeled sections of the library to guide you.

TEKS 5.24A
ELPS 2G, 3E

Understanding the Parts of a Book

Below, you will find a short description of each part of a nonfiction book.

- The **title page** is usually the first page with printing on it. It gives the title of the book, the author's name, the publisher's name, and the city where the book was published.

- The **copyright page** comes next. It gives the year the book was published.

- The **acknowledgement** or **preface** (if the book has one) comes before the table of contents. It tells what the book is about or why it was written.

- The **table of contents** tells how the book is organized. It gives the names and page numbers of the sections and chapters.

- The **body** is the main part of the book.

- A **cross-reference** sends the reader to another page for more information. *Example:* (See page **705**.)

- The **appendix** has extra information, such as maps, tables, lists, and explanations.

- The **glossary** (if there is one) explains special words used in the book. It's like a mini-dictionary.

- The **bibliography** (if there is one) lists books or articles used by the author in writing the book. You can use this list to find more information on the same topic.

- The **index** is an alphabetical list of all the topics in the book. It gives the page numbers where each topic is covered.

Practice

Find all of these parts in your science or social studies book. Turn and discuss this with a partner.

TEKS 5.24A, 5.24C
ELPS 2H, 3E, 4G

Using Encyclopedias

An **encyclopedia** is a set of books or a Web site with articles on almost every topic. Keep the following in mind as you use one.

- **Choose a reliable online encyclopedia.** Ask your teacher or librarian for help in finding the right online encyclopedia. Not all Web-based reference resources are trustworthy.

- **Notice how articles are organized.** Articles are written with the most basic information first, followed by more detailed information. Headings separate information into sections.

- **Take good notes.** Write names, dates, and other important information on index cards. Also take notes on data found in charts, time lines, or diagrams in the entry.

- **Jot down keywords.** As you read, keep an eye out for words that could lead to more useful information. For example, Daniel Boone created the Wilderness Trail. By looking up the phrase *Wilderness Trail,* you might find details that will make your report more interesting.

- **Look up related topics.** At the end of an article, you may find a list of related topics. Look them up to learn more about your topic. In an online encyclopedia, you can often just click on the related keywords.

- **Check the copyright date.** For scientific information or statistics that may have changed in the last few years, use an edition with a recent copyright date.

Practice

Choose a famous person who interests you. Use both a print encyclopedia and an online encyclopedia to conduct research. Turn to a partner and talk about what you found.

TEKS 5.24E
ELPS 2G, 3D, 3E

Paraphrasing and Plagiarism

Research turns up great ideas! You may want to use some of those ideas in your paper. Just be careful that you don't take another person's ideas and make them sound like your own. This is called *plagiarism,* and it is stealing.

Suppose you're researching police dogs and you find a great article written by Vivian Martinez, a police officer, who works with dogs.

> Working with Rusty is like working with a detective. He sniffs out hints that help solve crimes.

You will be guilty of plagiarism if you write something like this:

> Working with a police dog is like working with a detective. The dog sniffs out hints that help solve crimes.

Some students think they can avoid plagiarism by paraphrasing. Paraphrasing means using your own words to restate an idea.

> Police dogs and detectives have a lot in common. They both search for hints to help solve crimes.

But that still takes another person's idea! You must give credit to the source, or author, of an idea. Here is the one way to do that:

> Working with a police dog is like working with a detective who sniffs out clues to solve crimes, according to police officer Vivian Martinez, who works with a dog named Rusty.

Practice

Paraphrase information from a book and cite the source clearly. Exchange your work with a partner. Tell your partner whether the information was paraphrased and cited correctly.

Citing Sources

The sources you use and the information you note should be reliable, valid, and relevant to your report.

		Questions to Ask	What to Do
1	**Check for relevance, or usefulness.**	• Am I finding information that I will be able to use? • Will this information help me answer my research question?	• Focus on books, articles, and Web sites that are specific to your topic. • Turn directly to the chapter or section that has information you can use.
2	**Check for validity, or accuracy.**	• Are ideas explained accurately and clearly? • Is the information up-to-date?	• Check key facts and explanations in the source to make sure they match what you find elsewhere.
3	**Check for reliability, or trustworthiness.**	• Is the author biased? • Is the author an expert on the topic? • Does the writer sound knowledgeable? • Does the book include a list of sources?	• Choose sources that examine more than one side of the issue. • Learn about the group that published the source. • For Internet sources, if you can't determine who sponsors the Web site, it is not a reliable source.

Practice

Think about the famous person you began researching on page 321. Find a source that tells about that person. Evaluate whether the source is valid, reliable, and relevant. Discuss with a classmate why it is important to use sources that are trustworthy and accurate.

Bibliographic Information

As you research, keep track of the sources you are using and where you found your information. This will make citing your sources later on much easier.

- **Write down bibliographic information.** You will need to use bibliographic information to write a works-cited page at the end of your report. Sometimes it's easiest to photocopy the copyright page of a book or the "About us" page of a Web site so you can refer to it later. Here's the information that you will need to have:

  - For books: **Author, title, city** where the book was published, **publisher,** and **copyright date.**

  - For a Web site: **Author, page title, site title, date published, and date visited.**

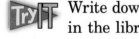 Write down the bibliographic information for a book you find in the library. Then write bibliographic notes for a Web site. Make sure you have every bit of information you need.

Taking Notes on Facts and Quotes

Here are a few more things to do as you research.

- **Write down page numbers.** Every time you write down a fact or idea, write the page number where you found it.

- **Find interesting quotes.** Look for quotes that you'd like to use to support your ideas, and copy them carefully. The best quotes explain an idea in a fun but clear way. Sometimes, quotes can help you imagine something. Find quotes from an expert to add interest to your report.

 Find a quote in the book you used earlier that could be used as support, or evidence. Write it down and cite it properly, using a page number and the name of the author.

Research Writing

Research Report

Writing a research report is an adventure of sorts. By searching sources like books, magazines, and Web sites, you can discover new and interesting facts about a topic. Are you interested in early explorers, Native American people, or past presidents?

In this chapter, you will choose an important person and go about the task of learning how he or she affected history. Then you will organize your facts and ideas into an informative and interesting report, one you can share with your classmates and others.

Writing Guidelines

Subject: An important person from history

Purpose: To find and share information about a historical person's life

Form: Research report

Audience: Classmates and parents

TEKS 5.15A, 5.18A(i), 5.26B
ELPS 4C, 4I

Research Report

In this report, student Isabella Rodriguez tells how Daniel Boone's life helped to shape early America. As you read Isabella's report, notice how important ideas are arranged and summarized. The side notes point out how the report is organized and presented.

The entire report is double-spaced.

1"

1/2"

Rodriguez 1   ← 1" →

Isabella Rodriguez

Ms. Alvarez

← 1" →   Social Studies

December 14, 2012

Daniel Boone, the Explorer

Beginning
Introduction catches the reader's interest and has a controlling idea, or thesis statement. (underlined)

Have you ever climbed to a high point and burned to explore the land beyond? That feeling was why Daniel Boone chose to blaze a trail through the Appalachian Mountains. Boone's explorations inspired many early Americans to head west.

Middle
The first body paragraph summarizes findings about how Boone got interested in exploration.

From an early age, Daniel Boone loved to explore the wilderness. As a child, he met Native Americans who taught him how to survive in the wild, track animals, and hunt for food (Chinn). While fighting in the French and Indian War, he met a hunter who told him about Kentucky (Chinn). Boone decided he wanted to see this place for himself (Filson 39–40).

1"

TEKS 5.18A(i), 5.26B, 5.26D
ELPS 4C, 4I

Rodriguez 2

Daniel Boone soon learned that Kentucky was risky as well as beautiful. The pristine, unexplored land was home to many Native Americans. Tensions rose between them and Boone's group of pioneers. Many of his people were captured (Salas 16–24). Boone returned from his first hunting trip penniless and almost alone. But he couldn't stay away from Kentucky (Salas 16–17).

> The next body paragraphs organize and summarize findings about Boone's adventures.

Boone's most important accomplishment was building a trail through the Appalachian Mountains to Kentucky in 1775. With the help of thirty settlers, he cut through 200 miles of thick forest before creating a settlement called Boonesborough (Salas 18–20). The trail they made became known as the Wilderness Road (Goldman). In 1792, Kentucky became a state, and the population boomed. Eventually, Boone said it was "too crowded," so he moved to West Virginia (Chinn).

> Sources are acknowledged in parentheses.

Boone's explorations encouraged pioneers to cross the Appalachians, settle in Kentucky and explore the West. According to Chinn, "More than any other man, Daniel Boone was responsible for the exploration and settlement of Kentucky." Boone's stories became legend, and his adventures inspired many to explore America.

> **Ending**
> The concluding paragraph uses a quote to add depth to the thesis statement.

TEKS 5.26D
ELPS 2C, 2H, 2I, 3G, 3H, 4G, 4I, 4J, 4K

Rodriguez 3

The writer's name and the page number appear on every page.

Works Cited

Chinn, Col. George M. "Daniel Boone." *American West.* Harrodsburg Historical Society, Apr. 1996. Web. 18 Nov. 2010.

Filson, John. "The Discovery, Settlement, and Present State of Kentucky." *American Journeys Collection.* Wisconsin Historical Digital Library and Archives, 2003. Web. 20 Nov. 2010.

Goldman, Lisa. "Going West: The Cumberland Gap." *Monkeyshines on America* Apr. 1999: 26. Print.

Salas, Laura Purdie. *The Wilderness Road, 1775.* Mankato, MN: Capstone Press, 2007. Print.

"Daniel Boone Wilderness Trail Interactive Map." Daniel Boone Trail. The Daniel Boone Wilderness Trail Association, 2006. Web. 19 Nov. 2010.

Sources are listed alphabetically by author.

Respond to the reading. Answer the following questions. Listen to your partner as you discuss thoughts, opinions, and ideas.

- **Focus and Coherence** (1) How did Isabella's conclusion connect to her thesis statement?

- **Development of Ideas** (2) Find a fact, detail, or example that supports one of the topic sentences.

- **Voice** (3) Is Isabella interested in her topic and knowledgeable about it? How do you know?

 **TEKS** 5.15A, 5.23A, 5.23B, 5.26B

Prewriting

 Go Online!

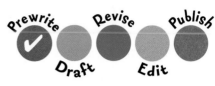 Prewrite ✓ · Draft · Revise · Edit · Publish

Before you start writing your report, you'll need to choose a topic, ask questions about it, and create a research plan. That's what prewriting is all about.

Keys to Prewriting

1. **Brainstorm, consult** with others, and **choose** an important person from history to write about.

2. **Formulate** open-ended questions you want to answer about this person.

3. **Generate** a research plan to gather information. **Use** a gathering grid and note cards to record information.

4. **Write** a thesis, or focus statement, with a controlling idea.

5. **Create** an organized list of details.

⭐ **TEKS** 5.15A, 5.23A
ELPS 3G

Prewriting **Selecting a Topic**

One way to select a topic is to brainstorm ideas. With help from her classmates, Isabella created the following cluster.

Cluster

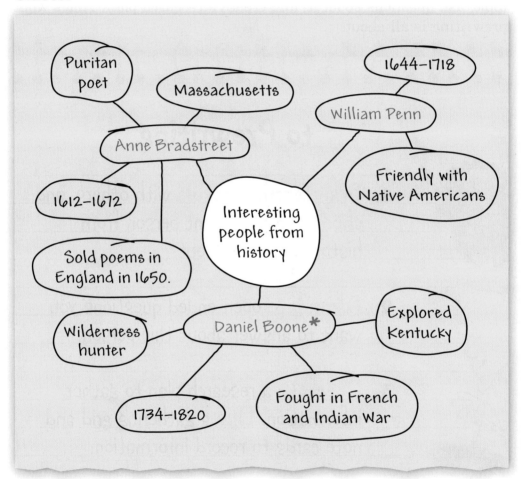

Puritan poet

Massachusetts

1644–1718

William Penn

Anne Bradstreet

Friendly with Native Americans

1612–1672

Interesting people from history

Sold poems in England in 1650.

Explored Kentucky

Wilderness hunter

Daniel Boone *

1734–1820

Fought in French and Indian War

Prewrite

Create a cluster. Choose three historical figures and brainstorm a few details about each person. Consult with others to come up with ideas. Put a star (✱) next to the person who interests you the most. That person will be the topic of your report.

 **TEKS** 5.23A, 5.25A
ELPS 3G

Writing Research Questions

The topic of your research report shouldn't be too broad or too narrow. To find the right focus, make a list of research questions you want to answer. Ask others to help you. Then ask yourself: *Which one is my main research question? Do all my questions address my main topic? Do they make sense together?* Here are Isabella's questions.

Research Questions

Too Broad

Who was Daniel Boone?

- As a boy, how did he make friends with Native Americans?
- What did he do in the French and Indian War?
- Why did he want to explore Kentucky?
- How did he build the Wilderness Road?
- How much time did he spend exploring Kentucky?
- Who did he marry, and who were his children?
- What other places did he live in?
- Did he help shape America?

Too Narrow

What is the Wilderness Road?

- How did Boone build the Wilderness Road?
- Who came with him?

Just Right (Focused)

Did Daniel Boone's exploration help shape America?

- Why is he famous?
- Why did he explore Kentucky?
- Did he face any problems?
- How did he build the Wilderness Road?

Prewrite

Consult with others to write questions. Write four or five focused questions that address your topic. Work in groups to make sure your questions are "just right."

Prewriting **Forming Open-Ended Questions**

Revisit your research questions to make sure they are open ended. Ask yourself two questions:

- Can my questions be answered with just one word?
- Does each question have only one right answer?

If you answered *yes*, you have a problem. Your questions are not open ended. Remember,

- An open-ended question should have more than just one right answer.
- Open-ended questions ask for examples, information, or explanations.
- Open-ended questions often ask *how, why,* or *what happened.*

Isabella looked at her questions. She realized that two of them could be answered with *yes* or *no*. Isabella decided to modify them to be more open ended. She added the words *how* and *why*.

Before
- Did Boone's explorations help shape America?
- Did he face any problems?

After
- How did Boone's explorations help shape America?
- Why did he face so many problems?

Now Isabella's questions might lead her to interesting or surprising facts. Answering open-ended questions will also give her report more depth.

Evaluate your questions. Read your questions. Are they open ended? If not, modify your questions by asking about *how, why,* or *what happened.*

TEKS 5.23B, 5.24B, 5.26A
ELPS 4K

Creating a Research Plan

Having a research plan will help you gather information about your topic. The steps below can guide you.

1 Decide where you will go to do research.

Your library is a good place to start. Then do an Internet search. Also think beyond that—brainstorm about experts, museums, and people to interview or observe. (See page 315 for ideas.)

2 Find good primary and secondary sources to use.

Always compile information from many sources and make sure to use both primary and secondary sources. You can create your own primary sources by conducting an interview or giving a survey.

Make sure your sources are trustworthy and accurate. Also check for relevance. If a source doesn't answer your research questions, don't take notes on it.

Isabella went to the library and found a few sources that she thought were trustworthy, accurate, and useful. Here's her research plan.

Research Plan

Where: school library, local library, Internet

Primary source: Daniel Boone's journal

Secondary sources: Encyclopedia article, Salas book, interactive map, Goldman magazine article, Chinn article on Web site

Prewrite

Create a research plan. Create a research plan using the steps above. Make sure you know the difference between a primary source and a secondary source. Include both in your plan.

TEKS 5.24A, 5.24E
ELPS 2C, 2G, 3D, 3E, 3G, 3H, 4G

Prewriting **Using Reference Texts**

A **reference text** is an excellent place to start gathering information. Print and online reference texts can help you build a foundation of knowledge for your report. Here's how to start:

- **Use the index.** Use the index to help you find related articles. The index is located in the back of a book or in the final volume of a set of reference texts.

- **Write down the basics.** Focus on information such as names, dates, places, and facts about the person's life. You will use this knowledge as you search other sources.

- **Look for more sources.** If any other sources are mentioned, search for them at your library. Also look for reference books that cover a period in history.

Isabella used an online encyclopedia article about Daniel Boone to begin her research. As she paraphrased information, she circled important dates. She underlined words that she planned to look up.

Notes

Daniel Boone
-Born 1734, in Pennsylvania; died 1820, in Missouri
-Blazed a trail through the <u>Cumberland Gap</u> in 1775
-Hunter and trapper for most of his life
-Paid to build the Wilderness Road, a main route West
-Founded <u>Boonesborough</u>, one of the first settlements in <u>Kentucky</u>

 tip Remember to write down bibliographic information. This will help prevent plagiarism when you paraphrase information. Discuss the difference between paraphrasing and plagiarism.

 Prewrite Use a reference text. **Look up your historical figure in a print or online reference text. Take notes on the names, dates, and facts you find. Don't forget to cite page numbers as you go.**

Using Periodicals

A **periodical** is something that is published on a regular basis, such as a magazine or a newspaper. Newspapers and magazines occasionally run articles about history or science, and some magazines specialize in these subjects.

Finding an Article

- **Visit the periodical section in the library.** For your report, look for history magazines. If you find a useful one, go online and search the archives for an article.

- **Do a search.** Narrow your Internet search to newspapers and magazines. At some libraries, magazine and newspaper articles are searchable in the catalog.

- **Make sure it's relevant.** You want an article that will help you answer your research questions. An article about Kentucky with one sentence about Daniel Boone probably won't be very helpful.

Reading the Article

If possible, make a photocopy of the article. Underline or highlight important facts as you read, like Isabella did. (See the model to the right.)

When you finish reading, write a sentence or two to summarize the main idea.

> Before the United States became a nation, this barrier kept colonists near the coastline. As populations increased, however, so did pressure to move west. In 1775, Daniel Boone led a party of 30 settlers into Kentucky through a natural break in the Appalachians. This pass is known as the Cumberland Gap, and the path the settlers blazed became the Wilderness Road. From 1775 to 1810, roughly a quarter million people traveled that road to begin settling the Central Plains.

Prewrite

Find and read an article. Choose an article from a newspaper or a magazine that you can use for your report. Read it carefully and take notes. Then summarize the main ideas.

 **TEKS** 5.24A, 5.24C
ELPS 4G

Prewriting **Using Online Sources**

Online searches can put hundreds of sources in front of you in seconds! The Internet has a wealth of information that can be tough to find in other places. Here are a few examples.

Pictures, paintings, and photographs.

Need a photo to jazz up your report? An online image search is an easy way to find one. Keep an eye out for historical photographs or paintings that show the people and events you describe in your report.

Video and audio.

Reliable sites might include short videos or news clips. If your historical person is from a more recent time, search for audio of his or her speeches.

Diagrams, time lines, charts, or maps.

Isabella typed in *Daniel Boone time line* and *Wilderness Trail map* to search for visual data. You can take written notes on any diagrams, time lines, charts, or maps you find and use the data in your report.

Interactive features.

Some Web sites have interactive features where you can click on graphics to see how things work. This can be helpful if you are struggling to understand a concept.

Search for online sources and take notes. Use a search engine to find pictures, video, audio, diagrams, time lines, or maps. Take notes on the most helpful sources. Print them out, if possible, or write down the link.

TEKS 5.24B, 5.24E, 5.25B
ELPS 4K

Evaluating Sources

After Isabella had gathered enough sources, she evaluated them to make sure they were relevant, valid, and reliable. (To review how to do this, turn to pages 314 and 323.)

She started with a primary source she had found: an excerpt from Daniel Boone's journals.

Evaluating a Primary Source

– <u>Is it relevant?</u> Yes. Boone's journal tells why he wanted to explore Kentucky and it talks about the problems he faced.

– <u>Is it valid?</u> Yes. The events I found here match the facts I found elsewhere.

– <u>Is it reliable?</u> Yes. It is from a university Web site, and the person who edited this source is an expert in the field. I found photos of the actual pages of the journal. Even though Boone only tells one side of the story, I still want to know what he thought about during his adventures.

 Primary sources such as journals and letters may only tell one side of history. Be careful about drawing conclusions based on one person's point of view.

Next, Isabella evaluated each of her secondary sources carefully. She checked important facts and researched the authors. She wanted to make sure everything in her paper was correct.

 Evaluate your sources. Evaluate the relevance, validity, and reliability of a primary source and a secondary source. (Make sure you know the difference between primary and secondary sources.) Then discuss with a partner why it is important to evaluate your sources.

TEKS 5.24A, 5.24C, 5.25A, 5.26B
ELPS 2C, 4G

Prewriting Using a Gathering Grid

A gathering grid is a way to organize and record your findings. Isabella used a grid to summarize facts from three of her sources.

Gathering Grid

Daniel Boone	The Wilderness Road, 1775 (book)	"Going West: The Cumberland Gap" (magazine article)	"Daniel Boone" (Internet article)
How did Daniel Boone's explorations help shape America?	Helped early Americans go west		
Why is Boone famous?	Established Boonesborough	Blazed the Wilderness Road	See card 1.
Why did he explore Kentucky?	Loved the wilderness		Heard about it from a hunter
Why did he face so many problems?	Many problems (See card 2.)		
How did he build the Wilderness Road?	30 settlers used axes to hack through the forest	Trail became known as the Wilderness Road	
Other interesting facts	Boone was hired to build the trail	The Wilderness Road crosses the Appalachians	Lived from 1734–1820; died in Missouri

Create a gathering grid. Refine your research questions, if necessary, and list them. Across the top, list sources. Write your findings in the boxes. Use a computer if one is available.

Creating Note Cards

If some answers are too long to fit on your gathering grid, write them on note cards. Number each card and write the research question at the top. Then write your answer and the page number. You can quote exact words (a quotation) or summarize in your own words (a paraphrase). Remember, it is important to cite your source.

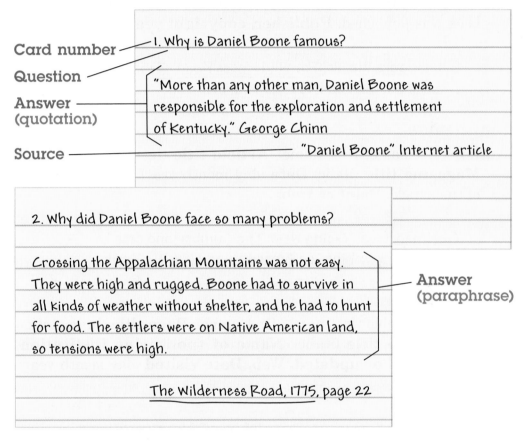

Card number —— 1. Why is Daniel Boone famous?

Question ——

Answer —— "More than any other man, Daniel Boone was
(quotation)   responsible for the exploration and settlement
            of Kentucky." George Chinn

Source ——   "Daniel Boone" Internet article

2. Why did Daniel Boone face so many problems?

Crossing the Appalachian Mountains was not easy.
They were high and rugged. Boone had to survive in   —— Answer
all kinds of weather without shelter, and he had to hunt   (paraphrase)
for food. The settlers were on Native American land,
so tensions were high.

            The Wilderness Road, 1775, page 22

 tip You must not copy any ideas and pretend they are yours. This is called *plagiarism,* and it is stealing. Explain to a partner the difference between paraphrasing and plagiarism.

Prewrite   **Create note cards.** Make note cards for your research. Include a quotation or a paraphrase that summarizes your findings.

TEKS 5.24D, 5.26D
ELPS 2C, 4G

Prewriting **Identifying Your Sources**

As you take notes, remember to record bibliographic information for your works-cited page. Here's how to write an entry.

Books

Author (last name, first name). **Title** (italic). **City, state** where the book was published: **Publisher, copyright year**. **Print** or **Web.**

> Salas, Laura Purdie. The Wilderness Road, 1775. Mankato,
>   MN: Capstone Press, 2007. Print.

Magazines

Author (last name, first name). **Article title** (in quotation marks). **Magazine title** (italic) **Date** (day month year): **Page numbers** of the article. **Print** or **Web.**

> Goldman, Lisa. "Going West: The Cumberland Gap."
>   Monkeyshines on America Apr. 1999: 26. Print.

Internet

Author, if available (last name, first name). **Page title** (in quotation marks). **Site title** (italic). **Name of sponsoring institution, date posted or updated. Web. Date visited** (day month year).

> Chinn, Col. George M. "Daniel Boone." American West.
>   Harrodsburg Historical Society, 1996. Web. 18 Nov. 2010.

Prewrite

Identify your sources. Write a bibliographic entry for each source you used while taking notes. Change the underlined text to italic when you type your works-cited page.

TEKS 5.15A, 5.24C, 5.26B
ELPS 2C, 4G, 4J, 5G

Organizing Ideas

Now that you've done your research, it's time to organize your ideas. Start by writing a thesis statement. Then arrange your details into an outline to see the relationships between ideas. (See page 342 for an example.) Use a computer if one is available.

Writing Your Thesis Statement

Your thesis statement tells what your report is all about. A good thesis statement starts with an interesting topic and then focuses on a controlling idea about the topic.

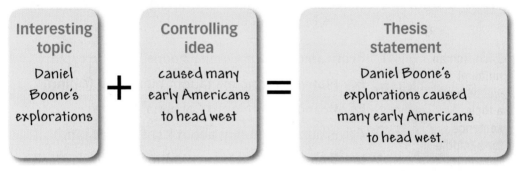

Interesting topic		Controlling idea		Thesis statement
Daniel Boone's explorations	**+**	caused many early Americans to head west	**=**	Daniel Boone's explorations caused many early Americans to head west.

Thesis Statements

The English Quaker William Penn (an interesting topic) founded the Pennsylvania colony to provide religious and political freedom. (a controlling idea)

Anne Bradstreet was a poet in the 1600s (an interesting topic) who wrote about family, women, faith, and politics. (a controlling idea)

Prewrite

Write a thesis statement. Write a thesis statement that explains the person's most important accomplishment.

TEKS 5.18A(iii), 5.24C, 5.26B
ELPS 4G, 4J, 5G

Prewriting Making an Outline

An outline is an organized list of ideas. Below is the beginning of Isabella's outline. Notice how the Roman numerals answer Isabella's research questions. These will become topic sentences in her report.

Outline

Thesis Statement

THESIS STATEMENT:

Daniel Boone's exploration caused many early Americans to head west.

Each Roman numeral will become a topic sentence for a middle paragraph.

I. From an early age, Daniel Boone loved to explore.
   A. Native Americans taught him skills. (Chinn)
   B. He moved to North Carolina. (Chinn)
   C. A hunter told him about Kentucky. (Chinn)
   D. Boone decided he wanted to see it for himself. (Filson)

Each capital letter uses a specific detail, fact, or example to support the topic sentence.

II. Kentucky was risky as well as beautiful.
   A. It was pristine but unexplored. (online map)
   B. It was home to Native Americans who did not want settlers on their land. (Salas)
   C. Boone returned from his first trip penniless and almost alone. (Salas)

Prewrite

Write your outline. Use a computer to organize the facts, details, and examples you've summarized into an outline. Include information from a map, diagram, chart, photo, or time line. Each topic sentence should relate to your thesis statement.

TEKS 5.15C, 5.18A(i), 5.18A(iii)
ELPS 4C

Drafting

Prewrite · Draft · Revise · Edit · Publish

Your planning is finished, and now you're ready to start writing! When you write your first draft, you put all your ideas on paper (or use a computer).

Keys to Drafting

1. **Synthesize** the research into a written presentation with strong beginning and ending paragraphs.

2. **Organize** supporting details, facts, and examples in paragraphs.

3. **Write** with your purpose, form, and audience in mind. Ask yourself:
   - Did I answer my research questions?
   - Did I support my topic sentences with evidence and cite the source of information and quotes?
   - Will I keep my classmates interested?

TEKS 5.18A(i), 5.26A, 5.26C
ELPS 4G, 5G

Drafting Starting Your Research Report

The opening paragraph of your report should grab your reader's attention, introduce the topic, and present your thesis statement. Isabella wrote two possible introductions for her report about Daniel Boone.

Beginning

Middle

Ending

Beginning Paragraph

This paragraph begins with a question and leads into the topic. It ends with the thesis statement.

Have you ever climbed to a high point and burned to explore the land beyond? That feeling was why Daniel Boone chose to blaze a trail through the Appalachian Mountains. Boone's explorations inspired many early Americans to head west.

This paragraph begins with a detail and ends with the thesis statement.

Daniel Boone loved the great outdoors. He knew how to track animals and survive in the wild (Chinn). He was the perfect person to explore the untamed Kentucky area. Boone's explorations inspired many early Americans to head west.

Draft

Write your opening paragraph. Write a beginning paragraph for your report. Use one of the examples above as a guide, or try an idea of your own. Think about what you learned from different sources.

TEKS 5.18A(ii), 5.18A(iii), 5.26A–D
ELPS 4G, 4J, 5G

Developing the Middle Part

Each middle paragraph should have a topic sentence followed by key ideas and evidence, including details, facts, and examples, that support the topic sentence. Research from multiple sources should be summarized and acknowledged.

Beginning
Middle
Ending

Middle Paragraphs

Find key evidence that supports each topic sentence (underlined).

From an early age, Daniel Boone loved to explore the wilderness. As a child, he met Native Americans who taught him how to survive in the wild, track animals, and hunt for food (Chinn). While fighting in the French and Indian War, he met a hunter who told him about Kentucky (Chinn). Boone decided he wanted to see this place for himself (Filson 39–40).

How are sources cited? Find two examples.

Daniel Boone soon learned that Kentucky was risky as well as beautiful. The pristine, unexplored land was home to many Native Americans. Tensions rose between them and Boone's group of pioneers. Many of Boone's people were captured (Salas 16–24). Boone returned from his first hunting trip penniless and almost alone. But he couldn't stay away from Kentucky (Salas 16–17).

Find a specific fact or example that adds interest to the report.

 **TEKS** 5.15B, 5.18A(iii), 5.26A–D
ELPS 5G

Final Middle Paragraph

> **Sentences flow together and build on ideas to create coherent writing.**
>
> **Specific facts and examples come from multiple sources.**

Boone's most important accomplishment was building a trail through the Appalachian Mountains to Kentucky in 1775. With the help of thirty settlers, Boone cut through 200 miles of thick forest before creating a settlement called Boonesborough (Salas 18–20). The trail they made became known as the Wilderness Road (Goldman). In 1792, Kentucky became a state, and the population boomed. Eventually, Boone said it was "too crowded," so he moved to West Virginia. (Chinn).

Citing Your Sources

You must always give credit for other people's ideas. As you write your research paper, be sure to do the following:

- **Set off exact words with quotation marks.** (See page 347.)
- **Add your sources in parentheses.** (See page 345.)
- **Include page numbers, if possible.** (See above.)
- **Give bibliographic information on your works-cited page.** (See pages 328, 340, 348, and 363 to learn how.)

Write your middle paragraphs. Use your outline as a guide. Compile your facts and main ideas in an organized and consistent way. Develop a topic sentence for each paragraph and use evidence, such as details and quotes, to support your ideas.

TEKS 5.18A(i), 5.18A(iii),
5.26A, 5.26.C, 5.26D
ELPS 5G

Drafting **Ending Your Research Report**

The ending paragraph should revisit your thesis statement and bring your report to a close. To do this, try one or more of the following ideas.

Beginning

Middle

Ending

- **Tell about the person's final years.**
- **Tell one last interesting fact, detail, or example about the person's life.**
- **Summarize the person's accomplishments or overall importance.**

Ending Paragraph

The ending tells why Boone's actions were important.	Daniel Boone's explorations encouraged pioneers to cross the Appalachians, settle in Kentucky, and explore the West. According to Chinn, "More than any other man, Daniel Boone was responsible for the exploration and settlement of Kentucky." Boone's stories became legend, and he inspired many to explore America.
The reader is reminded of the thesis (underlined).	

Draft

Write your final paragraph. Use one of the strategies above. Draw on all your sources as you sum up your report.

Look over your draft. Read through your first draft. Did you include evidence, such as examples, facts, and details? Is your report well-organized and easy to read? Review your notes and outline and write down changes you might want to make.

Drafting Creating Your Works-Cited Page

While you were doing your research, you wrote down bibliographic information. As you wrote your paper, you identified the source of each fact or quote in parentheses. Now you can arrange all your sources in alphabetical order on the works-cited page at the end of your report.

The title is centered at the top of the page.

Sources are listed alphabetically by author if available.

Underlined titles will be changed to italics when the page is typed.

Works Cited

Chinn, Col. George M. "Daniel Boone." American West. Harrodsburg Historical Society, 1996. Web. 18 Nov. 2010.

Filson, John. "The Discovery, Settlement, and Present State of Kentucky." American Journeys Collection. Wisconsin Historical Digital Library and Archives, 2003. Web. 20 Nov. 2010.

Goldman, Lisa. "Going West: The Cumberland Gap." Monkeyshines on America Apr. 1999: 26. Print.

Salas, Laura Purdie. The Wilderness Road 1775. Mankato, MN: Capstone Press, 2007.

The Wilderness Trail Interactive Map. Map. The Daniel Boone Wilderness Trail Association, 2006. Web. 19 Nov. 2012.

Draft

Create your works-cited page. Identify and list your sources on a works-cited page at the end of your report.

TEKS 5.15C

Revising

Revising may be the most important step in the writing process. When you revise, you check your report for *focus and coherence, organization, development of ideas,* and *voice.*

Keys to Revising

1. **Read** your report to yourself.

2. **Ask** yourself these questions:
   - Is my report informative?
   - Did I use the right form?
   - Have I included information and details that will engage my audience?

3. **Revise** for focus and coherence, organization, development of ideas, and voice. Rearrange sentences or paragraphs, if necessary, to make meaning clear.

Revising for **Focus** and **Coherence**

To revise your research report for *focus and coherence,* make sure your entire report is about your thesis, or controlling idea. Check that your beginning paragraph has a thesis statement, each middle paragraph supports your topic, and the final paragraph concludes and deepens your main ideas. As you revise, remove any facts or details that don't strongly support your thesis.

Does the beginning introduce my thesis?

Grab your audience's attention by making sure any attention-getting device leads right into your thesis. Your beginning should directly connect to your thesis, not be just somewhat related.

Practice

Read these two introductions. Decide with a partner which paragraph is the most effective and discuss how to improve the weaker paragraph.

1. "This old mutt shows me the world," Marty Manos tells his friends. Marty is visually impaired. His "old mutt" is Maxwell, a working dog. It's Maxwell's job to guide Marty through busy streets, up and down stairs, and around obstacles every day. Maxwell and dogs like him allow people with disabilities to live independently.

2. Some dogs like to play at the beach, chasing the waves and paddling through the surf. Some dogs herd sheep and keep them safe from harm. Some dogs retrieve or sniff out prey. But the most important dogs help people—by leading them through busy streets and being their eyes to the world.

 Revise

Check for a focused introduction. Read the first paragraph of your report. Does your attention-getting beginning lead into your thesis statement? If not, rewrite it.

 **TEKS** 5.15C

Do I have unnecessary information?

When you researched your historic person, not every detail you found supports your thesis statement, topic sentences, or research questions. To make your meaning clear, focus on only the most important facts, details, and examples.

Underline your thesis statement and topic sentences. Then read through your report. Ask yourself:

- Does each paragraph strengthen my thesis, or controlling idea?
- Does each detail help support the topic sentence of the paragraph?
- Are any of the facts, details, or explanations unnecessary?
- Did I repeat any ideas?

Revise

Check for unnecessary information. Make the meaning of your essay clear. Read through your report and delete any sentences or ideas that are unnecessary or repetitive.

Revising in Action

Below, Isabella deleted an unnecessary detail that did not help support the underlined topic sentence in this paragraph.

From an early age, Daniel Boone loved to explore the wilderness. As a child, he met Native Americans who taught him a lot about how to survive in the great outdoors. ~~When he was 15, Boone moved from Pennsylvania to North Carolina~~ (Chinn). While fighting in the French and Indian War, he met a man who told him about Kentucky. Boone decided he wanted to see this place for himself (Filson 39–40).

Revising for Organization

An *organized* piece of writing is easy for readers to follow. The ideas flow smoothly and in a logical order.

Are my ideas in order?

When revising, move ideas or details to improve the organization and clarity of your writing.

Revising in Action

Isabella read through her report and rearranged some sentences and paragraphs so that they were in time order.

> Boone's most important accomplishment was creating a trail through the Appalachian Mountains to Kentucky in 1775. The trail they made became known as the Wilderness Road (Goldman). With the help of thirty settlers, Boone cut through 200 miles of thick forest before creating a settlement called Boonesborough (Salas 18–20) Eventually, there were too many people for Boone, so he moved to West Virginia. In 1792, Kentucky became a state, and the population boomed (Chinn).

Revise

Check your organization. To make your meaning clear, rearrange sentences or paragraphs if necessary.

Do my ideas flow smoothly from one to another?

Your paragraphs and sentences should connect easily with one another. That means that

- paragraphs flow logically and smoothly.
- sentences and paragraphs build on ideas in an organized way.
- transition words and phrases help connect thoughts.

Practice

Read and then work in groups to revise the following essay about service dogs. Add, delete, combine, or rearrange paragraphs or sentences to help the ideas flow smoothly. Use transitions to connect ideas.

The best known service dogs are those that help visually impaired people walk from place to place. But there are other kinds of service dogs as well.

Well-trained service dogs can do amazing things, from opening doors to carrying objects such as phones. They can push wheelchairs or even help people get dressed.

Some service dogs aid hearing-impaired people. These dogs make sure their humans are aware of sounds like ringing phones or fire alarms.

There are service dogs that aid people who are unable to walk. The dogs turn lights off and on, help humans walk or move in a wheelchair, and retrieve things people in wheelchairs need. These service dogs are happy to help.

Revise

Check the flow of ideas. Read your report to make sure your paragraphs and sentences flow in a logical order. Add transition words as needed to connect ideas.

Revising for Development of Ideas

When revising for *development of ideas,* make sure all of your facts are specific and well-supported. Use only the strongest details.

Are my facts specific and well-supported?

Watch for general statements and unsupported opinions. Either remove them or replace them with strong, factual statements.

Revising in Action

When Isabella revised for ideas, she replaced a general sentence with a more detailed one. She also deleted an unsupported opinion.

From an early age, Daniel Boone loved to explore

the wilderness. As a child, he met Native Americans

who taught him ~~a lot about~~ how to survive in the ~~great~~

^ wild, track animals, and hunt for food

~~outdoors~~ (Chinn). While fighting in the French and Indian

War, he met a man who told him about Kentucky. Boone

decided he wanted to see this place for himself (Filson

39–40). ~~I think he was ready for a new adventure.~~

Revise

Check for strong, factual statements. Could specific facts be added to support your points? Should any opinions be deleted? Make changes to improve your paper.

TEKS 5.15C
ELPS 2G, 3E, 5G

How can I fix weak, superficial details?

When you find a weak detail, you have a few options.

- **Develop it.** If the sentence is vague, look for an example that illustrates your point, such as a story or a statistic. Add an interesting, specific fact that helps prove your point.
- **Explain it.** Use a simile or spell out your logic step-by-step.
- **Delete it.** Try crossing out that vague, general detail as you read the paragraph. If you don't miss the detail, then delete it!

Practice

Read the paragraph below. Identify weak details that do not help develop the paragraph. Work with a partner to develop one of the details further. Then choose two details that you can delete. If time allows, read your revised paragraph aloud to the class. Ask classmates to raise their hands when they hear strong details.

Search and rescue dogs are trained to find people who are lost or trapped in places like collapsed buildings. These dogs can smell things that people cannot. They have a strong sense of smell. Their sense of smell is amazing. A dog has 200 million smell receptors in its nose. That's 100 times as many as a person has! Their powerful noses can pick up scents underwater or under layers of rocks and rubble. Service dogs come in all shapes and sizes, and they like to keep busy. They have to be in good shape because searches can take hours and hours. Some can take even longer.

Revise

Review your details. Read through your report. Look for details that are vague, general, or repetitive. Develop them or delete them to improve each paragraph.

Revising for Voice

It's important show yourself in your report. *You* are the one guiding the reader through the topic and sharing insights and ideas.

When you revise for *voice,* strive to use words that are expressive and confident. Mine your research for clever, clear, or unique phrases, and use these quotes to spice up your report.

How can I make my writing unique?

Search through your report for lackluster words and replace them with vibrant ones that show your interest in this topic. Make sure to choose words that you know and use already—don't try to sprinkle in words you never would say. You may want to consult a thesaurus.

Revising in Action

As Isabella revised her first paragraph, she added words to show her interest in the topic. She focused on improving her action words.

> Have you ever climbed to a high point and ~~wanted~~ *burned*
>
> to explore the land beyond? That feeling was why Daniel
>
> Boone chose to ~~cut~~ *blaze* a trail through the Appalachian
>
> Mountains. Boone's explorations ~~caused~~ *inspired* many early
>
> Americans to head west.

Revise

Check for voice. Have a partner read your first paragraph aloud. Listen for vague words or words that don't sound like you. Revise the paragraph to include more interesting words.

TEKS 5.26D

Did I use quotes and paraphrases to add voice?

Look for quotes that express ideas in clever or interesting ways. Use those quotes as tools for expressing your ideas.

Revising in Action

Isabella wanted to add color and action to the sentence below. She decided to use a quote she had found.

Eventually, ~~there were too many people for Boone~~, so

Boone said it was "too crowded,"

he moved to West Virginia (Chinn).

Check for quotes. Did you use at least one interesting quote to express or support your ideas? If not, add one.

Did I write with confidence and authority?

You've done a lot of research and you now know a lot about your topic. Don't be timid or wishy-washy as you draw conclusions.

Practice

Rewrite the following sentences so that they sound strong and confident. Add your own twist to make them sound like you.

1. Amelia Earhart seemed to be a legend in her own time.
2. Her flight across the Pacific Ocean was kind of a big deal.
3. She may have been the most famous female aviator ever.

Check for confidence. Read your topic sentences. Revise them, if necessary, to make them strong and clear.

TEKS 5.15E
ELPS 3D, 3E

Revising Using a Checklist

Check your revising. Number a piece of paper from 1 to 9. If you can answer *yes* to a question, put a check mark after that number. If not, continue to work on that part of your report.

Focus and Coherence

_____ **1.** Did I write a focused beginning paragraph?

_____ **2.** Did I delete unnecessary or repetitive information?

Organization

_____ **3.** Are my sentences and paragraphs in order?

_____ **4.** Did I use transitions to connect ideas?

Development of Ideas

_____ **5.** Are all of my facts specific and well-supported?

_____ **6.** Have I deleted or developed any weak details?

Voice

_____ **7.** Do I sound interested in the topic?

_____ **8.** Did I use quotes and paraphrases to add voice?

_____ **9.** Do I sound knowledgeable and confident?

Make a clean copy. Ask your teacher or a classmate to read and respond to your report. Make the necessary edits. Create a clean copy for editing.

Editing

Editing becomes important after you've revised your first draft. When you edit, you make sure you have followed all grammar, sentence structure, punctuation, capitalization, and spelling rules.

Keys to Editing

1. **Use** a dictionary and the "Proofreader's Guide" in the back of this book for help.

2. **Edit** on a printed copy if you use a computer. Then make your changes on the computer.

3. **Double-check** your spelling, grammar, punctuation, and capitalization.

4. **Check** your report for proper formatting. (See pages 326–328.)

TEKS 5.20A(v)
ELPS 2I, 3E, 4C

Editing for Conventions

Grammar

When editing for *grammar*, make sure that you use prepositions and other parts of speech correctly.

How do I use prepositions?

A preposition is a word that introduces a prepositional phrase.

- Some prepositions indicate direction.

  Tall redwood trees grow toward the sky.

- Some prepositions indicate time.

  It is important to prune trees before their spring growth.

A prepositional phrase includes the preposition, the object of the preposition (noun or pronoun), and words that modify it.

Some animals hibernate during the long winter.

Grammar Practice

Create sentences using a word or phrase from each column. Read the sentences aloud. Have a partner identify the preposition and prepositional phrase in each.

Subject/Verb	Preposition	Object of Preposition
Bees stay busy	over	the mountains
Settlers journeyed	during	the long race
The runners rested	after	the hot summer

Check your use of prepositions. Make sure you have correctly used prepositions and prepositional phrases in your report. For more help, see pages 632–633.

TEKS 5.20A(v)
ELPS 2C, 2I, 3C, 3D, 3E, 4C

Have I used my prepositions correctly?

■ Prepositions may show location.

Small birds will fly behind an eagle to gain speed.

■ Prepositional phrases may provide details to the sentence.

Early colonists wrote letters about their early days in America.

Remember that a prepositional phrase may also show direction or time.

Grammar Practice

Write three sentences using prepositions from the list. Have a partner identify each prepositional phrase. Discuss whether the preposition shows direction, time, or location, and what details it provides.

about	between	from	since
after	down	in	throughout
behind	during	on	toward
beneath	for	past	under

Edit **Edit prepositions. Make sure you have used prepositions and prepositional phrases properly in your report.**

Learning Language

Read aloud the sentences below. Tell a partner the preposition and prepositional phrase in each sentence. Explain what information each preposition gives.

1. Some lakes stay frozen throughout the winter.
2. Bolivia is located below the Equator.
3. Daniel Boone led settlers through the mountains.
4. Austin's bats emerge at dusk.

Mechanics: Punctuation

When you edit for *mechanics,* you make sure you have used correct punctuation and styling, such as italics and underlining. When writing a report by hand, use underlining. When using a word processor to write, use italics.

When do I use italics and underlining?

- Underline or italicize book, magazine, and newspaper titles.

  I found a lot of information in <u>Sharks</u> by Patricia Corrigan.
  <u>National Wildlife</u> was a good resource for my report.
  We have a subscription to the <u>Dallas Morning News</u>.

- Underline or italicize words or phrases to show emphasis.

  Some people will <u>never</u> take sky diving lessons.
  That road is <u>extremely</u> dangerous.

Practice

Circle the word or words in each sentence that should be italicized or underlined. Explain why.

1. I read an interesting article in Owl magazine.
2. That meal was very delicious.
3. The Universe, by Seymour Simon, is a fascinating book.
4. A tornado is the worst kind of summer storm.
5. How to Knit Mittens can be found in the library.
6. My parents enjoy reading the Texas Herald each morning.

Edit

Check your use of underlines or italics. Make sure you have correctly used underlines or italics in your report. For more help with italics and underlining, see pages 546–547.

TEKS 5.24D, 5.26D

Editing Your Works Cited

Do I credit my sources correctly?

You might use books or magazines to find information for your report. Be sure to use a standard format to record bibliographic information. List sources alphabetically by author.

Magazine

Ransom, Cliff. "Hidden Giants." *National Geographic Adventure* Oct. 2009: 20–22. Print.

Book

Suzuki, David and Wayne Grady. *Tree, A Life Story*. Vancouver, BC: Greystone Books, 2004. Print.

Practice

Write the bibliographic information below in the correct format.
> **Author:** Gillian Richardson
> **Magazine title:** Cricket
> **Article title:** On Wings of Hope
> **Date:** Sept. 2009
> **Pages:** 30–34

Check your works cited. Make sure you have included the correct information and used the correct form of documentation when acknowledging sources in your report.

Editing in Action

In the sample below, changes are made to cite a source correctly.

Salas ⌃ Laura Purdie. <u>The wilderness Road</u>. 1775.

Mankato, MN: Capstone Press, 2007. ⌃ Print.

TEKS 5.15D, 5.20A(v), 5.21C
ELPS 2C

Editing Using a Checklist

Edit

Check your editing. Number a piece of paper from 1 to 10. If you can answer "yes" to a question, put a check mark before that number. If not, continue to edit for that convention.

Conventions

GRAMMAR

_____ 1. Have I used correct prepositions and prepositional phrases?

_____ 2. Have I used prepositions that convey location, time, or directions, or provide details?

MECHANICS

_____ 3. Have I used italics or underlining for titles and emphasis?

_____ 4. Have I used quotation marks correctly?

_____ 5. Have I correctly punctuated my works-cited page?

_____ 6. Have I started all my sentences with capital letters?

_____ 7. Have I capitalized proper nouns and titles?

SENTENCE STRUCTURE

_____ 8. Have I used a variety of sentence types?

SPELLING

_____ 9. Have I spelled all words correctly?

_____ 10. Have I double-checked the spelling of all names?

Creating a Title

■ Describe the main idea: **Leading Americans West**

■ Be creative: **A Boone to America's Growth**

■ Borrow words from the paper: **Daniel Boone, the Explorer**

TEKS 5.15E

Publishing

Go Online!

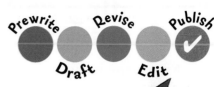

Prewrite · Draft · Revise · Edit · Publish ✓

You worked hard on your report. Be sure to share the results with family and friends.

Presentation

- Use black or blue ink and double-space the entire paper.
- Leave a one-inch margin on all four sides of your paper.
- Write your name, your teacher's name, the class, and the date in the upper left corner of page 1.
- Skip a line and center your title. Skip another line and start your report.
- Write your last name and the page number in the upper right corner of every page of your report.

Prepare an Electronic Presentation

Create a computer slide show of your report. (See "Multimedia Presentations" on pages 373–377 for more information.)

Develop an Illustrated Report

Draw a picture to illustrate the main point, or make a time line that shows important dates.

Go Online!

Upload your research report for others to read.

Publish

Make a final copy. Follow your teacher's instructions or use the guidelines above. (If you are using a computer, see pages 44–46.) Prepare a clean final copy of your research report.

ELPS 4I, 4K

Evaluating and Reflecting on Your Writing

After your research report is finished, complete the starter sentences below.

When you think about your writing, you will see how you are growing as a writer.

My Research Report

1. The best part of my research report is . . .

2. The most challenging part of writing the report was . . .

3. The main thing I learned about writing a report is . . .

4. The next time I write a research report, I would like to . . .

Giving Speeches

When you get really excited about something, you probably want to tell someone about it. Your latest interest—the secret lives of frogs, the mysterious Russian princess Anastasia, or the wonders of cyberspace—is a great topic for a speech. You can even turn a compelling research report into a speech. Your enthusiasm will capture your listeners and take them into the world of your favorite subject.

In this chapter, you will learn how to give a research-based speech. You will find tips on how to plan your speech, use visual aids, and keep your listeners' attention.

What's Ahead

- **Preparing Your Speech**
- **Organizing an Informative Speech**
- **Giving Your Speech**

Preparing Your Speech

The research report that you've already written can be turned into a great informative speech. Use your topic sentences to structure your speech and stay focused on important information, but rewrite your findings to appeal to a listening audience rather than a reading audience. Here's one way to rewrite your introduction.

Rewriting in Action

Below is the opening of the original essay "Daniel Boone, the Explorer" (pages 326–328). Notice that the new beginning (on gold paper) adds drama and a twist to grab the audience's attention.

Original Essay

> Have you ever climbed to a high point and burned to explore the land beyond? That feeling was why Daniel Boone chose to blaze a trail through the Appalachian mountains. Boone's exploration inspired many early Americans to head west.

Speech

> What makes a person venture into a dangerous land where few, if any, people have gone? Is it a feeling of adventure? A burning desire to explore something new? When you know the answers to these questions, you will know Daniel Boone. And you'll know why his explorations have inspired so many others. . .

 Prepare your speech. Rewrite the opening paragraph of your research report to add drama and to hook your audience. Make sure you have included the key idea from your topic sentence.

Organizing an Informative Speech

Organize your speech on note cards. Write the beginning and ending of your speech word for word. For details in between, use topic sentences or phrases that will spark your memory. You'll want to include evidence and quotations in your speech, too. Name sources rather than saying something like, "Research says . . ." Prepare and hand out a list of your sources.

Sample Note Cards

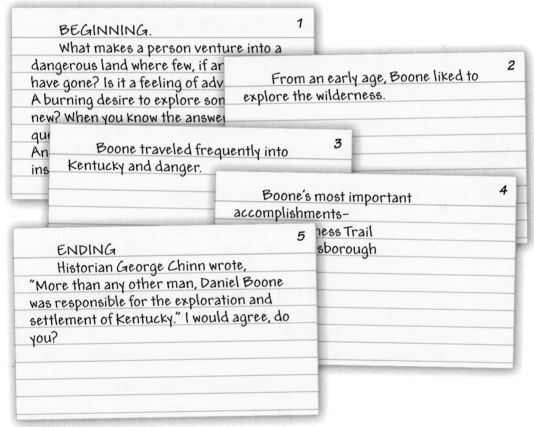

BEGINNING.   1
What makes a person venture into a
dangerous land where few, if ar
have gone? Is it a feeling of adv
A burning desire to explore son
new? When you know the answe
qu
An
ins

From an early age, Boone liked to   2
explore the wilderness.

Boone traveled frequently into   3
Kentucky and danger.

Boone's most important   4
accomplishments–
ess Trail
sborough   5

ENDING
Historian George Chinn wrote,
"More than any other man, Daniel Boone
was responsible for the exploration and
settlement of Kentucky." I would agree, do
you?

Create your note cards. Create a card for each part of your speech. Include a beginning and an ending that your listeners will remember. Other cards should have main ideas or quotes you'd like to read. You can also add notes to yourself about using visual materials.

TEKS 5.26B

Using Visual Aids

Revisit your research to locate any visual materials. Visual aids, like the ones listed below, help your listeners understand the details of your speech. They also provide evidence to support your conclusions.

Posters	show words, pictures, or both.
Photographs	help your audience see what you are talking about.
Charts	compare ideas or explain main points.
Transparencies	highlight key words, ideas, or graphics.
Maps	show specific places being discussed.
Objects	allow your audience to see the real thing.

Here are some tips for preparing your visual aids.

1 **Make them big.** The people in the back of the room should be able to see your visual aids.

2 **Keep them simple.** Avoid long sentences. Short labels, pictures, and graphs work best.

3 **Use a good design.** Make visual aids colorful and attractive.

 List visual aids. List four visual aids you could use during your speech. Then select two that you think will provide evidence that supports your conclusions.

Photograph	landscape of Kentucky
Poster	time line of Daniel Boone's life
Map	map of the Wilderness Road

Giving Your Speech

After you have planned your whole speech and outlined it on note cards, practice your speech and present it. Use these tips to make sure your speech will be presented clearly and consistently.

Practicing Your Delivery

Practice your speech several times, using the following tips and the checklist at the bottom of the page.

- Find a quiet place where you can listen to your own voice.
- Practice in front of friends or parents. Ask for suggestions.
- If possible, videotape or tape-record yourself.

Presenting Your Speech

When you give your speech, remember the following:

- Take a deep breath and relax.
- Look at your audience, or just over their heads.
- Stand up straight.
- Speak loudly, clearly, and slowly.

Using a Checklist

Use the following checklist as a guide when you practice your speech. Others can also use this list to give you comments.

_____ **1.** I have good posture, and I look relaxed.
_____ **2.** I look at my audience as I speak.
_____ **3.** My voice can be heard at the back of the room.
_____ **4.** I sound interested in my topic.
_____ **5.** I am not speaking too fast.
_____ **6.** I avoid "stalling" words like *um, er,* and *like.*
_____ **7.** My visual aids are large and easy to understand.
_____ **8.** I point out information on my visual aids.

⭐ **TEKS** 5.26B, 5.26C
ELPS 2G–2I, 3D, 3E

Speaking Tips

Before your speech . . .

- **Get everything organized.**
  To present your findings consistently, summarize your findings and put the main points of your speech on note cards. Make your visual aids.

- **Time your speech.**
  Read your note cards out loud. If your speech is too short or too long, add or remove details.

- **Practice.**
  The more you remember without looking at your notes, the easier it will be to give your speech.

During your speech . . .

- **Speak loudly.** Be sure that everyone can hear you.
- **Speak clearly and slowly.** Don't hurry.
- **Look at your audience.** Connect with your listeners.
- **Put visual aids where everyone can see them.**
  Point out the things that you are talking about.

After your speech . . .

- **Answer questions.**
  Ask if anyone has questions about your topic. Help classmates understand words they don't know.

- **Collect materials.**
  Gather your visual aids and note cards and return to your seat.

Prepare, practice, and present. Prepare your speech and practice one more time with a friend. After you present your speech in the classroom, listen for suggestions from your teacher or classmates.

Research Writing

Multimedia Presentations

What is a multimedia presentation? Since *multimedia* means "more than one form of communication," this kind of report shares information in several different ways. With the help of a computer, you can prepare a multimedia report using your voice, pictures, sounds, and the printed word. Think of it as a speech with a slide show on the side.

In this chapter, you will learn how to prepare a multimedia presentation using a report you have already written.

What's Ahead

- **Getting Started**
- **Presentation Checklist**

Getting Started

Your multimedia presentation begins with the research report you've already written. You list the topic sentences, or main ideas, from that paper, then use presentation software to make slides, add graphics (visuals), and include audio (sounds). Ask a friend or your teacher if you need help in doing this.

Prewrite **Get organized.** Make sure your computer has presentation software. Revisit your research to locate any visual materials.

Creating the Slides

1 **Find the main ideas in your research report.**

Each main idea should have its own slide. To plan your presentation, make a storyboard. Follow the format on page 376.

2 **Find audio and visuals for each slide.**

Use your research, computer software, and the Internet to find multimedia material. You can also create your images and sounds.

Draft **Gather ideas.** Use a cluster diagram to plan each slide. Write the main idea in the middle and add picture and sound ideas around it.

3 Design your slides.

Select fonts that are easy to read. Use the same fonts and some of the same colors on all your slides to tie your presentation together.

4 Build your slides one by one.

Each slide should be attractive and easy to understand. Write a main idea on each slide. Arrange your slides in a logical order.

Improving Your Presentation

A multimedia presentation should flow smoothly and present information in a clear and interesting way. Practice speaking and running the slide show at the same time.

Rehearse your presentation. Practice your presentation in front of friends and family. Ask for suggestions to make it better. Change any parts that are unclear.

It is also important that your slides are free of careless errors. You may ask an adult or a classmate to help you check your slides.

Make corrections. Check each slide for grammar, sentence structure, punctuation, capitalization, and spelling errors.

Giving a Multimedia Presentation

Your presentation should summarize what you learned from your research. Each slide should provide evidence, such as quotes, to support your conclusions and ideas. See pages 367–372 for information about speaking to groups.

Present your report. Before you begin, take a deep breath and relax. Enjoy presenting your hard work!

Multimedia Presentation Storyboard

This is a storyboard based on the report "Daniel Boone, the Explorer" on pages 326–328. Each box represents one slide. Create your storyboard similarly, making sure to use a variety of sources to support your ideas. Cite your sources on the last slide.

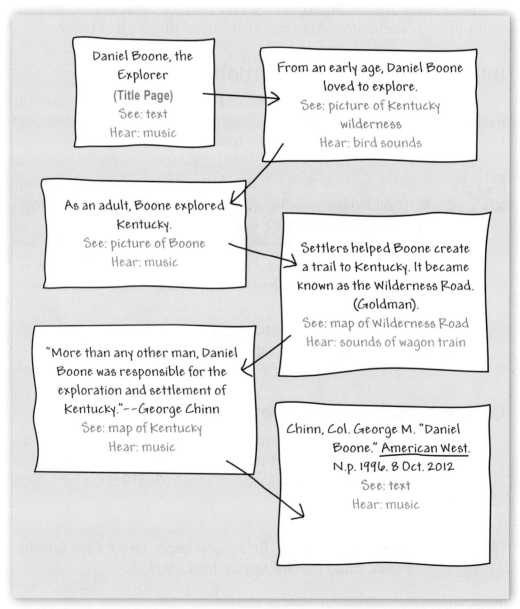

Daniel Boone, the
Explorer
(Title Page)
See: text
Hear: music

From an early age, Daniel Boone
loved to explore.
See: picture of Kentucky
wilderness
Hear: bird sounds

As an adult, Boone explored
Kentucky.
See: picture of Boone
Hear: music

Settlers helped Boone create
a trail to Kentucky. It became
known as the Wilderness Road.
(Goldman).
See: map of Wilderness Road
Hear: sounds of wagon train

"More than any other man, Daniel
Boone was responsible for the
exploration and settlement of
Kentucky."--George Chinn
See: map of Kentucky
Hear: music

Chinn, Col. George M. "Daniel
Boone." American West.
N.p. 1996. 8 Oct. 2012
See: text
Hear: music

TEKS 5.26A–D
ELPS 3D

Presentation Checklist

Use the following checklist to make sure your presentation is the best it can be. When you can answer all 11 questions with *yes*, you're ready to present!

Focus and Coherence

_____ **1.** Does each slide focus on the topic?

_____ **2.** Do my ideas connect to each other from one slide to the next?

Organization

_____ **3.** Do my slides follow a logical order?

_____ **4.** Have I summarized information in my presentation?

_____ **5.** Have I cited sources at the end?

Development of Ideas

_____ **6.** Is my information clear and interesting?

_____ **7.** Do I use quotes to support my ideas?

_____ **8.** Do I use evidence to support my conclusions?

Voice

_____ **9.** Do I show interest in my topic?

_____ **10.** Does my voice fit my audience and topic?

Conventions

_____ **11.** Is my presentation free of errors in grammar, sentence structure, punctuation, capitalization, and spelling?

⭐ **ELPS** 2C, 2G, 3E, 3G, 4G

The Tools of Language

Learning Language

Work with a partner. Read the meanings aloud and discuss your answers to the questions.

1. You participate when you take part in an activity.
   How do you participate in class?

2. Directions tell you what to do.
   Explain a set of directions in this book.

3. People cooperate when they work together.
   Tell about a way that you cooperate at home.

4. A strategy is a plan for doing something.
   What strategy do you use to learn a new word?

5. You use people skills to get along with others.
   What people skills do you use for group work?

Listening and Speaking

Did you know that you can hear someone without really listening to the person? When you listen, you think about the words you hear to understand their general meaning. Listening carefully will help you do well in school.

Speaking is also important. In school, you must ask and answer questions, give reports, and share information as you work in groups. This chapter can help you improve your listening and speaking skills.

What's Ahead

- Listening in Class
- Participating in a Group
- Speaking in Class

ELPS 2D, 2G, 2H, 2I

Listening in Class

Listening is more than just hearing someone talk. It's also thinking about what is being said. In fact, listening is one of the best ways to learn. The following tips will help you become a better listener.

1 **Know your purpose for listening.** Are you following directions for a science project? Are you learning about an important time in history? Are you reviewing main points about a certain topic as you prepare for a test?

2 **Listen carefully.** Hearing is not the same as listening. Hearing involves only your ears; listening involves your ears *and* your mind. Listen to the speaker. Take notes on what you hear and have questions about.

3 **Ask questions.** When the speaker is finished, ask any questions you have about specific ideas or concepts. Ask the speaker to clarify anything you don't understand.

Note Taking in Action

When you take notes, write down main points about the topic in your own words. Ask questions when you don't understand.

Sample Notes

> Kitchen Science   Mar. 9
>
> What does the salt in our ice-cream maker do?
> – Salt lowers the freezing point of water to about 28°.
> – The mixture of water and ice stays colder
>   than 32° so milk and cream can freeze.
>
> How much salt is needed?

Participating in a Group

When you work in a group, you must cooperate with others to solve a problem or reach a goal. Two important parts of cooperation are respecting yourself and respecting others.

Skills for Cooperating

In a group, you respect yourself when you . . .

- know that your own ideas are important.
- share your opinions, ideas, and feelings with the group.
- ask questions if you don't understand something.

In a group, you respect others when you . . .

- listen carefully.
- pay attention to others' opinions.
- take turns speaking or asking questions.
- avoid personal criticism.
- praise the ideas of others.
- encourage everyone to participate.

> Listening and cooperating are key people skills.

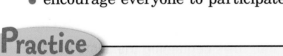

Practice

For each situation, decide which of the skills listed above would help the group work together more effectively. Discuss with a partner.

Situation 1

Someone in your group said something that you didn't understand. Now everyone is discussing it, and you're totally lost.

Situation 2

One member of your group sits quietly and listens to the others. She never says what she thinks or asks a question.

Speaking in Class

Speaking in class is an important classroom activity. The guidelines listed below will help you and your classmates become better classroom speakers.

Pay attention. Listen to understand the meaning of what others are saying. Stay on the topic being discussed.

Be respectful. Respond politely to what others say.

Make eye contact. Look at the person you are speaking to.

Wait your turn. Show respect for others by not interrupting.

Get to the point. State your ideas briefly and clearly.

> Hey, mates! Think before you speak so you're sure that you have something important to say.

Play "Pass It On." The following game requires you to listen and speak carefully.

1 The class is divided into rows containing the same number of students. Then the teacher whispers a sentence to the first person in each row.

2 When the teacher says, "Start," the first person in each row whispers the sentence to the next person in the row. That person whispers the sentence to the next person until it reaches the last person in the row.

3 The last person in the row goes to the board and writes the sentence the way that he or she heard it.

4 The first row to write the sentence exactly as the teacher whispered it wins.

Learning Language

When it comes to writing, there are many new words and ideas to learn. The *writing process, the Texas traits of writing, prewriting, drafting,* and *revising* are just a few of them.

If you play basketball, you know that there is a vocabulary, or certain group of words, related to this sport. Without words such as *lay up, jump shot, dribble,* and *rebound,* you would have a hard time playing the game.

The vocabulary related to writing works in the same way. Without knowing the meanings of the words *prewriting, drafting,* and *revising,* you would have a hard time writing a strong story or report. This section will help you hearn all about the language of writing so you can do your best work!

What's Ahead

- **Language of the Writing Process**
- **Language of the Writing Traits**
- **Language of the Writing Forms**

 ELPS 2C, 2D, 2G, 2H

Language Strategies

You hear new words in conversation every day. Here are some strategies to help you clarify, understand, remember, and use the new words you hear.

Ask for Help

When you don't know a word you hear, ask others for help or clarification.

You can say: I just heard a new word—*ladybug*. What is a ladybug?

Wait for the explanation and then thank the person for his or her help.

 Listen as a classmate explains a homework assignment. If you hear a word you don't know, use this strategy. Ask your friend to help you by explaining the word you don't understand.

Use Academic Language

Your teacher may use an instructional word in class that is unfamilar. Repeating the word will help you clarify and remember it. Then try using the word to show you understand its meaning.

You hear: Listen for information about an important concept.
You repeat: concept
You can use: Freedom is an important concept in American history.

 Listen in class and repeat words you think you may not remember. Then try using them in different sentences.

ELPS 2C, 2D, 2I, 3D, 3E

Talk Around the Problem Word

If you don't understand a word you hear, use familiar words instead. Then ask someone to tell you the word.

You can say: In the library, we talk very quietly. Can you tell me what that quiet kind of talking is called? (Whispering)

 The next time you don't know the right word to use, talk around it. Then ask a friend to tell you the word.

Teach a Friend

Use new words to teach someone you know, such as a friend, classmate, or someone in your family.

You hear: People recycle glass so it can be used again.
You can say: Use these containers to recycle glass and paper.

 Use a new word you have learned to explain something to a classmate.

Take Notes or Draw a Picture

Write new words that you hear in a notebook. Add information and your own drawings to help you remember their meanings.

You hear: A triangle is a shape that has three sides.
What you do: You write *triangle* and draw a picture of it.

 Keep a vocabulary notebook. The next time you hear a word you want to remember, draw it or write about it in your notebook.

TEKS 5.15A–E
ELPS 4C, 5B

Language of the Writing Process

Read each of the terms. Then read about what they mean.

The first step of the writing process is to prewrite, or plan your writing. You think about your purpose for writing, the topic, and your audience. Then brainstorm or use a graphic organizer to arrange your ideas Sometimes you will choose a genre, or form of writing. Other times, the genre will be given to you.

When you write a first draft, you build on ideas from prewriting to create a focused piece of writing. You put related ideas into groups. Then you write paragraphs about your groups of ideas. Remember to think about your audience and purpose as you write.

Next, you read your draft and revise, or make changes. You make sure that all the parts of your writing focus on the main idea. You check that you've included enough information to make your ideas clear. You look to see that your ideas fit your purpose and that you've arranged them in the right order. You check that the words you've used are right for your audience. Finally, you ask others for their opinions and make any last changes.

When you edit, you look for mistakes in grammar, mechanics (capitalization and punctuation), and spelling. You make sure that all your sentences make sense. Then you correct any errors that you find.

To publish, make a neat final copy and share.

ELPS 2C, 2G, 2I, 3A, 3D, 3E, 3G, 3H, 4C, 4G, 5B

Vocabulary: Writing Process

| draft | edit | prewrite |
| publish | revise | audience |

1. **Say the word.** Listen and read along as your teacher reads the words aloud. Then repeat each word. Some words have consonant blends. A consonant blend is two or more consonants that are together. The sounds blend together and each sound is heard, such as *dr-* in *drip* or *pr-* in *prize*. Which vocabulary words have consonant blends? Practice pronouncing these words with a partner.

2. **Discover the meaning.** Work with a partner to make a word web. Start with words you know. Discuss how each word you add to the web helps you better understand the word.

3. **Learn more.** Listen as your teacher explains the meanings of the words. Work with a partner to add words to your web.

4. **Show your understanding.** Work in a small group to answer the questions below. Share your ideas. Speak clearly and listen carefully to others.
   - Which step should you do first—draft or prewrite? Why?
   - What do you do when you revise?

5. **Write it, show it.** In your notebook, add key words to help you remember what the words mean. For example, you might draw a pencil next to the word *draft* and add the phrase *get your ideas down on paper*.

The Writing Process in Action

You have learned some key words that you can use to talk about the writing process. Now it's time to see the process in action! First, your teacher will show you how to do each step of the writing process. Then you will write together, responding to the questions.

Prewrite

1. Decide on a topic. For example, pick an outdoor activity you enjoy. What can you say about it?
2. Who might read your writing? Who is your audience?
3. What writing genre, or form, will you use to write?

Draft

1. How can you group your ideas to write paragraphs?
2. How can you organize your paragraphs to support your main idea, or focus statement?

The Writing Process in Action

These pages from the first unit in your book show the writing process in action.

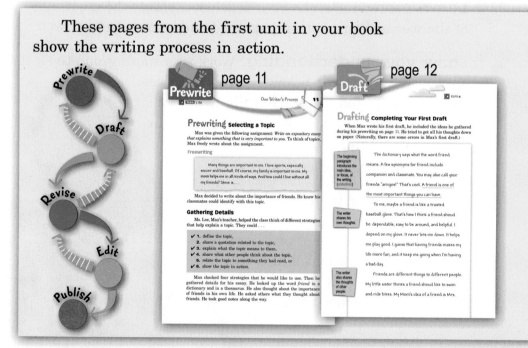

Revise

1. Do all your sentences support your focus statement?
2. Should you add, remove, or rearrange any sentences?

Edit

1. Did you follow all the rules of grammar and mechanics?
2. Does each sentence make sense?
3. Are all the words spelled correctly?

Publish

1. Have you used the feedback you received to make your writing better?
2. Is your writing neat and easy to read?

Turn and Talk

Talk to a classmate about the step in the writing process that you like best. Explain your opinion.

Example: The step I like best is _____.

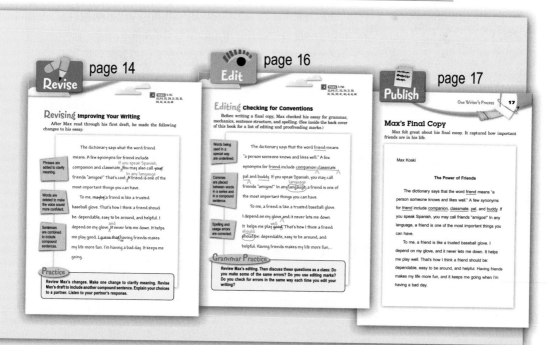

ELPS 4C, 5B

Language of the Writing Traits

Read each term, or writing trait. Then read what each means. Turn to a partner and explain the terms in your own words.

Focus and Coherence

Your writing has focus if you have written about one main idea. Your writing has coherence if all the sentences work together to tell something about that idea. There is no unnecessary information.

Organization

Your writing should be organized, or put together, so that it is easy for readers to follow from one idea to the next. Transition words and phrases show how sentences and paragraphs are linked.

Development of Ideas

You develop your ideas by adding unique and interesting details. Including details makes your writing clear and helps readers understand and appreciate your ideas.

Voice

Your writing voice shows the way you think and feel. It lets your personality shine through. Writing with an original voice makes readers pay attention.

Conventions

Your writing should follow conventions, or the rules for grammar, sentence structure, capitalization, punctuation, and spelling. Writing free of mistakes is easier to read.

ELPS 2C, 2G, 2H. 2I, 3D, 3E, 3G, 5B

Vocabulary: Writing Traits

coherence	conventions	development
focus	organization	voice

1 **Say the word.** Listen as your teacher reads the words aloud. Then repeat each word.

2 **Discover the meaning.** Work with a partner. List the words in your vocabulary notebook. Then use what you already know to write a general meaning for each word.

3 **Learn more.** Listen as your teacher explains the meaning of each word. Use the new information and work with your partner to correct or restate the meanings you wrote together.

4 **Show your understanding.** In a small group, take turns sharing ideas to answer the questions below. Listen to understand the main points, or important ideas, of others.

- How do you know if your writing has focus?
- How would you organize your ideas to write about a trip you took? What kinds of details would you include?
- Why should you pay attention to writing conventions?

5 **Write it, show it.** In your vocabulary notebook, add notes to help you remember new information you have about the vocabulary words. Then, make drawings in your partner's notebook for two words, and explain how the drawings connect to the words.

Language of Descriptive Writing

Descriptive writing is writing that gives a detailed picture of a person, a thing, or an event. A descriptive essay has three main parts: the beginning with a topic sentence, middle paragraphs with details, and an ending with a closing sentence. The graphic organizer shows how all the parts fit together.

Descriptive Essay Organization

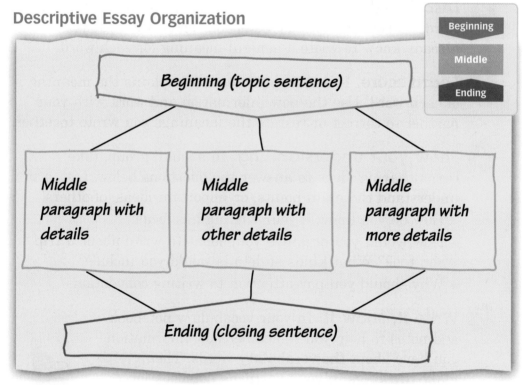

Beginning

Middle

Ending

Beginning (topic sentence)

Middle paragraph with details

Middle paragraph with other details

Middle paragraph with more details

Ending (closing sentence)

Turn and Talk

Talk with a partner and express your ideas about why writers use details to support their topic.

Details help support a topic because _____.

ELPS 2C, 2G, 2I, 3A, 3D, 5B

Vocabulary: Descriptive Writing

beginning	**describe**	**detail**
ending	**senses**	**subject**

1. **Say the word or phrase.** Listen as your teacher reads the words aloud. Repeat each word slowly to sound out each syllable. Some words have the short *e* sound as in *pencil* and *extra*. If a syllable has only one vowel, the vowel sound is usually short. Which two vocabulary words have a short *e* sound? Practice pronouncing these words with a partner.

2. **Discover the meaning.** Work with a partner. Find some of the vocabulary words on pages **56–57**. Look at the yellow boxes next to the writing model. Write notes about what you think the words mean.

3. **Learn more.** Listen as your teacher explains the meaning of each word. Work with your partner to check and add to your earlier notes. Write each word on an index card with its definition on the back. Hold up one card with the word facing your partner and have your partner say its definition. Take turns until you can define each word.

4. **Show your understanding.** Use your notebook to answer the questions below.
   - Would you start your writing with an ending or a beginning? Why?
   - What senses do you use every day?

5. **Write it, show it.** Write the vocabulary words in your notebook. Add drawings to help you remember the meanings. You might add synonyms, or words that mean the same thing. For example, near *senses* you could draw your nose.

Reading the Descriptive Model

What Do You Know?

Next you will read "Aunt Frankie" on pages **56–57**. It is a descriptive essay about a favorite aunt. Do you have a favorite relative or friend? How would you describe this person? What is his or her favorite hobby or pastime? What is your favorite hobby?

Build Background

Hobbies are activities people do to relax. Baking, collecting stamps, building models, and playing an instrument are some hobbies that help people feel comfortable and have fun. Sometimes clubs are formed so people with similar hobbies can share ideas.

Listening

Listen as your teacher or a classmate reads "Aunt Frankie" aloud. As you listen, make notes about the subject, main points, and important details. Work with a partner and share information to answer the questions below. Answering questions and taking notes will help you understand what happens in the story.

1. What is the subject of the essay?
2. What are three things Aunt Frankie likes to do?
3. How does the writer imply, or suggest, in the beginning paragraph the idea that Aunt Frankie might cook?

Key Descriptive Words

warm	sparkly	comfortable
favorite	glows	sticky

Look at the words in the box. With a partner, use the words to describe objects in your classroom. Tell why each word matches that object. Draw a picture of each object you describe and write the descriptive word beside the picture.

Read Along

Now it's your turn to read. Turn to pages 56–57. Read along as your teacher or a classmate reads the writing model aloud.

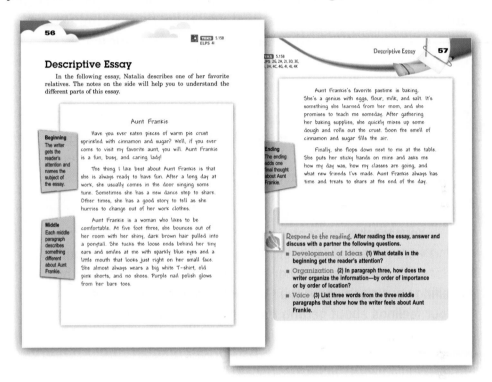

After Reading

On a sheet of paper write or draw answers to the following questions about the writing model. Answering questions will help you understand what you have read.

1. What does the writer like best about Aunt Frankie?
2. What does Aunt Frankie wear to make herself feel comfortable?
3. Which sense does the writer use to create the image of cinnamon and sugar in the air?

Oral Language: Descriptive Writing

The person or people who will listen to you or read your writing are called the audience. When you speak or write, it is important to choose just the right words that will reach your audience. To express your feelings in writing or speaking, the tone, or the words you choose, will be different for your best friend or for an adult.

 Read about the situation below. Then choose two audiences from the list above the picture. With a partner, discuss how the words you use to describe your gold star experience might be different for each audience.

Situation

Your teacher presented you with a gold star in school today. You were rewarded for being the most helpful student in your class this week. The teacher discussed the way you helped by telling your class about the things you did for others. Describe your feelings about getting the gold star and why you were so helpful.

Audiences

- A friend not in your school
- Your family
- The school newspaper

ELPS 3D, 3E, 3G, 4G, 4I

Effective Talk

When you answer a question, you might use a few words, a sentence, or a few sentences. When you use more details to tell about something, your audience will have a better understanding.

Read the question and the answers below. In the first box, there is only one word. In the second box, there is a short sentence that answers the question. The third answer contains more detail and does a better job answering the question.

How did you feel when you received the gold star this week?

good

▽

I started smiling.

▽

I was surprised! I didn't think I had done anything special. I cleaned the board one day, and watered the plants another. I did help Sal with his report. It was fun to help with different things.

Try IT Reread the question in blue. Talk with a partner about how each of you would answer the question. Think of additional questions, such as *Were you asked to help or did you help on your own? What made you want to help?* Responding to questions will help to express more feelings and give extra details. Add the new details to your answer. Review each other's answer again to make sure it does a better job answering the question.

ELPS 3G, 3H

Language of Narrative Writing

Narrative writing is writing that shares an event, feeling, or experience in the form of a story. The beginning introduces the main idea. The middle, or body, gives details about what happened. The ending might tell how the writer feels, tell what was learned, or give the reader something to think about.

Narrative Essay Organization

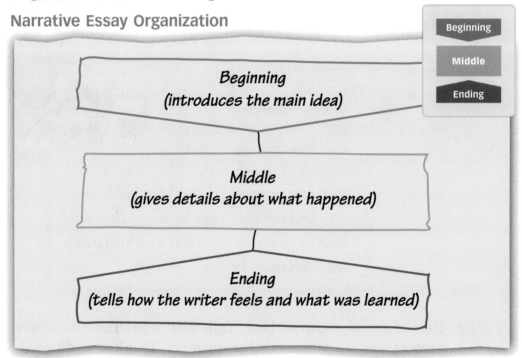

Beginning

Middle

Ending

Beginning
(introduces the main idea)

Middle
(gives details about what happened)

Ending
(tells how the writer feels and what was learned)

Turn and Talk

Talk with a partner about one part of the graphic organizer. Tell why you think that part is important to narrative writing.

This part is important because _____.

Vocabulary: Narrative Writing

closing	narrative	opinion
personal	time order	topic

1. **Say the word.** Listen as your teacher reads the words aloud. Then repeat each word, sounding out each syllable.

2. **Discover the meaning.** Work with a partner. Find some of the vocabulary words on pages **70** and **75–76**. Look at the yellow boxes next to the model paragraph and model essay. Write notes about what you think the words mean.

3. **Learn more.** Listen as your teacher explains the meaning of each word. Work with a partner to check and correct your earlier notes. Find examples of all the words and write their meanings in your notebook.

4. **Show your understanding.** Listen as your teacher reads the questions below. Discuss the answers with a partner. Use your notebook to help you answer each question.
   - Would you introduce your topic in the beginning or closing part of your essay? Why?
   - Is an opinion something personal? Why?
   - How do you know if the events that happen in a story are in time order?

5. **Write it, show it.** In your notebook, add pictures or drawings to help you remember what each word means. You may wish to add other words that mean the same thing. For example, near *personal* you could write *me*.

 **ELPS** 2C, 2G, 2I, 3E, 3G, 3H

Reading the Narrative Model

What Do You Know?

Next you will read "What Is It?" on pages 75–76. It is a personal narrative about being in an art contest. Have you been in an art show or attended one? Did you paint or draw, or did you make an object out of clay? How did you feel when everyone looked at your artwork? How did you feel when you looked at other's artworks?

Build Background

Art is an expression of a person's ideas and imagination. It is personal. Artwork can be as simple as drawing a line across a blank piece of paper. It can be as detailed as drawing a tree with every branch and every leaf.

Listening

Listen as your teacher or a classmate reads aloud "What Is It?" As you listen, take notes about the topic, colorful details, and the ending, or closing. Be prepared to answer the questions below. Taking notes and responding to questions will help you understand the important details.

    1. What is the topic of the personal narrative?

    2. Did the writer tell the story in time order? How do you know?

    3. How does the closing tell how the writer feels?

Key Words: Sensory and Time-Order Words

colorful	during	excited
experience	next	proud

Look at the words in the box. You will see these words when you read the writing model. With a partner, use the words to talk about a personal experience you've had and how it made you feel.

Read Along

Now it's your turn to read. Turn to page **75–76**. Read along as your teacher or a classmate reads the personal narrative aloud.

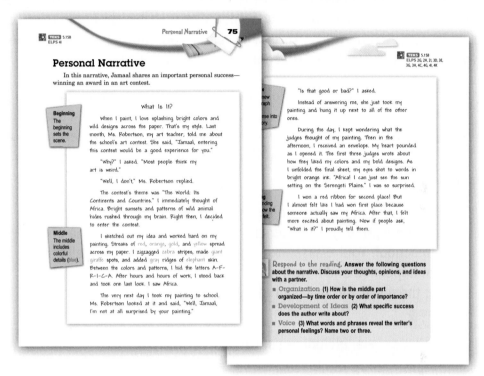

After Reading

Copy the following chart on a sheet of paper. A strong narrative includes sensory words that describe what you see, feel, smell, and hear. With your partner, look for sensory words in the writing model, such as *bright* and *splashing*. Write them in the chart. Use the words to retell what happened in the story.

See	Feel
bright	splashing

 **ELPS** 3D, 3G, 3H

Oral Language: Narrative Writing

The person or people who will listen to you or read your writing are called the audience. When you speak or write, it is important to choose just the right words that will reach your audience. Your tone, or way of writing, will be different for each audience.

 Read about the situation below. Then choose two audiences from the list above the picture. With a partner, discuss how you might tell your story about a school break differently for each audience. How would you change your tone?

Situation

You just got back from a school break. Your teacher wants to hear about an exciting experience you had during your time off from school. Your classmates want to hear, too! You will tell them what happened and how it made you feel. Use sensory words to help them see and feel your story.

Audiences

- Your class, including your teacher
- Your group of close friends after school
- Student teacher from the local college

Effective Talk

When you answer a question, you might use a few words, a sentence, or a few sentences. If you use sensory and time-order words, your audience will have a better understanding.

Read the question and the answers below. In the first box, there is a one word answer. In the second box, there is a short sentence that answers the question. The third answer does a better job of answering the question.

What was it like when the group first played music together?

terrible

We were all out of tune.

Our first time sounded like a scratchy jumble of noise. We couldn't keep a steady beat. Then the drummer thumped out one beat and we each added our instrument, one at a time. Finally, we had a rocking sound.

Try It With a partner, choose an experience your class shared at school. Ask each other *What happened, and how did you feel when it was over?* Take notes on the main ideas and important details as you each tell what happened. Circle the sensory and time-order words you wrote in your notes. Talk about how to keep the details in order and how adding other sensory details can make your answer more complete.

⭐ ELPS 3G, 3H

Language of Expository Writing

An expository essay is writing that provides information to explain something. The beginning has a focus statement that tells the main idea about a topic. The middle paragraphs organize specific facts and details about the topic. The ending gives a final thought that supports the main idea.

Expository Essay Organization

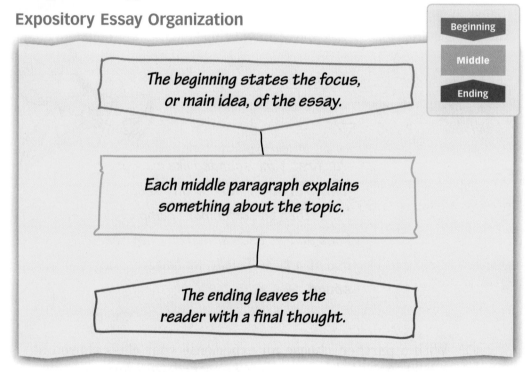

The beginning states the focus, or main idea, of the essay.

Each middle paragraph explains something about the topic.

The ending leaves the reader with a final thought.

| Beginning |
| Middle |
| Ending |

Turn and Talk

When you explain something, you make the meaning clear. Explain to a partner how the middle paragraphs of an expository essay are connected to the introduction.

The middle paragraphs explain _____.

Vocabulary: Expository Writing

explanation	**expository essay**	**fact**
focus statement	**introduction**	**detail**

1 **Say the word.** Listen as your teacher reads the words aloud. Then repeat each word.

2 **Discover the meaning.** Work with a partner. Find some of the vocabulary words on pages 135–136. Look at the yellow boxes next to the writing model. Discuss the words and write what you think they mean.

3 **Learn more.** Listen as your teacher explains the meaning of each word. With your partner, use this new information to revise the meanings you wrote earlier. Then find examples of these words in the writing model on pages 135–136.

4 **Show your understanding.** Answer the questions below in your notebook. Your teacher will give you directions. When following directions, listen for action words such as *write* and signal words such as *first, next,* and *finally.* These words tell you what to do and when to do it.
- Would the introduction come at the beginning or the end of an essay? Explain your answer.
- Would an expository essay give information or tell a story?
- Which of the following statements is a fact? *Some students in my class play soccer. Soccer is the most exciting sport.*

5 **Write it, show it.** Discuss your answers to the questions above with a partner. Make notes or draw pictures to show your understanding of his or her main points.

 ELPS 2G, 2H, 2I, 3E

Reading the Expository Model

What Do You Know?

Next you will read "Food for Everybody," an expository writing model about photosynthesis on pages 135–136. What do you know about the way plants grow? What plants are interesting to you? Have you ever tried to grow a plant? Describe what you did.

Build Background

Plants have a green substance called chlorophyll in their leaves. It uses sunlight to change carbon dioxide and water into food for the plant. All living things depend upon the food that plants make.

Listening

Listen as your teacher or a classmate reads "Food for Everybody" aloud. Make a note about the focus statement, the main idea of the essay. Listen for details, specific pieces of information that help you understand the main idea. You can also use these details to figure out things that the writer does not clearly state. The words in the box below show the order of the steps that happen during photosynthesis. Listen for these words. Then answer the questions.

1. What is the writer's focus?
2. What is the first step of photosynthesis? What happens next?
3. How does photosynthesis help you?

Key Words—Steps in the Process

> **Photosynthesis begins**   **In the next part**   **In the end**

You will see the words in the box when you read the writing model. With a partner, use the words to talk about the steps of an activity you enjoy. Discuss why it's important to explain the steps in a certain order.

Read Along

Turn to pages 135–136. Read the writing model as your teacher or a classmate reads it aloud. Think about the main idea and details as you read.

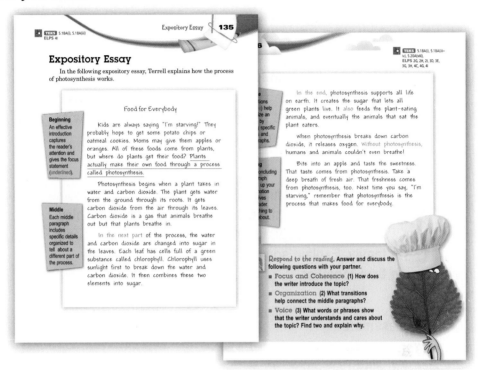

After Reading

When you summarize, you tell the most important points of something you have read. Copy the chart below on a sheet of paper. Use your chart to summarize the writing model with a partner.

Photosynthesis	
What Plants Use	What Plants Make

Oral Language: Expository Writing

The person or people who listen to you or read your writing are called the audience. When you speak or write, the words you choose will depend on your audience. Your tone, or way of writing, will be different for each audience, too.

 Read about the situation below. Then choose two audiences from the list above the picture. With a partner, discuss how the words you use to explain spending time with your family might be different for each audience.

Situation

Every Wednesday evening is family night in Sasha's home. All the members of her family spend time together. They play games, watch movies, or just talk to one another. Think about your own family. Explain some of the ways that you enjoy spending time together.

Audiences

- **A classmate**
- **Your teacher**
- **A cousin in another city**

ELPS 2G, 2I. 3G, 3H

Effective Talk

When you answer a question, you might use a few words, a sentence, or a few sentences. When you use more details to explain something, a listener will have a better understanding of your ideas.

Read the question and the answers below. In the first box, there are only two words. In the second box, there is a short sentence that answers the question. The third answer contains more detail and does a better job of answering the question.

Why should family members spend time together?

They play.

Family members play and have fun.

When family members spend time together, they play and have fun. Each person can talk about what's happening at school or at work. Kids and parents feel close to each other.

Try IT Choose a question to talk about with a partner. Write some ideas and details to help you as you explain your thoughts and opinions. Use the following ideas to get started.

1. What is a favorite thing that you do with your family? Why do you like that activity?
2. How is spending time with your family different than being with your friends? Why are both important?

Language of Persuasive Writing

Persuasive writing is writing that tries to persuade, or convince, the reader to believe in the writer's opinion. Persuasive essays use a beginning to tell the opinion, the middle to support the opinion with evidence and sound reasons, and the conclusion to tell the opinion again and encourage the reader to take action.

Persuasive Essay Organization

Beginning
Middle
Ending

Beginning
(tells the opinion, or what the writer believes)

Middle Paragraphs

Sound Reason 1
(important)

Sound Reason 2
(important)

Sound Reason 3
(most important)

Conclusion
(tells the opinion again and gives a call to action)

Turn and Talk

Talk with a partner and tell your ideas about why sound reasons are important to persuasive writing.

Sound reasons are important because _____.

Vocabulary: Persuasive Writing

call to action	**opinion**	**persuade**
sound reason	**support**	**transition**

1. **Say the word or phrase.** Listen as your teacher reads the words and phrases aloud. Then repeat each word and phrase.

2. **Discover the meaning.** Work with a partner. Find some of the vocabulary words on pages **195–196**. Look at the yellow boxes next to the writing model. Take notes about what you think the words mean.

3. **Learn more.** Listen as your teacher explains the meaning of each word. Take notes and write the meanings of the words you couldn't find. Work with your partner to check and make changes to the meanings you wrote earlier. This will help you understand the meaning of each word.

4. **Show your understanding.** Listen as your teacher reads the questions below. Use your notebook to help you with your answers. Then discuss your answers with a partner.
   - How are transition words used in a persuasive essay?
   - Why do you think it is important to give sound reasons?
   - Does a call to action help persuade the reader? How?

5. **Write it, show it.** In your notebook, you may wish to add synonyms, or words that mean the same thing. Add pictures or drawings to help you remember what each word means. For example, you could write the word *support* and draw a picture of you holding something up.

 ELPS 2C, 2G, 2I, 3D, 3G

Reading the Persuasive Model

What Do You Know?

Next you will read "Polish Your Pearly Whites," a persuasive essay about keeping your teeth clean. Did you know that *pearly whites* is another name for your teeth? Why would you need to polish them? What do you know about keeping your teeth clean?

Build Background

Teeth are an important part of your body. They help you bite and chew food so your body can digest it. If you don't take care of your teeth by brushing and flossing, you may lose them. It is very expensive to get new teeth. When teeth are crooked, braces are used to straighten them so you can bite and chew your food properly.

Listening

Listen as your teacher or a classmate reads "Polish Your Pearly Whites" aloud. As you listen, take notes about the writer's opinion and sound reasons. Taking notes about the important details and responding to questions will help you to understand the writer's purpose.

1. What is the writer's opinion?

2. Name one detail the writer uses to support flossing.

3. What call to action does the writer give in the ending?

Key Persuasive Words and Transition Phrases

advice	follow	for example
in addition	most important	should

Read the words in the box. You will see these words when you read the persuasive essay. With a partner, use the words to talk about ways to keep your body healthy. Then list your ideas in order of importance, from the most important to the least important.

Read Along

Now it's your turn to read. Turn to page 195–196. Read along as your teacher or a classmate reads the writing model aloud. As you read, think about how the writer supports the opinion.

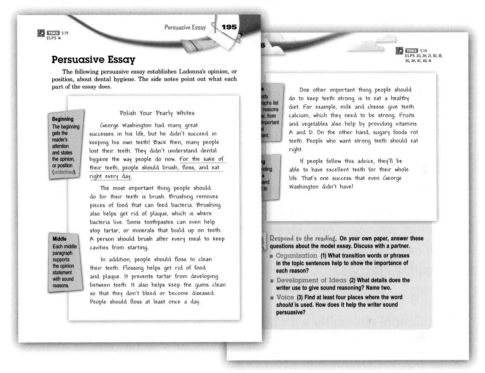

After Reading

Copy the following chart on a sheet of paper and fill it in with the writer's opinion, reasons, and call to action for keeping teeth clean. Use the chart to summarize the writing model with a partner.

Opinion	
Reason 1	
Reason 2	
Reason 3	
Call to Action	

⭐ ELPS 3E, 3G

Oral Language: Persuasive Writing

The person or people who will listen to you or read your writing are called the audience. When you speak or write, it is important to choose just the right words that will reach your audience. The tone you use to express your opinions, ideas, and feelings will be different for each audience.

 Read about the situation below. Then choose two audiences from the list above the picture. With a partner, discuss how the words you choose might be different for each audience.

Situation

You and two classmates have been assigned to write a report about why exercise is good for your health. Your report will express your opinions, ideas, and feelings with sound reasons on how exercise affects your body and why it is an important part of a healthy lifestyle.

Audiences

- School assembly with teachers and principal
- Your parents
- Kindergarten class

ELPS 3E, 3G, 3H

Effective Talk

When you answer a question, you might use a few words, a sentence, or a few sentences. When you use more details to tell about something, your audience will have a better understanding.

Read the question and the answers below. In the first box, there is only one word. In the second box, there is a short sentence that answers the question. The third answer contains more detail and does a better job answering the question.

Why is eating fruits and vegetables healthy for you?

vitamins

They taste good.

Fruits and vegetables are healthy food for your body. Most importantly, they are full of vitamins and nutrients that our bodies need to live. They taste good, too!

Try IT With a partner, identify the transition phrase in the third answer. Then think of two or three more sound reasons why fruits and vegetables are good for you. Add your ideas to the paragraph using transition phrases to connect the ideas. Complete your paragraph by adding an ending sentence that gives the reader a call to action. Read your paragraph aloud to another group.

Language of Response Writing

A response to a text is writing that tells about something the writer has read, and should include evidence from the text. The purpose is to help the reader decide if he or she would like to read the book. This type of writing has a beginning, middle, and ending.

Response Essay Organization

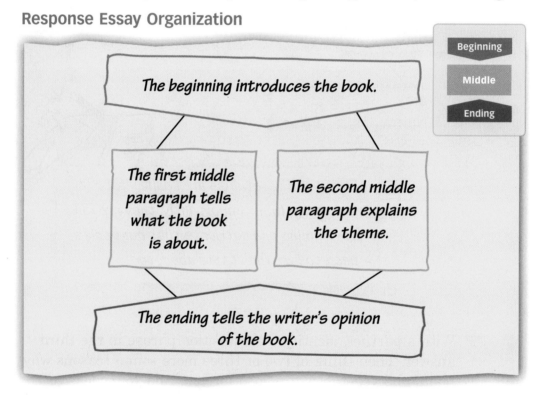

The beginning introduces the book.

Beginning

Middle

Ending

The first middle paragraph tells what the book is about.

The second middle paragraph explains the theme.

The ending tells the writer's opinion of the book.

 Turn and Talk

What book would you recommend to a friend? Why? Talk with a partner.

I would recommend _____ because _____.

ELPS 2C, 2G, 2I, 3A, 3D, 3E, 3G, 3H, 5B

Vocabulary: Response Writing

author	book review	character
fiction	novel	theme

1. **Say the word.** Listen as your teacher reads the words aloud. Then repeat each word. Some words have consonant digraphs. A consonant digraph is two consonants that are together. They stand for one sound such as *th-* in *thin* or *bathtub*. Which vocabulary words have consonant blends? Practice pronouncing these words with a partner.

2. **Discover the meaning.** Work with a partner. Find some of the vocabulary words on pages 256–257. Look at the yellow boxes next to the writing model. Share what you know about the words and write notes about what you think they mean.

3. **Learn more.** Listen as your teacher explains the meaning of each word. Work with your partner to add to your earlier notes on the general meanings of the words. Find examples of these words in the writing model on pages 256–257.

4. **Show your understanding.** Work in a group to answer the questions below. Speak clearly, using the words you learned to share your ideas. Listen carefully to understand the main points expressed by other members of the group.
   - What is one purpose for writing a book review?
   - Name a character you like from a book you've read. Why do you like this character?
   - How can you figure out the theme of a book?

5. **Write it, show it.** In your notebook, draw a scene from a novel that could be the topic of a book review. Write a few sentences about your drawing. Use words from the list.

ELPS 2G, 2H, 2I, 3E, 3G

Reading the Response Model

What Do You Know?

Next you will read *Treasure Island,* a model book review about an adventure novel on pages 256–257. How are adventure stories different from other kinds of novels? What makes adventure stories exciting? Have you ever read one? Tell about it.

Build Background

Long ago, pirates attacked and robbed merchant ships at sea. Sometimes the stolen goods were hidden in caves on nearby islands. Later, the pirates would go back and search for the hidden treasure.

Listening

Listen as your teacher or a classmate reads *Treasure Island* aloud. Then collaborate, or work with others, as you share your thoughts about its meaning. Use the background information to help you understand things about the novel that the writer does not directly state. Then discuss your answers to the questions below.

1. Why is Captain's map important to the story?
2. How does the writer feel about the book? What reasons are given to support this opinion?
3. Does the book review make you want to read the book? Why?

Key Words that Create Interest

adventure	discovers	mysterious
surprised	treasure	valuable

Read the words in the box. You will see these words when you read the writing model. With a partner, use these words to describe an adventure, such as going to a new place or trying a new thing. Discuss how the words make your story interesting and meaningful.

Read Along

Turn to pages 256–257. Read the model essay as your teacher or a classmate reads it aloud. As you read, think about the events in the novel, its theme, and the writer's opinion.

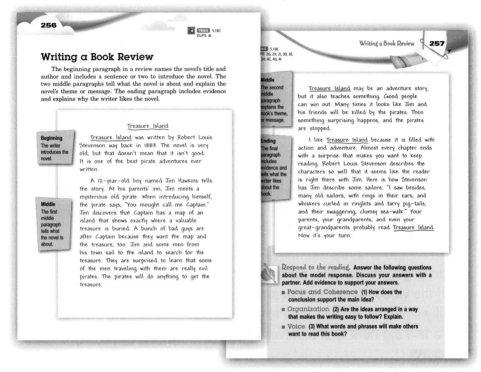

After Reading

When you summarize, you tell the most important points of something you have read. Copy the chart and fill it in. Use your chart to summarize the writing model with a partner.

Treasure Island	
What the book is about	
How the writer felt	

ELPS 3G, 3H

Oral Language: Response Writing

The person or people who will listen to you or read your writing are called the audience. When you speak or write to express ideas and feelings, it is important to choose words that are right for your audience. Your tone, or way of writing, should fit the audience, too.

 Read about the situation below. Then choose two audiences from the list. With a partner, discuss how the words you use to express your ideas and feelings might be different for each audience, depending on their age and experience.

Situation

Respond to the following story. Explain how you connect with the story and the characters in it. What characters interest you? Have you experienced something like this story?

Mario and his friends were bored and looking for something exciting to do on their summer vacation. They already had played all the video games and board games in Mario's house. Suddenly, Billy came up with an idea to go on a scavenger hunt. The group plans a big hunt that involves the entire neighborhood!

Audiences

- **Classmates**
- **Your teacher**
- **Family members**

 **ELPS** 2G, 2I, 3G, 3H

Effective Talk

When you answer a question, you might use a few words, a sentence, or a few sentences. When you use more details to explain something, the other person will have a better understanding.

Read the question and the answers below. In the first box, there is only one word. In the second box, there is a short sentence that answers the question. The third answer contains more detail and does a better job answering the question.

How do you connect with the story?

> *friends*

> *I like hanging out with friends.*

> *I always like hanging out with friends. Sometimes it seems like there is nothing to do, and I feel bored, just like the kids in the story. When I get together with a group of friends, someone always has an idea about fun things we can do.*

Try It Choose a story that you and a partner have both recently read. Talk about why you like the story and what interests you about it. Discuss details you can add to make the answer more complete. Listen carefully and make notes about the details. As you discuss the question together, help each other add more details to better explain your ideas.

⭐ **ELPS** 3D, 3E, 3G, 3H

Language of Creative Writing

Creative writing comes from the imagination. Some creative writing, such as historical fiction, may sound real, but it is not. A fictional story begins by introducing the characters and the setting. The middle, or rising action, presents a challenge for the characters. This challenge, or conflict, rises to a high point, and then the ending shows how the conflict worked out.

Creative Writing Organization

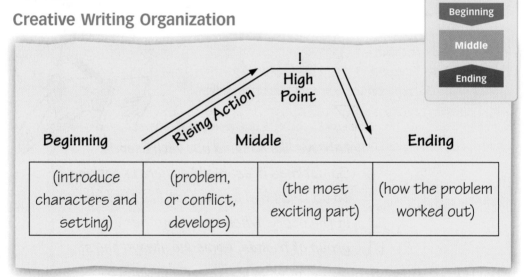

Beginning	Middle		Ending
(introduce characters and setting)	(problem, or conflict, develops)	(the most exciting part)	(how the problem worked out)

 Turn and Talk

Talk with a partner about the parts of this graphic organizer. Share why you think the conflict rises to a high point in a fictional story.

The problem rises to a high point because _____.

⭐ **ELPS** 2C, 2I, 3D, 4C, 5B

Vocabulary: Creative Writing

character	**conflict**	**fiction**
high point	**rising action**	**solution**

1. **Say the word.** Listen as your teacher reads the words aloud. Then repeat each one.

2. **Discover the meaning.** Work with a partner. Find some of the vocabulary words in the yellow boxes on pages 290–291. Take notes about what you think these words mean.

3. **Learn more.** Listen as your teacher explains the meaning of each word. Add to your notes and write the meanings of the words you didn't know. Work with your partner to make changes to the meanings you wrote earlier.

4. **Show your understanding.** Ask and answer the following questions with a partner. Use your notebook to help you. As your teacher reviews the questions, discuss your answers.
   - Can a story that is fiction tell about something that really happened? Why or why not?
   - What is the purpose of the rising action in a story?
   - What happens when the story reaches the high point?

5. **Write it, show it.** Use your notebook. Draw pictures and add notes to help you remember what each word means. For example, for *rising action* you could draw an arrow that points up. Add synonyms, or words that mean the same thing.

 ELPS 2C, 2I, 3E, 3G

Reading the Creative Model

What Do You Know?

Next you will read "My Best Friend, Ben," a story about a boy and his friend, Ben Franklin. What kind of things have you done with a friend? Have you wanted to do one thing when your friend wanted to do another? Was it a problem? How did you solve it?

Build Background

Ben Frankin was an American inventor who discovered electricity. He tied a metal key to the string of a kite and flew it during an electrical storm. "My Best Friend, Ben" is historical fiction.

Listening

Listen as your teacher or a classmate reads "My Best Friend, Ben" aloud. As you listen, take notes about the conflict, or problem between the two boys. Be prepared to answer the questions below. Taking notes and responding to questions will help you understand what happens in the story.

1. What is the conflict?
2. What is the rising action?
3. How is the conflict resolved?

Key Words

cluttered	discover	electricity
genius	meet	resolve

Look at the words in the box. You will see these words when you read "My Best Friend, Ben." "With a partner, use the words to talk about something you and a friend did that started out one way and ended up as another. Tell your feelings about the conflict. How was it was resolved?

ELPS 4C, 4G, 4I

Read Along

Now it's your turn to read. Turn to pages 290–291. Read along as your teacher or a classmate reads the writing model aloud. As you read, think about the conflict and how it is resolved.

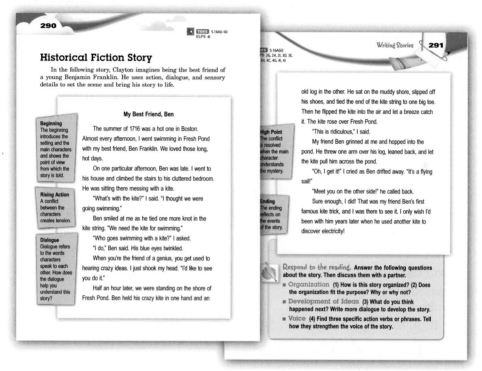

After Reading

Copy the following chart on a sheet of paper. Fill in the chart with the characters, the conflicts they each felt, and the solutions. With a partner, use your charts to orally summarize the writing model. Then tell what each character learned.

Character	Conflict	Solution

 ELPS 3D, 3G, 3H

Oral Language: Creative Writing

The person or people who will listen to you or read your writing are called the audience. When you speak or write, it is important to choose just the right words that will reach your audience. Your tone, or the way you write, will be different for each audience.

 Read about the situation below. Then choose two audiences from the list above the picture. With a partner, discuss how the words you choose for your writing might be different for each audience.

Situation

You went to the museum with your class and saw dinosaur fossils. As you were looking at them, you thought of a story idea about dinosaurs. You find a baby dinosaur and decide to take care of him. But the problem is he keeps getting bigger. What do you decide to do? Tell your story to different audiences.

Audiences

- A kindergarten class
- A group of classmates
- Your teacher

ELPS 3D, 3G, 3H

Effective Talk

When you answer a question, you might use a few words, a sentence, or a few sentences. When you use more details to tell about something, your audience will have a better understanding.

Read the question and the answers below. In the first box, there is only one word. In the second box, there is a short sentence that answers the question. The third answer contains more detail and does a better job answering the question.

What happened when the baby dinosaur grew bigger?

ate

He ate so much I didn't know what to do.

When the baby dinosaur grew bigger, I had to figure out what to do. He couldn't stay in our house any more. I decided to take him where other dinosaurs went for food. Maybe he would stay with them.

 How would you answer the question in blue? Write down two or three ideas and talk about it with a partner. Expressing your ideas will help you decide which ones work best for your answer. Ask your partner what details could be added to help make your answer more complete. Take notes and add the new details. Then say your new answer aloud. Ask your partner if the details help make it a better, more interesting answer.

Language of Research Writing

Research writing is writing that shares facts and conclusions that a writer has reached about a topic. Doing research is a way to find out more about something that interests you. You search through sources, such as books, magazines, and Web sites, and use that information to write a report. Research reports begin with a thesis statement, the main idea. The middle paragraphs support the thesis, and the ending reminds readers about the thesis.

Research Report Organization

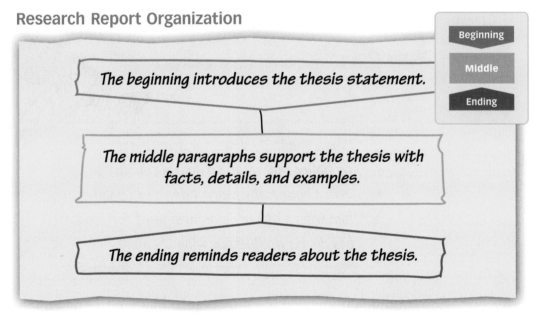

Beginning

Middle

Ending

The beginning introduces the thesis statement.

The middle paragraphs support the thesis with facts, details, and examples.

The ending reminds readers about the thesis.

Turn and Talk

Turn to a partner. Discuss your opinions and ideas about why it is important to begin and end with a thesis statement.

Beginning with a thesis statement is important because _____.

Ending with the thesis statement is important because _____.

⭐ ELPS 2C, 2H, 2I, 4C, 5B

Vocabulary: Research Writing

thesis statement	**evidence**	**summarize**
works cited	**source**	**open ended**

1 **Say the word.** Listen as your teacher reads the words aloud. Then repeat each word.

2 **Discover the meaning.** Work with a partner. Find some of the vocabulary words on pages **326–328**. Look at the yellow boxes next to the writing model. Discuss the words you know and take notes about what you think the other words mean.

3 **Learn more.** Listen as your teacher explains the meaning of each word. Write down the meanings of the words you didn't know. Work with a partner to find examples of some of these words in the writing model on pages **326–328**.

4 **Show your understanding.** Use your notebook to answer the questions below. Your teacher will give you directions. When following directions, listen for action words such as *find* and *write*. Also listen for the vocabulary words.

- What is the purpose of a thesis statement?
- What kind of information can you use as evidence?
- Where do you list your sources, on a works cited page or in a thesis statement?

5 **Write it, show it.** In your notebook, draw pictures that will help you remember what each word means. You may wish to add synonyms, or words that mean the same thing. For example, for *thesis statement* you could write "main idea."

 ELPS 2G, 2I, 3E, 3G, 3H, 4C

Reading the Research Model

What Do You Know?

Next you will read "Daniel Boone, the Explorer," a model research report on pages 326–328. What do you know about Daniel Boone? What other early American explorers can you name?

Build Background

Can you find the Appalachian Mountains on a map? Before 1775, people could not get across these mountains. Most people stayed east of the mountains. After a while, that area became crowded. Daniel Boone and his group of pioneers built the Wilderness Road. They made a Native American trail wider and longer, and they cut through many miles of woods.

Listening

Listen as your teacher or a classmate reads "Daniel Boone, the Explorer" aloud. As you listen, write notes about the thesis statement. Answer the questions below.

1. What is the thesis statement? Retell it using your own words.
2. What is the most interesting fact you learned?
3. What is one source the writer used?

Key Words

exploration	wilderness	pioneer
captured	settlement	population

Read the words in the box. You will see these words when you read the writing model. With a partner, use the words to talk about what it would be like to join Daniel Boone's group. Would you want to explore Kentucky? Would you be afraid of the wilderness? Explain your opinions and feelings in detail.

ELPS 2G, 4G, 4I

Read Along

Read along as your teacher or classmate reads pages 326–328 aloud. Think about the main idea and supporting details.

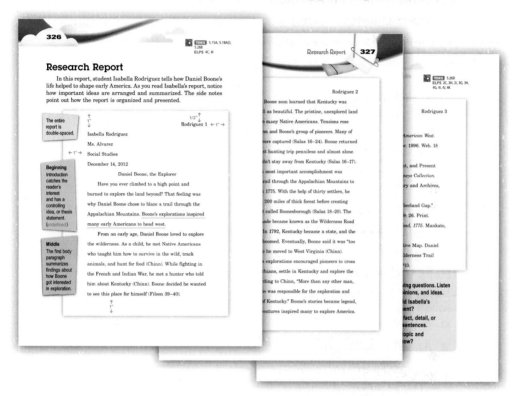

After Reading

Copy this chart on a sheet of paper. Work with a partner to take notes as you read the writing model again. Then use these questions to summarize the report. Your chart will help you remember details.

1. What words describe Daniel Boone's personality?
2. Why did Daniel Boone want to explore Kentucky?
3. What was the most important thing Daniel Boone did?

Early life	Kentucky	The Wilderness Road

Oral Language: Research Writing

The person or people who will listen to you or read your writing are called the audience. When you speak or write, it is important to choose just the right words that will reach your audience. The tone, or the way you write, will be different for each audience.

 Read about the situation below. Then choose two audiences from the list. With a partner, discuss how the words you choose to express your opinions and ideas might be different for each audience.

Situation

Jaguars are powerful hunters that are at the top of the food chain. But they are endangered animals. Why are they endangered? Use a print or online source to find out facts and details that will explain why jaguars are endangered.

Audiences

- A 5-year-old cousin
- An adult who likes animals
- A classmate

Effective Talk

When you answer a question, you might use a few words, a sentence, or a few sentences. When you use more details to tell about something, the other person will have a better idea of what you are talking about.

Read the question and the answers below. In the first box, there is a one word answer. In the second box, there is a short sentence that answers the question. The third answer contains more detail and does a better job answering the question.

Why are jaguars endangered?

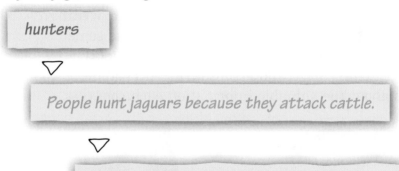

hunters

▽

People hunt jaguars because they attack cattle.

▽

When cattle ranches first appeared in the jaguar's habitat, jaguars began to attack the cattle. Some thought that the population of jaguars grew. To protect their cattle, ranchers began to hire people to hunt jaguars.

 Choose a question to talk about with a partner. Write down a few ideas for answering the question. Add details that will help your partner understand your ideas. As your partner speaks, listen for important details.

1. What makes jaguars such good hunters?
2. Why are jaguar habitats getting smaller?

Using Reference Materials

Sometimes your writing is going well and then you are stumped by how to spell a word. You may notice that you keep repeating the same word over and over. Where can you go for help? How can you add sparkle to your writing?

In this section, you will learn how to use some important reference tools. You will see examples of a dictionary page and a thesaurus entry and learn about the valuable information each contains.

What's Ahead

- **Checking a Dictionary**
- **Using a Thesaurus**

Checking a Dictionary

A **dictionary** is the fastest way to find the meaning of a word. Dictionaries provide the following aids and information.

- **Guide words** These words are listed at the top of each page. They tell the first and last words on that page.

- **Entry words** The entry words are defined on the dictionary page. The most commonly used meaning is usually listed first.

- **Stress marks** A stress (or accent) mark (´) shows which syllable should be stressed when you say a word.

- **Word history** Some words have stories about their origins or how their meanings have changed through the years.

- **Spelling and capital letters** If you don't know how to spell a word, try looking it up by how it sounds. If a word is capitalized, capitalize it in your writing.

- **Pronunciation** A dictionary respells each word phonetically (as it sounds). Special markings are linked to a *pronunciation key*.

- **Synonyms** Synonyms (words with the same or similar meanings) are listed. Antonyms (words with opposite meanings) may also be listed.

- **Parts of speech** A dictionary tells how a word can be used *(noun, verb, adjective)*.

- **Syllable division** A dictionary shows where to divide a word.

Practice

Open a dictionary to any page and do the following:
1. Write the guide words on that page.
2. Write a word that has more than one meaning.
3. Find a word with more than one syllable. Write the word's pronunciation.

Dictionary Page

Guide words ⟶ **dandelion ▸ dangle**

Entry word ⟶ **dandelion** *noun* A plant with bright yellow flowers and long notched leaves that is a common weed. Its leaves are sometimes eaten in salads.
dan·de·li·on (dăn′dl ī′ən) ◊ *noun, plural* **dandelions**

Stress marks

Word history ⟶

Word History

dandelion

Dandelion comes from an old French phrase meaning "tooth of a lion." The leaves of a dandelion have jagged edges that look a little like lions' teeth.

dandruff *noun* Small white flakes of dead skin that are shed from the scalp.
dan·druff (dăn′drəf) ◊ *noun*

Spelling and capital letters ⟶ **Dane** *noun* A person who was born in or lives in Denmark.
Dane (dān) ◊ *noun, plural* **Danes**

danger *noun* **1.** The chance of harm or destruction; peril: *the danger of a cave-in.* **2.** The condition of being exposed to harm or loss: *in danger of falling.* **3.** Something that may cause harm.
dan·ger (dān′jər) ◊ *noun, plural* **dangers**

Pronunciation

Synonyms

Synonyms ⟶ **danger, hazard, risk**

The explorer faced many *dangers* in the jungle. ▶ People who live near active volcanoes face certain *hazards.* ▶ It is a *risk* to swim so far, but if you succeed, you will win a prize.

Part of speech ⟶ **dangerous** *adjective* **1.** Full of danger; risky. **2.** Able or likely to cause harm.
dan·ger·ous (dān′jər əs) ◊ *adjective*

dangle *verb* To swing or cause to swing loosely: *A key dangled from the chain.*
Syllable division ⟶ **dan·gle** (dăng′gəl) ◊ *verb* **dangled, dangling**

Pronunciation key

ă	pat	ĭ	pit
ā	pay	ī	ride
â	care	î	fierce
ä	father	ŏ	pot
ĕ	pet	ō	go
ē	be	ô	paw, for
oi	oil	th	bath
ŏŏ	book	*th*	bathe
ōō	boot	ə	ago, item
ou	out		pencil
ŭ	cut		atom
û	fur		circus

ELPS 4K

Using a Thesaurus

A **thesaurus** is a book of synonyms (words with similar meanings). A thesaurus also lists antonyms (words with opposite meanings). You can use a thesaurus to improve your writing and to expand your vocabulary. A thesaurus helps you . . .

- find just the right word for a specific sentence and
- keep from using the same words again and again.

Thesaurus Entry

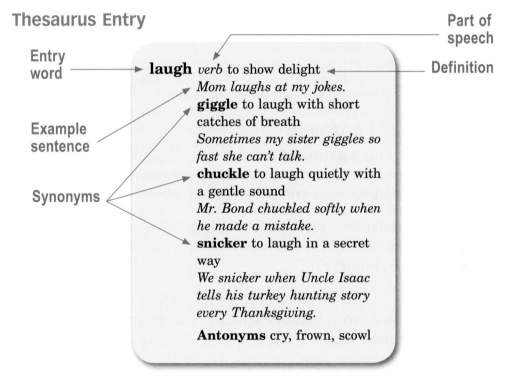

Entry word → **laugh** *verb* to show delight ← **Definition**
Mom laughs at my jokes.
giggle to laugh with short catches of breath
Sometimes my sister giggles so fast she can't talk.
chuckle to laugh quietly with a gentle sound
Mr. Bond chuckled softly when he made a mistake.
snicker to laugh in a secret way
We snicker when Uncle Isaac tells his turkey hunting story every Thanksgiving.

Antonyms cry, frown, scowl

Part of speech

Example sentence

Synonyms

Practice

Use the thesaurus entry above to find the right synonym for *laughed* in the sentence below.

I asked the doorman where the Bronx Hotel was, and he laughed as he politely told me, "You're standing in front of it, son."

⭐ **ELPS** 2C, 2G, 2H, 2I, 3D, 3E, 3G, 3H, 4C, 4G

Basic Grammar and Writing

Learning Language

Work with a partner. Read the meanings aloud and share answers to the questions. Listen to make sure your partner uses complete sentences.

1. A function is what something is used for, its purpose.
   What is the function of a desk? A book? A telephone?

2. If a word is specific, it tells exactly what you mean.
   Which word is more specific, *run* or *scamper*? Explain why.

3. Something personal belongs to a certain person.
   Describe some of your personal belongings.

4. Something is compound if it is made from two or more smaller parts.
   What is an example of a compound word?

Working with Words

Do you look for something to do on a rainy afternoon? Try working on a crossword puzzle. Every day, thousands of people exercise their brains by working on these word puzzles.

Our language includes eight types of words called the parts of speech. The parts of speech are *nouns, pronouns, verbs, adjectives, adverbs, prepositions, conjunctions,* and *interjections.* This chapter will help you learn about the parts of speech and how to use words effectively in your writing. It might help you do crossword puzzles, too!

Mini Index

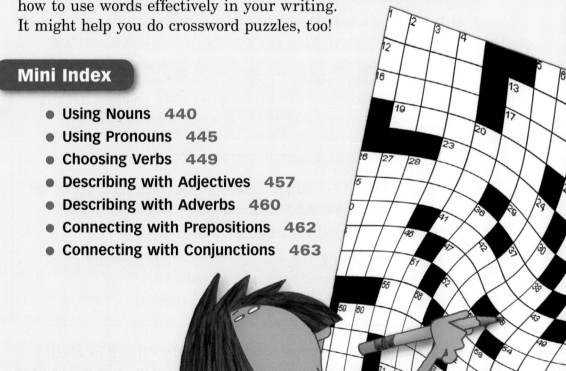

Using Nouns

A **noun** is a word that names a person, a place, a thing, or an idea. (Also see page 604.)

Kinds of Nouns

There are two kinds of nouns. A **proper noun** names someone or something specific. Proper nouns are capitalized. **Common nouns** do not name specific people or things. They are not capitalized.

Proper Nouns	Common Nouns
Josie, Echo Park, Labor Day	girl, park, holiday

Number of Nouns

A **singular noun** names *one* person, place, thing, or idea. A **plural noun** names *more than one* person, place, thing, or idea.

Singular Nouns	Plural Nouns
president, child, airport	presidents, children, airports

Grammar Practice

On your paper, write the noun in each sentence and label it "C" for common or "P" for proper. Add "S" for singular or "PL" for plural.

1. Many books are filled with wonderful journeys.
2. My favorite story is about a girl growing up in Canada.
3. Doris lived with her mother and two sisters.
4. Life was hard, but the children had fun times.

Learning Language Tell a partner about the neighborhood in which you grew up. Ask your partner to write down any nouns you use and tell whether they are common, proper, singular, or plural.

Collective Nouns

A **collective noun** names a group of people, animals, or things. The word *team* is a collective noun. It is a single unit that names a group. Read the paragraph below for examples of collective nouns.

> **Collective Nouns**
>
> A company of actors performed *Wagons West* at our school. My class was invited to attend the play. After the show, the cast answered questions from the audience. It was interesting to learn that the play was based on the diaries of a caravan of pioneers heading west.

Here are some more common collective nouns.

People	Animals	Things
army	army	collection
team	flock	batch
company	herd	bunch
class	pack	clump
public	litter	cluster

tip Some collective nouns can name two different groups, such as a military *army* of men and women or an *army* of ants.

Grammar Practice

With a partner, choose a collective noun for each group below. Together, write a sentence for each collective noun. Then choose another collective noun from the list above and say a sentence.

1. the third graders in Ms. Cata's room
2. the voters in a city
3. the cattle grazing in a pasture
4. five mushrooms growing together
5. fifty saved baseball cards

ELPS 2C, 2G, 2I, 3C, 3E, 4C, 5E

Possessive Nouns

A **possessive noun** shows ownership. An apostrophe is used to show that a noun is possessive. If a noun is singular, an apostrophe and the letter *s* are added to the end of the word. For plural nouns ending in *s*, an apostrophe is placed after the *s*. The possessive form for plurals like *women* or *children* is created by adding an apostrophe and the letter *s*. (See page **536** for more information.)

Singular Possessive Nouns	Plural Possessive Nouns
boy's father (one boy)	**boys' father** (more than one boy)
child's game (one child)	**children's games** (more than one child)

Grammar Practice

For each sentence, write the correct possessive in parentheses.

■ Four *(girl's, girls')* bicycles were parked by the tree. girls'

1. The friends had decided to hike along the *(river's, rivers')* edge.
2. The *(dolphin's, dolphins')* tails splashed when they jumped.
3. My *(grandfather's, grandfathers')* car is spotless.
4. The *(wrestler's, wrestlers')* families cheered them on.
5. In the science contest, my *(friend's, friends')* report won an award for best individual project.

Learning Language Tell a partner about a few things that might be found around your house. Which family member owns each thing? Work together to write sentences about these things. Use possessive nouns.

ELPS 3G, 3H, 5G

How can I improve my writing with nouns?
Use Specific Nouns

Your writing will be more interesting, clear, and precise if you use **specific nouns**. The chart below shows how specific nouns can help you describe things vividly.

General Nouns	Specific Nouns
woman	Harriet Tubman
country	Thailand
car	convertible
emotion	joy

Grammar Practice

Rewrite sentences 1 through 5 twice. Each time, replace the underlined general noun with a more specific one. See the difference specific nouns can make!

■ The <u>man</u> turned and walked away.

   The <u>police officer</u> turned and walked away.
   <u>Our coach</u> turned and walked away.

1. Later that day, Alice walked down the <u>road</u>.
2. I enjoyed the <u>show</u> very much.
3. At recess, Carley got mud on her <u>clothes</u>.
4. Darren studied the <u>material</u> before the test.
5. After school we met at our favorite <u>place</u>.

Learning Language Say a few sentences that tell your feelings about a sport. Have your partner repeat them, replacing any general nouns with specific nouns.

Use Nouns with the Right Feeling

The nouns you include in your writing should have the right feeling, or **connotation**.

Suppose you are writing about a dream that really scared you. The word *dream* may not have a strong enough feeling for this situation. You could look in a thesaurus and find synonyms for *dream* such as *fantasy, illusion,* and *nightmare*. The word with the right feeling is *nightmare* because it means "a frightening dream."

> Don't settle for just any word. Find the word with the right feeling.

Grammar Practice

Choose a synonym to replace each underlined noun below. Pick the word that best describes the feeling of the situation. Use a dictionary if you need help making your choices. Explain to a partner why that word is best. Then work together to say or write sentences using the words that you didn't pick.

■ Our class had disappointed our teacher. The look *(frown, smile, surprise)* on her face told us that everyone was in big trouble. A frown usually shows that someone is mad.

1. Our family visited San Simeon, a huge, showy house *(cottage, mansion, building)* where a rich family lived.

2. My dad wears special steel-toed shoes *(sneakers, boots, clogs)* when he works at dangerous construction sites.

3. I have thought about being a doctor, a job *(profession, trade, position)* that would require years of training.

4. Because of the severe rain *(drizzle, downpour, shower)*, the baseball game was canceled.

Using Pronouns

A **pronoun** is a word used in place of a noun. The noun it replaces or refers to is called the pronoun's **antecedent**. (Also see 610.1.)

The phoenix **is an imaginary beast, but** it **has become a symbol of hope.** (*Phoenix* is the antecedent of the pronoun *it*.)

Personal Pronouns

Personal pronouns are the most common pronouns. (See page 612 for a full list.) Study these words until you know them by sight.

Personal Pronouns						
I	you	he	she	it	we	they
me		him	her		us	them

Person and Number of a Pronoun

Pronouns can vary in person (*first, second,* or *third*) and in number (*singular* or *plural*).

	Singular	Plural
First person (*the person speaking*)	I ride.	We ride.
Second person (*the person spoken to*)	You ride.	You ride.
Third person (*the person spoken about*)	He/She/It rides.	They ride.

Grammar Practice

Work with a partner. Write a sentence using each type of pronoun given below as the subject. Underline the pronoun that is the subject. Then take turns saying more sentences with pronouns as subjects.

■ second-person singular You should sit next to me.

1. third-person singular
2. first-person plural
3. third-person plural
4. first-person singular

TEKS 5.20A(vi)
ELPS 2C, 3C, 4C

Indefinite Pronouns

An **indefinite pronoun** refers to people or things that are not named or known. Some indefinite pronouns are singular, some are plural, and some can be either singular or plural.

Indefinite Pronouns	
Singular	another, something, nobody, neither, either, everybody, everyone, anybody, anyone, no one, somebody, anything, someone, one, each, everything, nothing
Plural	both, few, many, several
Singular or Plural	all, any, most, none, some

When you use an indefinite pronoun as a subject, the verb must agree with it in number.

Singular: Nobody wants the special lunch today.

Plural: Few of us eat breakfast at 6:00 a.m.

When the indefinite pronouns *all, any, more, most, none,* or *some* comes before a prepositional phrase, the pronoun may be singular or plural depending on the meaning in the sentence.

Singular or Plural:
All of the pizza disappears. All of my friends like pizza.

Grammar Practice

Number your paper from 1 to 9. Write a sentence for each indefinite pronoun below. Underline the pronoun and verb. Then pick an indefinite pronoun on this page and use it in an oral sentence with a prepositional phrase. Say your sentence to a partner.

■ everyone Everyone wants an easy math assignment.

1. some
2. many
3. all

4. something
5. both
6. few

7. nobody
8. none
9. someone

TEKS 5.20A(vi)
ELPS 2C, 3C, 3E, 4C, 5D, 5E

How can I use pronouns properly?

Forming the Possessive of Pronouns

Possessive pronouns are used to show ownership. Some of these pronouns can stand alone. Others are used before a noun and function as adjectives.

You found your coat. Where is mine? (*Your* comes before the noun *coat* and functions as an adjective. *Mine* can stand alone.)

My coat is bright red. (*My* functions as an adjective before *coat*.)

> **Possessive Forms of Personal Pronouns**
>
> **my, mine, your, yours, his, her, hers, its, our, ours, their, theirs**

Possessive indefinite pronouns are formed by simply adding an apostrophe and *-s* to the word.

No one's project is graded yet.

I can't remember everybody's name!

Grammar Practice

Number your paper from 1 to 6. Find the numbered possessive pronouns below. If a pronoun is correct, write "C" after the number. If it is incorrect, write the possessive form correctly. Finally, say a sentence using a possessive indefinite pronoun correctly. Share it with a partner.

1. hers

I went to Mrs. Lee's house to see if the gray kitten was
(1) her's. She said that her family loves cats, but this one wasn't
(2) theirs. I wanted to help the kitten find (3) it's home, so I took it
to the next house. The people there said that the kitten wasn't (4)
their's either. Then I checked with Mrs. Brown. She would know if
(5) someone's cat was missing. She said, "That kitten is (6) our's!"

How can pronouns improve my writing?

Avoid Repeating Nouns

Use pronouns so that you don't repeat the same nouns over and over again. This will make your sentences flow more smoothly. Notice how the writer of the paragraph below replaced nouns with pronouns.

John Alden was one of the settlers who came to Cape Cod on

the *Mayflower* in 1620. ~~John Alden~~ ^{He} was hired as a barrel maker for

the voyage. After the ship landed, ~~Alden~~ ^{he} decided to stay rather than

return to England. Priscilla Mullens was a young woman who also

settled in Plymouth Colony. In about 1622, ~~Priscilla~~ ^{she} and Alden were

married. ~~John Alden and Priscilla~~ ^{They} had 10 children, and they became

one of Plymouth's most important families.

Grammar Practice

Rewrite the paragraph below. Change some of the underlined nouns to pronouns so the paragraph will read more smoothly. Then tell a partner about a person who interests you. Make sure to use correct pronouns.

<u>William Bradford</u> was one of the many people who came to Plymouth for religious freedom. <u>William Bradford</u> and his wife, <u>Dorothy</u>, were on the *Mayflower*. Tragically, <u>Dorothy</u> died in Cape Cod Bay. <u>Bradford</u> was selected as a replacement for the colony's leader. From that point on, <u>Bradford's</u> life was linked with Plymouth Colony. <u>Bradford</u> married his second wife, Anne, at Plymouth.

TEKS 5.20A(i)
ELPS 2C, 3G, 4C

Choosing Verbs

A **verb** either shows action or links the subject to another word in the sentence. There are three types of verbs: action verbs, linking verbs, and helping verbs. (Also see page 616.)

Action Verbs

An **action verb** tells what the subject is doing. Always try to use specific action verbs and an active voice to bring life to your writing. Avoid passive verbs such as *are, am, is, was,* and *were.*

General Action Verbs	Specific Action Verbs
Paul left.	Paul disappeared.
Hungry dogs eat food.	Hungry dogs gobble food.
We are hugged by Grandma.	Grandma always hugs us.

> A thesaurus and dictionary will help you find specific action verbs. Be sure you know the exact meaning of a verb before using it.

Grammar Practice

Rewrite each sentence, replacing the general verb with a more specific one. Then work with a partner to tell a story about Kit's adventure. Use an active voice and specific, interesting action verbs in your sentences.

■ The mountain <u>stood</u> over Kit.
  The mountain towered over Kit.

1. She <u>walked</u> through the deep snow.
2. The bitter wind <u>hurt</u> her face.
3. The snow <u>was</u> all around her.
4. The temperature <u>dropped</u> very quickly.
5. Kit <u>looked</u> at her map of the trail.

⭐ ELPS 2C, 2I, 3E, 3G, 4C

Linking and Helping Verbs

A **linking verb** connects a subject to a noun or an adjective in the predicate.

Artichokes are **unusual vegetables.**

(The linking verb *are* connects the subject *artichokes* to the noun *vegetables*.)

Linking Verbs
Forms of the verb *be*—is, are, was, were, being, been, am
Other linking verbs—appear, become, feel, grow, look, remain, seem, smell, sound, taste

Helping verbs come before the main verb and help form verb tenses such as past tense or future tense. (See page **451**.)

We will **eat the artichokes tomorrow.**

Helping Verbs
Forms of the verb *be*—is, are, was, were, being, been, am
Other helping verbs—shall, will, should, would, could, must, can, may, have, had, has, do, did, does

Grammar Practice

Write five sentences using the following linking verbs.

1. is   **2.** were   **3.** become   **4.** look   **5.** smell

Write five sentences using the following helping verbs.

1. are   **2.** will   **3.** would   **4.** have   **5.** did

Learning Language With a partner, take turns saying sentences that use linking or helping verbs. Listen to your partner and add ideas to create a funny story.

TEKS 5.20A(i)
ELPS 2C, 2I, 3E, 4C

Tenses of Verbs

The **tense** of a verb tells *when* the action takes place. Verb tenses may be either simple or perfect. (Also see pages **452** and **618**.)

Simple Tenses

The **simple** tenses include **present, past,** and **future**.

The **present tense** of a verb states an action that is *happening now* or that *happens regularly.*

> I practice multiplication.　　I study for my tests.

The **past tense** of a verb states an action or a state of being that *happened at a specific time in the past.*

> I practiced multiplication.　　I studied for my tests.

The **future tense** of a verb states an action that *will take place.* It needs a helping verb such as *will* or *shall* before the main verb.

> I will practice multiplication.　　I shall study for my tests.

Form the past tense of irregular verbs, like "give," by changing the spelling: "gave."
(See pages 620 and 622.)

Grammar Practice

Number your paper. Identify the tense of each underlined verb below.

■ I <u>like</u> to visit my uncle in Arizona. present
1. He <u>invites</u> us every year.
2. Next summer we <u>will spend</u> an entire week with him.
3. Last time we <u>visited</u> the Hopi Reservation near Flagstaff.
4. Huge, flat mountains, called mesas, <u>rise</u> above the flat land.

Learning Language Say a sentence in the past, present, or future, and have a partner identify the verb tense. Listen to your partner's sentence.

Perfect Tenses

The **perfect tenses** include **present perfect**, **past perfect**, and **future perfect**. (See page 618 for more information.)

The **present perfect tense** states an action that *began in the past but is still happening*. The helping verb *has* or *have* is added before the past-participle form of the main verb.

Derek has practiced **his cello every day this week.**

The **past perfect tense** states an action that *began and was completed in the past*. The helping verb *had* is added before *practiced*, the past-participle form of the main verb.

He had practiced **for an hour yesterday.**

The **future perfect tense** states an action that *will begin in the future and end at a specific time*. The helping verbs *will have* are added before *practiced*, the past-participle form of the main verb.

By concert time, he will have practiced **enough.**

Grammar Practice

Number your paper from 1 to 4. Identify the tense of each underlined verb below. Then write another sentence using the same tense.

■ Our band teacher, Mr. Huan, has planned this concert for months. *present perfect*

1. We have practiced the music for "Peter and the Wolf."
2. A month ago, we had asked our principal to read the script.
3. She has performed the spoken part many times.
4. After this concert, she will have narrated the piece five times.

Learning Language **With a partner, take turns sharing a musical experience. Speak carefully and use at least three perfect tense verbs. If you hear an error, let your partner know.**

TEKS 5.20C
ELPS 2G, 3E, 4C, 5D

How can I use verbs correctly?

Number of a Verb

Make sure that the subjects and verbs in your sentences agree in number. If you use a singular subject, use a singular verb (with an *s*). If you use a plural subject (with an *s*), use a plural verb. (See 620.3.)

Subject-Verb Agreement

The chart below shows how subject-verb agreement works.

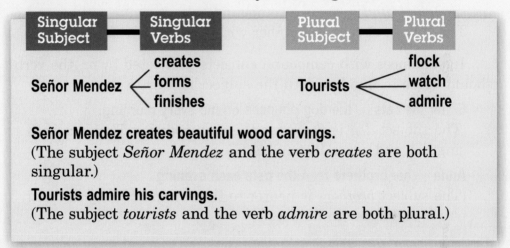

Singular Subject	Singular Verbs		Plural Subject	Plural Verbs
Señor Mendez	creates, forms, finishes		Tourists	flock, watch, admire

Señor Mendez creates beautiful wood carvings.
(The subject *Señor Mendez* and the verb *creates* are both singular.)

Tourists admire his carvings.
(The subject *tourists* and the verb *admire* are both plural.)

Grammar Practice

Match each subject below with the best verb. Make sure the subject and verb agree in number. Then write a sentence for each subject-verb pair. Check that the subject and verb agree in each sentence.

Subjects: cats   Lila   coach   vegetables

Verbs: complains   sleep   contain   instructs

Learning Language Talk with a partner about a favorite sport or activity, paying attention to subject-verb agreement. Ask questions if you hear something that you don't understand.

 **TEKS** 5.20C
ELPS 2C, 2G, 3C, 3E, 4C, 5D

Agreement in Sentences with Compound Subjects

In sentences with compound subjects connected by *and*, the verb should be plural.

Latrelle, Michael, and Jason sing well together.
(*Latrelle, Michael, and Jason* is a compound subject connected by *and*. The subject agrees in number with the plural verb *sing*.)

Spaghetti and tacos are my favorite foods.
(*Spaghetti and tacos* is a compound subject connected by *and*. The subject agrees in number with the plural verb *are*.)

In sentences with compound subjects connected by *or,* the verb should agree in number with the subject nearer to it.

Either the cats or the dog pounces on me every morning.
(The subject *dog* is nearer to the verb *pounces*. They are both singular and agree in number.)

Anna or her brothers feed the pets each evening.
(The subject *brothers* is nearer to the verb *feed*. They are both plural and agree in number.)

Grammar Practice

Match each compound subject below with a verb that agrees in number. Write a sentence for each pair and tell it to a partner.

Compound Subjects	Verbs
Rosa and Pasha	plans
diet and exercise	make
assistants or the head coach	eat
brother or sisters	improve

Learning Language Talk with a partner about your favorite foods. Listen for subject-verb agreement, especially in compound subjects. Correct sentences with errors.

Agreement in Compound Sentences

In a compound sentence, each verb should agree in number with its subject. The subject and verb before the conjunction should agree in number. The subject and verb after the conjunction should also agree in number.

Pay attention to subject-verb agreement as you read the sentences below.

> **Scientists worry** that some plants may become extinct, so a seed bank preserves those seeds.
> (*Scientists* and *worry* are both plural; *seed bank* and *preserves* are both singular.)

> The vault in the world's largest seed bank contains over one billion seeds, but many wild plants still face extinction.
> (*Vault* and *contains* are both singular; *plants* and *face* are both plural.)

 Don't get confused by words that separate the subject and the verb. Cross them out if necessary.

Grammar Practice

Write each sentence. Choose the verb that agrees with the subject.

1. The seeds (*comes, come*) from endangered plants, so some (*is, are*) very rare.

2. Dr. Smith (*collects, collect*) seeds in the United States, and she (*stores, store*) them in a seed bank in Oregon.

3. The air in the vaults (*is, are*) very cold and dry, so Dr. Smith and her helper (*wears, wear*) coats and gloves as they work.

Learning Language Work with a partner to say three compound sentences about the work scientists do. Make sure that each verb agrees in number with its subject.

⭐ **ELPS** 2C, 2H, 2I, 3E, 3G, 3H, 4C

How can I improve my writing with verbs?

Share the Right Feeling

Strong action verbs create clear word pictures for the reader. The feeling, or **connotation,** of a verb should fit the picture you want to create. For example, in the sentence below, the verb *walks* suggests "moving at a normal pace." Substitute each synonym below and notice how the feeling of the sentence changes each time.

John walks through the park.

Synonym	Definitions
strolls	to walk slowly, in a relaxed way
strides	to walk briskly, with long steps
trudges	to walk very slowly, with effort
struts	to walk in a very confident, showy way
stomps	to walk with heavy, aggressive steps
hobbles	to walk with difficulty, usually because of pain

Make sure the connotation, or feeling, of a word clearly matches the picture you want to create for your reader.

Grammar Practice

Write a sentence using the verb *smile.* Rewrite the sentence twice, using a new synonym for *smile* in each sentence. Share your sentences with a partner. Explain how each verb changes the connotation of the sentence. Repeat the exercise with the verbs *see* and *run.*

Describing with Adjectives

An **adjective** is a word that describes a noun or a pronoun. An adjective tells what kind, how much, how many, or which one. The adjectives *a, an,* and *the* are called **articles.** (See page 624.)

Example Adjectives			
What kind?	woolly **socks**	blue **eyes**	Chinese **cabbage**
How many? How much?		six **eggs**	full **glass**
Which one?	that **girl**	these **notes**	this **problem**

Proper and Common Adjectives

Proper adjectives (in red) are formed from proper nouns and are always capitalized. **Common adjectives** (in blue) are any adjectives that are not proper.

A Chicago **pizza has a** thick **crust and** spicy **sausage.**

Grammar Practice

Number your paper from 1 to 7. List the adjectives, including articles, that you find in each line. There are 32 adjectives.

1   Every year, our city has a street fair with food from around
2   the world. I like starting with *samosas*, Indian pastries that are
3   crispy on the outside and savory on the inside. Our next stop is
4   Japanese food. My dad loves fresh sushi, but my favorite thing is
5   the soba noodles with their tasty soy and citrus sauce. We never
6   forget the local Italian restaurant, which serves delicious, cheesy
7   pizza. I save just a little room for dessert, sweet Cuban plantains!

Tell a partner a sentence with a common adjective and a proper adjective. Write down the adjectives from your partner's sentence. Then write a new sentence that uses those words.

 **TEKS** 5.20A(iii)
ELPS 2C, 3C, 3E, 4C

Forms of Adjectives

Use the **comparative form** of an adjective to compare two things. Use the **superlative form** to compare three or more things. For most one-syllable adjectives, add *-er* for the comparative form and *-est* for the superlative form. (See page 626.)

Positive	Comparative	Superlative
hot	hotter	hottest

Comparative: **It's hotter today than yesterday.**

Superlative: **Tomorrow is predicted to be the hottest day of the week.**

 Place *more* or *most* in front of most multi-syllable adjectives to form the comparative and superlative forms.

Positive	Comparative	Superlative
amazing	more amazing	most amazing

Comparative: **Today's episode was more amazing than yesterday's.**

Superlative: **Ants are the most amazing insects on earth.**

Grammar Practice

On your own paper, write the correct form of each adjective.

I took my three cousins to their baseball game. My (1. young) cousin, Kyle, wore a mitt that was (2. big) than he was. He also wore a smile that was even (3. wide). The star player on the other team came up to bat. He is the (4. strong) hitter in the league. He slammed the first pitch. It was (5. loud) than thunder. The ball soared into left field, and Kyle caught it to make the last out in the inning. Kyle's catch was the (6. exciting) part of the game up to that point. When Kevin, one of my other cousins, came to bat, he drove in two runs. His double was the (7. important) hit in the inning.

Then think of a sentence using *taller* and another sentence using *tallest*. Tell your sentences to a partner.

How can I improve my writing with adjectives?

Use Specific Adjectives

Adjectives need to be specific in order to create interesting and clear word pictures for the reader. Some adjectives like *good* and *nice* should be avoided because they are overused. When you see one of these adjectives, replace it with a better word.

> **Overused adjectives**
>
> good, neat, big, pretty, small, cute, fun, bad, nice, dumb, great
>
> I get a good feeling when I think of my grandmother's house.
> I get a cozy feeling when I think of my grandmother's house.

Grammar Practice

Write each of the following sentences twice. Each time, replace the overused adjective (underlined) with an adjective that is more specific.

1. That was a good lunch!
2. The poster looks bad.
3. My mom makes nice sweaters.
4. This is a great apple.

Include Sensory Details

Effective adjectives often appeal to the senses. Each adjective below helps you *see, hear, smell,* and *feel* an autumn day.

> The October sky was framed by the glowing, golden leaves. The air smelled musty from the powdery leaves that crunched beneath my feet. Swirling winds blew in gusts, and the crackling chatter of the dry leaves drowned out any other sound.

Grammar Practice

Describe to a partner your favorite kind of day. Use adjectives that help your partner see, hear, smell, and feel the experience.

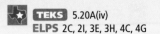 **TEKS** 5.20A(iv)
ELPS 2C, 2I, 3E, 3H, 4C, 4G

Describing with Adverbs

An **adverb** is a word that describes a verb, an adjective, or another adverb. An adverb usually tells how, when, where, how often, or how much. (For more information, see page 628.)

Kim runs daily **to get into shape.**
(The adverb *daily* tells how often. It describes the frequency.)
I can scarcely **hear you over the crowd's cheering.**
(The adverb *scarcely* tells how much. It describes the intensity.)

Forms of Adverbs

Adverbs come in three different forms: **positive, comparative,** and **superlative.** For most one-syllable adverbs, add *-er* to make the comparative form and *-est* to make the superlative form.

Positive	Comparative	Superlative
late	later	latest

Comparative: **Pepe goes to bed** later **than his sister does.**
Superlative: **He goes to bed** latest **on Saturday night.**

tip Place the word *more* or *most* in front of most multi-syllable adverbs to form the comparative and superlative forms.

Positive	Comparative	Superlative
often	more often	most often

Comparative: **Jordan wins races** more often **than Ellie does.**
Superlative: **He races** most often **in 100-yard dashes.**

Learning Language Tell a partner sentences using the comparative and superlative forms of *cheerful*. Then write a paragraph about a weekend activity using the words *usually* and *almost*. Read your paragraph aloud and have a partner retell it.

How can I improve my writing with adverbs?

Describe Actions

Use adverbs to help describe the action in a sentence. Remember that adverbs often end in *-ly*.

Sentence without an adverb:
We squeezed through the subway door before it closed.

Sentence with an adverb:
We barely squeezed through the subway door before it closed.
(The adverb *barely* makes the action clearer. It tells how much.)

Grammar Practice

Write four interesting sentences using the adverbs listed below. Each adverb should help describe the action in the sentence.

■ gladly   I gladly gave Steve some of my sunflower seeds.

1. quickly   **2.** constantly   **3.** smoothly   **4.** carefully

Modify Adjectives

Also use adverbs to make the meaning of adjectives clearer and more exact in a sentence.

Sentence without an adverb: **That writer's stories are scary.**

Sentence with an adverb: **That writer's stories are sometimes scary.**

(The adverb *sometimes* makes the meaning of the adjective *scary* more exact. It tells how often.)

Grammar Practice

Tell your partner four sentences using the adverbs listed below. Each adverb should make the meaning of an adjective more exact.

■ often   Little children are often noisy.

1. always   **2.** extremely   **3.** very   **4.** uncomfortably

★ **TEKS** 5.20A(v)
ELPS 2C, 3E, 4C, 4F

Connecting with Prepositions

A **preposition** introduces a prepositional phrase. A prepositional phrase usually provides details to show location, time, or direction.

My dog scampered under **the bed.** (The preposition *under* introduces the prepositional phrase *under the bed*, which shows location.)

I do my homework after **school.** (The preposition *after* introduces the prepositional phrase *after school*, which shows time.)

The children ran toward **the school.** (The preposition *toward* introduces the phrase *toward the school*, which shows direction.)

A **prepositional phrase** includes a preposition, the object of the preposition (a noun or a pronoun), and any modifying words.

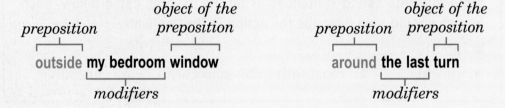

preposition	*object of the preposition*		*preposition*	*object of the preposition*
outside	my bedroom window		around	the last turn

modifiers   *modifiers*

Grammar Practice

Tell a partner the prepositional phrases in the sentences below. Then create two sentences using prepositional phrases from the sentences. Write them down and share them with your partner.

■ Thuan broke his leg during the game. during the game

1. He was rushed to the emergency room in the hospital.
2. A doctor took X-rays of his leg.
3. Thuan and the doctor waited for the results.
4. A nurse put ice on Thuan's injured leg.
5. The doctor applied a temporary cast on the leg.
6. After a few weeks, the leg will be ready for a more permanent cast.

TEKS 5.20A(vii)
ELPS 2C, 3C, 4C, 5F

Connecting with Conjunctions

A **conjunction** connects individual words or groups of words.

The river is wide and deep.

(The conjunction *and* connects the words *wide* and *deep*.)

We can take the ferry or walk across the bridge.

(The conjunction *or* connects the phrases *take the ferry* and *walk across the bridge*.)

Kinds of Conjunctions

There are three kinds of conjunctions. (Also see page 634.)

Coordinating

Coordinating conjunctions (and, but, for, nor, so, yet) connect equal words, phrases, or clauses:

Anita cleaned the yard, and Luis washed the car.

Correlative

Correlative conjunctions are used in pairs (either/or, neither/nor) to connect words or groups of words:

Either they got tired, or they ran out of time.

Subordinating

Subordinating conjunctions (after, although, because, when) introduce the dependent clauses in complex sentences: (Dependent clauses cannot stand alone as sentences.)

After the two stopped, they had something to eat.

Grammar Practice

Write sentences using the following conjunctions. Then make up a new sentence for each conjunction and tell it to a partner.

1. but   **2.** either/or   **3.** because   **4.** and   **5.** while

 **TEKS** 5.20A(v), 5.20A(vii)

ELPS 3C, 3E, 5F

How can I use prepositions and conjunctions?

Add Information

You can use prepositional phrases to add useful information.

Without prepositional phrases: **Ben reads many books.**

With prepositional phrases: During study time, **Ben reads many books** about space exploration.

Grammar Practice

Make each of the sentences more informative by adding one or more prepositional phrases. Share your new sentence with a partner.

1. Justin threw the football.
2. Claudia played her favorite song.
3. The clerk answered my question.

Connect Short Sentences

You can use conjunctions to combine short sentences. Combining short sentences will help your writing read more smoothly.

Two short sentences: **The marching band performed at Rockville. The drill team stayed home.**

The two sentences combined: Although **the marching band performed at Rockville, the drill team stayed home.**

Grammar Practice

Combine each pair of sentences using the conjunction in parentheses.

1. *(but)* Jason loves music. Sondra's favorite class is math.
2. *(because)* We can't play hockey. The pond isn't frozen.
3. *(either/or)* You can have an apple. You can have an orange.

Learning Language With a partner, take turns saying four new sentences using the conjunctions *while, if, or,* and *neither/nor.*

Building Effective Sentences

A sentence is like a railroad track. If the track is incomplete or damaged, the train can't get through. In the same way, if a sentence is incomplete or incorrect, the idea can't get through—it won't make sense to the reader.

Writing complete, correct sentences will put your ideas on the right track. This chapter will show you how to build effective sentences.

Mini Index

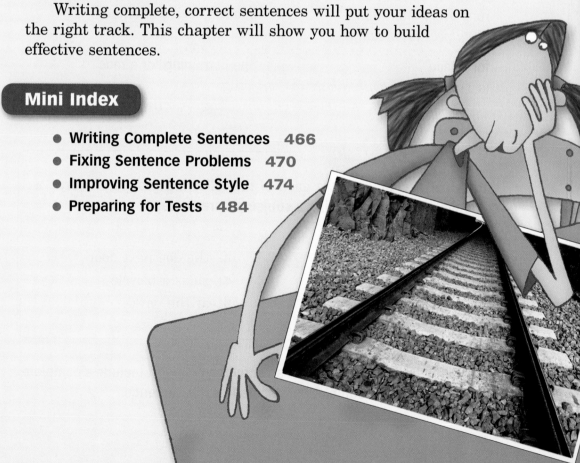

 **TEKS** 5.20B
ELPS 2C, 3E, 4C, 4F, 5F

Writing Complete Sentences

A **complete sentence** is a group of words that expresses a complete thought.

How can I make sure my sentences are complete?

A sentence must have a **subject**, which tells who or what is doing something. A sentence must also have a **predicate**, which tells what the subject is doing or what is being done to the subject.

Incomplete Thought	Complete Sentence
My cousin Jillian *(a predicate is missing)*	**My cousin Jillian runs.**
runs every afternoon *(a subject is missing)*	**She runs every afternoon.**
for a race *(a subject and a predicate are missing)*	**She is training for a race.**

Grammar Practice

With a partner, orally make each of the following groups of words a complete sentence by adding a subject, a predicate, or both.

■ in the summer
 I play baseball in the summer.

1. run around the yard

2. my little brother

3. the dog next door

4. rides a bicycle

5. at the park

Write NOW Write five sentences about an activity you enjoy. Include a complete subject and a complete predicate in each sentence.

TEKS 5.20B
ELPS 2C, 2G, 2H, 3C, 3E, 3H, 4C

Complete Subjects and Predicates

The **complete subject** in a sentence includes the simple subject and its modifiers. The **complete predicate** includes the simple predicate (the verb) and its modifiers.

Complete Subject	Complete Predicate
Who or what is doing something?	*What is being done?*
Our new bus driver	likes to tell jokes.
Janelle and I	planned the class picnic.
The noise in the background	spoiled the concert.
Mr. Cosford, our neighbor,	is very friendly.

Grammar Practice

Copy sentences 1 to 5. Draw a line between the complete subject and the complete predicate in each sentence. Then say to a partner a new sentence with a complete subject and predicate.

■ The members of my team visited the hospital yesterday.

The members of my team | visited the hospital yesterday.

1. A volunteer in a blue uniform showed us around.
2. Another person gave each of us a first-aid booklet.
3. The surgery room was the most interesting place.
4. We asked some good questions afterward.
5. My teammates and I learned about sports medicine.

Learning Language Create five sentences about a trip you took. Make sure each sentence has a complete subject and a complete predicate. Say your sentences to a partner.

ELPS 2C, 2G, 2H, 2I, 3F, 4C

Simple Subjects and Predicates

A **simple subject** (shown in orange) is the subject without the words that describe or modify it. A **simple predicate** (shown in blue) is the verb without any of the other words that modify it.

Simple Subject	Simple Predicate
My friend Jan	bought her ticket at the door.
The entire audience	waited patiently.
We	cheered.

Sometimes the simple subject or predicate serves as the complete subject or predicate. (We cheered.)

Grammar Practice

Rewrite the following sentences. Underline the simple subject with one line and the simple predicate with two lines.

■ The school cooks announced a new menu.

The school <u>cooks</u> <u>announced</u> a new menu.

1. Hungry students choose from a large variety of foods.
2. The school copied the idea from food courts.
3. Most students prefer healthful foods to junk food.
4. Salads are a popular choice.
5. Nutritious snacks give students energy.

Learning Language Tell your partner a few sentences about your school lunch program or the lunch you bring to school. Ask your partner to identify the simple subject and the simple predicate in each sentence.

Compound Subjects and Predicates

A **compound subject** includes two or more simple subjects. A **compound predicate** includes two or more simple predicates. The simple subjects (in orange) and the simple predicates (in blue) are shown in each sentence below.

Compound Subject	Compound Predicate
Harry and Lana	caught and released three fish.
My brother and my cousin	sing and dance in the musical.
Tim and Colin	ran outside and played soccer after dinner.

> Compound subjects or compound predicates are usually joined by "and," "but," or "or."

Grammar Practice

Write these sentences. Underline each subject with one line and each predicate with two lines. Use two or three of the words you underlined to write a new sentence with a compound subject and predicate.

■ Jake and Elijah gathered and packed their fishing gear.

  Jake and Elijah gathered and packed their fishing gear.

1. Their uncle took them to Blue Lake and rented a boat.
2. The fish and the mosquitoes always bite.
3. The boys caught the fish and slapped the mosquitoes.
4. The uncle and his nephews joked and laughed a lot.
5. The small boat rocked and rolled in the choppy water.

Learning Language Tell your partner about an outdoor activity. Use a compound subject or a compound predicate in each of your sentences.

Fixing Sentence Problems

How can I be sure my sentences are correct?

One way to check your sentences for correctness is to look for **fragments**, or incomplete sentences. A fragment is an incomplete sentence that is missing a subject, a predicate, or both.

Fragment	Sentence
Eats chips with dip.	Saul eats chips with dip.
Many people.	Many people like salty chips.
Not a healthful snack.	Salty chips are not a healthful snack.

Practice

Write "C" for each complete sentence and "F" for each fragment below. Rewrite each fragment to make it a complete sentence. Tell your new sentences to a partner.

■ Got back from the skating rink.
  F | We got back from the skating rink.

1. My little sister was ready for dessert.
2. Maurice and his friends after school.
3. Close to the end of class.
4. Ling and her puppy won the grand prize.
5. All the other dogs.

> A fragment is part of a sentence, but it doesn't express a complete thought.

Write NOW Write five sentences about a favorite snack. Be sure your sentences are complete and punctuated correctly.

Check for Run-On and Rambling Sentences

Run-on sentences are two or more sentences that run together. One type of run-on is called a *comma splice* because the sentences are connected incorrectly (spliced together) with a comma.

Rambling sentences occur when several sentences are connected with coordinating conjunctions such as *and, or,* and *but.*

Incorrect Sentence	Corrected
Run-On (Comma Splice): The pet show was fun, the crowd loved Jenn's friendly dog, Brenna.	The pet show was fun. The crowd loved Jenn's friendly dog, Brenna.
Rambling: I knew that Maya's parrot would get an award and I also thought that Lem's cat would win something but I was not so sure that Jenn's dog would do well.	I knew that Maya's parrot would get an award, and I also thought that Lem's cat would win something. I was not so sure that Jenn's dog would do well.

Check your sentences for too many conjunctions.

Practice

Rewrite this rambling sentence. Keep any necessary conjunctions.

> Tara's monkey jumped on David's shoulder and his dog, Kip, started barking and the monkey jumped on Kip's back and Kip began to turn in circles trying to get the monkey off his back.

Learning Language Tell your partner about something funny that happened to you. Don't use any rambling or run-on sentences. Listen for places to pause.

 **TEKS** 5.20C
ELPS 3C, 3E, 5D

Watch for Subject-Verb Agreement

Make sure that the subjects and the verbs agree in the sentences you write. When you use a singular subject, use a singular verb. When you use a plural subject, use a plural verb.

Singular Agreement	Plural Agreement
That girl loves tap dancing.	Those girls love ballet.
My watch ticks softly.	The boys' watches tick loudly.
Anna creates dried flower art.	Anna and Lily create dried flower art.
Dad cooks while Mom bakes.	Mom and Dad cook while we bake.

Most nouns ending in "s" or "es" are plural.
Most verbs ending in "s" are singular.

Grammar Practice

Rewrite each sentence with the subject or verb that agrees with the underlined words. Then write two new sentences, one simple and one compound. Make sure the subjects and verbs agree.

■ My <u>mother</u> (*think, thinks*) we need an air purifier. thinks

1. <u>She</u> (*say, says*) that clean air is important.
2. (*We, My brother*) <u>agree</u> that it's a good idea.
3. Our <u>dog</u> and <u>cat</u> (*raises, raise*) a lot of dust.
4. The (*window, windows*) <u>get</u> very dirty, too.
5. The <u>carpets</u> (*is, are*) new, but <u>they</u> still (*collect, collects*) dust.

Learning Language Tell a partner about a housekeeping job. Use three simple sentences and a compound sentence. Use both singular and plural subjects. Make sure the subjects and verbs agree.

Avoid Double Negatives

A **double negative** is an error that occurs when you use two negative words in the same sentence. Double negatives change the meaning of your ideas and should be avoided.

Negative Words

barely	hardly	neither	never	nobody
none	not	nothing	nowhere	

Contractions that end in *n't*, meaning "not," are also negative words.

can't	couldn't	didn't	don't
hadn't	shouldn't	won't	wouldn't

> Since a contraction like "can't" is already negative, don't use it with another negative word.

Grammar Practice

Rewrite the paragraph below, correcting the double negatives you find. (Hint: There are four of them.)

■ Hardly nobody showed up for the party.

Hardly anybody showed up for the party.

Allie was upset that very few people came to her party. She hadn't never thrown a party before, and she had worked really hard. There wasn't nothing missing, or so she thought. Then she found a pile of invitations in a desk drawer. She hadn't never sent them out. Allie won't never make that mistake again!

Learning Language Tell a partner about a funny mistake you once made. Hide a double negative in your story and ask your partner to identify and correct it.

Improving Sentence Style

How can I add variety to my writing?

Here are five ways to improve your writing by adding variety to your sentences.

1. **Try different kinds of sentences.**

2. **Use different types of sentences.**

3. **Combine short sentences.**

4. **Expand sentences by adding words and phrases.**

5. **Model sentences other writers have created.**

Sentences Lacking Variety

I love going to pick apples. We go to an orchard in autumn. I like Jonathans the best. My brother likes Macintoshes. Mom chooses Granny Smiths. The best part is when we get home. We make apple pies and applesauce. We also make caramel apples. It's a tasty time of year.

Sentence Variety Improved

I love going to pick apples in an orchard in autumn. My favorite apples are Jonathans, my brother likes Macintoshes, and my mom prefers Granny Smiths. Do you know what the best part is? When we get home, we make apple pies, applesauce, and caramel apples. It's a tasty time of year!

> Adding variety to your sentences is a simple way to add style to your writing.

TEKS 5.18A(iv)
ELPS 2C, 3F, 4C, 4G, 5G

Try Different Kinds of Sentences

You can use four kinds of sentences to add variety and punch to your writing.

Kinds of Sentences

Declarative .	Makes a statement about a person, a place, a thing, or an idea	I am looking forward to the movie.	This is the most common kind of sentence.
Interrogative ?	Asks a question	Can we get there in time?	A question gets the reader's attention.
Imperative . or !	Gives a command	Find your glasses.	Commands often appear in dialogue or directions.
Exclamatory !	Shows strong emotion or feeling	Oh no, we'll never get there in time!	These sentences emphasize a point.

Practice

Number your paper. Punctuate each sentence and label it "DEC" for declarative, "INT" for interrogative, "IMP" for imperative, or "EX" for exclamatory. Then say a new sentence to a partner. Ask your partner to identify what kind of sentence it is.

■ Do you want to see that movie on Saturday night? INT

1. It should be really funny and our friends will be there
2. Are you listening to the radio
3. Quiet down for one minute until the song ends
4. We'll leave in an hour if everyone is ready
5. You are so sure about the answer

Write NOW On your paper, write a paragraph describing a movie. Use at least one of each kind of sentence. Read your paragraph aloud to a partner.

 **TEKS** 5.18A(iv), 5.20C
ELPS 2C, 3C, 3H, 4C

Use Different Types of Sentences

There are three types of sentences: **simple**, **compound**, and **complex**. Use all three types to add variety to your writing.

Use Simple Sentences

A **simple sentence** is one independent clause. It has a subject and a predicate and expresses a complete thought.

Simple Sentences	
Single subject with single predicate	Mount Saint Helens **erupted violently in 1980.**
Single subject with compound predicate	**The** volcano **rumbled and** spewed **ash.**
Compound subject with compound predicate	Scientists **and** photographers watched **and snapped** pictures.

Practice

Copy the sentences below. In each sentence, underline each simple subject once and each simple predicate twice. Then tell a partner a simple sentence using correct subject-verb agreement.

■ The United States and Canada boast a number of volcanoes.

The United States and Canada boast a number of volcanoes.

1. Volcanoes and earthquakes tell us about the Earth.
2. However, they seldom erupt.
3. Mount Saint Helens rumbled and then exploded.
4. Geologists and other scientists measure volcanic activity.

Write NOW Write four simple sentences that describe a storm or flood that happened in your area. Include compound subjects and predicates, and check for subject-verb agreement.

TEKS 5.18A(iv), 5.21B(i)
ELPS 2C, 4C, 5B 5F, 5G

Form Compound Sentences

A **compound sentence** is made up of two or more simple sentences joined together. One way to join simple sentences is by using a comma and a coordinating conjunction *(and, but, or)*.

> At the zoo, my sister Wanda rode a camel, **and** I took her picture.
> My brother fed the seals, **but** I preferred just to watch.
> Next, we can go to the lion house, **or** we can watch the monkeys.

In a compound sentence, the coordinating conjunction often separates two different ideas.

Practice

Work with a partner to combine the pairs of sentences below. Rewrite the sentences, using the coordinating conjunction in parentheses. Add a comma before the connecting word, or conjunction.

■ My parents planned a trip. They asked us for ideas. *(and)*
My parents planned a trip, and they asked us for ideas.

1. Wanda wanted to go to the desert. I'm not fond of hot weather. *(but)*

2. Nevada is beautiful. It is one day's drive from home. *(and)*

3. We could hike up Mount Washington. We could reach the top by car. *(or)*

4. Dad said we could see for miles from the peak. The top of the mountain was covered with clouds. *(but)*

Write NOW **Write about a place you have visited. Include simple sentences and at least three compound sentences. Be sure to punctuate your compound sentences correctly. Share your work with a partner.**

Create Complex Sentences

A **complex sentence** contains one independent clause and one or more dependent clauses. A dependent clause contains a subject and a verb, but it does not express a complete thought. A dependent clause often begins with a subordinating conjunction like *because* or *although*. (See page **634** for more on subordinating conjunctions.)

COMPLEX SENTENCE =

A Dependent Clause	+	An Independent Clause
After the rain stopped,		the air smelled fresh and clean.

An Independent Clause	+	A Dependent Clause
We were amazed at the rainbow		when the sun came out.

Use a variety of sentence structures to add interest.

 Practice

Number your paper from 1 to 5. Find the dependent clause in each of the following sentences, and write it on your paper.

■ Because the storm brought strong winds, damage was heavy.
   Because the storm brought strong winds

1. We walked to the park after it was dark.
2. Since the power went out, the streetlights haven't worked.
3. City workers tried to clean up, although it was hard to see.
4. When we saw branches on the ground, we picked them up.
5. We became very hot while we worked.

 Write NOW **Write a short paragraph about a time when you experienced the power of nature. Then revise your draft to include at least two compound and two complex sentences.**

Combine Short Sentences

Use Key Words and Phrases

One way you can combine short, choppy sentences is by moving a key word or phrase from one sentence to another.

Short Sentences	Combined Sentences
My shoes are red. They are <u>new</u>. *(The key word is underlined.)*	**My new shoes are red.** *(The adjective* new *has been moved to the first sentence.)*
We play volleyball. We play <u>on sand courts</u>. *(The prepositional phrase is underlined.)*	**We play volleyball on sand courts.** *(The prepositional phrase has been moved to the first sentence.)*

Practice

On your own paper, combine the pairs of short sentences in numbers 1 to 5 below. Move a key word or phrase from one sentence to the other.

■ Alberto hit a long drive. He hit it to left field.

   Alberto hit a long drive to left field.

1. Anne got a new sweater. The sweater is made of wool.
2. Dimitri's jacket is new. His jacket is leather.
3. Our cat curls up. He curls up on our couch.
4. Jerome cleans his bedroom. He cleans it on Saturdays.
5. The child slid down the slope on an inner tube. The child was squealing.

Learning Language Describe your favorite item of clothing to a partner in two or three short sentences. Ask your partner to combine the sentences aloud.

 ELPS 3E, 4C, 5F

Use a Series of Words or Phrases

Sentences can be combined using a key word or phrase. Sentences can also be combined using a **series of words or phrases**. All the words or phrases in a series should be parallel—stated in the same way—and punctuated with commas. (See **526.1**.)

Short Sentences	Combined Sentences
Children like to ride bicycles. They ride skateboards, too. Other children ride scooters.	Children like to ride bicycles, skateboards, and scooters.
Ellie had paint in her hair. She had it on her clothes. She had it under her fingernails.	Ellie had paint in her hair, on her clothes, and under her fingernails.

Practice

Combine each group of sentences with a series of words or phrases. (Some words may need to be changed to make the sentences work.)

■ The fifth-grade boys get exercise by climbing the monkey bars. They play kickball. They run around the schoolyard.

The fifth-grade boys get exercise by climbing the monkey bars, playing kickball, and running around the schoolyard.

1. The fourth-grade girls play volleyball at recess. The fifth-grade girls play volleyball at recess. The sixth-grade girls play volleyball, too.

2. When it rains, we enjoy working on jigsaw puzzles. We read books. Some of us do art projects.

3. The huge green gumball rolled out of Breanne's pocket. It rolled down the aisle. It went under the teacher's desk.

 Write NOW Write three sentences for a classmate to combine. Make sure your sentences can be combined using a series of words or phrases.

Combine Sentences with Compound Subjects and Predicates

Sometimes you can combine two sentences by moving a subject or a predicate from one sentence to another. This creates a **compound subject** or a **compound predicate**. (See page 469.)

Short Sentences	Combined Sentences
I raked the leaves. I piled them high.	I raked the leaves and piled them high. (a compound predicate)
Conall jumps in the leaves. Katie jumps in the leaves, too.	Conall and Katie jump in the leaves. (a compound subject)

Combining short sentences can make your writing smoother and easier to read!

Practice

Combine each of the short sentences below. Create a compound subject or a compound predicate. Continue the story by telling a partner two more sentences with compound subjects or predicates.

■ The gym filled quickly. The gym rang with excitement.
  The gym filled quickly and rang with excitement.

1. The players laughed as they changed. They joked, too.
2. Coach blew his whistle. He told the team to go into the gym.
3. The crowd cheered. They yelled for their team.
4. Referees added to the noise. Cheerleaders added to the noise.
5. Our team played well. We won the game.

TEKS 5.20A(v)
ELPS 2C, 3C, 3E, 4C

Expand Sentences with Prepositional Phrases

A **prepositional phrase** can provide details or add important information about location, time, or direction. Prepositions include *on, in, above, at, with, for, until, toward,* and *under.* (Also see page 632.)

Prepositional Phrases

I looked for my glasses. (Where did I look?)
I looked for my glasses on Dad's desk **and** under my bed.

> Prepositional phrases can add details to your sentences.

Practice

Write down the prepositional phrases you find in the sentences below. Say new sentences to a partner using the phrases you found.

■ I left my permission slip on the table in the hall.
on the table, in the hall

1. We will hike through the forest.
2. The lake lies at the bottom of the valley.
3. We have reservations at the campground.
4. At night, we sleep on cots in the cabins.

Write **NOW** **Use one or two prepositional phrases to add details or information to each of the sentences.**

1 Salvador will join the camping trip.
2 He brought a sleeping bag.
3 We're leaving.

Model Sentences

Artists learn to paint by studying the works of other artists. You can learn to write effective sentences by studying or modeling the work of professional writers. **Modeling** is following a writer's use of words, phrases, and punctuation in sentences of your own.

Professional Model	Student Model
Walking through the woods, I listened to the wind, and I pulled my coat tighter around my body.	Rushing toward school, I heard the call of my friends, and I shifted my backpack more comfortably across my shoulders.

Guidelines for Modeling

- **Varying Sentence Beginnings**

  Try starting sentences with a dependent clause or a phrase.
  Perhaps if people talked less, **animals would talk more.**
  —Charlotte's Web by E. B. White

- **Moving Adjectives**

  Sometimes you can vary a sentence by placing an adjective or two after the noun it modifies.
  And because it was autumn, the leaves were lovely colors, orange-red, reddish-orange, deep yellow.
  —Afternoon of the Elves by Janet Taylor Lisle

- **Repeating a Word**

  You can repeat a word to emphasize a particular idea or feeling.
  The baying of the hounds grew nearer, **then still** nearer, nearer, **ever** nearer.
  —The Most Dangerous Game by Richard Connell

Practice

Write three sentences of your own, modeled after the examples above. Follow the pattern of the original sentence as closely as you can.

Preparing for Tests

How can I check my sentence knowledge?

Read the following questions. Select the correct answers.

1 **Which sentence is complete?**
Ⓐ He saw the doctor and took the medicine.
Ⓑ The cough and the runny nose and sneeze.
Ⓒ Missed school for one week.
Ⓓ His teacher and the principal and his parents.

2 **Which sentence has the comma in the correct place?**
Ⓐ What is the first, thing you will do?
Ⓑ Next, the cat will have to be fed.
Ⓒ He didn't, eat all the food in his dish.
Ⓓ I think that the cat, was ill.

3 **In which sentence does the subject agree with the verb?**
Ⓐ Those classes joins the team every year.
Ⓑ Mrs. Smith like her students to participate.
Ⓒ She encourage her entire class to sign up for an event.
Ⓓ They always win a ribbon for best student participation.

4 **You are writing about getting a new pet. Which sentence best helps the reader picture your pet?**
Ⓐ On the way to the pet store, the traffic was horrible.
Ⓑ There were puppies, kittens, and birds in the first room.
Ⓒ Our kitten looks like a little tiger with white paws.
Ⓓ We could hardly wait to get home with our pet.

5 **Which sentence is correct?**
Ⓐ Climbed the hill, ran all the way down, and got on her bike.
Ⓑ Laughed at the ending and read it again.
Ⓒ The fifth graders finished the project before it was due.
Ⓓ Was the time for everyone to try their best.

Writing Paragraphs

A paragraph is a group of sentences sharing details about one specific topic. The first sentence in a paragraph usually identifies the topic, or main idea, and the other sentences give details and facts about it.

Here are four main reasons to write a paragraph.

1. **Describe** someone or something.
2. **Share** an event or an experience.
3. **Explain** or give information about a topic.
4. **Give your opinion** about something.

Mini Index

ELPS 2G, 3G, 3H, 4I, 4K

The Parts of a Paragraph

A paragraph has three main parts. (1) It begins with a **topic sentence** that states the main idea. (2) The sentences in the **body** share details about the main idea. (3) The **closing sentence** sums up the paragraph's message.

Topic Sentence

Body

Closing Sentence

Roughing It

During the winter, the Korth family in Alaska lives almost totally off the land. Much of their time is spent setting trap lines for pelts. They also hunt caribou and moose for meat. Meat is stored outside because the temperature stays below freezing. In addition, the family members either break through the ice on a river for water, or they melt snow. They live in a small, one-room cabin that is heated by wood that they cut. If there is an emergency, someone in the family will write a huge message in the snow, in hopes that an airplane pilot will see it. Few people are able to live the way this family does.

Respond to the reading. (1) What is the main idea of this paragraph? (2) Which details stand out the most? (3) How does the title fit the paragraph? Discuss with a partner.

A Closer Look at the Parts

The Topic Sentence

The **topic sentence** tells the reader what the paragraph is about. An effective topic sentence (1) names the topic and (2) states an important detail or feeling about it.

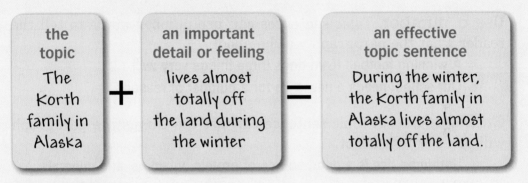

the topic
The Korth family in Alaska

+

an important detail or feeling
lives almost totally off the land during the winter

=

an effective topic sentence
During the winter, the Korth family in Alaska lives almost totally off the land.

The Body

The sentences in the **body** include the information the reader needs in order to understand the topic.

- **Use specific details.** The following sentences include specific details (in blue):
  Much of their time is spent setting trap lines for pelts. **They also** hunt caribou and moose for meat. Meat is stored outside **because the** temperature stays below freezing. **In addition, the family members either** break through the ice on a river for water, **or they** melt snow.

- **Organize the sentences.** The sentences in the paragraph on page 486 are organized in a logical order. (See pages 490–491 for other methods of organization.)

The Closing Sentence

The **closing sentence** sums up the information in the paragraph or reminds the reader of the topic.
    Few people are able to live the way this family does.

Writing Strong Topic Sentences

An effective paragraph starts with a strong topic sentence. Remember that a topic sentence should (1) name the topic and (2) state an important detail or feeling about it. Use the following strategies to help you write topic sentences. (See page 502 for more strategies.)

Use a number. Topic sentences can use number words to tell the reader what the paragraph will be about.

- A winning football team does three things very well.
- Our school needs a new gym for a number of reasons.

Create a list. A topic sentence can list the things the paragraph will cover or talk about.

- Unrefined rice is a good source of protein, vitamins, and minerals.
- Before any test, review your assignments, re-read any handouts, and study your notes.

Start with "to" and a verb. A topic sentence that starts with "to" and a verb clearly introduces the paragraph's topic.

- To guard a great shooter, a defender must keep totally focused.
- To appreciate what immigrants went through, visit Ellis Island.

Join two ideas. A topic sentence can combine two ideas by using a comma and a coordinating conjunction: *and, but, or, for, so, nor, yet.*

- Our coach wants morning practices, but many players don't like the idea.
- Lewis and Clark did reach the Pacific Ocean, yet their trip was not easy.

Practice

Reread the information above and write a topic sentence using each of the four strategies listed. Share your sentences with a partner.

Using Different Levels of Detail

The sentences in the body, or middle part, of a well-written paragraph usually contain at least three levels of detail.

Level 1: Topic Sentence The topic sentence tells what the paragraph will be about. The closing sentence sums up the ideas.

> Ms. Burke taught me how to plant lettuce and radish seeds early in the year.

Level 2: Supporting Sentences The second level of detail supports the topic sentence or makes it clearer.

> The key is to plant the seeds just below the surface.

Level 3: Completing Sentence The third level of detail completes the supporting idea.

> That way, they will be warmed by the sun.

tip The graphic below shows you how the different levels of details would be arranged in an effective paragraph.

> Ms. Burke taught me how to plant lettuce and radish seeds early in the year. The key is to plant the seeds just below the surface. That way, they will be warmed by the sun. Also, Ms. Burke used some fast-growing seeds and some slow-growing seeds. She said this would make the garden come up sooner and last longer. Ms. Burke and I can't wait to taste our first salads!

The **topic sentence** connects to the **closing sentence**.

Practice

Write a topic sentence about a way to earn money. Add at least one supporting sentence and one or two completing sentences. Share your sentences with a partner. Discuss the purpose of each level of detail.

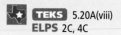

TEKS 5.20A(viii)
ELPS 2C, 4C

Organizational Patterns

The sentences in your paragraph must be organized so that the reader can follow your ideas. Some common organizational patterns are *logical order, time order, order of location,* and *order of importance.*

Logical Order

Use a **logical order** in expository paragraphs to organize your details in a way that makes the best sense. The following paragraph from page 486 is organized in this way.

> During the winter, the Korth family in Alaska lives almost totally off the land. Much of their time is spent setting trap lines for pelts. They also hunt caribou and moose for meat. Meat is stored outside because the temperature stays below freezing. In addition, the family members either break through the ice on a river for water, or . . .

Transitions to use with logical order

also   therefore   in fact   in addition   another   for example

Time Order

Use **time order** in narrative or expository paragraphs to organize details in the order in which they happened.

> Our class play about the Aztecs came to a surprise ending. During the big moment, Cortés and his soldiers were waiting for Montezuma II. Then the Aztec leader arrived. After the two leaders exchanged greetings, Cortés suddenly drew his sword.

Transitions to use with time order

during   next   second   then   soon   third   after   first   finally

TEKS 5.20A(viii)
ELPS 2C, 2G, 3E, 4C

Order of Location

Use **order of location** in descriptive paragraphs. The details can be arranged from left to right, front to back, and so on.

> In the old photograph, my great-great-grandmother's dark hair is twisted high on top of her head. Under it, her face looks very serious, with dark eyes and no smile. She is wearing a long black dress. Beneath the hem of the dress appear her narrow black boots.

Transitions to use with order of location

on top of   beside   inside   beneath   under   in front of   between   over

Order of Importance

Use **order of importance** when writing persuasive and expository paragraphs. Arrange the details from the most important to the least important—or the other way around.

> Students should be able to choose their school clothes rather than wear uniforms. For one reason, allowing students to wear regular clothes saves money. For another reason, giving students a choice says, "We trust you." Most importantly, having a choice makes students more responsible.

Transitions to use with order of importance

for one reason   for another reason   most importantly   in addition

Practice

Write a paragraph using one of the organizational patterns shown on these two pages. Use some of the transitions for that type of organization. With a partner, choose another organizational pattern and say a few sentences. Don't forget to use transitions!

ELPS 4C, 5G

Writing Guidelines

Prewriting Selecting a Topic

Often, your teacher will give you a *general subject area* to write about. Then it will be your job to select a *specific topic* that truly interests you. Look around you for inspiration—at words on books, signs, and advertisements. (See page **497** for topic ideas.) Here are the ideas Julio came up with.

General subject area	Specific topic
an unforgettable experience	winning an art contest
the circulation system	measuring your heart rate
the Oregon Trail	guide Jim Bridger
a health issue	people should wear bike helmets
a natural wonder	the Grand Canyon

Gathering and Organizing the Details

Collect details about your topic using the following information.

For a . . .	you'll need . . .
descriptive paragraph	details showing how the topic looks, sounds, feels, tastes, and smells.
narrative paragraph	details about an experience—how it began, continued, and ended.
expository paragraph	details that give information or explain the topic.
persuasive paragraph	facts and examples that support your opinion.

After you've gathered your details, write a topic sentence that states the main idea of your paragraph. (See pages **487–488.**) Also decide on the best way to organize the details. (See pages **490–491.**)

Drafting Creating Your First Draft

When you write your first draft, your goal is to get all your ideas on paper. Start with your topic sentence. Then write the supporting and completing sentences in the body of your paragraph. Make sure to organize these sentences in the best order. End with a closing sentence that sums up the paragraph's message. (See page **489**.)

Revising Improving Your Paragraph

Use the following questions as a guide when you begin revising your paragraph.

1 Is my topic sentence clear?

2 Have I included the important details in the best order?

3 Do I sound interested in the topic?

4 Do I use specific nouns and action verbs?

5 Do I vary my sentence lengths?

6 Do my sentences read smoothly?

Editing Checking for Conventions

Carefully edit your revised paragraph for conventions using these questions as a guide.

1 Do I use correct punctuation and capitalization?

2 Do I use the correct word (*to, too,* or *two*)?

3 Do I spell words correctly? Have I used my spell-checker?

Practice

Plan and write a paragraph that explains something about a remarkable person. Refer to the paragraph on page 486. Use the writing guidelines on these pages as a guide. Discuss your paragraph with a partner.

ELPS 2C, 2G, 2H, 2I, 3E, 3G, 3H, 4C, 4G

A Writer's Resource

Learning Language

Work with a partner. Read the meanings aloud and share answers to the questions.

1. A genre is a form of writing.
   What genre of writing do you prefer, narrative or expository? Why?

2. A graphic organizer such as a chart or diagram is a visual way to express ideas and information.
   Tell about a graphic organizer that helped you understand something.

3. Writers who get stuck can't think of new ideas.
   If you get stuck, how do you find new ideas?

4. A transition is a change from one idea to another.
   What words can signal a transition in writing?

A Writer's Resource

Writers sometimes get stuck and need a little help. Finding a good topic to write about or looking for just the right word can be challenging. If you're in class when questions come up, you can ask your teacher for help. What happens, though, when you're somewhere else, like at home?

This chapter is a great place to find answers to your questions! When you can't find a topic, you aren't sure how to organize your details, or your sentences sound boring—look here for help.

Mini Index

You will learn how to . . .

How can I find a good topic to write about?

Try a Topic-Selecting Activity

If you get stuck, try one of the topic-selecting activities below.

Clustering Begin a cluster by writing a word connected with your assignment in the middle of a piece of paper. Then write related words around it. Circle and connect the words. (See the cluster on page **498**.)

Freewriting With your general topic in mind, write freely for 3 to 5 minutes. Do not stop to make corrections or look up facts—just write. As you freewrite, you may find one or two topics you could use.

Environmental Print Use signs for restaurants or shops, advertisements, and warning signs you see in the real world to help you brainstorm topic ideas. Choose a topic that interests you.

Sentence Completion Another way to develop ideas is to complete a sentence starter in as many ways as you can. Make sure that your sentence starter relates to your assignment. Here are some samples:

I remember when . . .	I wonder how . . .
One thing I know about . . .	I just learned . . .

"Basics-of-Life" List

Look at the list below for possible topic areas. Here's how to use the "Basics-of-Life" list. (Also see page **138**.)

1. Choose a topic category. *(environment)*

2. Decide what part of this subject fits your assignment. *(report on oceans)*

3. List possible subjects. *(farming algae and pearls)*

animals	school	clothing	sports	food
friends	community	family	faith	environment
health	computers	games	rules	books
movies	science	exercise	money	television

What else can I do to get started?

Choose a Writing Form

Remember to select the form, or genre, that best fits your assignment. The following topics are organized according to the four basic forms of writing. Look through these lists to find topic ideas.

Descriptive Writing

People: a relative, a teacher, a friend, a neighbor, yourself, someone you spend time with, someone you admire, someone from history

Places: a room, a garage, a basement, an attic, a rooftop, the alley, the gym, the library, a museum, a lake, the zoo, a barn, a park

Things: a pet, a cartoon, a video game, a junk drawer, a photograph, a favorite possession, a Web site, a stuffed animal

Narrative Writing

Tell about . . . getting caught, getting lost, making a mistake, helping someone, being surprised, making the news, learning to do something

Expository Writing

How to . . . make a burrito, care for a pet, organize your life, earn money, get in shape, be a good friend, eat a balanced diet, saddle a horse

The causes of . . . pollution, rust, hurricanes, infections, success in school, happiness, accidents, volcanoes

Kinds of . . . music, commercials, clouds, heroes, clothes, restaurants, fun, books, games, animals, houses, vehicles

The definition of . . . friendship, courage, a hero, geology, rap, freedom, love, a team, family

Persuasive Writing

Issues: school rules, homework, recycling, helmets (bicycle, skateboard), things that need to be improved, favorite causes, pet peeves, something that deserves support, a need for more or less of something

How can I collect details for my writing?

Try Graphic Organizers

A graphic organizer is a good way to gather and organize details for writing. Use a **5 W's chart** (page **79**) for a personal narrative or a news story and a **Venn Diagram** for comparison-contrast writing. Four more graphic organizers are shown on these two pages. See which one works best for you.

Cluster A cluster or web will help you gather facts and ideas for reports, narratives, and poems. Begin by writing the subject in the middle of the page. Then list related words around it. Circle and connect your words.

Personal Narrative: A Trip to a Water Park

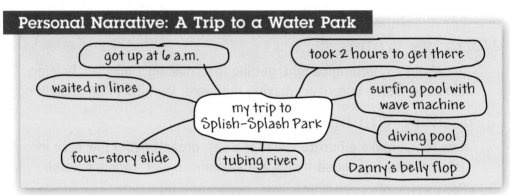

got up at 6 a.m.

took 2 hours to get there

waited in lines

surfing pool with wave machine

my trip to Splish-Splash Park

diving pool

four-story slide

tubing river

Danny's belly flop

Sensory Chart This organizer will help you collect details for observation reports and descriptions. Make a chart with five columns— one for each sense. Under each sense, list your details.

Observation Report: Growing Baker's Yeast

Sight	Sound	Smell	Taste	Touch
– tan – thick and puffy – bubbles pop slowly	– little "poof poof" sounds	– like bread baking – a bit like vinegar	– sour, not sweet	– cold – wet

Time Line Time lines organize events in chronological (time) order. Personal narratives and how-to essays often follow this pattern. Write the topic at the top of your time line. Then list the events or steps in order, from first to last.

How-To Essay: Feeding a Cat

1 — Buy two heavy bowls—one for water, one for food.
2 — Buy cat food that is dry and nutritious.
3 — Place food and water away from litter pan.
4 — Fill each bowl twice a day.

Process Diagram Science-related writing often tells how events are connected. To make a process diagram, start with the first event in the process. Then write the second event, the third event, and so on. Connect the events with arrows.

Science Report: How Water Boils

1. Heat transfers from stove to pot of water. → 2. Water circulates in pot.

4. Water boils when whole pot reaches 212 degrees. ← 3. Water heats evenly.

5. Boiling water changes from liquid to vapor (steam).

TEKS 5.15B
ELPS 4C, 4F

How can I organize my details effectively?

Put Ideas in Order

After you choose your topic and collect your details, you need to organize your information. First, decide on an order and then make an outline. Here are three ways to put your information in order.

Time Order

It's easy to follow ideas when the facts or events are explained in the order in which they happened *(before, during, after)*. Time order works for stories, explanations, directions, and reports.

> First, we used a rope to raise the wood up into the tree. Next, our parents helped us make a frame for the floor. After we nailed boards to the frame, we put up the walls and roof.

Order of Location

When details are described in the order in which they are located *(above, behind, beneath, beside),* the description usually goes from left to right or from top to bottom. Order of location works well in directions and descriptions.

> The trunk of our tree-house tree is so wide that I can't reach my arms around it. The patterns in the bark seem to crawl up the tree, and the tips of its branches reach for the sky.

Order of Importance

News stories are often organized by order of importance. The most important detail usually comes *first,* but it may come *last.* Persuasive and expository writing can also be organized in this way.

> All kids need a place to call their own, and a tree house is the perfect place. It is a place to get away from televisions, computers, and little brothers and sisters. Most importantly, a tree house is a place to just hang out with your friends.

Build a Topic Outline

After you have decided how to organize your details, you can write an outline. First, you need to select the main points that support your topic. Then, under each main point, list the details that help explain it. A *topic outline* contains only words and phrases, but if you want to express your ideas in complete sentences, you can write a *sentence outline*.

Topic Outline

   I. Daniel Boone's early adventures
       A. Moved often
       B. Fought in French and Indian War
       C. Got interested in Kentucky
  II. Famous as Kentucky explorer
       A. Several trips from 1767 to 1774
       B. Blazed the Wilderness Trail
       C. Started Boonesborough
 III. Kentucky beautiful but dangerous
       A. Hunting and warring ground
       B. French and British opposition
       C. Settlers often attacked

Sentence Outline

   I. Daniel Boone had many adventures.
       A. He moved often when he was young.
       B. He fought in the French and Indian War.
       C. He became interested in Kentucky.
  II. Boone became a famous Kentucky explorer.

TEKS 5.15A
ELPS 5F, 5G

How can I write effective topic sentences?

Try a Special Strategy

A **topic sentence** gives the main idea of a paragraph. A good topic sentence (1) names the topic and (2) states a detail, idea, or feeling about it. The following strategies will help you write terrific topic sentences.

Use a Number

Use number words to tell what the paragraph will be about.

> **Here are three reasons why our class should serve a meal at the homeless shelter.**

> **I'm having several problems training our new puppy.**

Create a List

Create a list of the things that the paragraph will include.

> **Trees add beauty to nature, give shelter to wildlife, and make shade for people and plants.**

> **The setting of a story is the time and the place it happens.**

Use Word Pairs

Use conjunctions that come in pairs to connect ideas in a topic sentence.

> **Either keep dogs on a leash or keep them in fenced yards.**

> **My doctor said that both a balanced diet and regular exercise are needed to stay healthy.**

> **Word Pairs**
> either . . . or
> not only . . . but also
> both . . . and
> whether . . . or

Quote an Expert

Quote someone who knows something about your topic.

> **Walt Disney once said,** "All our dreams can come true."

> **Amelia Earhart said,** "It is easier to start something than it is to finish it."

TEKS 5.15A
ELPS 2C, 4C

What forms can I use for my writing?

Try These Forms of Writing

Finding the right form, or genre, for your writing is very important. When you choose a form, think about *who* you're writing for (your *audience*) and *why* you're writing (your *purpose*). Listed below are a few different forms of descriptive, narrative, expository, and persuasive writing.

Autobiography	The story of the writer's own life.
Biography	The story of someone else's life.
Book Review	Writing that shares your thoughts and feelings about a book (See pages **255–270**.)
Descriptive Writing	Writing that uses details to help the reader clearly imagine a certain person, place, thing, or idea (See pages **50–67**.)
Essay	A piece of writing in which ideas are presented, explained, argued, or described in an interesting way
Expository Writing	Writing that explains by presenting the steps, the causes, or the kinds of something (See pages **128–187**.)
Narrative Writing	Writing that relates an event, an experience, or a story (See pages **68–127**.)
Persuasive Writing	Writing that is meant to persuade the reader to agree with the writer about someone or something (See pages **188–249**.)
Short Story	A short piece of literature with only a few characters and one problem or conflict (See pages **288–295**.)

TEKS 5.15C
ELPS 5G

How can I create an effective voice?

Make Your Voice Fit Your Purpose and Audience

Your writing will have an effective voice if it fits your purpose. Write with your purpose in mind, and think about your readers.

Descriptive Voice

A good descriptive voice sounds *interested*. One way to improve your descriptive voice is to follow this rule: "*show,* don't *tell.*"

- **Telling:** Here a writer tells what a mongoose is like.

  He was a mongoose, and he looked sort of like a cat and sort of like a weasel. He ran around a lot and made a strange noise.

- **Showing:** Here the author Rudyard Kipling describes a mongoose in a story from *The Jungle Book*:

  He was a mongoose, like a little cat in his fur and his tail but like a weasel in his head and his habits. He could scratch himself anywhere he pleased with any leg. . . . His war cry as he scuttled through the long grass was *Rikk-tikk-tikki-tikki-tchk!*

Narrative Voice

A good narrative voice sounds *natural* and *personal*. Your narrative writing should sound as if you are telling a story to a friend.

- **Unnatural and Impersonal:** This narrative sounds too dull.

  Last Saturday I couldn't find Moses, my pet ferret. I gave up looking and went to bed. Later I woke up. Moses was hiding in my bed.

- **Natural and Personal:** Here is the same story told in a more personal voice.

  Last Saturday I couldn't find Moses, my pet ferret. I was afraid he had run out the back door, so I looked for him for hours. Finally, I gave up and went to bed. At about midnight, I woke up because something was licking my toe. I screamed and threw off the covers! You guessed it—Moses had found a warm place to hide in my bed.

Expository Voice

An expository voice should sound *well-informed* and *enthusiastic*. Use interesting facts and specific details to get and hold your reader's attention.

- **Uninterested:** This writer simply presents the facts.

  Seaweed is sometimes served as a vegetable. Seaweed is also used in many foods. Some of the foods are ice cream, hot fudge, and stir-fry.

- **Well-informed and enthusiastic:** This writer sounds truly interested.

  Have you ever had a long strand of seaweed wrap around your leg at the beach? Don't panic—it's not going to eat you! You have probably eaten several forms of seaweed, however. Some kinds of ice cream and hot fudge use seaweed to make them creamy. Seaweed is also served as a vegetable. Your favorite stir-fried food may contain some of the delicious green stuff!

Persuasive Voice

A persuasive voice should sound *convincing* and *positive*. Support your opinion with good reasons and positive solutions.

- **Unconvincing and negative:** This writer simply complains and offers no solutions.

  Monday mornings are awful. My brother and I have to get up early and go to school while we're still sleepy. The teachers aren't very happy, either. Why doesn't someone do something about Monday mornings?

- **Convincing and positive:** This writer has a more positive attitude and proposes a solution.

  Wouldn't it be great if our class did something that was fun every Monday? I think our class should have a Monday Morning Talent Show. That would be one way to put the teachers and students in a good mood for the rest of the week.

TEKS 5.16A(ii), 5.16A(iii), 5.16B(ii)
ELPS 2C, 4C, 5G

How can I spice up my writing style?

Use Writing Techniques

You can develop a lively writing style by using some special effects. For example, you can add dialogue to your stories or poems to make them sound more natural and real. (See pages **82** and **290–291**.) Below are additional techniques you can experiment with in your own writing.

Exaggeration Overstating the truth to make a point
> **Gramps is** the funniest man in the world.

Idiom Using a word or phrase in a way that is different from its usual or dictionary meaning
> **Maha and Jake** ironed out **their problems.**
> (In this sentence, *ironed out* means "solved.")
> **My sister and I don't** see eye to eye **about how to clean our room.**
> (In this sentence, *see eye to eye* means "agree.")

Metaphor Comparing two different things without using the word *like* or *as*
> **That** player **in the red jersey is a regular** roadrunner.
> **Mom's chicken** soup **was the best** medicine **for my cold.**

Personification Giving human qualities to nonhuman things, such as an idea, an object, or an animal
> **That** stubborn **rock** refused to move.

Sensory Details Details that help the reader *hear, see, smell, taste,* or *feel* what is being described
> **When the book** crashed to **the floor, our cat** jumped three feet straight up, **giving me** the chills.

Simile Comparing two things using the word *like* or *as*
> **The new hamburgers at Brute Burger are** as big around as a pizza.
> **The ice was** as smooth as glass **before the skaters arrived.**

ELPS 2C, 2I, 3B, 3D, 3E, 3H, 4C

How can I learn to talk about my writing?

Study Writing Terms

This glossary includes terms that name important parts of the writing process. Read each word and definition aloud with a partner. Take turns using these words to describe something you wrote.

Audience	The people who read or hear your writing
Dialogue	Written conversation between two or more people
Focus Statement	The statement that focuses on the controlling or main idea and tells what specific part of a topic is written about in an essay (See page **23**.)
Point of View	The angle or viewpoint from which a story is told (See page **300**.)
Purpose	The main reason for writing a certain piece to describe to narrate to explain to persuade
Style	The way a writer puts words, phrases, and sentences together
Supporting Details	Specific details used to develop a topic or bring a story to life
Theme	The main idea or message in a piece of writing
Topic	The specific subject of a piece of writing
Topic Sentence	The sentence that expresses the main idea of a paragraph (See page **502**.)
Transition	A word or phrase that ties ideas together in essays, paragraphs, and sentences (See pages **515–516**.)
Voice	The tone or feeling a writer uses to express ideas

ELPS 2C, 4C, 4F, 4J

How can I increase my vocabulary skills?

Use Context

You can often figure out an unfamiliar word by looking at the words surrounding it. Here are some strategies you can use:

- Study the sentence containing the unfamiliar word, as well as the sentences that come before and after it.

  On his first day at the mine, Harold took an elevator deep into the earth. He never knew subterranean spaces were so dark. Working underground would be an adventure. (*Subterranean* means "under the earth.")

- Search for **synonyms** (words with the same meaning).

  Because I plan to be a lawyer, Dad calls me a barrister. (A *barrister* is a "lawyer.")

- Search for **antonyms** (words with the opposite meaning).

  Dad says that fishing is tedious, but I think it's exciting. (*Tedious* means "boring," the opposite of "exciting.")

- Search for a **definition** of the word.

  We saw yuccas, common desert plants, on our drive to the Grand Canyon. (*Yuccas* are common desert plants.)

- Search for **familiar words in a series** with the new word.

  In the South, many houses have a veranda, porch, or patio. (A *veranda* is a large, open porch.)

- Watch for **idioms** (words that have different uses from their most typical dictionary meanings).

  My cell phone is cutting out. (The dictionary meaning of this phrase could be "removing something using scissors," but here it means "disconnecting.")

Learn About Word Parts

Beginning with Prefixes

Prefixes are word parts that come before the root or base word (*pre-* means "before"). Prefixes can change the meaning of a word. *Kind* means "gentle." Add the prefix *un-*, meaning "not," and the resulting word, *unkind*, means "not gentle." Here are some other common prefixes:

de *(remove, take away)*
   defog (to remove the fog)

ex *(out)*
   expel (to drive out)

inter *(among, between)*
   international (between two or more nations)

mal *(bad, poor)*
   malnutrition (poor nutrition)

non *(absence of, not)*
   nonfat (without fat)

pre *(before)*
   preview (to show something before the regular time)

re *(again, back)*
   rewrite (to write again)

semi *(half, partly)*
   semicircle (a half circle)

sub *(under, less than)*
   subway (a way or road that goes under the street)

Ending with Suffixes

Suffixes are word parts that come at the end of a word. Sometimes a suffix will tell you what part of speech a word is. For example, many adverbs end in the suffix *-ly*. Add the suffix *-able*, which means "able to," to the word *agree*, and the resulting word, *agreeable*, means "able or willing to agree." Here are some other suffixes:

ful *(full of)*
   playful (full of play)

ion *(state of)*
   infection (state of being infected)

less *(without)*
   careless (without care)

ly *(in some manner)*
   bashfully (in a bashful manner)

ment *(act of, result of)*
   shipment (result of shipping)

ness *(state of)*
   carelessness (state of being careless)

ology *(study, science)*
   biology (study of living things)

ous *(full of)*
   joyous (full of joy)

y *(tending to)*
   itchy (tending to itch)

Knowing Your Roots

A **root** is the main part of a word. If you know the root of a difficult word, you may be able to figure out the word's meaning.

Suppose that you hear your friend say, "I couldn't understand what the speaker said because his voice wasn't *audible*." If you know that the root *aud* means "hear or listen," you will know that your friend couldn't hear the speaker's voice. Here are some other roots:

alter *(other)*
  alternate (another choice)

bio *(life)*
  biography (book about a person's life)

chron *(time)*
  chronological (in time order)

cise *(cut)*
  incision (a thin, clean cut)

dem *(people)*
  democracy (ruled by the people)

equi *(equal)*
  equinox (a day and night of equal length)

fin *(end)*
  final (the last or end of
    something)

flex *(bend)*
  flexible (able to bend)

fract, frag *(break)*
  fracture (to break)
  fragment (a small piece)

geo *(earth)*
  geography (the study of the earth's surface)

graph *(write)*
autograph (writing one's name)

ject *(to force, to throw)*
inject (to force inward)

multi *(many, much)*
multicultural (including many cultures)

port *(carry)*
export (to carry out)

pos *(place)*
position (a person or thing's place in relation to others)

scope *(see, watch)*
microscope (an instrument used for viewing objects too small to be seen with the naked eye)

scribe *(write)*
inscribe (to write on or in)

tele *(over a long distance)*
telephone (machine used to speak over a distance)

therm *(heat)*
thermostat (a device for controlling heat)

voc *(call)*
vocalize (to use the voice; sing)

TEKS 5.18A(iv)
ELPS 5F

How can I vary my sentences?

Study Sentence Patterns

Use a combination of sentence patterns to make your writing more interesting. Some basic sentence patterns are shown below.

1 Subject + Action Verb

    S   AV
Samantha smiled. (Some action verbs, like *smiled,* do not need a direct object to make a complete thought.)

2 Subject + Action Verb + Direct Object

    S   AV   DO
Stan threw the ball. (Some action verbs, like *threw,* need a direct object, like *ball,* to make a complete thought.)

3 Subject + Action Verb + Indirect Object + Direct Object

     S   AV IO   DO
Latesha gave me a penny.

4 Subject + Action Verb + Direct Object + Object Complement

       S   AV   DO   OC
Coach Allison named Rodney captain.

5 Subject + Linking Verb + Predicate Noun

    S   LV   PN
Frogs are amphibians.

6 Subject + Linking Verb + Predicate Adjective

    S   LV   PA
Toads are bumpy.

In the patterns above, the subject comes before the verb. In the patterns below, the verb comes before the subject.

    LV S   PN
7 **Is Lanette your sister?** (A question)

     LV   S
8 **Here is my jacket.** (A sentence beginning with *there* or *here*)

ELPS 4F

Practice Sentence Diagramming

Diagramming a sentence can give you a "picture" of how the parts fit together. Below are diagrams of the sentences from page 513.

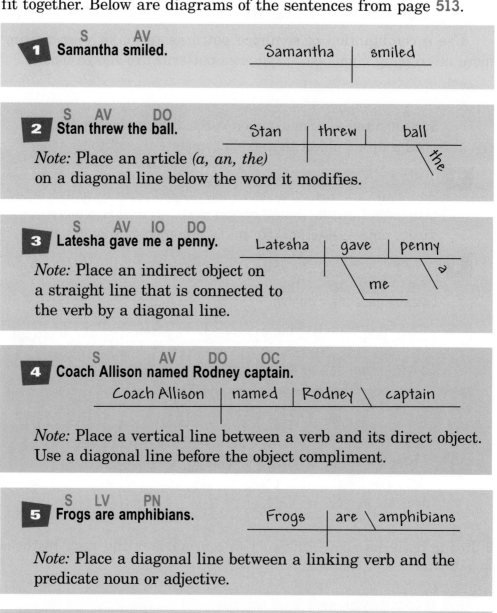

1
S AV
Samantha smiled.

Samantha | smiled

2
S AV DO
Stan threw the ball.

Stan | threw | ball
      the

Note: Place an article (*a, an, the*) on a diagonal line below the word it modifies.

3
S AV IO DO
Latesha gave me a penny.

Latesha | gave | penny
    me a

Note: Place an indirect object on a straight line that is connected to the verb by a diagonal line.

4
S AV DO OC
Coach Allison named Rodney captain.

Coach Allison | named | Rodney \ captain

Note: Place a vertical line between a verb and its direct object. Use a diagonal line before the object compliment.

5
S LV PN
Frogs are amphibians.

Frogs | are \ amphibians

Note: Place a diagonal line between a linking verb and the predicate noun or adjective.

6
S LV PA
Toads are bumpy.

Toads | are \ bumpy

TEKS 5.15C, 5.18A(iv),
5.20A(viii)
ELPS 3C, 3E, 3H

How can I connect my ideas?

Use Transitions

Transitions can be used to connect sentences and paragraphs. With a partner, take turns telling a silly story. Use the transitions below to link sentences and paragraphs. Write your story down.

Words that show location:

above	around	between	inside	outside
across	behind	by	into	over
against	below	down	near	throughout
along	beneath	in back of	off	to the right
among	beside	in front of	on top of	under

> We saw a flock of green ducks. Among them was one white one.

Words that show time:

about	during	until	yesterday	finally
after	first	meanwhile	next	then
at	second	today	soon	as soon as
before	third	tomorrow	later	when

> On the day that I was supposed to meet Robbie at 9:00 a.m., I didn't wake up until 9:15. Meanwhile, Robbie had slept late, too.

Words that show comparisons (similarities):

in the same way	likewise	as	while
similarly	like	also	

> You should always wear protective gear at the skate park. Similarly, you should always wear a helmet when you ride a bike.

 **TEKS** 5.15C, 5.18A(iv), 5.20A(viii)

ELPS 4F

Words that show contrast (differences):

on the other hand	otherwise	but	although
even though	however	still	yet

> Dogs that play and exercise on grassy yards must have their toenails trimmed regularly. On the other hand, dogs that are walked on pavement seldom need to have their toenails trimmed.

Words that emphasize a point:

again	truly	especially	for this reason
to repeat	in fact	to emphasize	

> The coach might announce a last-minute change in a play. For this reason, it's important to listen carefully to his calls.

Words that add information:

again	for instance	and	as well
also	besides	next	along with
another	for example	finally	in addition

> The best reason for saving energy is to make resources last longer. Another important reason is to cut down on pollution.

Words that summarize:

as a result	finally	in conclusion
therefore	lastly	because

> During her serve, the judges said Sela stepped over the line. As a result, Sela's opponent was given the point that won the match.

How can I make my final copy look better?

Add Diagrams and Graphs

Diagrams are simple drawings that include labels.

■ **Picture diagrams** show how something is put together, how the parts relate to each other, or how the object works.

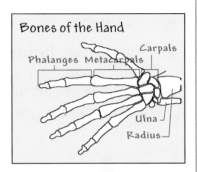

Bones of the Hand

Carpals
Phalanges Metacarpals
Ulna
Radius

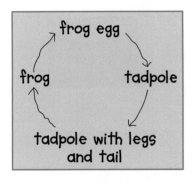

frog egg
frog
tadpole
tadpole with legs and tail

■ A **cycle diagram** shows how something happens over time. The process always leads back to the starting point.

Graphs show information about how things compare to each other. They help show information that includes numbers.

■ **A circle graph** shows what part (or percentage) of the total number each portion contains.

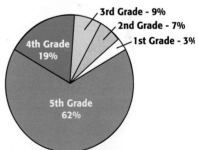

Percentage of Guppies in Each Grade

3rd Grade - 9%
2nd Grade - 7%
1st Grade - 3%
4th Grade 19%
5th Grade 62%

■ **A bar graph** compares two or more things at one point in time—like a snapshot. Bars on a graph can go up and down or sideways.

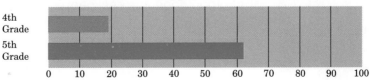

Number of Guppies in Grades 4 and 5

4th Grade
5th Grade

0 10 20 30 40 50 60 70 80 90 100

Add Pictures

Pictures will help make your final copy clear and interesting. Use photos from magazines or newspapers or download them from the Internet. (*Note:* Web sites, newspapers, or magazines often have rules for using their pictures. Check with your teacher first.)

■ **To Inform** . . . Pictures can help the reader understand your topic. They can add color and interesting details in the body of a report or an essay or can decorate a report cover. You can wrap your text around a picture, as shown in this example from a how-to essay:

If you've never used a computer, just looking at one can make you ask lots of questions. How do I get the screen to light up? What are all the buttons for? Do I have to know how to type? What does the mouse do? Don't worry; computers are easy to use. If you can use the remote for a TV, you can use a computer. There are three basic things you should know.

■ **To Set the Tone** . . . Pictures can show the reader how you feel about your topic. The photo below, included in a report on occupations, says that being a chef is fun. The words and the picture work together.

Have you ever thought about being a chef? There are many jobs available for cooks. Even if you don't know how to cook, you can go to school to learn. The pay is good, and you can move around the country because there are restaurants everywhere. The best part of the job is that good food makes people happy. Being a chef could be fun.

TEKS 5.18B
ELPS 2C, 3D, 3E, 3G, 4C, 4G

How should I set up my practical writing?

Follow Guidelines for Letters

Friendly letters and **business letters** have the same basic parts—*heading, salutation, body, closing,* and *signature.* In addition, a business letter also has an *inside address.* Discuss the letter below.

Friendly Letter

Heading Include your address and date. (1) Why is the date important?

Salutation Write a greeting and the person's name, followed by a comma. (2) What greetings would be best for an informal letter? A formal letter?

Body Each paragraph is indented. (3) What information and ideas does Michael share? (4) How does he bring the letter to a close?

Closing Capitalize the first word and end with a comma.

Signature Written signature

> 1040 Tolman Street
> Williamsburg, VA 23185
> January 8, 2010
>
> Dear Phillipe,
>
> My name is Michael, and I am your new pen pal. I'm in fifth grade at Page Elementary School in Williamsburg, Virginia, and I'm eleven years old.
> Here's my favorite thing to do: crouch by the pool, listen for a starting pistol, then dive into the pool and pump my arms and legs furiously until I reach the finish. I'm a swimmer, and I just started to compete with teams at other pools. My coach says swimming is really good exercise. It builds endurance and muscles, and it burns calories. But I just think it's fun!
> Please write back and tell me about yourself. What's the thing you do best?
>
> Your pen pal,
> Michael Fritz

Write a letter to a pen pal about an activity you enjoy. Convey ideas and information, and make sure your letter has all the parts shown above.

 **TEKS** 5.18B
ELPS 2C, 4C, 4F

Business Letter

All the parts of a business letter start at the left margin. Notice that there are spaces between paragraphs. Read the notes below.

Heading Include your address and the date. (1) How might a business use this information?

Inside Address Name and address of the person or company

Salutation A formal greeting followed by a colon

Body State your purpose for writing, and tell what you need. Show a sense of closure at the end. (2) What important information and ideas did Luke convey? (3) How did Luke wrap up the letter?

Closing Capitalize the first word and end with a comma.

Signature Include a written signature and a typed name. (4) Why might this be helpful?

4824 Park Street
Richland Center, WI 53581
January 20, 2010

Mr. David Shore
Box 168
Yellowstone Park, WY 82190

Dear Mr. Shore:

We're having a contest in my family to see who can plan the best summer vacation. I want to convince everyone to travel to Yellowstone National Park. I think seeing herds of buffalo stampeding by our car and watching Old Faithful erupt would be much more exciting than going to the seashore.

I would appreciate any help you could give me. I am interested in brochures with photos and maps of the park. I will also need some information about where we can stay and what special activities we can do in the park.

Thank you for your help. Maybe I'll see you next summer.

Sincerely yours,

Luke Johnson

Luke Johnson

 Write a business letter asking for information about a place you would like to visit. Convey ideas and information, and bring your letter to a polite close. Make sure your letter has all of the parts shown above.

Editing and Proofreading Marks

Use the symbols and letters below to show where and how your writing needs to be changed. Your teachers may also use these symbols to point out errors in your writing.

Symbol	Meaning	Example	Corrected Example
≡	Capitalize a letter.	Roald Dahl wrote the book _the BFG_.	Roald Dahl wrote the book _The BFG_.
/	Make a capital letter lowercase.	Sophie is an Ørphan.	Sophie is an orphan.
⊙	Insert (add) a period.	A giant takes Sophie from her bed⊙	A giant takes Sophie from her bed.
◯ or *sp.*	Correct spelling.	The giant (caries) Sophie away.	The giant carries Sophie away.
✐	Delete (take out) or replace.	The giant he takes her to Giant Country.	The giant takes her to Giant Country.
∧	Insert here.	Sophie is afraid the giant wants ∧to eat her.	Sophie is afraid the giant wants to eat her.
∧ ∧̇ ∧̦	Insert a comma, a colon, or a semicolon.	Because the giant tells her he means no harm∧Sophie stops worrying.	Because the giant tells her he means no harm, Sophie stops worrying.
∨ ∨∨ ∨∨	Insert an apostrophe or a quotation mark.	The giant∨s way of talking is unusual.	The giant's way of talking is unusual.
? ! ∧ ∧	Insert a question mark or an exclamation point.	Who blows dreams through a trumpet?∧	Who blows dreams through a trumpet?
∼	Switch words or letters.	Sophie and the BFG try to stop the giants bad from taking children.	Sophie and the BFG try to stop the bad giants from taking children.
¶	Start a new paragraph.	The BFG and Sophie needed help. ¶The next morning, they started off . . .	The BFG and Sophie needed help. The next morning, they started off . . .

Proofreader's Guide

Learning Language

Work with a partner. Read the meanings aloud and share answers to the questions.

1. A guide provides information.
   How might a guide to your town or city be helpful?

2. If something is basic, it is a simple yet main part.
   Tell a basic spelling rule.

3. To see something in your mind's eye is to picture it in your mind.
   When you think of summer, what do you see in your mind's eye?

Editing for Mechanics

Periods

A **period** is used to end a sentence. It is also used after initials, after abbreviations, and as a decimal point.

523.1
**At the End
of a Sentence**

Use a period to end a sentence that is a statement, a command, or a request.

Taro won the pitching contest. (statement)

Take his picture. (command)

Please loan me your baseball cap. (request)

523.2
After an Initial

Use a period after an initial in a person's name. (An initial is the first letter of a name.)

B. B. King (blues musician)

A. A. Milne (writer)

523.3
**As a Decimal
Point**

Use a period as a decimal point and to separate dollars and cents.

Robert is 99.9 percent sure that the bus pass costs $2.50.

523.4
**In
Abbreviations**

Use a period after an abbreviation. (See page 562 for more about abbreviations.)

Mr.   Mrs.   Jr.   Dr.   B.C.E.   U.S.A.

Use only one period when an abbreviation is the last word in a sentence.

A library has books, CD's, DVD's, magazines, etc.

ELPS 2C, 4C

Question Marks

A **question mark** is used after a direct question (an interrogative sentence). Sometimes it is used to show doubt about the correctness of a detail.

524.1

In Direct Questions

Place a question mark at the end of a direct question.

Do air bags make cars safer?

No question mark is used after an indirect question. (In an indirect question, you tell about the question you or someone else asked.)

I asked if air bags make cars safer.

524.2

In Tag Questions

A question mark is used when you add a short question to the end of a statement. (This type of statement is called a *tag question*.)

The end of this century is the year 2099, isn't it?

524.3

To Show Doubt

Place a question mark in parentheses to show that you aren't sure a fact is correct.

The ship arrived in Boston on July 23(?), 1652.

Exclamation Points

An **exclamation point** is used to express strong feeling. It may be placed after a word, a phrase, or a sentence.

524.4

To Show Strong Feeling

Surprise! (word)

Happy birthday! (phrase)

Wait for me! (sentence)

TIP: Never use extra exclamation points (Hooray!!!) in school writing assignments or in business letters.

Practice

End Punctuation

▶ For each of the following sentences, write the correct end-punctuation mark (a period, a question mark, or an exclamation point).

Example: Do you know what the capital of Ohio is **?**

1. Ooh, I know, I know—it's O

2. No, I'm not asking about capital letters

3. Darla, you tell me the answer

4. The state capital of Ohio is Columbus

5. What city is South Carolina's capital

6. I'll give you a hint

7. It starts the same way as Ohio's capital

8. It sounds like the name of a South American country

9. Is it Columbia

10. Yes, you're right

Next Step: Write a question about a state capital. Then write another sentence that answers it. Make sure that you use the correct end punctuation.

Commas . . .

Commas keep words and ideas from running together. They tell your reader where to pause, which makes your writing easier to read.

526.1
Between Items in a Series

Place commas between words, phrases, or clauses in a series. (A series is three items or more in a row.)

Hanae likes pepperoni, pineapple, and olives on her pizza. (words)

During the summer I read mysteries, ride my bike, and play basketball. (phrases)

526.2
To Set Off Dialogue

Use a comma to set off the words of the speaker from the rest of the sentence.

The stranded frog replied, "I'm just waiting for the toad truck."

If you are telling what someone has said but are not using the person's exact words, do *not* use commas or quotation marks.

The stranded frog told me that he was just waiting for the toad truck.

526.3
In Compound Sentences

Use a comma between two independent clauses that are joined by coordinating conjunctions like *and, but, or, nor, for, so,* or *yet.*

Aunt Carrie offered to pay my way, so I am going to the amusement park with her.

We'll try to get on all the rides, and we'll see one of the stage shows.

TIP: Do not connect two independent clauses with a comma only. That is called a comma splice. (See **600.2** for more information about independent clauses.)

TEKS 5.21B(i)
ELPS 4C, 5G

Practice

Commas 1

■ Between Items in a Series
■ To Set Off Dialogue
■ In Compound Sentences

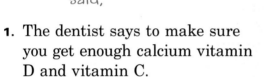 For each sentence below, write the word or words that should be followed by a comma. Write the commas, too.

Example: Gloria said "I have a dentist appointment today."

said,

1. The dentist says to make sure you get enough calcium vitamin D and vitamin C.

2. "These vitamins and minerals are important for healthy teeth" Dr. Green said.

3. Gloria asked "Doesn't milk have calcium and vitamin D?"

4. "Yes, and so does cheese" said the dentist.

5. Good sources of vitamin C are oranges green peppers and strawberries.

6. Gloria vowed to have a healthy diet so she looked for recipes online.

Next Step: Write four sentences of dialogue between a dentist and a patient. Place commas correctly.

Commas . . .

528.1
To Separate Introductory Phrases and Clauses

Use a comma to separate a long phrase or clause that comes before the main part of the sentence.

> After checking my knee pads, I started off. (phrase)

> If you practice often, skating is easy. (clause)

You usually do not need a comma when the phrase or the clause comes after the main part of the sentence.

> **Skating is easy if you practice often.**

Also, a comma is usually unnecessary after a short opening phrase.

> In time you'll find yourself looking forward to practice.

(No comma is needed after *In time*.)

528.2
In Dates and Addresses

Commas are used to set off the different parts in addresses and dates. (Do *not* use a comma between the state and ZIP code.)

> **My family's address is 2463 Bell Street, Atlanta, Georgia 30200.**

> **I will be 21 years old on January 15, 2015.**

Do not use a comma if only the month and year are written (January 2015).

528.3
In Large Numbers

Place commas between hundreds, thousands, millions, and billions.

> **Junji's car has 200,000 miles on it. He's trying to sell it for $1,000.**

When a number refers to a year, street address, or ZIP code, no comma is used. Also, write numbers in the millions and billions this way: 7.5 million, 16 billion. (See **566.2**.)

> **Brazil is a country of 184 million people.**

ELPS 4C, 5G

Practice

Commas 2

■ To Separate Introductory Phrases and Clauses
■ In Dates and Addresses

Rewrite the paragraph below. Be sure to add commas to dates, address parts, and introductory word groups that should be followed by a comma.

Example: When Dad was young he
played soccer.

When Dad was young,

1   The International Children's Games began on July 30

2   2004. During the five-day event in Ohio more than 2,000

3   kids from 12 to 15 years old competed in 10 different sports.

4   Contestants played table tennis and baseball at John Carroll

5   University 20700 North Park Boulevard University Heights

6   Ohio. They played basketball at Cleveland State University

7   2121 Euclid Avenue Cleveland Ohio. When the Games

8   returned on July 6 2005 kids from 150 cities around the

9   world met in Coventry, England.

Next Step: Write two sentences about a friend who enjoys
athletics. Tell when your friend was born and give
his or her address.

ELPS 2C, 4C

Commas . . .

530.1
To Set Off Interruptions

Use commas to set off a word, phrase, or clause that interrupts the main thought of a sentence.

> **You could, for example, take the dog for a walk instead of watching TV.**

Here is a list of words and phrases that you can use to interrupt main thoughts.

for example	to be sure	moreover
however	as a matter of fact	in fact

TESTS: Try one of these tests to see if a word or phrase interrupts a main thought:

1. Take out the word or phrase. The meaning of the sentence should not change.

2. Move the word or phrase to another place in the sentence. The meaning should not change.

530.2
To Set Off Interjections

Use a comma to separate an interjection or a weak exclamation from the rest of the sentence.

> **Wow, look at that sunrise!**
>
> **Hey, we're up early!**

If an interjection shows very strong feeling, an exclamation point (!) may be used after it.

> **Whoa! Let's slow down.**

The following words are often used as interjections.

Hello	Hey	Ah
Oh my	No kidding	Hmm
Really	Wow	Well

530.3
In Direct Address

Use commas to separate a noun of direct address (the person being spoken to) from the rest of the sentence.

> **Yuri, some computers do not need keyboards.**
>
> **I know that, Maria. They respond to voice commands.**

 ELPS 4C, 5G

Practice

Commas 3

■ To Set Off Interruptions
■ To Set Off Interjections

For each sentence below, write the word or words that should be followed by a comma. Write the commas, too.

Example: Wow did you know that the seasons in the United States are the opposite of Australia's seasons?

Wow,

1. Well it's true!

2. In Australia for example winter is from June to August.

3. In most areas of Australia however even winter temperatures don't fall below 50 degrees Fahrenheit.

4. In the southern part of Argentina on the other hand it gets quite cold in July and August.

5. No kidding you can ski down a mountain then!

6. Hmm that would be different.

Next Step: Write two sentences describing your favorite season. Use an interruption in one and an interjection in the other. Use commas correctly.

TEKS 5.18B
ELPS 2C, 4C

Commas . . .

532.1
To Separate Equal Adjectives

Use commas to separate two or more adjectives that equally modify a noun.

> **There are plenty of nutritious, edible plants in the world.**
> (*Nutritious* and *edible* are separated by a comma because they modify *plants* equally.)

> **We may eat many unusual plants in the years to come.**
> (*Many* and *unusual* do not modify *plants* equally. No comma is needed.)

TESTS: Use one of the tests below to help you decide if adjectives modify equally:

1. Switch the order of the adjectives. If the sentence is still clear, the adjectives modify equally.

2. Put the word *and* between the adjectives. If the sentence sounds clear, the adjectives modify equally.

Remember: Do not use a comma to separate the last adjective from the noun.

532.2
To Set Off Explanatory Phrases and Appositives

Use commas to set off an explanatory phrase from the rest of the sentence. (*Explanatory* means "helping to explain.")

> **Sonja, back from a visit to Florida, showed us some seashells.**

Use commas to set off appositives. An appositive is a word or phrase that is another way of saying the noun or pronoun before it. (See 602.5.)

> **Mrs. Chinn, our science teacher, says that the sun is an important source of energy.**

> **Solar power and wind power, two very clean sources of energy, should be used more.**

532.3
In Letter Writing

Place a comma after the salutation, or greeting, in a friendly letter and after the closing in all letters.

> **Dear Uncle Jim,** (greeting)   **Love,** (closing)

TEKS 5.18B
ELPS 4C, 5G

Practice

Commas 4

■ To Separate Equal Adjectives
■ To Set Off Appositives
■ In Letter Writing

For each sentence below, write the
word or words that should be followed
by a comma. Write the commas, too.

Example: Clyde my brother was
at the fair.

Clyde, my brother,

1. Dear Ted

2. Clyde saw a round red-haired clown selling helium balloons.

3. The clown had tied about 30 colorful balloons to an old rusty fence post.

4. Suddenly Mrs. Flanders our neighbor shouted, "The balloons are getting away!"

5. Clyde ran as fast as he could, trying to reach the bright weightless bundle of color.

6. As Clyde grabbed the strings, Ricky our older cousin yelled, "No, Clyde! Let go!"

Next Step: Write an ending to this story. If you use an appositive or two equal adjectives, use commas correctly with them.

Apostrophes . . .

An **apostrophe** is used to form contractions, to show possession, to form some plurals, or to show that letters have been left out of a word.

534.1 In Contractions

Use an apostrophe to show that one or more letters have been left out of a word, forming a contraction. The list below shows some common contractions.

couldn't (could not)	**it's** (it is; it has)
didn't (did not)	**I've** (I have)
doesn't (does not)	**she's** (she is; she has)
don't (do not)	**they'll** (they will)
hasn't (has not)	**they're** (they are)
haven't (have not)	**we've** (we have)
I'll (I will)	**wouldn't** (would not)
isn't (is not)	**you'd** (you would)

534.2 To Form Singular Possessives

Form the possessive of most singular nouns by adding an apostrophe and -s.

My sister's hobby is jazz dancing.

When a singular noun ends with an s or a z sound, the possessive may be formed by adding just an apostrophe.

Carlos' weather chart is very detailed.
(or) **Carlos's chart**

If the singular noun is a one-syllable word, form the possessive by adding both an apostrophe and -s.

Chris's lab report is incomplete.

TIP: An apostrophe is never used with a possessive pronoun (its, hers, yours).

The horse had its hooves trimmed.

Practice

Apostrophes 1

■ In Contractions
■ To Form Singular Possessives

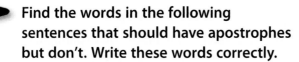 **Find the words in the following sentences that should have apostrophes but don't. Write these words correctly.**

Example: Lately Ive been wondering who invented the compact disc (CD).

I've

1. The CD was James Russells invention.

2. He didnt like the hiss and the scratches that he heard on his records.

3. To play a record, youd put a stylus, or "needle," right on the vinyl disc.

4. This wasnt very good for the record, which would become more worn with each play.

5. In the late 1960s, Russell asked for his employers permission to work at his idea.

6. He recorded code onto a discs special surface; then a laser light beam "read" it without touching the CD.

7. Russell figured out that a recording wouldnt wear out this way.

ELPS 2C, 4C

Apostrophes . . .

536.1
To Form Plural Possessives

Add just an apostrophe to make the possessive form of plural nouns ending in *s*.

> **The visitors' ideas were helpful.**
>
> **The girls' washroom should be expanded.**

For plural nouns not ending in *s,* add an apostrophe and an *-s*.

> **The children's team practices today, and the men's league starts this weekend.**

Remember: The word before the apostrophe is the owner.

> **Justin's CD** (The CD belongs to Justin.)
>
> **the boys' shoes** (The shoes belong to the boys.)

536.2
To Form Possessives with Indefinite Pronouns

Form the possessive of an indefinite pronoun *(someone, everyone, no one, both, anyone)* by adding an apostrophe and *-s*.

> **everyone's idea**   **no one's fault**
>
> **somebody's book**   **another's suggestion**

536.3
To Form Shared Possessives

When possession is shared by more than one noun, add an apostrophe and *-s* to the last noun only.

> **Danetta, Sasha, and Olga's science project deals with electricity.**

536.4
To Form Some Plurals

An apostrophe and *s* are used to form the plural of a letter, a number, or a sign.

> **A's   B's   3's   10's   +'s   &'s**

536.5
In Place of Omitted Letters or Numbers

Use an apostrophe to show that one or more letters or numbers have been left out.

> **class of '15** (*20* is left out)
>
> **fixin' to go** (*g* is left out)

ELPS 4C, 5G

Practice

Apostrophes 2

■ To Form Plural Possessives
■ To Form Shared Possessives

Find the words in the following sentences that should have apostrophes but don't. Write these words correctly.

Example: Someone rang the
Lombards doorbell.

Lombards'

1. Roderick and Antoines dog barked when the doorbell rang.

2. A teenager said, "I have the Hoffmans pizza here."

3. "They live down the street," Roderick said, "next to the Singers house."

4. "That must be Leanna and Kaleys pizza," Antoine said.

5. Roderick said to the delivery boy, "Look for their parents car, a green minivan, in the driveway."

6. But there were green minivans parked in both the Singers and the Hoffmans driveways!

7. The pizza became Sovann and Howies dinner.

Next Step: Write a sentence about two of your neighbors who share possession of something. Place the apostrophe correctly.

 **TEKS** 5.21B(ii)
ELPS 2C, 4C

Quotation Marks

Quotation marks are used to enclose the exact words of the speaker, to show that words are used in a special way, and to punctuate some titles.

538.1

To Set Off Dialogue

Place quotation marks before and after the spoken words in dialogue.

> Martha asked, "How long did you live in Mexico?"

538.2

Placement of Punctuation

Put periods and commas *inside* quotation marks.

> Trev said, "Let's make tuna sandwiches."

> "Sounds good," said Rich.

Place question marks or exclamation points *inside* the quotation marks when they punctuate the quotation.

> "Do we have any apples?" asked Trev.

> "Yes!" replied Mom.

Place them *outside* the quotation marks when they punctuate the main sentence.

> Did you hear Rich say, "We're out of pickles"?

538.3

To Punctuate Titles

Place quotation marks around titles of songs, poems, short stories, book chapters, and titles of articles in encyclopedias, magazines, or electronic sources. (See 546.1 for information on other kinds of titles.)

> "Oh! Susanna" (song)   "Casey at the Bat" (poem)
> "McBroom Tells the Truth" (short story)
> "Local Boy Wins Competition" (newspaper article)

(See 556.2 for information on capitalization of titles.)

538.4

For Special Words

Quotation marks may be used to set apart a word that is being discussed or that is used in a special way.

> The word "scrumptious" is hard to spell.

> The queen wanted to sell the royal chairs rather than see them "throne" away.

TEKS 5.21B(ii)
ELPS 4C, 5G

Practice

Quotation Marks

■ To Set Off Dialogue
■ To Punctuate Titles

For each sentence, write the words, including any periods or commas, that should be enclosed in quotation marks.

Example: Tyra said, I love to dance.
"I love to dance."

1. She wrote a poem about it called Dance Cake.

2. She especially likes dancing to the song Georgia Express.

3. That song rocks! said Ahmad.

4. Do you dance? asked Tyra.

5. He replied, I am just learning.

6. He had read Learn Basic Dance Steps, an article in a magazine.

7. Let's dance together sometime, Tyra suggested.

8. Ahmad hinted that he could dance only to an easy song like Hokey Pokey.

Next Step: Write a few lines of dialogue between two friends. Use quotation marks correctly.

Hyphens

A **hyphen** is used to divide a word at the end of a line. Hyphens are also used to join or create new words.

540.1
To Divide a Word

Use a hyphen to divide a word when you run out of room at the end of a line. A word may be divided only between syllables *(ex-plor-er)*. Always refer to a dictionary if you're not sure how to divide a word. Here are some guidelines for hyphenating words:

- Never divide a one-syllable word *(act, large, school)*.
- Try not to divide a word of five or fewer letters *(older, habit, loyal)*.
- Never divide a one-letter syllable from the rest of the word *(apart-ment,* not *a-partment)*.
- Never divide abbreviations or contractions *(Mrs., Dr., don't, haven't)*.

540.2
In Compound Words

Use a hyphen in certain compound words.

the two-year-old   sister-in-law

540.3
In Fractions

Use a hyphen between the parts of a fraction.

one-half (1/2)   five-tenths (5/10)

540.4
To Create New Words

Use a hyphen to form new words beginning with the prefixes *all-, self-, ex-,* or *great-*. A hyphen is also used with suffixes such as *-elect* and *-free*.

all-star team   self-respect   president-elect
great-grandmother   ex-hero   smoke-free

Use a hyphen to join two or more words that work together to form a single adjective *before* a noun.

school-age children   lightning-fast skating

540.5
To Join Letters and Words

A hyphen is often used to join a letter to a word.

T-shirt   X-ray   e-mail   U-turn

ELPS 4C

Practice

Hyphens

- ■ To Divide a Word
- ■ In Compound Words

If a word at the end of a line is hyphenated incorrectly, or if a compound word needs a hyphen, write the word correctly on your paper.

Example: Uncle Jay, who is Mom's brother in law, is an artist.

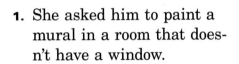
brother-in-law

1. She asked him to paint a mural in a room that does-n't have a window.

2. Uncle Jay said he would paint a couple of fake wi-ndows along with the scene outside them.

3. It turned out to be a time consuming project.

4. First, Mom painted the whole room in a medium bei-ge color.

5. Uncle Jay sketched the outline using a felt tip pen.

6. Then he used a many colored palette of paints to complete the mural.

7. He said, "Since the paint won't dry for a while, do-n't touch it!"

8. Mom will invite her friends to a get together to show them the mural.

TEKS 5.18B
ELPS 2C, 4C

Colons

A **colon** may be used to introduce a list or a quotation. Colons are also used in business letters and between the numbers expressing time.

542.1
To Introduce a List

Use a colon to introduce a list that follows a complete sentence.

> **The following materials can be used to build houses: plants, shells, sod, and sand.**

When introducing a list, the colon often comes after summary words like *the following* or *these things*.

> **On cleaning day, I do these things: sweep the floor, clean the bathroom mirror, and take out the garbage.**

TIP: It is incorrect to use a colon after a verb or after a preposition.

542.2
As a Formal Introduction

Use a colon to introduce an important quotation in a serious report, essay, or news story.

> **President Lincoln concluded the Gettysburg Address with these famous words: " . . . government of the people, by the people, for the people, shall not perish from the earth."**

542.3
In Business Letters

A colon is used after the greeting in a business letter.

> **Dear Ms. Kununga: Dear Sir:**
> **Dear Dr. Watts:**

542.4
Between Numbers in Time

Place a colon between the parts of a number that shows time.

> **7:30 a.m.   1:00 p.m.   12:00 noon**

ELPS 4C

Practice

Colons

■ To Introduce a List
■ Between Numbers in Time

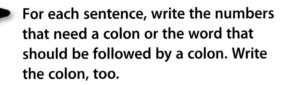 **For each sentence, write the numbers that need a colon or the word that should be followed by a colon. Write the colon, too.**

Example: We're leaving the house to go river tubing at 800 tomorrow morning.

8:00

1. Before you go tubing, make sure you have these things a swimsuit, a T-shirt, a hat, and some shoes.

2. You may also want to bring the following lip balm, sunglasses, and sunscreen.

3. The sun can be quite strong between the hours of 1100 a.m. and 200 p.m.

4. Here are some words that describe river tubing cool, relaxing, and scenic.

5. We will probably be back home by about 600 p.m.

Next Step: Write a sentence that includes a list of things you'd bring on a long car trip. Use a colon to introduce your list.

Semicolons

A **semicolon** sometimes works in the same way that a comma does. At other times, it works like a period and indicates a stronger pause.

544.1

To Join Two Independent Clauses

You can join two independent clauses with a semicolon when there is no coordinating conjunction (like *and* or *but*) between them. (See **600.2** for more information about independent clauses.)

In the future, some cities may rest on the ocean floor; other cities may float like islands.

Floating cities sound great; however, I get seasick.

TIP: Independent clauses can stand alone as separate sentences.

544.2

To Separate Groups in a Series with Commas

Use a semicolon to separate a series of phrases that already contain commas.

We crossed the stream; unpacked our lunches, cameras, and journals; and finally took time to rest.

(The second phrase contains commas.)

Ellipses

An **ellipsis** (three periods with a space before, between, and after) is used to show omitted words or sentences and to show a pause in dialogue.

544.3

To Show Omitted Words

Use an ellipsis to show that one or more words have been left out of a quotation.

"Give me liberty or give me death."

"Give me liberty or . . . death."

544.4

To Show a Pause

Use an ellipsis to indicate a pause in dialogue.

"That's . . . incredible!" I cried.

ELPS 4C, 5G

Practice

Semicolons

For the sentences below, write the words that should be separated by a semicolon. Write the semicolon, too.

Example: Troy's family went on a unique trip they went to Iqaluit (pronounced *ĭ-kăl′ ōō-ĭt*).

trip; they

1. Iqaluit is the capital city of Nunavut this Canadian territory was created in 1999.

2. Troy visited a museum and a theater exercised at an ice arena, a health club, and a swimming pool and ate at some great restaurants.

3. Iqaluit is located north of Quebec its Arctic climate means there is snow nine months of the year.

4. Visitors can eat clams, shrimp, and caribou travel by dogsled, kayak, and snowmobile and see polar bears, seals, and walrus.

5. Most of Iqaluit's people are Inuit they are one of the native peoples of the far north.

Next Step: Write a compound sentence describing an unusual place. Use a semicolon to join the independent clauses.

 **TEKS** 5.21C
ELPS 2C, 4C

Italics and Underlining

Italics is a style of type that is slightly slanted, like this: *girl*. It is used for some titles and special words. If you use a computer, you should use italics. In handwritten material, underline words that should be in italics.

546.1
In Titles

Use italics (or underlining) for the titles of books, plays, very long poems, magazines, and newspapers; the titles of television programs, movies (videos and DVD's), and albums of music (cassettes and CD's); and the names of ships and aircraft. (See **538.3** for information on other kinds of titles.)

> *The Giver* OR <u>The Giver</u> (book)
>
> *National Geographic* OR <u>National Geographic</u> (magazine)
>
> *Air Bud* OR <u>Air Bud</u> (movie)
>
> *Dance on a Moonbeam* OR <u>Dance on a Moonbeam</u> (CD)
>
> *Los Angeles Times* OR <u>Los Angeles Times</u> (newspaper)
>
> *Titanic* OR <u>Titanic</u> (ship)
>
> *Discovery* OR <u>Discovery</u> (spacecraft)

546.2
For Special Words

Use italics (or underlining) for scientific names and for words or letters being discussed or used in a special way.

> The marigold's scientific name is *Tagetes*.
>
> The word *friend* has different meanings to different people.

546.3
For Emphasis

Use italics (or underlining) to add emphasis to a key word or idea.

> The tiny sprout was a symbol of life, of hope, of our *future*.
>
> We were stuck in traffic for hours, but now we were *free*.

TEKS 5.21C
ELPS 3G

Practice

Italics and Underlining

▶ For each sentence, write the words that should be italicized and underline them.

Example: Consuela read the book The Polar Express.

<u>The Polar Express</u>

1. She said that it was muy bien, and I know that means "very good."

2. Tom Hanks is in the movie based on the book; he was also in the movie Cast Away.

3. Mom read a review of the movie in the San Antonio Express-News, the newspaper she usually reads.

4. She told me that the movie is not about Ursus maritimus, the polar bear.

5. "I know," I said. "It's the name of a train, just as Queen Elizabeth 2 is the name of a ship."

6. "Oh, have you been reading my Cruising the World magazine?" she said.

7. "No, but I would love to go on a cruise," I replied.

8. "How could you bear to miss school?" Mom joked.

Next Step: Write a sentence that includes the name of a popular book or movie. Remember to underline the title. Tell your opinion to a partner.

ELPS 2C, 4C

Dashes

A **dash** is used to show a break in a sentence, to emphasize certain words, or to show that a speaker has been interrupted.

548.1

To Show a Sentence Break

A dash can show a sudden break in a sentence.

> Because of computers, our world—and the way we describe it—has changed greatly.

> With a computer—or a cell phone—people can connect to the Internet.

548.2

For Emphasis

Use a dash to emphasize a word, a series of words, a phrase, or a clause.

> You can learn about customs, careers, sports, weather—just about anything—on the Internet.

548.3

To Show Interrupted Speech

Use a dash to show that someone's speech is being interrupted by another person.

> Well, hello—yes, I—that's right—yes, I—sure, I'd love—I'll be there!

Parentheses

Parentheses are used around words that add extra information to a sentence or make an idea clearer.

548.4

To Add Information

Use parentheses when adding information or making an idea clearer.

> I accidentally left the keys to Mom's car (a blue convertible) on the front seat.

> Five of the students provided background music (very quiet humming) for the singer.

Practice

Dashes and Parentheses

▶ **For each sentence, write whether you would use parentheses or a dash (or dashes) to set off the underlined words.**

Example: A real taco is a corn tortilla filled with meat, onions, and spice <u>nothing else</u>.
dash

1. People make different kinds of sauces with *chipotle* <u>smoked jalapeño pepper</u>.

2. Although lima beans first came from Guatemala, their name came from <u>you guessed it</u> Lima, Peru.

3. People in Costa Rica eat *gallo pinto* <u>a rice and bean dish</u> for breakfast, lunch, or dinner.

4. Mango <u>a fruit native to India</u> is used in many Latino dishes.

5. *Gazpacho* is a soup made of tomatoes, cucumbers, and garlic <u>and it's served cold!</u>

6. In Spain, a tortilla is an egg omelet <u>not a flat, thin bread as it is known in the United States</u>.

Next Step: Write a sentence about an unusual food. Add extra information and enclose it in parentheses.

★ **TEKS** 5.21A(i–iii)
ELPS 2C, 4C

Capitalization . . .

550.1 Proper Nouns and Adjectives

Capitalize all proper nouns and proper adjectives. A proper noun names a specific person, place, thing, or idea. A proper adjective is formed from a proper noun.

Proper Nouns:

Golden Gate Bridge	Utah Jazz	Thanksgiving Day

Proper Adjectives:

American citizen	Chicago skyline
New Jersey shore	Belgian waffle

550.2 Names of People (including initials)

Capitalize the names of people as well as the initials or abbreviations that stand for those names.

John Steptoe	Harriet Tubman
C. S. Lewis	Sacagawea

550.3 Titles Used with Names

Capitalize titles used with names of persons.

President Lincoln	Dr. Li Tam	Mayor Rita Gonzales

TIP: Do not capitalize titles when they are used alone: *the president, the doctor, the mayor.*

550.4 Abbreviations and Acronyms

Capitalize abbreviations of titles, organizations, and acronyms.

M.D. (doctor of medicine)   **Mr. Martin Lopez**

ADA (American Dental Association)

NATO (North Atlantic Treaty Organization)

550.5 Organizations

Capitalize the name of an organization, an association, or a team, as well as its members.

Girl Scouts	the Democratic Party
Chicago Bulls	Republicans

TEKS 5.21A(i–iii)
ELPS 3E, 3G, 4C

Practice

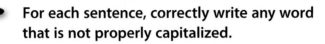

Capitalization 1

- Abbreviations and Acronyms
- Names and Initials
- Organizations

For each sentence, correctly write any word that is not properly capitalized.

Example: My neighbor, ms. hobbs, is a photojournalist.
              Ms. Hobbs

1. She wrote an interesting book about nasa and the space program.

2. The superintendent, dr. Girard, introduced her at a book talk at our school one night last week.

3. Principal jeff stone had great praise for Ms. Hobbs and her book.

4. He had heard her speak at an nsta convention.

5. Some members of the chamber of commerce were in the audience.

6. The Mayor was also in attendance.

7. After her presentation, Ms. Hobbs offered a dvd of her photographs for purchase.

8. My friend b. j. saunders bought one to use for a report.

Learning Language With a partner, talk about why people use abbreviations. Make a list of abbreviations you know.

Capitalization . . .

552.1
Words Used as Names

Capitalize words such as *mother, father, aunt,* and *uncle* when these words are used as names.

> **Ask Mother what we're having for lunch.**
> (*Mother* is used as a name; you could use her first name in its place.)

Words such as *dad, uncle, mother,* and *grandma* are not usually capitalized if they come after a possessive pronoun (*my, his, our*).

> **Ask my mother what we're having for lunch.**
> (In this sentence, *mother* refers to someone but is not used as a name.)

552.2
Days, Months, and Holidays

Capitalize the names of days of the week, months of the year, and holidays.

> **Wednesday   March   Easter**
> **Arbor Day   Passover   Juneteenth Day**

TIP: Do not capitalize the seasons.

> **winter   spring   summer   fall** (or **autumn**)

552.3
Names of Religions, Nationalities, and Languages

Capitalize the names of religions, nationalities, and languages.

> **Christianity, Hinduism, Islam** (religions)
> **Australian, Somalian, Chinese** (nationalities)
> **English, Spanish, Hebrew** (languages)

552.4
Official Names

Capitalize the names of businesses and official product names. (These are called trade names.)

> **Budget Mart   Crispy Crunch cereal   Smile toothpaste**

TIP: Do not capitalize a general word like *toothpaste* when it follows the product name.

Practice

Capitalization 2

- Names of Religions, Nationalities, and Languages
- Official Names

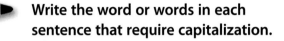 Write the word or words in each sentence that require capitalization.

Example: This ad for mountain man boots claims they'll protect you from snake bites.
Mountain Man

1. The zippy boot company makes them.

2. It is a canadian company.

3. Nayeli's favorite kind of car is the newmobile fastcar.

4. Her puerto rican grandparents have one.

5. Her grandfather used to work for island electric.

6. The people of Chile speak spanish.

7. Some young jewish people study the hebrew language.

8. Many europeans immigrating to the United States in the late 1800s were catholics.

Next Step: Write a sentence describing a product you enjoy using. Capitalize its name correctly.

Capitalization . . .

554.1
Names of Places

Capitalize the names of places that are either proper nouns or proper adjectives.

Planets and heavenly bodies	**Earth, Jupiter, Milky Way**
Continents	**Europe, Asia, South America, Australia**
Countries	**Mexico, Haiti, Greece, Chile, Jordan**
States	**New Mexico, West Virginia, Delaware**
Provinces	**Alberta, British Columbia, Quebec, Ontario**
Cities	**Montreal, Portland**
Counties	**Wayne County, Dade County**
Bodies of water	**Hudson Bay, North Sea, Lake Geneva, Saskatchewan River, Gulf of Mexico**
Landforms	**Appalachian Mountains, Bitterroot Range**
Public areas	**Vietnam Memorial**
Roads and highways	**New Jersey Turnpike, Interstate 80, Central Avenue**
Buildings	**Pentagon, Will Rogers Coliseum, Empire State Building**
Monuments	**Eiffel Tower, Statue of Liberty**

554.2
Sections of the Country

Capitalize words that name particular sections of the country. (Also capitalize proper adjectives formed from these words.)

A large part of the United States' population lives on the East Coast. (*East Coast* is a section of the country.)

Southern cooking   out West

Do *not* capitalize words that simply show direction.

If you keep driving west, you will end up in the Pacific Ocean. (direction)

western Brazil   northeasterly wind

ELPS 4C, 5G

Practice

Capitalization 3

■ Names of Places

▶ **For each sentence, write the word or words that should be capitalized.**

Example: A group of people had gathered at villa road and 30th street.

Villa Road, Street

1. They waited in line to buy tickets for a ride across lake erie.

2. They would take a restful trip from the united states to canada.

3. The ferry would take passengers from cleveland, ohio, to port stanley, ontario.

4. Winding through the town, kettle creek empties into the lake at pierside beach.

5. Canadians making the trip to cleveland might like to visit the rock 'n' roll hall of fame.

6. The 125-foot-tall soldiers and sailors monument is located in public square.

7. There is also a lot to do at cleveland lakefront state park.

Next Step: Write a sentence or two describing a trip, stating where you started and where you ended up.

ELPS 2C, 4C

Capitalization . . .

Capitalize the names of historical events, documents, and periods of time.

> **Boston Tea Party**
>
> **Emancipation Proclamation**
>
> **Stone Age**

Capitalize the first word of a title, the last word, and every word in between except short prepositions, coordinating conjunctions, and articles *(a, an, the).*

> ***National Geographic World*** (magazine)
>
> **"The Star-Spangled Banner"** (song)
>
> ***Beauty and the Beast*** (movie)
>
> ***In My Pocket*** (book)

Capitalize the first word of every sentence.

> **We play our first basketball game tomorrow.**

Capitalize the first word of a direct quotation.

> **Jamir shouted, "Keep that ball moving!"**

Capitalize	Do Not Capitalize
January, March	winter, spring
Grandpa (as a name)	my grandpa
Mayor Sayles-Belton	the mayor
President Washington	our first president
Ida B. Wells Elementary School	the local elementary school
Lake Ontario	the lake area
the South (section of the country)	south (a direction)
planet Earth	a mound of earth (dirt)

Practice

Capitalization 4

- ■ Historical Events
- ■ Titles

For each sentence, write the word or words that should be capitalized but are not.

Example: A good book about space journeys is *Our space program*.

Space Program

1. In a way, astronauts are like the explorers on the lewis and clark expedition.

2. Some missiles built during world war II were used to launch the first satellites.

3. The United Nations created the outer space treaty of 1967, which encouraged peaceful space exploration.

4. An article in the magazine *National geographic* explains the many dangers that astronauts face.

5. The movie *apollo 13* also showed how risky space travel can be.

6. Millions still watch the old TV show *star trek*.

7. The book *timeline* is about students who travel back in history to rescue their professor.

Next Step: List some magazines in your home, books you have read, and important historical events you have learned about. Capitalize them correctly.

Plurals . . .

558.1
Most Nouns

Form the **plurals** of most nouns by adding *-s*.

balloon—balloons   **shoe**—shoes

558.2
Nouns Ending in *sh, ch, x, s,* and *z*

Form the plurals of nouns ending in *sh, ch, x, s,* and *z* by adding *-es* to the singular.

brush—brushes   **bunch**—bunches   **box**—boxes
dress—dresses   **buzz**—buzzes

558.3
Nouns Ending in *o*

Form the plurals of most words that end in *o* by adding *-s*.

patio—patios   **rodeo**—rodeos

For most nouns ending in *o* with a consonant letter just before the *o*, add *-es*.

echo—echoes   **hero**—heroes

However, musical terms and words of Spanish origin form plurals by adding *-s;* check your dictionary for other words of this type.

piano—pianos   **solo**—solos
taco—tacos   **burrito**—burritos

558.4
Nouns Ending in *-ful*

Form the plurals of nouns that end with *-ful* by adding an *-s* at the end of the word.

two spoonfuls   **three** tankfuls
four bowlfuls   **five** cupfuls

558.5
Nouns Ending in *f* or *fe*

Form the plurals of nouns that end in *f* or *fe* in one of two ways.

1. If the final *f* is still heard in the plural form of the word, simply add *-s*.

    goof—goofs   **chief**—chiefs   **safe**—safes

2. If the final *f* has the sound of *v* in the plural form, change the *f* to *v* and add *-es*.

    calf—calves   **loaf**—loaves   **knife**—knives

ELPS 3E, 4C

Practice

Plurals 1

- Nouns Ending in *sh, ch, x, s,* and *z*
- Nouns Ending in *-ful*

Write the plural of each of the following words.

Example: lunch
lunches

1. tax

2. class

3. forkful

4. ash

5. mix

6. eyelash

7. batch

8. mouthful

9. rush

10. handful

11. fax

12. fox

13. dish

14. bus

15. six

16. ditch

17. plateful

18. mess

19. watch

20. waltz

Learning Language Make a list of four or five other nouns that end in *sh, ch,* or *-ful*. Write their plurals. Tell a partner a sentence using both a singular and a plural noun.

⭐ ELPS 2C, 4C

Plurals . . .

560.1
Nouns Ending in *y*

When a common noun ends in a consonant + *y*, form its plural by changing the *y* to *i* and adding *-es*.

sky—skies	bunny—bunnies
story—stories	musky—muskies

For proper nouns, do *not* change the letters—just add *-s*.

area Bargain Citys　　**the Berrys**　　**two Timmys**

For nouns that end in a vowel + *y,* add only *-s*.

donkey—donkeys　　**monkey—monkeys**　　**day—days**

560.2
Compound Nouns

Form the plurals of most compound nouns by changing the most important word in the compound to its plural form.

sisters-**in-law**	maids **of honor**	life **jackets**
secretaries **of state**	houses **of assembly**	

560.3
Irregular Nouns

Some nouns form plurals using an irregular spelling.

child—children	goose—geese	foot—feet
man—men	woman—women	tooth—teeth
ox—oxen	mouse—mice	
cactus—cacti *or* cactuses		

A few words have the same singular and plural forms.

Singular:	Plural:
That sheep wanders away.	The other sheep follow it.
I caught one trout.	Dad caught three trout.

Others: deer, moose, buffalo, fish, aircraft

560.4
Adding an *'s*

The plurals of symbols, letters, numerals, and words discussed as words are formed by adding an apostrophe and *-s*.

two ?'s **and two** !'s　　**five** 7's　　*x*'s **and** *y*'s

TIP: For more information on forming plurals and plural possessives, see page 536.

Practice

Plurals 2

- Compound Nouns
- Irregular Nouns

For each of the following sentences, write the correct plural form of the underlined word.

Example: Grandpa counted 68 <u>sheep</u> before falling asleep.

sheep

1. Moose have bigger <u>foot</u> than deer.

2. Park rangers say there are more <u>deer</u> in the United States now than there were 400 years ago.

3. Wild <u>goose</u> will not fly south for the winter if they can find open water and food.

4. Hikers in Glacier National Park sometimes see many <u>mountain goat</u>.

5. Did you know that <u>mouse</u> are wild animals?

6. Some fish have very sharp <u>tooth</u>.

7. My mother's two <u>brother-in-law</u> like to photograph sandhill cranes.

Learning Language Write one or two sentences using the correct plural forms of *child* and *vice president*. Tell a partner another sentence using the plural form of a word.

TEKS 5.21A(i), 5.21A(ii)
ELPS 2C, 4C

Abbreviations . . .

An **abbreviation** is the shortened form of a word or phrase.

562.1
Common Abbreviations (names, titles, initials, time)

Most abbreviations begin with a capital letter and end with a period. In formal writing, do *not* abbreviate the names of states, countries, months, days, or units of measure. Also, do *not* use symbols (%, &) in place of words.

TIP: The following abbreviations are always acceptable in both formal and informal writing:

Mr.	Mrs.	Ms.	Dr.	Jr., Sr.
M.D.	B.C.E.	C.E.	a.m., p.m. (A.M., P.M.)	

562.2
Acronyms

An **acronym** is made up of the first letter or letters of words capitalized in a phrase. An acronym is pronounced as a word, and it does not have any periods.

SADD (Students Against Destructive Decisions)

PIN (personal identification number)

562.3
Initialisms

An **initialism** is like an acronym, except the capital letters that form the abbreviation are pronounced individually (not as a word).

TV (**t**ele**v**ision)   DA (**d**istrict **a**ttorney)

CD (**c**ompact **d**isc)   PO (**p**ost **o**ffice)

Common Abbreviations

a.m.	ante meridiem (before noon)	**Inc.**	incorporated	**oz.**	ounce
ATM	automatic teller machine	**kg**	kilogram	**pd.**	paid
B.C.E.	before the Common Era	**km**	kilometer	**p.**	page
C.E.	the Common Era	**lb.**	pound	**p.m.**	post meridiem (after noon)
etc.	and so forth	**M.D.**	doctor of medicine	**qt.**	quart
FYI	for your information	**mpg**	miles per gallon		
		mph	miles per hour		

TEKS 5.21A(i), 5.21A(ii)
ELPS 4C

Practice

Abbreviations 1

■ Common Abbreviations
■ Acronyms
■ Initialisms

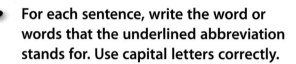

For each sentence, write the word or words that the underlined abbreviation stands for. Use capital letters correctly.

Example: <u>Mr.</u> Al E. Gator met some pals in the swamp.

Mister

1. They had a meeting every Friday at 2:30 <u>p.m.</u>

2. A speedboat went by, going about 60 <u>mph</u>.

3. "Those boats get only 6 <u>mpg</u> of fuel," Al said.

4. "Did you know that a gallon is about the same as eight <u>lbs.</u>?" asked C. Rocky Dile.

5. "I learned that fact on a <u>TV</u> program," he said.

6. Then little Green Tree Frog, <u>Jr.</u>, piped up, "Would anyone like to hear some music?"

7. "I have a new <u>CD</u>," he said.

8. "It's called *Horns in the <u>U.S.A.</u>*"

9. "<u>FYI</u>, the CD is a fund-raiser for school bands," he added.

Next Step: Write a silly sentence that includes an acronym you make up. Write what the abbreviation stands for.

TEKS 5.21A(i)
ELPS 2C, 4C

Abbreviations . . .

564.1
State and Address Abbreviations

You may use a state or address abbreviation when it is part of an address on a letter or envelope. Capitalize both letters of a state abbreviation. Do not use these abbreviations in sentences. Use all capital letters and no punctuation on an envelope.

On a letter:

2323 N. Kipp St.
Cleveland, OH 52133

On an envelope:

7828 E FIRST AVE
ORONO ME 04403

In sentences:

Jasper lives at 2323 North Kipp Street, Cleveland, Ohio.

His old address was 7828 East First Avenue, Orono, Maine 04403.

State Postal Abbreviations

Alabama	AL	Idaho	ID	Missouri	MO	Pennsylvania	PA
Alaska	AK	Illinois	IL	Montana	MT	Rhode Island	RI
Arizona	AZ	Indiana	IN	Nebraska	NE	South Carolina	SC
Arkansas	AR	Iowa	IA	Nevada	NV	South Dakota	SD
California	CA	Kansas	KS	New Hampshire	NH	Tennessee	TN
Colorado	CO	Kentucky	KY	New Jersey	NJ	Texas	TX
Connecticut	CT	Louisiana	LA	New Mexico	NM	Utah	UT
Delaware	DE	Maine	ME	New York	NY	Vermont	VT
District of		Maryland	MD	North Carolina	NC	Virginia	VA
Columbia	DC	Massachusetts	MA	North Dakota	ND	Washington	WA
Florida	FL	Michigan	MI	Ohio	OH	West Virginia	WV
Georgia	GA	Minnesota	MN	Oklahoma	OK	Wisconsin	WI
Hawaii	HI	Mississippi	MS	Oregon	OR	Wyoming	WY

Address Abbreviations

Apartment	Apt.	Expressway	Expy.	Parkway	Pkwy.	Square	Sq.
Avenue	Ave.	Heights	Hts.	Place	Pl.	Station	Sta.
Boulevard	Blvd.	Highway	Hwy.	Road	Rd.	Street	St.
Court	Ct.	Lane	Ln.	Route	Rte.	Terrace	Terr.
Drive	Dr.	North	N.	Rural	R.	Turnpike	Tpke.
East	E.	Park	Pk.	South	S.	West	W.

TEKS 5.21A(i)
ELPS 4C

Practice

Abbreviations 2

■ State and Address Abbreviations

Imagine that you are addressing envelopes. Write each of the following addresses using the correct abbreviations. Use correct capitalization.

Example: 3999 West Fourman Court, Waukegan, Illinois 60085

3999 W FOURMAN CT
WAUKEGAN IL 60085

1. 620 South Highway 187, Dallas, Texas 75019

2. 161 Saturn Parkway North, Dayton, New Jersey 08810

3. 950 Splice Heights, Eagan, Minnesota 55121

4. 2256 Benton Harbor Road, Route 44, Duluth, Georgia 30096

5. 26123 East Francis Lane, Lake Forest, California 92630

Next Step: Write your own address as if you were addressing an envelope.

Numbers

566.1 Numbers from 1 to 9

Numbers from one to nine are usually written as words. (Most of the time, numbers 10 and higher are written as numerals.)

> **one   three   nine   10   115   2,000**

Keep any numbers that are being compared in the same style, either as words or numerals.

> **Students from 8 to 11 years old are invited.**

> **Students from eight to eleven years old are invited.**

566.2 Very Large Numbers

You may use a combination of numerals and words for very large numbers.

> **15 million   1.2 billion**

You may spell out large numbers that can be written as two words, but if you need more than two words to spell out a number, write it as a numeral.

> **three million   fifteen thousand   3,275,100   7,418**

566.3 Sentence Beginnings

Use words, not numerals, to begin a sentence.

> **Fourteen new students joined the jazz band.**

> **Fifty-two cards make up a deck.**

566.4 Numerals Only

Use numerals for numbers in the following forms:

decimals	**25.5**
with dollar signs	**$3.97**
percentages	**6 percent**
chapters	**chapter 8**
pages	**pages 17–20**
addresses	**445 E. Acorn Dr.**
dates	**June 10, 1923**
times with a.m. or p.m.	**1:30 p.m.**
statistics	**a vote of 5 to 2**

Practice

Numbers

■ Sentence Beginnings
■ Numerals Only

For each sentence, write the number the correct way. (If it is already correct, write "C.")

Example: 26 chickens got loose from the Jones farm yesterday.

Twenty-six

1. The date was May thirty.

2. Some of the chickens actually crossed Highway 9.

3. Some of them hid in the bushes near the house at fifty National Road.

4. By one p.m., I was tired of chasing chickens.

5. 11 chickens were still missing.

6. Farmer Jones wouldn't be happy until one hundred percent of the birds were found.

7. Twenty-five chickens were back in the coop by sunset.

8. The last chicken didn't turn up until June six, but it was fine.

Next Step: Write a short paragraph about a time when you lost something. Include one sentence that begins with a number.

Improving Spelling

568.1

i before e

Write *i* before *e*—except after *c* or when rhyming with *say*, as in *neighbor* and *weigh*.

believe   chief   receive freight

Exceptions to the *i* before *e* rule include the following:

either   neither   heir   leisure   species
foreign   height   seize   weird

568.2

Silent e

If a word ends with a silent *e*, drop the *e* before adding a suffix (ending) that begins with a vowel.

judge—judging   **continue**—continual
create—creative—creation   **relate**—relating—relative

568.3

Words Ending in y

When a word ends in a consonant + *y*, change the *y* to *i* before adding a suffix. Do not, however, change the *y* when adding the *-ing* suffix.

happy—happiness   **try**—tries—trying
lady—ladies   **cry**—cried—crying

When forming the plural of a word that ends in *y* with a vowel just before it, add *-s*.

holiday—holidays   **key**—keys   **boy**—boys

568.4

Words Ending in a Consonant

When a one-syllable word ends in a consonant that has a single vowel before it, double the final consonant before adding a suffix that begins with a vowel.

beg—begging   **hop**—hopped   **sit**—sitting

When a word with more than one syllable ends with a vowel + consonant, double the final consonant only if the accent is on the last syllable and the suffix begins with a vowel.

admit—admitting   **occur**—occurrence

Practice

Spelling 1

- *i* before *e*
- Silent *e*

For each sentence, write any misspelled words correctly.

Example: In the Olympics, judgeing is an important part of each sport.

judging

1. Many foriegn visitors attend Olympic events.

2. Each athlete beleives that he or she can win a gold medal.

3. An athlete's hieght is not important in most of the sports.

4. Figure skateing is a crowd favorite in the Winter Olympics.

5. The top three athletes in each sport recieve medals.

6. You'll see the winners raiseing their medals above their heads for everyone to see.

Next Step: Write a list of five words that are spelled with *i* before *e*. Then write a list of five words that end with a silent *e*; add a suffix to each of the five words, spelling the new words correctly.

Practice

Spelling 2

■ Words Ending in *y*
■ Words Ending in a Consonant

For each sentence, write the correct spelling of the underlined word or words.

Example: Pirates left <u>buryed</u> treasure on Cat Island.

buried

1. Nate imagined his family's <u>happyness</u> if he were to find a chest of jewels.

2. He <u>grined</u> from ear to ear.

3. It would be the <u>begining</u> of the good life!

4. Nate <u>grabed</u> a shovel and started <u>diging</u>.

5. The <u>dustyness</u> of the dry sand bothered his eyes.

6. He grunted as he <u>jabed</u> the shovel into the hard ground.

7. He was not <u>enjoing</u> this work.

8. The shovel wasn't <u>hiting</u> anything hard.

9. <u>Worryed</u> that he was wasting his time, Nate <u>faned</u> himself for a minute.

10. Then he <u>droped</u> the shovel and <u>hurryed</u> home to dinner.

Practice

Spelling Review

For each sentence, write the correct spelling of the underlined word.

1. Dwight had books from two <u>librarys</u>.

2. He <u>carryed</u> the books to the study area of the second library.

3. After almost an hour of <u>writeing</u>, he finished his essay.

4. He looked up at the <u>cieling</u> and sighed.

5. "Oh, my <u>acheing</u> hand!" Dwight moaned.

6. He had a <u>breif</u> cramp in his right hand.

7. He <u>rubed</u> it to ease the cramp.

8. All of a sudden, he realized that it was <u>geting</u> late.

9. He <u>journied</u> home before it got dark.

10. His mom was a bit <u>exciteable</u>, and Dwight did not want her to worry.

11. She had a <u>feirce</u> need to protect her child (as many mothers do).

12. When Dwight got home, he discovered he had <u>forgoten</u> his essay at the library.

Proofreader's Guide to Improved Spelling

Be patient. Becoming a good speller takes time and practice. Learn the basic spelling rules.

Check your spelling by using a dictionary or a list of commonly misspelled words.

Check a dictionary for the correct pronunciation of each word you are trying to spell. Knowing how to pronounce a word will help you remember how to spell it.

Look up the meaning of each word. Knowing its meaning will help you to use it and spell it correctly.

Study the word in the dictionary. Then look away from the dictionary page and picture the word in your mind's eye. Next, write the word on a piece of paper. Finally, check its spelling in the dictionary. Repeat these steps until you can spell the word correctly.

Make a spelling dictionary. In a special notebook, write down any words you frequently misspell.

A

abbreviate	adjust	already	another	architect
aboard	admire	although	answer	arctic
above	adventure	altogether	antarctic	aren't
absence	advertisement	aluminum	anxious	argument
absent	advise	always	anybody	arithmetic
absolute	afraid	ambulance	anyone	around
accept	afterward	amendment	anything	arrange
accident	again	American	anyway	arrival
according	against	among	anywhere	article
account	agreeable	amount	apartment	artificial
ache	agreement	ancient	apologize	asleep
achieve	aisle	angel	appearance	assign
acre	alley	anger	appetite	assist
across	allowance	angle	appointment	associate
actual	all right	angry	appreciate	association
addition	almost	animal	approach	assume
address	alone	anniversary	approval	athlete
	along	announce	approximate	athletic
	a lot	annual	April	attach

attack
attempt
attendance
attention
attitude
attractive
audience
August
author
authority
automobile
autumn
available
avenue
average
awful
awkward

B

baggage
baking
balance
balloon
banana
bandage
barber
bargain
barrel
basement
battery
beautiful
beauty
because
becoming
been
before
beginning
behave
behavior
behind
belief
believe

belong
beneath
between
bicycle
blizzard
bother
bottom
bought
bounce
boundary
breakfast
breath
breathe
breeze
bridge
brief
bright
brilliant
brother
brought
buckle
budget
build
built
burglar
bury
business
busy

C

cafeteria
calendar
cancel
candidate
candle
canoe
canyon
captain
cardboard
career
carpenter
carriage

casual
catalog
catcher
caught
ceiling
celebration
cemetery
century
certain
certificate
challenge
champion
change
channel
character
chief
chocolate
choice
choir
choose
chorus
church
circle
citizen
city
clear
climate
climb
closet
clothes
coach
cocoa
cocoon
college
color
column
comedy
coming
commercial
commit
committed
committee
communicate
community

company
comparison
competitive
complain
complete
concern
concert
concrete
condition
conference
confidence
congratulate
connect
continue
continuous
convenient
convince
cooperate
cough
could
country
county
courage
courageous
cousin
coverage
cozy
crawl
cried
criticize
cruel
crumb
curiosity
curious
current
customer

D

daily
damage
danger
dangerous

daughter
December
decide
decision
decorate
definite
definition
delicious
describe
description
design
develop
dictionary
difference
different
difficulty
disappear
disastrous
discipline
discover
discuss
discussion
disease
distance
divide
division
doctor
doesn't
dollar
doubt

E

eager
early
easily
easy
edge
eight
eighth
either
electricity
elephant

embarrass
emergency
encourage
enormous
enough
entertain
entrance
environment
equal
equipment
escape
especially
every
everybody
exactly
excellent
excited
exercise
exhausted
expensive
experience
experiment
explain
explanation
extinct
extreme
eyes

F

face
familiar
family
famous
fashion
favorite
February
field
fierce
fifty
finally
foreign
fortunate

forty
forward
fountain
fragile
Friday
friend
frighten
fuel

G

gadget
gauge
general
generous
genius
gentle
genuine
geography
ghost
gnaw
goes
government
governor
graduation
grammar
grateful
great
grief
grocery
group
guarantee
guard
guess
guilty
gymnasium

H

half
handsome
happen

happiness
hazardous
headache
health
heavy
height
history
holiday
honor
horrible
hospital
humorous
hundreds
hygiene

I

icicle
ideal
identical
illustrate
imaginary
imagine
imitate
imitation
immediately
immigrant
impatient
important
impossible
incredible
independence
independent
individual
initial
innocent
instead
intelligence
intelligent
interest
interrupt
invitation
island

J

January
jealous
jewelry
journal
journey
judgment
July
June

K

knew
knife
knives
knowledge

L

label
language
laugh
lawyer
league
leave
leisure
length
library
license
lightning
liquid
listen
loose
lovable

M

machine
magazine
manufacture

March
marriage
material
mathematics
May
mayor
meant
measure
medicine
message
millions
miniature
minute
mirror
mischief
misspell
Monday
morning
mountain
multiplication
muscle
music
musician
mysterious

N

national
natural
necessary
neighbor
neither
nephew
nervous
nickel
niece
nineteen
ninth
noisy
no one
nothing
November
nuclear

O

obey
occasion
occur
occurred
o'clock
October
office
official
often
once
operate
opinion
opportunity
opposite
ordinary
original

P

package
paid
paragraph
parallel
participate
particular
patience
people
perfect
permanent
personal
persuade
physical
picture
pleasant
please
point
poison
popular
possess
possible
practical

practice
precious
preparation
president
pretty
privilege
probably
problem
produce
protein

Q

quarter
quickly
quiet
quit
quite
quotient

R

raise
ready
realize
really
reason
receive
recipe
recognize
recommend
relieve
remember
responsibility
restaurant
review
rhyme
rhythm
ridiculous
right
rough
route

S

safety
said
salary
Saturday
says
scared
scene
schedule
science
scissors
secretary
seize
sentence
separate
September
serious
several
similar
since
sincerely
skiing
soldier
spaghetti
special
statue
stomach
straight
strength
stretch
studying
subtraction
succeed
success
suddenly
sugar
Sunday
suppose
sure
surprise
surround
symptom
system

T

table
teacher
tear
temperature
terrible
Thanksgiving
theater
thief
though
thought
thousand
through
Thursday
tired
together
tomorrow
tongue
touch
toward
treasure
tried
trouble
truly
Tuesday

U

unconscious
unfortunately
unique
universe
until
unusual
usually

V

vacation
vacuum
valuable
various
vegetable
vehicle
violence
visitor
voice
volume
volunteer

W

wander
weather
Wednesday
weight
weird
welcome
what
when
where
which
while
whole
women
write
wrong
wrote

Y

yellow
yesterday
young
yourself

⭐ ELPS 2C, 2G, 4C, 5B

Using the Right Word

You need to use "the right words" in your writing and speaking, and this section will help you do that. First, look over the commonly misused words on this and the next 19 pages. Then, whenever you have a question about which word is the right word, come back to this section for help. (Remember to look for your word in a dictionary if you don't find it here.)

576.1
a, an

We took a ride to look for wildlife.
(Use *a* before words beginning with a consonant sound.)
José saw an eagle and an antelope.
(Use *an* before words beginning with a vowel sound.)

576.2
accept, except

Zachary walked up to accept his award.
(*Accept* means "to receive" or "approve of.")
Except for his sister, the whole family was there.
(*Except* means "other than.")

576.3
allowed, aloud

We are allowed to read to partners in class.
(*Allowed* means "permitted.")
We may not read aloud in the library, however.
(*Aloud* is an adverb meaning "out loud" or "clearly heard.")

576.4
a lot

A lot of my friends like chips and salsa.
(*A lot* is always two words.)

576.5
already, all ready

I already finished my homework.
(*Already* is an adverb telling when.)
Now I'm all ready to shoot some buckets.
(*All ready* is a phrase meaning "completely ready.")

576.6
ant, aunt

A large black ant crawled across the picnic blanket.
Aunt Lucinda, my mom's sister, got out of its way.

ELPS 3H, 5B

Grammar Practice

Using the Right Word 1

■ accept, except; **allowed, aloud;** a lot, alot; **already, all ready**

▶ **For each of the following sentences, write the correct word or words from the pair in parentheses.**

Example: At the start of every school day, we say the Pledge of Allegiance *(aloud, allowed)*.
aloud

1. Our teacher wants us to read *(alot, a lot)* of books this year.

2. I guess I have a head start because I often read *(aloud, allowed)* to my little sister.

3. My teachers do not *(accept, except)* late homework.

4. Our new classmate will be *(aloud, allowed)* to hand in his book report next week.

5. Zed volunteered to help clean the blackboard, but Cree had *(already, all ready)* washed it.

6. Everyone in the class *(accept, except)* Bria takes the bus home.

7. Sean says he is *(already, all ready)* to go fishing after school.

Learning Language Tell a partner a sentence using a word from the list at the top of the page. Explain what the word means. Then write a sentence using another word from the list.

ELPS 2C, 2G, 4C, 5B

578.1
ate, eight

I ate a bowl of popcorn.
He had eight pieces of candy.

578.2
bare, bear

She put her bare feet into the cool stream.
She didn't see the bear fishing on the other side.

578.3
blew, blue

I blew on my cold hands.
The tips of my fingers looked almost blue.

578.4
board, bored

One board in the wooden floor was loose.
With nothing to do, I felt bored.

578.5
borrow, lend

It's so cold—could I borrow a sweater?
(*Borrow* means "receive.")
It's so cold—could you lend me a sweater?
(*Lend* means "give.")

578.6
brake, break

Pump the brake to slow down.
You could break a bone if you skateboard without protection.

578.7
breath, breathe

Take a deep breath and calm down. (*Breath* is a noun.)
My nose is so stuffed up that it's hard to breathe.
(*Breathe* is a verb.)

578.8
bring, take

Please bring me my glasses.
(*Bring* means "to move toward the speaker.")
Take your dishes to the kitchen.
(*Take* means "to carry away.")

578.9
by, buy

Chuck stopped by the store window.
He wanted to buy a new baseball glove.

Grammar Practice

Using the Right Word 2

■ bare, bear; **board, bored;** borrow, lend; **brake, break;**
breath, breathe; **bring, take**

▶ **For each of the following sentences, write the correct word from the pair in parentheses.**

Example: Kelvin was feeling a little *(board, bored)* during his family camping trip.
bored

1. He was surprised to see a *(bare, bear)* helping itself to a peanut butter sandwich.

2. He whispered, "Tamela—quick! May I *(borrow, lend)* your camera?"

3. Tamela said, "Okay, but don't *(brake, break)* it."

4. "And *(bring, take)* it back to me when you're done," she added.

5. Kelvin held his *(breath, breathe)* as he clicked the shutter.

6. "Will you *(borrow, lend)* me that picture of the bear?" Tamela asked.

7. "I want to *(bring, take)* it to school to show my friends," she said.

Learning Language **With a partner, take turns telling a story about the picture. Use these words in your sentences:** *bare, bear, board, bring, break,* **and** *breathe.* **Then write a sentence using the word** *blue.*

580.1
can, may

Do you think I can go off the high dive?
(I am asking if I have the *ability* to do it.)
May I go off the high dive?
(I am asking for *permission* to do something.)

580.2
capital, capitol

The capital city of Texas is Austin.
Be sure to begin Austin with a capital letter.
My uncle works in the capitol building.
(*Capitol,* with an *ol,* refers to a government building.)

580.3
cent, scent, sent

Each rose cost one cent less than a dollar.
The scent of the flowers is sweet.
Dad sent Mom a dozen roses.

580.4
choose, chose

David must choose a different instrument this year.
Last year he chose to take drum lessons.
(*Chose* [chōz] is the past tense of the verb *choose* [cho͞oz].)

580.5
close, clothes

Please close the window.
Do you have all your clothes packed for your trip?

580.6
coarse, course

A cat's tongue feels coarse, like sandpaper.
I took a course called "Caring for Cats."

580.7
creak, creek

Old houses creak when the wind blows hard.
The water in the nearby creek is clear and cold.

580.8
dear, deer

Amber is my dear friend.
The deer enjoyed the sweet corn in her garden.

Grammar Practice

Using the Right Word 3

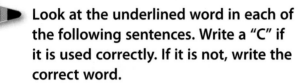

■ can, may; **capital, capitol;** cent, scent, sent; **close, clothes;** coarse, course

▶ Look at the underlined word in each of the following sentences. Write a "C" if it is used correctly. If it is not, write the correct word.

Example: <u>May</u> you eat five pieces of chicken? *Can*

1. The fox caught the <u>cent</u> of the chicken farm.

2. We're not going anywhere until you <u>close</u> the car door!

3. My brother wants to take a <u>coarse</u> in car mechanics.

4. The state <u>capitol</u> of Alaska is Juneau.

5. Jill says she <u>sent</u> the package last Friday.

6. Tai asked the coach, "<u>Can</u> we play softball instead of running today?"

7. The <u>capitol</u> building of North Dakota is designed to look like a giant grain elevator.

8. That pine tree has <u>coarse</u> bark.

9. Mom took lots of old <u>close</u> to the rummage sale.

10. This book cost only one <u>scent</u> at last year's sale!

Learning Language Tell a partner a sentence using one of the underlined words on the page. Explain the meaning of the word. Then write a sentence using another underlined word.

ELPS 2C, 2G, 4C, 5B

582.1 desert, dessert

Cactuses grow in the desert near our house.

My favorite dessert is strawberry pie.

582.2 dew, do, due

The dew on the grass got my new shoes wet.

I will do my research after school since the report is due on Wednesday.

582.3 die, dye

The plant will die if it isn't watered.

The red dye in the sweatshirt turned everything in the wash pink.

582.4 doesn't, don't

She doesn't like green bananas.
(*Doesn't* is the contraction of "does not.")

I don't either.
(*Don't* is the contraction of "do not.")

582.5 fewer, less

We had fewer snow days this winter than we did last year.
(*Fewer* refers to something you can count.)

That meant less time for ice-skating.
(*Less* refers to an amount that you cannot count.)

582.6 flower, flour

A tulip is a spring flower.

Flour is the main ingredient in bread.

582.7 for, four

The friends looked for a snack.

They found four apples on the table.

582.8 forth, fourth

We set forth on our journey through the forest.

Reggie was the fourth player to get hurt during the game.

582.9 good, well

Ling looks good in that outfit. (*Good* is an adjective modifying *Ling*.)

It fits her well. (*Well* is an adverb modifying "fits.")

Grammar Practice

Using the Right Word 4

■ desert, dessert; **dew, do, due;** die, dye; **doesn't, don't;**
  fewer, less; **forth, fourth;** good, well

▶ **For each of the following sentences,
write the correct word from each
pair of choices in parentheses.**

Example: A baby crocodile named
Liz was the *(forth, fourth)*
animal born at the zoo.
fourth

1. Crocodiles *(doesn't, don't)* give birth
   to live young.

2. They *(do, due)* lay eggs, from which the babies hatch.

3. Since they feed on fish and other small water animals,
   they would *(die, dye)* in a *(desert, dessert)*.

4. A croc's *(good, well)* hearing allows it to hear prey.

5. A frog *(doesn't, don't)* have a chance against a croc.

6. Swamps and riverbanks with lots to eat serve
   crocodiles *(good, well)*.

7. Their bellies are *(fewer, less)* scaly than their backs.

8. They use their powerful tails to charge *(forth, fourth)*.

9. There are *(fewer, less)* crocodiles than alligators
   in Florida.

Learning Language Tell a partner a funny story that uses two of
these words: *dessert, dew, due,* and *dye.* Then write a sentence
using the word *fewer.*

584.1
hair, hare

Celia's hair is short and curly.
A hare looks like a large rabbit.

584.2
heal, heel

Most scrapes and cuts heal quickly.
Gracie has a blister on her heel.

584.3
hear, here

I couldn't hear your directions.
I was over here, and you were way over there.

584.4
heard, herd

We heard the noise, all right!
It sounded like a herd of charging elephants.

584.5
hi, high

Say hi to the pilot for me.
How high is this plane flying?

584.6
hole, whole

A donut has a hole in the middle of it.
Montel ate a whole donut.

584.7
hour, our

It takes one hour to ride to the beach.
Let's pack our lunches and go.

584.8
its, it's

This backpack is no good; its zipper is stuck.
(*Its* shows possession and never has an apostrophe.)
It's also ripped. (*It's* is the contraction of "it is.")

584.9
knew, new

I knew it was going to rain.
I still wanted to wear my new shoes.

584.10
knot, not

I have a knot in my shoelaces.
I am not able to untie the tangled mess.

584.11
knows, nose

Mr. Beck knows at least a billion historical facts.
His nose is always in a book.

Grammar Practice

Using the Right Word 5

■ heal, heel; **hear, here;** hole, whole; **hour, our;** its, it's; **knew, new;** knot, not

For the following sentences, write the correct word from each pair of choices in parentheses.

Example: Adrian did *(knot, not)* feel
well; he *(knew, new)* he had
to get some rest.

not, knew

1. The train would not leave
   for an *(hour, our)*, but Ebony
   wanted to *(hear, here)* the train whistle.

2. Tera dug a *(hole, whole)* in the garden to plant a
   (knew, new) rose bush.

3. Gretchen cut her *(heal, heel)* on some broken glass
   when she dropped a *(hole, whole)* bottle of juice.

4. Wesley ties a *(knot, not)* so tight that *(its, it's)*
   impossible to untie!

5. This is *(hour, our)* cat right *(hear, here)*; that one does
   (knot, not) belong to us.

6. When Ira's gerbil got a sore on *(its, it's)* back, Ira's
   mom assured him that it would *(heal, heel)* just fine.

Learning Language **Talk with a partner about running a race.
Use these words:** *heel, hour, it's, knot, not.* **Then write a sentence
using the word** *knew.*

586.1
lay, lie

Just lay the sleeping bags on the floor.
(*Lay* means "to place.")

After the hike, we'll lie down and rest.
(*Lie* means "to recline.")

586.2
lead, led

Today I will lead (lēd) the ponies around the show ring.
Yesterday I led (lĕd) them, too.
(*Led* is the past tense of the verb *lead*.)

Some old paint contains the metal lead (lĕd).

586.3
learn, teach

I need to learn these facts about the moon.
(*Learn* means "to get information.")

Tomorrow I have to teach the science lesson.
(*Teach* means "to give information.")

586.4
loose, lose

Lee's pet tarantula is loose!
(*Loose* [lōōs] means "free or untied.")

No one but Lee could lose a big, fat spider.
(*Lose* [lōōz] means "to misplace" or "fail to win.")

586.5
made, maid

Yes, I have made a big mess.

I need a maid to help me clean it up!

586.6
mail, male

Many people get more mail on their computers than in their mailboxes.

Men are male; women are female.

586.7
meat, meet

I think meat can be a part of a healthful diet.

We were so excited to finally meet the senator.

586.8
metal, medal

Gold is a precious metal.

Is the Olympic first-place medal actually made of gold?

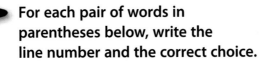

Grammar Practice

Using the Right Word 6

▪ lay, lie; **lead, led;** learn, teach; **loose, lose;** metal, medal

For each pair of words in parentheses below, write the line number and the correct choice.

Example: 1 The teacher *(lead, led)* the
        2 first graders.

   1. led

1   Larry was ready to *(learn, teach)* us how to pan for gold.

2 He said that early gold miners used *(lead, led)* pans. Today

3 most pans are made of plastic, not *(metal, medal)*.

4   "The first thing a prospector should *(learn, teach)*,"

5 Larry said, "is which streams have gold." Then he *(lead, led)*

6 the following demonstration.

7   He put a few handfuls of *(loose, lose)* gravel from a

8 stream into a pan. He submerged the pan just under some

9 water. He shook the pan gently and removed bigger rocks.

10   "After repeating the process a few times," he explained,

11 "only a bit of black sand should *(lay, lie)* in the pan. You may

12 see little nuggets or flakes of gold, too!"

13   Larry said to pick out the gold and *(lay, lie)* the pieces

14 aside. "Don't *(loose, lose)* sight of them. Start all over again,

15 and soon you may have enough gold for a *(metal, medal)*!"

Learning Language Tell a partner a sentence using the word *learn* and a sentence using the word *teach*. Then write a sentence using the word *lose*.

ELPS 2C, 2G, 4C, 5B

588.1
plain, plane

Toni wanted a plain (basic) white top.

The coyote ran across the flat plain.

A stunt plane can fly upside down.

588.2
poor, pore,
pour

The poor man had no money at all.

Every pore on my nose is clogged with oil.

Please pour the lemonade.

588.3
principal,
principle

Our principal visits the classrooms often.
(The noun *principal* is a school administrator.)

Her principal job is to be sure we are learning.
(The adjective *principal* means "most important.")

She asks students to follow this principle: Respect each other, and I'll respect you.
(*Principle* means "idea" or "belief.")

588.4
quiet, quit,
quite

Libraries should be quiet places.

Quit talking, please.

I hear quite a bit of whispering going on.

588.5
raise, rays

Please don't raise (lift) the shades.

The sun's rays are very bright this afternoon.

588.6
read, red

Have you read any books by Betsy Byars?

Why are most barns painted red?

588.7
real, really

Mom gave me a stuffed animal, but I wanted a real dog.
(Use *real* as an adjective.)

I was really disappointed.
(*Really* is an adverb.)

588.8
right, write

Is this the right (correct) place to turn right?

I'll write the directions on a note card.

Grammar Practice

Using the Right Word 7

■ plain, plane; **principal, principle;** raise, rays; **real, really;** right, write

▶ **Look at each underlined word in the following sentences. Write a "C" if it is used correctly. If it is not, write the right word.**

Example: Sarai will <u>right</u> her uncle a
             thank-you note.
             write

1. He gave her a present in a <u>plain</u> cardboard box.

2. She opened it and saw a model jet <u>plain</u>.

3. Sarai <u>really</u> wants to be a pilot someday.

4. She knows one <u>principal</u> of flight: rotating blades provide lift.

5. It was <u>plane</u> to see she was <u>real</u> happy with her gift.

6. Her name was printed on the <u>right</u> side of the <u>plane</u>.

7. She could <u>rays</u> and lower the landing gear just as a <u>real</u> pilot would.

8. <u>Rays</u> of light shone from the jet's headlights.

9. Sarai took her gift to school to show her class, and she could tell that the <u>principle</u> was impressed.

Learning Language Use the words *real* and *really* to tell a partner about a gift you've received. Then write a sentence using the word *right*.

590.1
road, rode, rowed

My house is one block from the main road.
I rode my bike to the pond.
Then I rowed the boat to my favorite fishing spot.

590.2
scene, seen

The movie has a great chase scene.
Have you seen it yet?

590.3
sea, see

A sea is a body of salty water.
I see a tall ship on the horizon.

590.4
seam, seem

The seam in my jacket is ripped.
I seem to always catch my sleeve on the door handle.

590.5
sew, so, sow

Shauna loves to sew her own clothes.
She saves her allowance so she can buy fabric.
I'd rather sow seeds and watch my garden grow.

590.6
sit, set

May I sit on one of those folding chairs?
Yes, if you help me set them up first.

590.7
some, sum

I have some math problems to do.
What is the sum of 58 + 17?

590.8
son, sun

Joe Jackson is the son of Kate Jackson.
The sun is the source of the earth's energy.

590.9
soar, sore

We watched hawks soar above us.
Our feet and legs were sore after the long hike.

590.10
stationary, stationery

A stationary bike stays in place while you pedal it.
Wu designs his own stationery (paper) on the computer.

ELPS 3H, 5B

Grammar Practice

Using the Right Word 8

■ road, rode, rowed; **scene, seen;** seam, seem; **sew, so, sow;** sit, set; **soar, sore;** stationary, stationery

▶ **For each underlined word below, write "C" if it is correct or the right word if it isn't.**

Example: Can a dragon <u>sore</u>
through the sky?
soar

Mom and Dad drove down a **(1)** <u>rode</u> we had never
(2) <u>seen</u> before. They said they had a special treat. They
were taking us to the drive-in theater!

Marla and I **(3)** <u>rowed</u> in the back seat on the way
there. A **(4)** <u>stationary</u> car didn't **(5)** <u>seam</u> like the ideal
place to watch a movie, **(6)** <u>so</u> Mom said we could **(7)** <u>set</u> on
some lawn chairs. Dad **(8)** <u>set</u> them up right next to the car.

This was the best **(9)** <u>seen</u> in the movie: It was dark.
The bad guy had just **(10)** <u>rode</u> a small boat across a lake.
He was spying on people in a cabin through the torn
(11) <u>seem</u> of a curtain. (Gosh, too bad no one knew how to
(12) <u>sow</u>!) Then a dragon breathed fire on the bad guy. I'll
bet he was **(13)** <u>soar</u> for a few days!

Learning Language To a partner, describe a scene from a play.
Use the words *set* and *stationery*. Then write a sentence using the
word *rowed*.

ELPS 2C, 2G, 4C, 5B

592.1
steal, steel

Our cat tries to steal our dog's food.
The food bowl is made of stainless steel.

592.2
tail, tale

A snake uses its tail to move its body.
"Sammy the Spotted Snake" is my favorite tall tale.

592.3
than, then

Jana's card collection is bigger than Erica's.
(*Than* is used in a comparison.)
When Jana is finished, then we can play.
(*Then* tells when.)

592.4
their, there, they're

What should we do with their cards?
(*Their* shows ownership.)
Put them over there for now.
They're going to pick them up later.
(*They're* is a contraction of "they are.")

592.5
threw, through

He threw the ball at the basket.
It swished through the net.

592.6
to, too, two

Josie passed the ball to Maria.
Lea was too tired to guard her. (*Too* means "very.")
Maria made a jump shot and scored two points.
The fans jumped and cheered, too. (*Too* can mean "also.")

592.7
waist, waste

My little sister's waist is tiny.
Do not waste your time trying to fix that bike chain.

592.8
wait, weight

I can't wait for the field trip.
Many students complain about the weight of their bookbags.

592.9
way, weigh

What is the best way to get to the park?
Birds weigh very little because of their hollow bones.

ELPS 3H, 5B

Grammar Practice

Using the Right Word 9

■ steal, steel; **than, then;** their, there, they're; **threw, through;** waist, waste; **way, weigh**

▶ **For each of the following sentences, write the correct word from the pair in parentheses.**

Example: Only one superhero is the "man of *(steal, steel)*."

steel

1. He is faster *(than, then)* a speeding bullet.

2. He can see right *(threw, through)* brick walls.

3. A big safe might *(way, weigh)* a thousand pounds, but it's easy for him to lift.

4. People trust this hero with *(they're, their)* lives.

5. At lunch, Nina *(threw, through)* her cookies away.

6. Ms. Sabb said, "Nina! Don't *(waist, waste)* food!"

7. *(Than, Then)* Nina's face turned red.

8. "But *(there, they're)* too hard," she complained.

9. "*(There, Their)* must be someone who would like them."

10. A young boy made his *(way, weigh)* to Ms. Sabb to claim the cookies.

Learning Language Tell sentences to a partner that use the words *steal* and *waist*. Explain what each word means. Then write a sentence using the word *they're*.

ELPS 2C, 2G, 4C, 5B

594.1
weak, week

The opposite of strong is weak.

There are seven days in a week.

594.2
wear, where

Finally, it's warm enough to wear shorts.

Where is the sunscreen?

594.3
weather, whether

I like rainy weather.

My dad goes golfing whether it's nice out or not.

594.4
which, witch

Which book should I read?

You'll like *The Lion, the Witch, and the Wardrobe.*

594.5
who, that, which

The man who answered the phone had a loud voice.
(*Who* refers to people.)

The puppy that I really wanted was sold already. Its brother, which had not been sold yet, came home with me.
(*That* and *which* refer to animals and things. Use commas around a clause that begins with *which.*)

594.6
who, whom

Who ordered this pizza?

And for whom did you order it?

594.7
who's, whose

Who's that knocking at the door?
(*Who's* is a contraction of "who is.")

Mrs. Lang, whose dog ran into our yard, came to get him.

594.8
wood, would

Some baseball bats are made of wood.

Would you like to play baseball after school?

594.9
your, you're

You'll get your ice cream; be patient.

You're talking to the right person!
(*You're* is a contraction of "you are.")

ELPS 3E, 5B

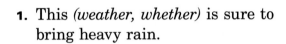

Grammar Practice

Using the Right Word 10

■ weather, whether; **who, that, which;** who, whom; **who's, whose;** your, you're

For the following sentences, write the correct word from each pair in parentheses.

Example: *(You're, Your)* going to get wet
if you forget an umbrella.

You're

1. This *(weather, whether)* is sure to bring heavy rain.

2. *(Who, Whom)* knows *(weather, whether)* it will rain cats and dogs . . . or fish and frogs?

3. Fred Hodgkins, *(who, which)* lives in England, said it rained fish there in 2000.

4. The fish *(that, who)* rained down in his yard actually came from the North Sea.

5. A waterspout, *(that, which)* is a tornado over water, picked the fish up and then dropped them over land.

6. Mr. Hodgkins, *(who's, whose)* garden the fish fell into, was quite surprised.

7. You would be surprised, too, if fish fell from the sky into *(you're, your)* garden.

Learning Language Tell a partner a sentence using a word from the list at the top of the page. Have your partner point to the word you used. Then write a sentence using another word from the list.

⭐ **TEKS** 5.20B
ELPS 2C, 4C

Understanding Sentences

A **sentence** expresses a complete thought. Usually it has a subject and a predicate. A sentence begins with a capital letter and ends with a period, a question mark, or an exclamation point.

Parts of a Sentence . . .

596.1
Subject

A **subject** is the part of a sentence—a noun or pronoun— that names who or what is doing something.

Marisha **baked a chocolate cake.**

A subject can also be the part that is talked about.

She **is a marvelous cook.**

596.2
Simple Subject

A simple subject is the subject without the words that describe or modify it.

Marisha's little sister **likes to help.**

596.3
Complete Subject

The complete subject is the simple subject along with all the words that describe it.

Marisha's little sister **likes to help.**

596.4
Compound Subject

A compound subject has two or more simple subjects joined by a conjunction *(and, or).*

Marisha **and her** sister **worked on the puzzle.**

TEKS 5.20B
ELPS 4C, 5G

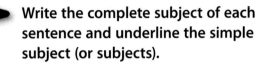

Parts of a Sentence 1

■ Subjects

Write the complete subject of each sentence and underline the simple subject (or subjects).

Example: Mom and Dad built a small tree house for me.

Mom and Dad

1. My little tree house sits in our cedar tree.

2. Three tree branches support the structure.

3. A homemade wooden ladder leads up to it.

4. Some people build tree houses to live in.

5. They are like playhouses for adults.

6. Those tree houses have electricity and plumbing.

7. Most kids' tree houses have light, too—from the sun and moon!

8. My friends and I read, write, talk, and dream in my tree house.

9. We eat snacks up there, too.

10. This private place gives us space to be ourselves.

Learning Language Write two sentences describing a special place. Underline the complete subject and circle the simple subject. Tell a partner a new sentence and identify the complete subject.

TEKS 5.20B
ELPS 2C, 4C

Parts of a Sentence . . .

598.1
Predicates

A **predicate** is the part of the sentence that contains the verb. The predicate can show action by telling what the subject is doing.

Marisha baked the cake for my birthday.

A predicate can also say something about the subject.

She is a good cook.

598.2
Simple Predicates

A simple predicate is the verb without any of the other words that modify it.

Marisha baked the cake yesterday.

598.3
Complete Predicates

The complete predicate is the verb along with all the words that modify or complete it.

Marisha baked the cake yesterday.

She had made cupcakes, too.

598.4
Compound Predicates

A compound predicate has two or more verbs.

She decorated the cake and hid it in a box in the cupboard.

598.5
Modifiers

A modifier is a word (an adjective or an adverb) or a group of words that describes another word.

My family planned a surprise party. (*My* modifies *family*; *a* and *surprise* modify *party*.)

They hid behind the door and waited quietly. (*Behind the door* modifies *hid*; *quietly* modifies *waited*.)

TEKS 5.20B
ELPS 4C

Practice

Parts of a Sentence 2

■ Predicates

> Write the complete predicate of each
> sentence. Then underline the simple
> predicate (the verb or verbs).

Example: Angelita has made a wish.

<u>has made</u> a wish

1. She wished for diamonds.

2. A diamond is one of the hardest
   materials known.

3. A diamond can scratch just about anything else.

4. Diamonds are formed from carbon deposits.

5. Anthracite, a shiny black coal, is also a form of carbon.

6. Constant underground pressure and heat may cause a
   change in a carbon deposit.

7. Sometimes it becomes a colorless crystal called a
   diamond.

8. Anthracite does not produce diamonds.

9. This type of coal is usually burned for heat or power.

10. It burns very cleanly.

Learning Language Write a sentence about diamonds. Underline
the complete predicate. Circle the simple predicate. Tell a partner
another sentence. Identify the complete predicate and the simple
predicate.

Parts of a Sentence . . .

600.1
Clauses

A **clause** is a group of words that has a subject and a predicate. A clause can be independent or dependent.

600.2
Independent Clauses

An independent clause expresses a complete thought and can stand alone as a sentence.

> **I ride my bike to school.**

> **Bryan gets a ride from his dad.**

600.3
Dependent Clauses

A dependent clause does not express a complete thought, so it cannot stand alone as a sentence. Dependent clauses often begin with subordinating conjunctions like *when* or *because*. (See **634.2**.)

> **when the weather is nice**

Some dependent clauses begin with relative pronouns like *who* or *which*. (See **614.1**.)

> **who works near our school**

A dependent clause must be joined to an independent clause. The result is a complex sentence.

> **I ride my bike to school when the weather is nice. Bryan gets a ride from his dad, who works near our school.**

ELPS 3E, 4C

Practice

Parts of a Sentence 3

■ Clauses

For each clause below, write an "I" for independent clause or a "D" for dependent clause.

Example: all of Geeta's friends were
wearing sunglasses
I

1. because her outfit was so bright

2. Geeta often wears colorful clothes

3. once she colored her hair to match her outfit

4. which was a pair of pink polka-dot overalls

5. last spring, if it was a rainy day

6. she wore a neon-yellow rain slicker

7. when we went to the zoo on a field trip

8. Geeta dressed in safari clothes

9. she says she gets her fashion sense from her grandmother

10. who has traveled around the world

Learning Language With a partner, choose a dependent clause from the list above. Take turns adding words to it to form complete sentences.

ELPS 2C, 4C

Parts of a Sentence . . .

602.1
Phrases

A **phrase** is a group of related words. Phrases cannot stand alone as sentences since they do *not* have both a subject and a predicate.

602.2
Noun Phrases

A noun phrase doesn't have a predicate. A noun and the adjectives that describe it make up a noun phrase.

> **the new student**

602.3
Verb Phrases

A verb phrase doesn't have a subject. It includes a main verb and one or more helping verbs.

> **could have written**

602.4
Prepositional Phrases

A prepositional phrase doesn't have a subject or a predicate. However, it can add important information to a sentence. (See page **632**.)

> **about George Washington**

602.5
Appositive Phrases

An appositive phrase is another way of saying or renaming the noun or pronoun before it.

> **George Washington,** our first president

NOTE: When you put these phrases together, they become a sentence.

> **The new student could have written about George Washington, our first president.**

 ELPS 3H, 4C

Practice

Parts of a Sentence 4

■ Phrases

Identify the underlined phrases. Write "N" for a noun phrase, "V" for a verb phrase, "P" for a prepositional phrase, and "A" for an appositive phrase.

Example: Look at this book showing the
flags <u>of the world</u>.
P

1. A flag <u>might have</u> horizontal bars or stripes.

2. I <u>have seen</u> that one many times before!

3. Red, <u>a popular flag color</u>, is in the flags of the three largest North American countries.

4. Our class will have its own flag <u>by the end</u> of the week.

5. <u>Your own family flag</u> can fly in front of your home.

6. You could also hang it <u>on the refrigerator door</u>.

7. George's flag has a Komodo dragon, <u>a monitor lizard</u>, on it.

8. <u>My older brother</u> would like that one.

Learning Language Tell a partner about a flag you would design. Try to include each type of phrase (noun, verb, prepositional, and appositive) in your description. Have your partner identify the phrases.

 **TEKS** 5.20A(ii)
ELPS 2C, 4C

Using the Parts of Speech
Nouns . . .

A **noun** is a word that names a person, a place, a thing, or an idea.

Kinds of Nouns

604.1
Proper Nouns

A proper noun names a specific person, place, thing, or idea. Proper nouns are capitalized.

Roberta Fischer   Millennium Park   *Shrek*   Labor Day

604.2
Common Nouns

A common noun does *not* name a specific person, place, thing, or idea. Common nouns are not capitalized.

woman   park   movie   holiday

604.3
Concrete Nouns

A concrete noun names a thing that you can experience through one or more of your five senses. Concrete nouns are either common or proper.

magazine   rose   Washington Monument   chocolate

604.4
Abstract Nouns

An abstract noun names a thing that you can think about but cannot see, hear, or touch. Abstract nouns are either common or proper.

love   democracy   Judaism   Wednesday

604.5
Compound Nouns

A compound noun is made up of two or more words.

busboy (spelled as one word)

blue jeans (spelled as two words)

two-wheeler   sister-in-law (spelled with hyphens)

604.6
Collective Nouns

A collective noun names a group of persons or things.

Persons: **class   team   clan   family**

Animals: **herd   flock   litter   pack   colony**

Things: **bunch   batch   collection**

 **TEKS** 5.20A(ii)
ELPS 4C

Grammar Practice

Nouns 1

■ Common, Proper, Concrete, and Abstract Nouns

▶ **For each sentence, write whether the first underlined noun is common or proper.**

Example: What is a fair <u>price</u> for a movie <u>ticket</u>?
common

1. In the <u>United States</u>, <u>wealth</u> is measured in dollars.

2. The dollar bill has a <u>drawing</u> of <u>George Washington</u> on its face.

3. A picture of <u>Sacagawea</u>, a Native American woman who helped Lewis and Clark, is on the dollar <u>coin</u>.

4. Most <u>bills</u> and coins have little real <u>worth</u> by themselves.

5. For money to have value, <u>people</u> must agree on it as a symbol of fair <u>trade</u>.

6. For instance, <u>Americans</u> agree that the bill with Ben Franklin's <u>picture</u> on it is worth $100.

7. And when you trade it for 10 <u>Yellowstone National Park Passes</u>, you've determined the <u>value</u> of $100!

Learning Language Write whether the second underlined noun is concrete or abstract. Then name some collective nouns. Tell a partner a sentence using a collective noun.

Nouns . . .
Number of Nouns

606.1
Singular Nouns

A singular noun names just one person, place, thing, or idea.

room   **paper**   **pen pal**   **hope**

606.2
Plural Nouns

A plural noun names more than one person, place, thing, or idea.

rooms   **papers**   **pen pals**   **hopes**

Gender of Nouns

606.3
Noun Gender

The gender of a noun refers to its being *feminine* (female), *masculine* (male), *neuter* (neither male nor female), or *indefinite* (male or female).

Feminine **(female): mother, sister, women, cow, hen**

Masculine **(male): father, brother, men, bull, rooster**

Neuter **(neither male nor female):**
tree, closet, cobweb

Indefinite **(male or female):**
child, pilot, parent, dentist

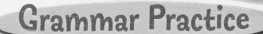

Grammar Practice

Nouns 2

■ Number of Nouns
■ Gender of Nouns

Identify the underlined noun in each sentence as "F" for feminine, "M" for masculine, "N" for neuter, or "I" for indefinite.

Example: <u>Frank</u> wanted to go fishing.
M

1. He gathered fishing <u>rods</u> and bait.

2. He walked down to the <u>pier</u>.

3. Before he even got there, he heard his <u>mom</u> calling.

4. He looked at his watch and realized it was time to walk the neighbor's <u>dogs</u>.

5. Frank's neighbor, <u>Mr. Wise</u>, was ill.

6. <u>Mrs. Wise</u> was working and couldn't walk the dogs.

7. Frank put <u>leashes</u> on Bo and Spot and took them out.

8. Frank saw one of his <u>friends</u> riding a bike.

9. He shouted, "Hey, Sandy! Let's go to the <u>lake</u>!"

10. Sandy said, "Okay! My <u>cousin</u> will come, too."

Learning Language Tell a partner a story about caring for a dog. Use three singular and three plural nouns in your story. Have your partner tell which nouns are singular and which are plural.

ELPS 2C, 4C

Nouns . . .
Uses of Nouns

608.1
Subject Nouns

A noun may be the subject of a sentence. (The subject is the part of the sentence that does something or is being talked about.)

Joe ran away from the bee.

608.2
Predicate Nouns

A predicate noun follows a form of the verb *be (is, are, was, were)* and renames the subject.

The book is a mystery.

608.3
Possessive Nouns

A possessive noun shows ownership. (See **534.2** and **536.1** for information on forming possessives.)

The book's **ending is a big surprise.**

The books' **bindings are torn and weak.**

608.4
Object Nouns

Direct Object: A direct object is the word that tells *what* or *who* receives the action of the verb. The direct object completes the meaning of the verb.

Nadia spent all her money. (*What* did Nadia spend? The verb *spent* would be unclear without the direct object, *money.*)

Indirect Object: An indirect object names the person *to whom* or *for whom* something is done.

Joe gave Nadia **the book.** (The book is given *to whom*? The book is given to *Nadia*, the indirect object.)

Object of a Preposition: An object of a preposition is part of a prepositional phrase. (See page **632**.)

Nadia put the book on the shelf. (The noun *shelf* is the object of the preposition *on.*)

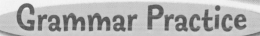

Grammar Practice

Nouns 3

■ Uses of Nouns

▶ **Work with a partner. For each sentence below, tell whether the underlined noun is a subject, an object, or a predicate noun.**

Example: People like to look at <u>stars</u>.
                    object

1. Long ago, <u>people</u> thought certain groups of stars looked like bears, lions, and people.

2. One <u>group</u> of seven stars is known as the Big Dipper.

3. Three bright stars in a row are <u>part</u> of Orion the Hunter.

4. In rural areas, as many as 2,500 stars might be visible to the human <u>eye</u>.

5. People in the <u>city</u> don't see that many stars.

6. One <u>woman</u> in the city painted stars on her house.

7. For the most part, stars are simply great <u>balls</u> of gas.

8. Just like the sun, stars produce <u>energy</u> as a result of nuclear reactions.

Learning Language Talk with a partner about predicate nouns you could use to complete this sentence: *When I looked at the sky, the clouds were _____ .*

⭐ ELPS 2C, 4C

Pronouns . . .

A **pronoun** is a word used in place of a noun.

610.1
Antecedents

An antecedent is the noun that a pronoun refers to or replaces. All pronouns have antecedents.

Anju's brother has his own skateboard now.
(*Brother* is the antecedent of the pronoun *his*.)

Number of a Pronoun

610.2
Singular and Plural

Pronouns can be either singular or plural.

I grabbed my skateboard and joined LeRon.
We were going to the skate park.

Person of a Pronoun

The *person* of a pronoun tells whether the antecedent of the pronoun is speaking, being spoken to, or being spoken about.

610.3
First-Person Pronouns

A first-person pronoun is used in place of the name of the speaker.

Petra said, "I like raspberry ice cream." (*I* replaces the name *Petra,* the person who is speaking.)

610.4
Second-Person Pronouns

A second-person pronoun names the person spoken to.

Su, have you decided on a flavor? (*You* replaces the name *Su,* the person being spoken to.)

610.5
Third-Person Pronouns

A third-person pronoun is used to name the person or thing spoken about.

Jon said that he wants pumpkin ice cream because it is so good. (*He* refers to *Jon,* the person being spoken about, and *it* refers to *ice cream,* the thing being spoken about.)

ELPS 3E, 4C

Grammar Practice

Pronouns 1

■ Number of a Pronoun
■ Person of a Pronoun

▶ In the following sentences, write whether the underlined pronoun is first, second, or third person.

Example: Carey asked Aunt Dulcie, "Will <u>you</u> be picking up Mac at the airport?"

second person

1. "Yes," <u>she</u> replied.

2. "May <u>we</u> join you?" asked Cleo.

3. "Are <u>you</u> both ready?" asked Aunt Dulcie.

4. When <u>they</u> reached the airport, they watched for Mac's plane.

5. Carey said, "<u>I</u> can't wait to see Mac!"

6. "I wonder if <u>he</u> will look different," Cleo said.

7. "Maybe he won't recognize <u>us</u>!" Carey worried.

8. When Mac got off the plane, he went to get <u>his</u> bags.

9. Aunt Dulcie, Carey, and Cleo were waiting there, and Mac immediately waved at <u>them</u>.

10. "Boy, that makes <u>me</u> feel good!" Carey exclaimed.

Learning Language Tell a partner about a person you would like to visit. Use at least two singular pronouns.

ELPS 2C, 4C

Pronouns . . .
Uses of Pronouns

612.1
Subject Pronouns

A subject pronoun is used as the subject of a sentence.

I can tell jokes well.

They really make people laugh.

612.2
Object Pronouns

An object pronoun is used as a direct object, an indirect object, or the object of a preposition.

Mr. Otto encourages me. (direct object)

Mr. Otto gives us help with math. (indirect object)

I made a funny card for him. (object of the preposition)

612.3
Possessive Pronouns

A possessive pronoun shows ownership. It can be used before a noun, or it can stand alone.

Gloria finished writing her story.
(*Her* comes before the noun *story*.)

The idea for the plot was mine. (*Mine* can stand alone.)

Before a noun: *my, your, his, her, its, our, their*

Stand alone: *mine, yours, his, hers, ours, theirs*

Uses of Personal Pronouns

	Singular Pronouns			Plural Pronouns		
	Subject Pronouns	Possessive Pronouns	Object Pronouns	Subject Pronouns	Possessive Pronouns	Object Pronouns
First Person	I	my, mine	me	we	our, ours	us
Second Person	you	your, yours	you	you	your, yours	you
Third Person	he	his	him	they	their, theirs	them
	she	her, hers	her			
	it	its	it			

ELPS 2G, 2I, 4C

Grammar Practice

Pronouns 2

■ Uses of Pronouns

For the underlined pronoun in each sentence below, write "SP" if it is a subject pronoun, "OP" if it is an object pronoun, or "PP" if it is a possessive pronoun.

Example: What is <u>your</u> favorite kind of fruit?

PP

1. <u>I</u> like apples.

2. <u>My</u> mom likes oranges and peaches the best.

3. Dad gave <u>her</u> a whole basket of fruit.

4. <u>She</u> was thrilled!

5. First, she set aside some of <u>her</u> favorites.

6. Then she shared the rest with <u>us</u>.

7. We divided <u>them</u> all in no time.

8. Boy, <u>they</u> were good!

9. Poor Dad—there were none left for <u>him</u>.

10. Mom said, "Next time I'll save some for <u>you</u>."

Learning Language With a partner, take turns telling about your favorite kind of fruit. Use at least three personal pronouns. Retell what your partner says.

TEKS 5.20A(vi)
ELPS 2C, 4C

Pronouns . . .

Types of Pronouns

614.1
Relative Pronouns

A relative pronoun connects a dependent clause to a word in another part of the sentence.

Any fifth grader who wants to join our music group should see Carlos.

Relative pronouns: *who, whose, whom, which, what, that, whoever, whomever, whichever, whatever*

614.2
Interrogative Pronouns

An interrogative pronoun asks a question.

Who is going to play the keyboard?

Interrogative pronouns: *who, whose, whom, which, what*

614.3
Demonstrative Pronouns

A demonstrative pronoun points out or identifies a noun without naming it. The demonstrative pronouns are *this, that, these,* and *those.*

That sounds like a great idea!

TIP: When *this, that, these,* and *those* are used before nouns, they are adjectives, not pronouns.

614.4
Intensive and Reflexive Pronouns

An intensive pronoun stresses the word it refers to. A reflexive pronoun refers back to the subject. These pronouns have *-self* or *-selves* added at the end.

Carlos himself taught the group. (intensive)

Carlos enjoyed himself. (reflexive)

614.5
Indefinite Pronouns

An indefinite pronoun refers to people or things that are not named or known. (See page 446.)

Nobody is here to videotape the practice.

Indefinite pronouns: *all, another, any, anybody, anyone, anything, both, each, each one, either, everybody, everyone, everything, few, many, most, much, neither, nobody, none, no one, nothing, one, others, several, some*

TEKS 5.20A(vi)
ELPS 3E, 4C, 5B, 5G

Grammar Practice

Pronouns 3

■ Relative, Demonstrative, and Indefinite Pronouns

▶ **For each underlined pronoun in the sentences below, write "R" if it is a relative pronoun, "D" if it is demonstrative, or "I" if it is indefinite.**

Example: Giant pandas, <u>whose</u> natural habitat is in China, can eat 30 pounds of bamboo daily.

R

1. <u>Some</u> can eat more than 80 pounds in a day.

2. <u>That</u> is a lot of food, even for a 300-pound animal!

3. Ask <u>someone</u> what kind of animal a panda is.

4. <u>Many</u> will say a panda is a bear.

5. <u>Others</u> will call it a member of the raccoon family.

6. With such a lean diet, pandas don't build up the fat <u>that</u> is needed for a long winter sleep.

7. <u>This</u> makes them unlike most other bears.

8. They are also active mainly at night, <u>which</u> is when raccoons are active.

9. <u>Everyone</u> was sad when giant pandas were placed on the endangered species list.

Learning Language Write a sentence describing another unusual animal. Use an indefinite pronoun. To a partner, tell another sentence with an indefinite pronoun.

Verbs . . .

A **verb** shows action or links the subject to another word in the sentence. The verb is the main word in the predicate.

Types of Verbs

616.1
Action Verbs

An action verb tells what the subject is doing.

The wind blows.   **I pull my sweater on.**

616.2
Linking Verbs

A linking verb links a subject to a noun or an adjective in the predicate part of the sentence.

That car is a convertible. (The verb *is* links the subject *car* to the noun *convertible*.)

A new car looks shiny. (The verb *looks* links the subject *car* to the adjective *shiny*.)

616.3
Helping Verbs

Helping verbs (also called auxiliary verbs) come before the main verb and give it a more specific meaning.

Lee will write in his journal. (The verb *will* helps state a future action.)

Lee has been writing in his journal. (The verbs *has* and *been* help state a continuing action.)

Linking Verbs

is, are, was, were, am, being, been, smell, look, taste, remain, feel, appear, sound, seem, become, grow, stand, turn

Helping Verbs

shall, will, should, would, could, must, can, may, have, had, has, do, did, does

The forms of the verb *be (is, are, was, were, am, being, been)* may also be helping verbs.

ELPS 3G, 4C

Grammar Practice

Verbs 1

■ Types of Verbs

In the following sentences, write whether the underlined verb is an action verb, a linking verb, or a helping verb.

Example: My dogs, Butch and Bailey, <u>learned</u> how to "sing."
action verb

1. They <u>can</u> bark several tunes.

2. Butch's deep "woof" <u>supplies</u> the low notes.

3. Bailey <u>is</u> the soprano of the duo.

4. They <u>sound</u> funny!

5. They <u>have</u> performed at local talent shows.

6. They <u>are</u> very popular.

7. The audience <u>cheers</u> for more.

8. Everyone <u>will</u> gather around Butch and Bailey at the end of a show.

9. The dogs just <u>love</u> all the attention!

10. Maybe someday they'll <u>be</u> famous.

Learning Language To a partner, tell how you feel about dogs. Use two linking verbs.

Verbs . . .

Simple Verb Tenses

The tense of a verb tells when the action takes place. The simple tenses are *present, past,* and *future.* (See page 451.)

618.1 Present Tense Verbs

The present tense of a verb states an action (or state of being) that is *happening now* or that *happens regularly.*

I like soccer.   We practice every day.

618.2 Past Tense Verbs

The past tense of a verb states an action (or state of being) that *happened at a specific time in the past.*

Anne kicked the soccer ball.   She was the goalie.

618.3 Future Tense Verbs

The future tense of a verb states an action (or state of being) that *will take place.*

I will like soccer forever.   We will practice every day.

Perfect Verb Tenses

Perfect tense is expressed with certain helping verbs.

618.4 Present Perfect Tense Verbs

The present perfect tense states an action that is *still going on.* Add *has* or *have* before the past participle form of the main verb.

Alexis has slept for two hours so far.

TIP: The past participle is the same as the past tense of most verbs.

618.5 Past Perfect Tense Verbs

The past perfect tense states an action that *began and ended in the past.* Add *had* before the past participle.

Jondra had slept for eight hours before the alarm rang.

618.6 Future Perfect Tense Verbs

The future perfect tense states an action that *will begin in the future and end at a specific time.* Add *will have* before the past participle form of the main verb.

Riley will have slept for 12 hours by 9:00 a.m. tomorrow.

Grammar Practice

Verbs 2

■ Simple Verb Tenses

▶ **Write the tense—*past, present,* or *future*—of the underlined verbs in the following sentences.**

Example: Isabel <u>loves</u> clothes.

  present

1. She <u>will show</u> me her new poncho tomorrow.

2. She <u>saw</u> some great new styles in *Latina* magazine.

3. Many of her clothes <u>are</u> quite colorful.

4. She <u>enjoys</u> wearing ruffled skirts in green, purple, orange, and yellow.

5. Designers Carolina Herrera and Oscar de la Renta <u>brought</u> Latin flavor into their styles.

6. They <u>mixed</u> different textures in one outfit.

7. Famous people like Jennifer Lopez and Carlos Santana <u>design</u> their own lines of clothing.

8. Perhaps many people <u>will choose</u> to wear more Latin-flavored items.

Learning Language Tell a partner about your favorite clothes. Use two different verb tenses. Ask your partner about his or her favorite clothing. Compare your answers.

★ **TEKS** 5.20A(i)
ELPS 2C, 4C

Verbs . . .
Forms of Verbs

620.1
Transitive and Intransitive Verbs

An action verb is called a transitive verb if it is followed by a direct object (noun or pronoun). The object makes the meaning of the verb complete.

> Direct Object: **Ann Cameron** writes books **about Julian.**

A transitive verb may also be followed by an indirect object. An indirect object names the person *to whom* or *for whom* something is done.

> Indirect Object: **Books** give children **enjoyment.**
> (*Children* is the indirect object. *Give* is a transitive verb, and *enjoyment* is the direct object.)

A verb that is not followed by a direct object is intransitive.

> **Ann Cameron** writes **about Julian in her books.** (The verb is followed by two prepositional phrases.)

620.2
Active and Passive Verbs

A verb is active if the subject is doing the action.

> **Tia** threw **a ball.** (The subject *Tia* is doing the action.)

A verb is passive if the subject does not do the action.

> **A ball** was thrown **by Tia.** (The subject *ball* is not doing the action.)

620.3
Singular and Plural Verbs

A singular verb is used with a singular subject.

> **Ben** likes **cream cheese and olive sandwiches.**

A plural verb is used when the subject is plural. (A plural verb usually does not have an *s* at the end, which is just the opposite of a plural subject.)

> **Black olives** taste **like wax.**

620.4
Irregular Verbs

Some verbs in the English language are irregular. Instead of adding *-ed,* the spelling of the word changes in different tenses. See page **622** for a chart of irregular verbs.

> **I** speak.   **Yesterday I** spoke.   **I have** spoken.

TEKS 5.20A(i)
ELPS 4C

Grammar Practice

Verbs 3

■ Active and Passive Verbs

Decide whether the subject (underlined) does or does not do the action in the following sentences. If it does, write "active verb"; if not, write "passive verb."

Example: A <u>mother mallard duck</u> protects her babies.

active verb

1. <u>She</u> doesn't need an umbrella to protect them, though.

2. <u>Ducklings</u> are protected by their feathers.

3. Their <u>feathers</u> help them stay warm and dry.

4. Within a day of hatching, the <u>babies</u> are led to the water by their mother.

5. The <u>ducklings</u> can already feed themselves!

6. In 50 or 60 days, <u>they</u> fly off to independence.

7. <u>Adult feathers</u> are molted by the ducks every summer.

8. By October, <u>they</u> have all their feathers again and can begin to fly south.

9. Their <u>quacking</u> can be heard by everyone!

Learning Language Write Sentence 4 above as an active sentence. Circle the irregular verb. To a partner, tell another sentence that uses an active, irregular verb.

Verbs . . .

Forms of Verbs

Common Irregular Verbs

The principal parts of some common irregular verbs are listed below. The past participle is used with the helping verbs *has, have,* or *had.*

Present Tense	**I** hide.	**She** hides.
Past Tense	**Yesterday I** hid.	**Yesterday she** hid.
Past Participle	**I have** hidden.	**She has** hidden.

Present Tense	Past Tense	Past Participle	Present Tense	Past Tense	Past Participle	Present Tense	Past Tense	Past Participle
am, is, are	was, were	been	give	gave	given	shrink	shrank	shrunk
begin	began	begun	go	went	gone	sing	sang, sung	sung
bite	bit	bitten	grow	grew	grown	sink	sank, sunk	sunk
blow	blew	blown	hang	hung	hung	sit	sat	sat
break	broke	broken	hide	hid	hidden, hid	sleep	slept	slept
bring	brought	brought	hold	held	held	speak	spoke	spoken
buy	bought	bought	keep	kept	kept	spring	sprang, sprung	sprung
catch	caught	caught	know	knew	known	stand	stood	stood
come	came	come	lay (place)	laid	laid	steal	stole	stolen
dive	dived, dove	dived	lead	led	led	swear	swore	sworn
do	did	done	leave	left	left	swim	swam	swum
draw	drew	drawn	lie (recline)	lay	lain	swing	swung	swung
drink	drank	drunk	make	made	made	take	took	taken
drive	drove	driven	ride	rode	ridden	teach	taught	taught
eat	ate	eaten	ring	rang	rung	tear	tore	torn
fall	fell	fallen	rise	rose	risen	throw	threw	thrown
fight	fought	fought	run	ran	run	wake	woke	woken
fly	flew	flown	see	saw	seen	wear	wore	worn
freeze	froze	frozen	shake	shook	shaken	weave	wove	woven
get	got	gotten	shine (light)	shone	shone	write	wrote	written

* The following verbs are the same in each of the principal parts: *burst, cost, cut, hurt, let, put, set,* and *spread.*

TEKS 5.20A(i)
ELPS 3C, 4C

Grammar Practice

Verbs 4

■ Irregular Verbs

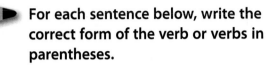

For each sentence below, write the correct form of the verb or verbs in parentheses.

Example: I *(sit)* in the park for five hours yesterday.
sat

1. Sarah had *(eat)* a sandwich just before supper.

2. Jasmine *(set)* the dictionary on the teacher's desk last Friday.

3. Jamal has already *(go)* home.

4. For some reason, Omar *(leave)* eight copies of the newspaper in our mailbox.

5. Olive *(swim)* 22 laps during the races last summer.

6. When Yadira's parakeet *(fly)* out of its cage, she *(run)* to catch it and *(put)* it back in its cage.

7. When he was little, my dad *(keep)* a squirrel as a pet.

8. The teacher *(lead)* the class to the museum's prehistoric exhibit.

Learning Language Write sentences with active verbs. Use the past tense of the irregular verbs *bring, write,* and *speak.* Tell a partner another active sentence using one of the words.

Adjectives . . .

Adjectives are words that modify (describe) nouns or pronouns. Adjectives tell *what kind, how many,* or *which one.* (See pages **457–459**.)

624.1
Articles

The adjectives *a, an,* and *the* are called articles.

> **"Owlet" is the name for a baby owl.**

The article *a* comes before singular words that begin with consonant sounds. Also use *a* before singular words that begin with the long *u* sound.

> **a shooting star**   **a unique constellation**

The article *an* comes before singular words that begin with any vowel sounds except for long *u.*

> **an astronaut**   **an inquiring mind**   **an unusual outfit**

624.2
Proper and Common Adjectives

Proper adjectives are formed from proper nouns. They are always capitalized. (See page **457**.)

> **On a cold Minnesota day, a Hawaiian trip sounds great.**

Common adjectives are any that are *not* proper.

> **I'll pack my big blue suitcase for a weeklong trip.**

624.3
Predicate Adjectives

Predicate adjectives follow linking verbs and describe subjects. (See page **513**.)

> **The apples are juicy. They taste sweet.**

624.4
Compound Adjectives

Compound adjectives are made up of more than one word. Some are spelled as one word; others are hyphenated.

> **white-throated sparrows**   **evergreen tree**

624.5
Demonstrative Adjectives

Demonstrative adjectives point out specific nouns.

> **This nest has four eggs, and that nest has two.**

> **These eggs will hatch before those eggs will.**

TIP: When *this, that, these,* and *those* are not used before nouns, they are pronouns, not adjectives.

ELPS 3H, 4C, 5G

Grammar Practice

Adjectives 1

■ Common and Proper Adjectives
■ Predicate Adjectives

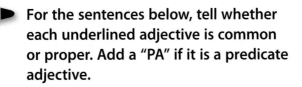

For the sentences below, tell whether each underlined adjective is common or proper. Add a "PA" if it is a predicate adjective.

Example: My dog Ramona makes some noises that are quite <u>unusual</u>.
common, PA

1. I wish I knew what the <u>poor</u> animal is trying to say!

2. She barks a lot, but she's really <u>sweet</u>.

3. She is an <u>Australian</u> cattle dog.

4. She was born in Montana, though, so she is <u>American</u>.

5. Cattle dogs are <u>muscular</u> and have a lot of energy.

6. Whenever I throw a ball, Ramona makes some <u>amazing</u> catches.

7. The breed is also very <u>protective</u>.

8. Ramona's <u>low</u> growl alerts us if a stranger approaches our house.

Learning Language Write two sentences describing a pet. Use a proper adjective in one and a predicate adjective in the other. To a partner, tell another sentence using an adjective that describes your pet.

TEKS 5.20A(iii)
ELPS 2C, 4C

Adjectives . . .

626.1
Indefinite Adjectives

Indefinite adjectives tell approximately (not exactly) *how many* or *how much*.

> Most **students love summer.**
>
> Some **days are rainy, but** few **days are boring.**

Forms of Adjectives

626.2
Positive Adjectives

The positive (base) form of an adjective describes a noun without comparing it to another noun. (See page 458.)

> A hummingbird is small.

626.3
Comparative Adjectives

The comparative form of an adjective compares two people, places, things, or ideas. The comparison is formed by adding *-er* to one-syllable adjectives or the word *more* or *less* before longer adjectives.

> A hummingbird is smaller **than a sparrow.**
>
> Hummingbirds are more colorful **than sparrows.**

626.4
Superlative Adjectives

The superlative form of an adjective compares three or more people, places, things, or ideas. The superlative is formed by adding *-est* to one-syllable adjectives or the word *most* or *least* before longer adjectives.

> The hummingbird is the smallest **bird I've seen.**
>
> The parrot is the most colorful **bird in the zoo.**

626.5
Irregular Forms of Adjectives

The comparative and superlative forms of some adjectives are different words. *More* or *most* is not needed with these words.

Positive	Comparative	Superlative
good	better	best
bad	worse	worst
many	more	most
little	less	least

TEKS 5.20A(iii)
ELPS 3C, 4C

Grammar Practice

Adjectives 2

■ Indefinite Adjectives
■ Forms of Adjectives

▶ **For each underlined adjective below, write whether it is positive, comparative, or superlative. Add an "I" if the adjective is indefinite.**

Example: <u>Many</u> theaters have afternoon shows. positive, I

1. The audience for a matinee is <u>smaller</u> than the audience for a show at night.

2. Since there are <u>fewer</u> viewers in the afternoon, a good seat is easy to find.

3. <u>Most</u> people who see a movie go on the weekend.

4. That is my <u>least favorite</u> time to see a movie.

5. The <u>best</u> movie I've ever seen is the new version of *Charlie and the Chocolate Factory.*

6. It is <u>more faithful</u> to the book than the old movie is.

7. For instance, the Oompa-Loompas had <u>orange</u> skin in the old movie but not in the book.

8. Forty years after Roald Dahl wrote the book, it is still a <u>great</u> story.

Learning Language Write two sentences. Use a comparative adjective in one and a superlative adjective in the other. To a partner, tell two more sentences using the same types of adjectives.

 **TEKS** 5.20A(iv)
ELPS 2C, 4C

Adverbs . . .

Adverbs are words that modify (describe) verbs, adjectives, or other adverbs. (Also see pages **460–461**.)

> **The softball team practices** faithfully.
> (*Faithfully* modifies the verb *practices*.)
>
> **Yesterday's practice was** extra **long.**
> (*Extra* modifies the adjective *long*.)
>
> **Last night the players slept** quite **soundly.**
> (*Quite* modifies the adverb *soundly*.)

Types of Adverbs

628.1 **Adverbs of Time**	Adverbs of time tell *when, how often,* or *how long.* **Max batted** first. (when) **Katie's team plays** weekly. (how often) **Her team was in first place** briefly. (how long)
628.2 **Adverbs of Place**	Adverbs of place tell *where.* **When the first pitch curved** outside, **the batter leaned** forward. **"Hit it** there!" **urged the coach, pointing to right field.**
628.3 **Adverbs of Manner**	Adverbs of manner tell *how* something is done. **Max waited** eagerly **for the next pitch.** **He swung** powerfully **but missed the ball.**
628.4 **Adverbs of Intensity**	Adverbs of intensity tell *how much.* **Andrew could** almost **see the scene that Max described so well.** **Kara reads** a lot **on weekends.**

TEKS 5.20A(iv)
ELPS 4C

Grammar Practice

Adverbs 1

■ Types of Adverbs

▶ Identify the type of each underlined adverb. Write "T" for time, "P" for place, "M" for manner, or "I" for intensity.

Example: My little brother put a peanut butter sandwich in our DVD player <u>yesterday</u>.

1. He told Mom he was putting <u>away</u> his sandwich.

2. Karina <u>cleverly</u> solved the puzzle.

3. Nelson had never been to a movie theater <u>before</u>.

4. When we got to Pine Lane, Rae shouted, "Turn <u>here</u>!"

5. Emilio was <u>completely</u> exhausted.

6. <u>Finally</u>, he turned the lights off and went to bed.

7. You need to slide your feet <u>backward</u> to do this dance.

8. I had <u>hardly</u> gotten to sleep when it was time for me to get up again.

9. The coach said, "We'll have something to drink <u>shortly</u>."

Learning Language For the adverbs of time above, write whether they tell *when, how often,* or *how long.* Tell a partner another sentence using an adverb that shows time.

TEKS 5.20A(iv)
ELPS 2C, 4C

Adverbs . . .

Forms of Adverbs

630.1
Positive Adverbs

The positive (base) form of an adverb does not make a comparison. (See page 460.)

Max plays hard **from the first pitch to the last out.**

630.2
Comparative Adverbs

The comparative form of an adverb compares how two things are done. The comparison is formed by adding *-er* to one-syllable adverbs or the word *more* or *less* before longer adverbs.

Max plays harder **than his cousin plays, and he plays** more often **than his cousin does.**

630.3
Superlative Adverbs

The superlative form of an adverb compares how three or more things are done. The superlative is formed by adding *-est* to one-syllable adverbs or the word *most* or *least* before longer adverbs.

Max plays hardest **in close games. He plays** most often **in center field.**

630.4
Irregular Forms of Adverbs

The comparative and superlative forms of some adverbs are different words. *More* or *most* is not needed with these words.

Positive	Comparative	Superlative
well	**better**	**best**
badly	**worse**	**worst**

TIP: Do not confuse *well* and *good*. *Good* is an adjective and *well* is usually an adverb. (See 626.5.)

TEKS 5.20A(iv)
ELPS 4C

Grammar Practice

Adverbs 2

■ Forms of Adverbs

▶ **For each sentence, write the comparative or superlative form of the adverb given in the blank.**

Example: My cat could predict the weather ___*(well)*___ than Channel 29's forecaster can!

better

1. I think Debra Lynch, the forecaster on Channel 6, predicts weather ___*(well)*___ of all.

2. When we read aloud in class, I thought I was reading ___*(quietly)*___ of anyone.

3. Then Reuben read after me, and he read ___*(quietly)*___ than I did.

4. The zoologist told us we could move ___*(close)*___ to the snake than we were.

5. Rosanna was the bravest; she moved ___*(close)*___ to it.

6. When Terrence explained the math homework to me, I understood it ___*(clearly)*___ than I did before.

7. He explains math ___*(clearly)*___ of anyone in class.

Learning Language Write sentences using the comparative and superlative forms of *close*. Tell a partner sentences using *faster*. Then tell a sentence using *fastest*.

TEKS 5.20A(v)
ELPS 2C, 4C

Prepositions

Prepositions are words that introduce prepositional phrases. They can show location, time, or direction, or they can provide details.

Our cats do what they please in our house.

632.1
Prepositional Phrases

Prepositional phrases include a preposition, the object of the preposition (a noun or pronoun that comes after the preposition), and any words that modify the object.

Jo-Jo sneaks toward the gerbil cage. (*Toward* is the preposition, and *cage* is the object of the preposition. *The* and *gerbil* modify *cage.*)

Smacker watches from the desk drawer and then ducks inside it. (The noun *drawer* is the object of the preposition *from,* and the pronoun *it* is the object of the preposition *inside.*)

Smacker hid silently until Jo-Jo's bedtime. (The noun *bedtime* is the object of the preposition *until. Jo-Jo's* modifies *bedtime.*)

Common Prepositions

aboard	around	but	into	over	until
about	at	by	like	past	up
above	before	down	near	since	up to
across	behind	during	of	through	upon
across from	below	except	off	throughout	with
after	beneath	except for	on	till	within
against	beside	for	on top of	to	without
along	besides	from	onto	toward	
along with	between	in	out	under	
among	beyond	inside	outside	underneath	

 TEKS 5.20A(v)
ELPS 4C, 5G

Grammar Practice

Prepositions

▶ Write down the prepositional phrase from each sentence. (There are two prepositional phrases in one of the sentences.) Underline the preposition in each phrase.

Example: As you learn about fractions, you might wonder how you'll ever use them.

about fractions

1. Well, suppose you are making a cake for your friend.

2. Double the size of the cake so you can share it.

3. The recipe lists 2 1/4 cups of flour and 2/3 cup of sugar.

4. How do you add one fraction to another?

5. Before your math lessons, you wouldn't have known.

6. Now you know that the numerator is the number before the slash.

7. The denominator is after the slash.

8. As long as there is a common denominator, you add only the numbers in the numerator.

Learning Language Write a sentence about some other school subject. Use a preposition. Then tell a partner three more sentences about the subject. Use the following prepositions correctly: *over, until,* and *from.*

Conjunctions

Conjunctions connect individual words or groups of words.

634.1
Coordinating Conjunctions

A coordinating conjunction connects equal parts: two or more words, phrases, or clauses.

> **The river is wide and deep.** (words)
>
> **We can fish in the morning or in the evening.** (phrases)
>
> **The river rushes down the valley, and then it winds through the prairie.** (clauses)

634.2
Subordinating Conjunctions

A subordinating conjunction is often used to introduce the dependent clause in a complex sentence.

> **Our trip was delayed when the snowstorm hit.**
>
> **Until the snow stopped, we had to stay in town.**

TIP: Relative pronouns can also be used to connect clauses. (See 600.3.)

634.3
Correlative Conjunctions

Correlative conjunctions are used in pairs.

> **Either snow or wind can make the trip dangerous.**

Common Conjunctions

Coordinating Conjunctions
and, but, or, nor, for, so, yet

Correlative Conjunctions
either/or, neither/nor, not only/but also, both/and, whether/or, as/so

Subordinating Conjunctions
after, although, as, as if, as long as, as though, because, before, if, in order that, since, so, so that, that, though, unless, until, when, where, whereas, while

TEKS 5.20A(vii)
ELPS 3C, 4C

Grammar Practice

Conjunctions

- ■ Coordinating Conjunctions
- ■ Subordinating Conjunctions

Write the conjunction from each sentence below. Then write "C" for coordinating or "S" for subordinating.

Example: Rusty and Ahmed went camping with their scout troop. *and, C*

1. The scouts talked around a campfire until it was time to turn in.

2. Ahmed heard some noise, so he crawled back out of the tent.

3. While he was looking around, he saw a flying saucer!

4. As Ahmed stared, Rusty came out of their tent.

5. Before he left home, Rusty put a cell phone in his bag.

6. He found the phone, and he called the police.

7. The police were not happy when they discovered the source of the "spacecraft."

8. Some older boys had been on a nearby hill, where a toy flying saucer now lay on the ground.

Learning Language Write two sentences. Use a coordinating conjunction in one and a subordinating conjunction in the other. Tell a partner two more sentences using those types of conjunctions.

ELPS 2C, 4C

Interjections

Interjections are words or phrases that express strong emotion. Commas or exclamation points are used to separate interjections from the rest of the sentence.

Wow, look at those mountains!

Hey! Keep your eyes on the road!

Quick Guide: Parts of Speech

Nouns	Words that name a person, a place, a thing, or an idea **(Bill, office, billboard, confusion)**
Pronouns	Words used in place of nouns **(I, me, her, them, who, which, those, myself, some)**
Verbs	Words that express action or state of being **(run, jump, is, are)**
Adjectives	Words that describe a noun or pronoun **(tall, quiet, three, the, neat)**
Adverbs	Words that describe a verb, an adjective, or another adverb **(gently, easily, fast, very)**
Prepositions	Words that show position or direction and introduce prepositional phrases **(on, near, over, on top of)**
Conjunctions	Words that connect words or groups of words **(and, or, because)**
Interjections	Words (set off by commas or exclamation points) that show emotion or surprise **(Wow, Oh, Yikes!)**

Grammar Practice

Parts of Speech Review

Write down the part of speech for each underlined word or words in the following sentences.

(1) Marcella is dreaming of her summer <u>vacation</u>. **(2)** She knows she <u>will</u> be swimming a lot. **(3)** <u>She</u> will go hiking on nature trails near her home. **(4)** Also, Marcella will not set her <u>dreadful</u> alarm clock for 6:15 a.m.!

(5) <u>If</u> her mom can take some time off work, Marcella's family will go on a trip. **(6)** <u>Oh</u>, how Marcella would like to see the Statue of Liberty! **(7)** However, that would be quite a <u>long</u> drive. **(8)** It is more than a thousand miles <u>from</u> their apartment in New Orleans to New York City. **(9)** Marcella would have to work hard to convince her family to go so <u>far</u>.

(10) Marcella is also looking forward to spending time <u>with</u> her friends. **(11)** They could rent movies <u>and</u> listen to their CD's. **(12)** <u>They</u> could have picnics out in the courtyard. **(13)** Maybe they could go fishing <u>sometimes</u>. **(14)** For sure, they will also go to the <u>library</u> a lot. **(15)** Marcella <u>knows</u> that she'll enjoy this summer.

Credits

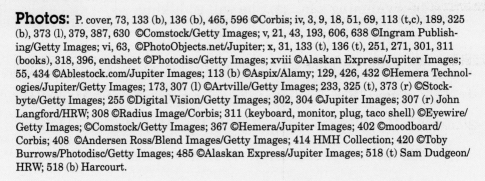

Texas Essential Knowledge and Skills (TEKS) for English Language Arts

The TEKS are the skills you need to master by the end of Grade 5. The first column in the chart below lists the English Language Arts TEKS. The second column shows were these TEKS are taught in *Texas Write Source*.

★ TEKS 5.15 Writing/Writing Process

Students use elements of the writing process (planning, drafting, revising, editing, and publishing) to compose text. Students are expected to:

A plan a first draft by selecting a genre appropriate for conveying the intended meaning to an audience, determining appropriate topics through a range of strategies (e.g., discussion, background reading, personal interests, interviews), and developing a thesis or controlling idea;	pages 5, 6, 11, 53, 58, 65, 67, 70, 71, 78, 115, 119, 123, 126, 130, 131, 137, 138, 175, 176, 183, 186, 191, 198, 235, 245, 248, 258, 260, 326, 329, 330, 341, 386, 496, 497, 502, 503
B develop drafts by choosing an appropriate organizational strategy (e.g., sequence of events, cause-effect, compare-contrast) and building on ideas to create a focused, organized, and coherent piece of writing;	pages 25, 52, 54, 56, 57, 59–62, 64–67, 70, 72, 75, 76, 80, 84–88, 117, 119, 132, 143–148, 174, 176, 204, 205, 207, 208, 278, 346, 386, 500
C revise drafts to clarify meaning, enhance style, include simple and compound sentences, and improve transitions by adding, deleting, combining, and rearranging sentences or larger units of text after rethinking how well questions of purpose, audience, and genre have been addressed;	pages 5–7, 14, 15, 54, 83, 89, 91–93, 103, 126, 143, 149, 150, 152–158, 162, 186, 203, 209–212, 214, 216, 217, 248, 265, 343, 349, 351–355, 386, 478, 504, 505, 515, 516
D edit drafts for grammar, mechanics, and spelling; and	pages 16, 54, 72, 100, 101, 104, 119, 160, 161, 164, 219–221, 224, 248, 254, 266, 279, 283, 287, 295, 364, 386 pages 100–103, 105–107, 112, 201, 202

*Page References in *Student Edition*
*Page References in *SkillsBook*

E   revise final draft in response to feedback from peers and teacher and publish written work for appropriate audiences.

pages 7, 15, 41, 62, 98, 105, 158, 165, 218, 225, 241, 305, 358, 365, 386

⭐ (TEKS) 5.16 Writing/Literary Texts

Students write literary texts to express their ideas and feelings about real or imagined people, events, and ideas. Students are expected to:

A   write imaginative stories that include:

pages 290–300, 506

   (i)   a clearly defined focus, plot, and point of view;

   (ii) a specific, believable setting created through the use of sensory details; and

   (iii) dialogue that develops the story; and

B   write poems using:

pages 302, 304–309, 506

   (i)   poetic techniques (e.g., alliteration, onomatopoeia);

   (ii) figurative language (e.g., similes, metaphors); and

   (iii) graphic elements (e.g., capital letters, line length).

⭐ (TEKS) 5.17 Writing

Students write about their own experiences. Students are expected to write a personal narrative that conveys thoughts and feelings about an experience.

pages 74, 81, 84, 86–88, 94

⭐ (TEKS) 5.18 Writing/Expository and Procedural Texts

Students write expository and procedural or work-related texts to communicate ideas and information to specific audiences for specific purposes. Students are expected to:

A   create multi-paragraph essays to convey information about the topic that:

pages 135, 136, 139–148, 150, 151, 153–155, 162, 163, 174, 177, 184–187, 326, 327, 342–347, 354, 474–478, 513, 515, 516

   (i)   present effective introductions and concluding paragraphs;

   (ii) guide and inform the reader's understanding of key ideas and evidence;

   (iii) include specific facts, details, and examples in an appropriately organized structure; and

   (iv) use a variety of sentence structures and transitions to link paragraphs;

*Page References in *Student Edition*
*Page References in *SkillsBook*

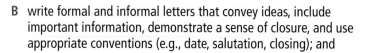
B write formal and informal letters that convey ideas, include important information, demonstrate a sense of closure, and use appropriate conventions (e.g., date, salutation, closing); and

C write responses to literary or expository texts and provide evidence from the text to demonstrate understanding.

⭐ (TEKS) 5.19 Writing/Persuasive Texts

Students write persuasive texts to influence the attitudes or actions of a specific audience on specific issues. Students are expected to write persuasive essays for appropriate audiences that establish a position and include sound reasoning, detailed and relevant evidence, and consideration of alternatives.

⭐ (TEKS) 5.20 Oral and Written Conventions/Conventions

Students understand the function of and use the conventions of academic language when speaking and writing. Students continue to apply earlier standards with greater complexity. Students are expected to:

A use and understand the function of the following parts of speech in the context of reading, writing, and speaking:
  (i) verbs (irregular verbs and active voice);
  (ii) collective nouns (e.g., class, public);
  (iii) adjectives (e.g., descriptive, including origins: French windows, American cars) and their comparative and superlative forms (e.g., good, better, best);
  (iv) adverbs (e.g., frequency: usually, sometimes; intensity: almost, a lot);
  (v) prepositions and prepositional phrases to convey location, time, direction, or to provide details;
  (vi) indefinite pronouns (e.g., all, both, nothing, anything);
  (vii) subordinating conjunctions (e.g., while, because, although, if); and
  (viii) transitional words (e.g., also, therefore);

B	use the complete subject and the complete predicate in a sentence; and	pages 466, 467, 596–599 pages 90, 91
C	use complete simple and compound sentences with correct subject-verb agreement.	pages 100, 101, 453–455, 472, 476 pages 108, 109, 112, 113

⭐ TEKS 5.21 Oral and Written Conventions/Handwriting, Capitalization, and Punctuation

Students write legibly and use appropriate capitalization and punctuation conventions in their compositions. Students are expected to:

A	use capitalization for: (i) abbreviations; (ii) initials and acronyms; and (iii) organizations;	pages 550, 551, 562, 563–565 pages 49–54, 57, 58
B	recognize and use punctuation marks including: (i) commas in compound sentences; and (ii) proper punctuation and spacing for quotations; and	pages 102, 477, 526, 527, 538, 539 pages 6, 7, 17–19, 24–28, 43, 44, 46, 61, 62, 190, 192
C	use proper mechanics including italics and underlining for titles and emphasis.	pages 254, 362, 364, 546, 547 pages 36–40, 46, 64

⭐ TEKS 5.23 Research/Research Plan

Students ask open-ended research questions and develop a plan for answering them. Students are expected to:

A	brainstorm, consult with others, decide upon a topic, and formulate open-ended questions to address the major research topic; and	pages 131, 138, 139, 253, 258, 312, 329–332
B	generate a research plan for gathering relevant information about the major research question.	pages 139, 175, 312, 329, 333

*Page References in *Student Edition*
*Page References in *SkillsBook*

⭐ TEKS 5.24 Research/Gathering Sources

Students determine, locate, and explore the full range of relevant sources addressing a research question and systematically record the information they gather. Students are expected to:

A	follow the research plan to collect data from a range of print and electronic resources (e.g., reference texts, periodicals, web pages, online sources) and data from experts;	pages 139, 175, 259, 261, 312, 314, 316–321, 334–336, 338
B	differentiate between primary and secondary sources;	pages 312, 315, 333, 337
C	record data, utilizing available technology (e.g., word processors) in order to see the relationships between ideas and convert graphic/visual data (e.g., charts, diagrams, timelines) into written notes;	pages 180, 181, 312, 313, 321, 336, 338, 341, 342
D	identify the source of notes (e.g., author, title, page number) and record bibliographic information concerning those sources according to a standard format; and	pages 312, 324, 340, 348, 363
E	differentiate between paraphrasing and plagiarism and identify the importance of citing valid and reliable sources.	pages 312, 314, 322, 323, 334, 337, 339

⭐ TEKS 5.25 Research/Synthesizing Information

Students clarify research questions and evaluate and synthesize collected information. Students are expected to:

A	refine the major research question, if necessary, guided by the answers to a secondary set of questions; and	pages 313, 331, 332, 338
B	evaluate the relevance, validity, and reliability of sources for the research.	pages 313, 314, 323, 337

⭐ TEKS 5.26 Research/Organizing and Presenting Ideas

Students organize and present their ideas and information according to the purpose of the research and their audience. Students are expected to synthesize the research into a written or an oral presentation that:

A	compiles important information from multiple sources;	pages 139–141, 313, 333, 344–347, 369, 376, 377
B	develops a topic sentence, summarizes findings, and uses evidence to support conclusions;	pages 140, 141, 313, 326, 327, 329, 338, 339, 341, 342, 345, 346, 368–370, 372, 375, 377
C	presents the findings in a consistent format; and	pages 313, 344–347, 369, 371, 372, 374–377
D	uses quotations to support ideas and an appropriate form of documentation to acknowledge sources (e.g., bibliography, works cited).	pages 313, 324, 327, 328, 340, 345–348, 357, 363, 369, 375–377

English Language Proficiency Standards (ELPS)

The English Language Proficiency Standards (ELPS) outline expectations for students who are learning English. The first column in the chart below lists selected ELPS for English Language Arts. The second column shows where these ELPS are taught in *Texas Write Source*.

⭐ ELPS 2 Listening

Cross-curricular second language acquisition/listening. The ELL listens to a variety of speakers including teachers, peers, and electronic media to gain an increasing level of comprehension of newly acquired language in all content areas. ELLs may be at the beginning, intermediate, advanced, or advanced high stage of English language acquisition in listening. In order for the ELL to meet grade-level learning expectations across the foundation and enrichment curriculum, all instruction delivered in English must be linguistically accommodated (communicated, sequenced, and scaffolded) commensurate with the student's level of English language proficiency. The student is expected to:

D	monitor understanding of spoken language during classroom instruction and interactions and seek clarification as needed	pages 380, 384, 385

*Page References in Student Edition
*Page References in SkillsBook

⭐ ELPS 3 Speaking

Cross-curricular second language acquisition/speaking. The ELL speaks in a variety of modes for a variety of purposes with an awareness of different language registers (formal/informal) using vocabulary with increasing fluency and accuracy in language arts and all content areas. ELLs may be at the beginning, intermediate, advanced, or advanced high stage of English language acquisition in speaking. In order for the ELL to meet grade-level learning expectations across the foundation and enrichment curriculum, all instruction delivered in English must be linguistically accommodated (communicated, sequenced, and scaffolded) commensurate with the student's level of English language proficiency. The student is expected to:

A practice producing sounds of newly acquired vocabulary such as long and short vowels, silent letters, and consonant clusters to pronounce English words in a manner that is increasingly comprehensible

pages 387, 393, 417

G express opinions, ideas, and feelings ranging from communicating single words and short phrases to participating in extended discussions on a variety of social and grade-appropriate academic topics

pages 2, 4, 5, 10, 15, 16, 19, 25, 26, 28, 29, 33, 41, 50, 52, 57, 68, 70, 76, 125, 128, 136, 155, 185, 188, 196, 247, 250, 252, 257, 288, 291, 302, 310, 312, 313, 328, 330, 331, 334, 378, 381, 387, 389, 391, 392, 396–398, 400, 402–404, 408–410, 412, 414–418, 420–422, 424, 426–428, 430, 432, 433, 438, 440, 443, 449, 450, 456, 459, 486, 494, 519, 547, 551, 609, 617

H narrate, describe, and explain with increasing specificity and detail as more English is acquired

pages 2, 4, 5, 10, 13–16, 19, 24–27, 29, 33, 50, 52, 57, 68, 70, 76, 125, 128, 130, 136, 185, 188, 190, 196, 247, 250, 257, 288, 291, 298, 302, 310, 314–316, 328, 334, 383, 387, 389, 392, 396, 398, 400, 402–404, 408–410, 415–417, 420–422, 426–428, 430, 432, 433, 438, 440, 443, 444, 456, 459–461, 467, 476, 479, 486, 494, 507, 515, 522, 577, 579, 581, 583, 591, 593, 603, 607, 625

*Page References in *Student Edition*
*Page References in *SkillsBook*

⊠ ELPS 4 Reading

Cross-curricular second language acquisition/reading. The ELL reads a variety of texts for a variety of purposes with an increasing level of comprehension in all content areas. ELLs may be at the beginning, intermediate, advanced, or advanced high stage of English language acquisition in reading. In order for the ELL to meet grade-level learning expectations across the foundation and enrichment curriculum, all instruction delivered in English must be linguistically accommodated (communicated, sequenced, and scaffolded) commensurate with the student's level of English language proficiency. For kindergarten and first grade, certain of these student expectations apply to text read aloud for students not yet at the stage of decoding written text. The student is expected to:

C develop basic sight vocabulary, derive meaning of environmental print, and comprehend English vocabulary and language structures used routinely in written classroom materials

pages 2, 8, 10, 13–16, 19, 22–29, 32–35, 40, 50, 52, 57, 68, 70, 76, 125, 128, 130, 136, 185, 188, 190, 196, 242, 247, 250, 257, 268, 276, 280, 284, 288, 291, 299, 300, 302, 308–310, 317, 319, 326, 327, 343, 350, 352, 354, 356, 360, 361, 386, 387, 390, 401, 405, 423, 425, 429, 430, 438, 440–442, 445–447, 449–458, 460, 462, 463, 466–471, 473, 475–478, 480–483, 487, 488, 490–492, 494, 496, 497, 500, 503, 506–511, 517, 519, 520, 522–546, 548–566, 568, 576, 578, 580, 582, 584, 586, 588, 592, 594, 596–636

pages 2–65, 86–89, 91–133, 136–149, 151–170, 172–200

⭐ ELPS 5 Writing

Cross-curricular second language acquisition/writing. The ELL writes in a variety of forms with increasing accuracy to effectively address a specific purpose and audience in all content areas. ELLs may be at the beginning, intermediate, advanced, or advanced high stage of English language acquisition in writing. In order for the ELL to meet grade-level learning expectations across foundation and enrichment curriculum, all instruction delivered in English must be linguistically accommodated (communicated, sequenced, and scaffolded) commensurate with the student's level of English language proficiency. For kindergarten and first grade, certain of these student expectations do not apply until the student has reached the stage of generating original written text using a standard writing system. The student is expected to:

B	write using newly acquired basic vocabulary and content-based grade-level vocabulary	pages 386, 387, 390, 391, 393, 399, 405, 417, 423, 429, 444, 477, 478, 576–595, 615
		page 68
G	narrate, describe, and explain with increasing specificity and detail to fulfill content area writing needs as more English is acquired	pages 24, 28, 47, 53, 54, 58–62, 65, 67, 71, 72, 77–88, 90, 94, 95, 98, 115–117, 119, 121, 123, 126, 131, 132, 137–155, 158, 175–177, 179, 181, 183, 186, 191, 192, 197–215, 218, 235–237, 239, 241, 245, 248, 253, 254, 258–265, 273–275, 277–279, 281–283, 285–287, 292–297, 303–307, 309, 341, 342, 344–347, 354–356, 443, 444, 459, 475, 477, 478, 483, 485, 487, 489, 492, 493, 498, 499, 502, 504–506, 527, 529, 531, 533, 537, 539, 545, 549, 553, 555, 597, 615, 625, 633
		pages 142, 170, 175, 176, 186

*Page References in *Student Edition*
*Page References in *SkillsBook*

Index

This **index** will help you find specific information in the handbook. Entries in italic are words from the "Using the Right Word" section. The colored boxes contain information you will use often.